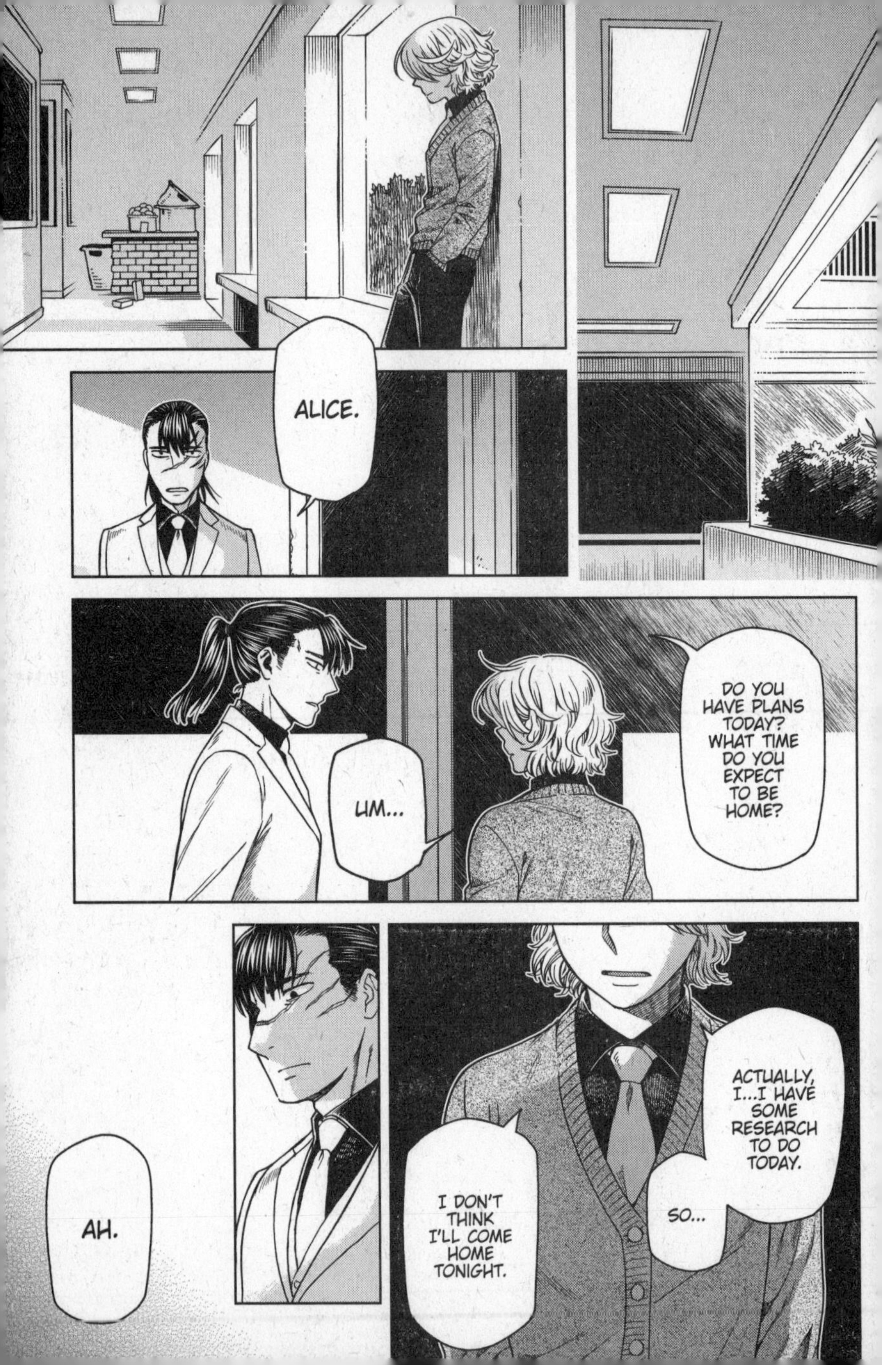
ALICE.
DO YOU HAVE PLANS TODAY? WHAT TIME DO YOU EXPECT TO BE HOME?
UM...
ACTUALLY, I...I HAVE SOME RESEARCH TO DO TODAY.
SO...
I DON'T THINK I'LL COME HOME TONIGHT.
AH.

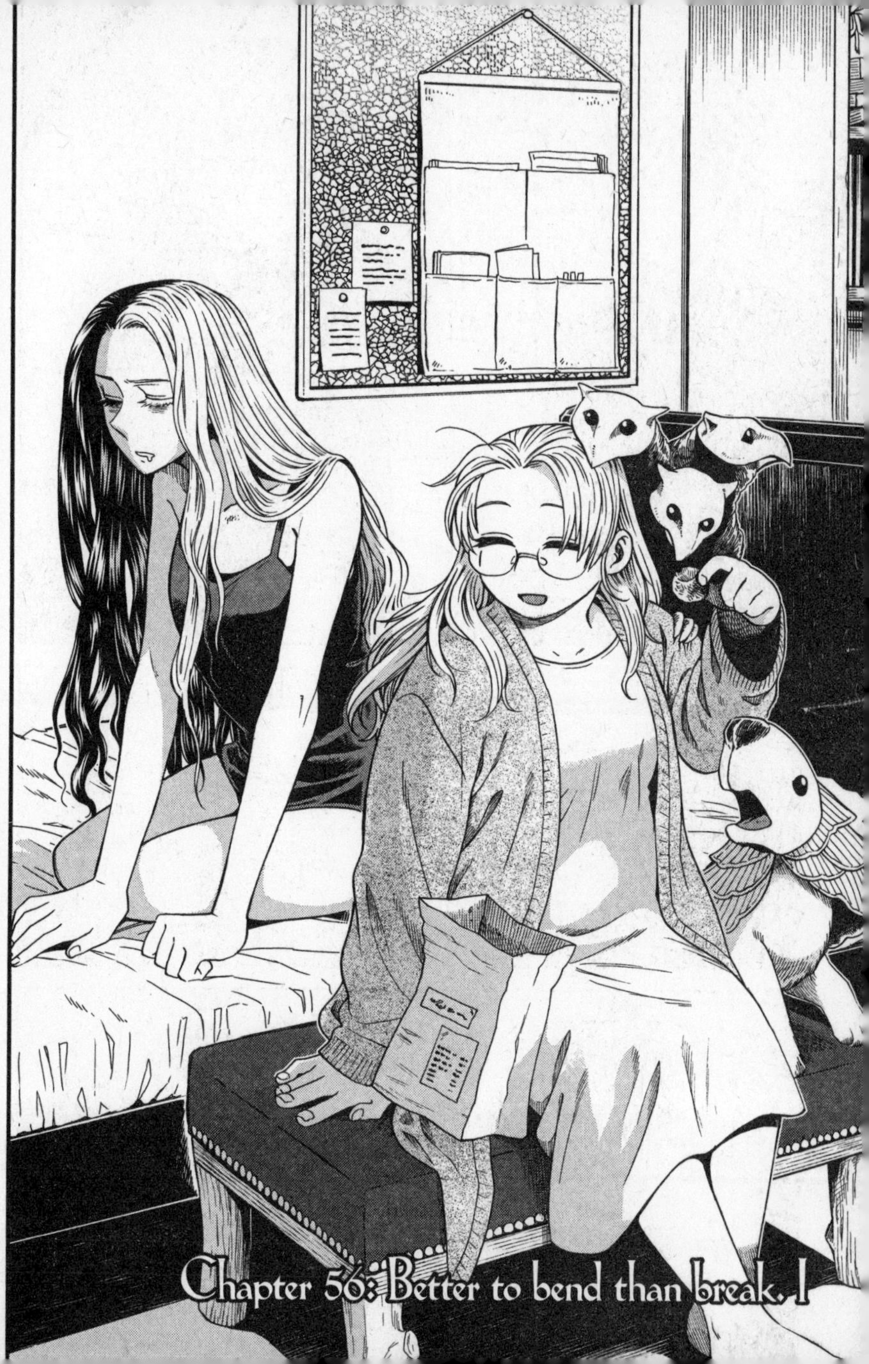
Chapter 56: Better to bend than break. I

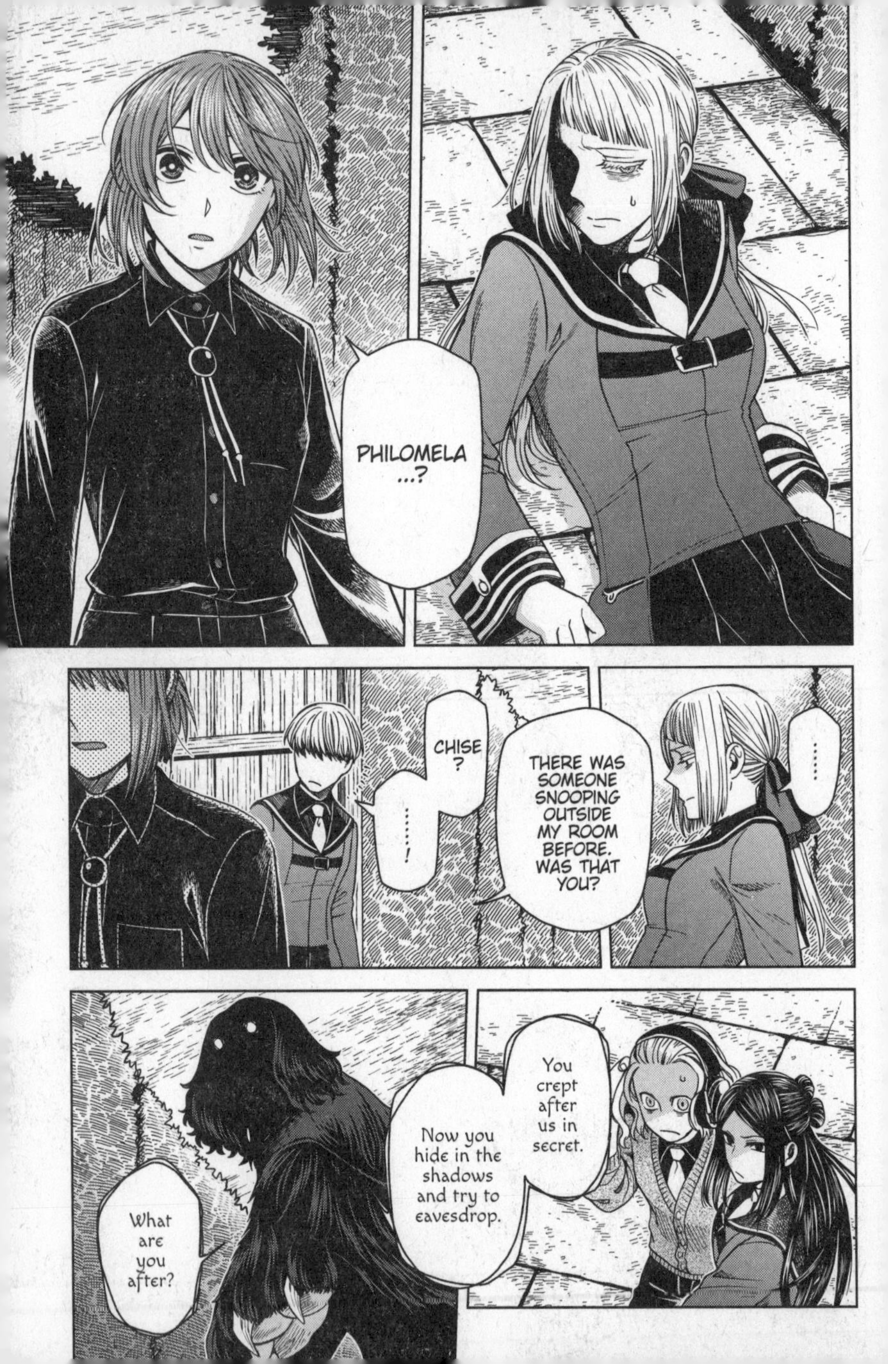
PHILOMELA ...?
......
THERE WAS SOMEONE SNOOPING OUTSIDE MY ROOM BEFORE. WAS THAT YOU?
CHISE ?
......!
You crept after us in secret.
Now you hide in the shadows and try to eavesdrop.
What are you after?

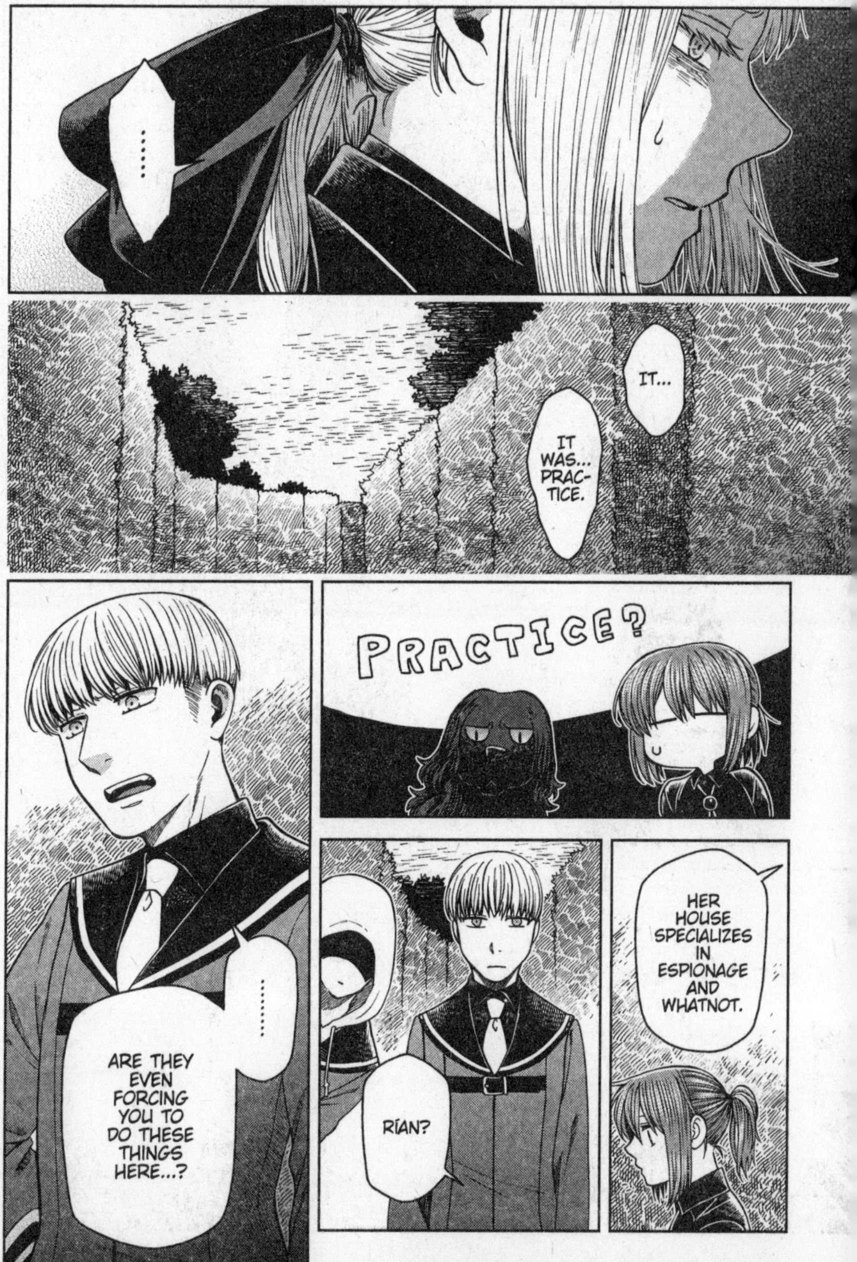
......
IT...
IT WAS... PRACTICE.
PRACTICE?
HER HOUSE SPECIALIZES IN ESPIONAGE AND WHATNOT.
RÍAN?
......
ARE THEY EVEN FORCING YOU TO DO THESE THINGS HERE...?

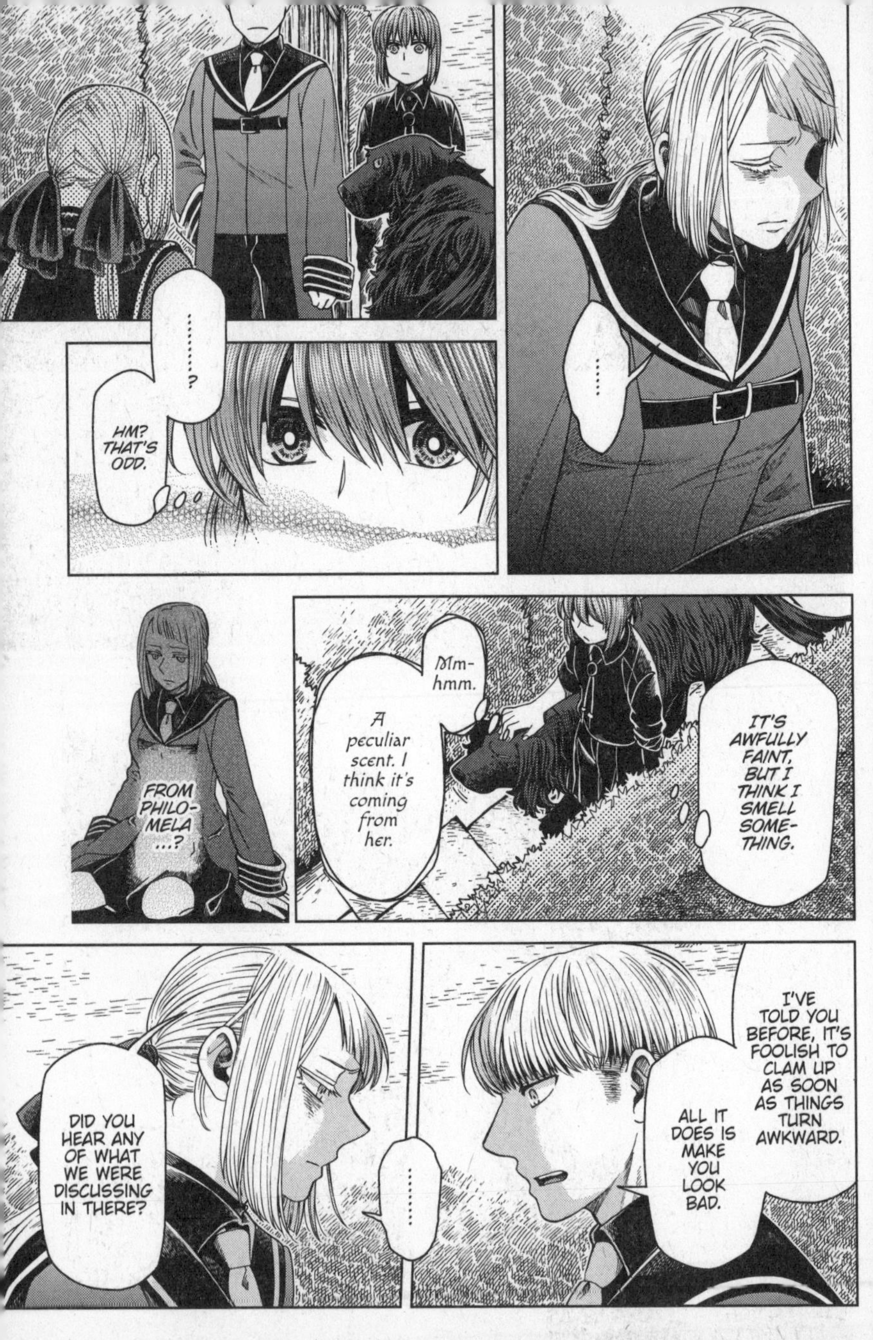
......
........?
HM? THAT'S ODD.
IT'S AWFULLY FAINT, BUT I THINK I SMELL SOMETHING.
Mm-hmm.
A peculiar scent. I think it's coming from her.
FROM PHILOMELA ...?
I'VE TOLD YOU BEFORE, IT'S FOOLISH TO CLAM UP AS SOON AS THINGS TURN AWKWARD.
ALL IT DOES IS MAKE YOU LOOK BAD.
......
DID YOU HEAR ANY OF WHAT WE WERE DISCUSSING IN THERE?

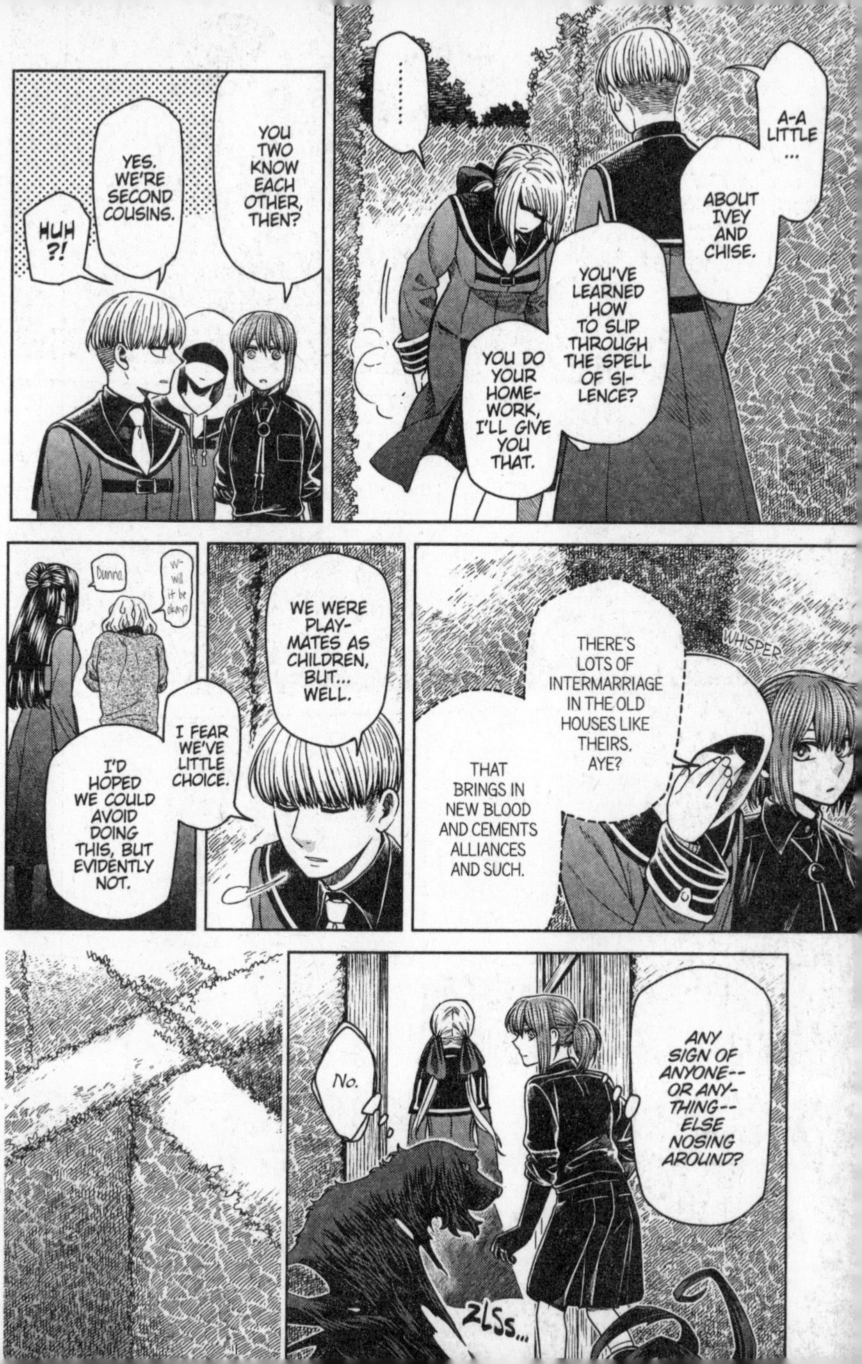
A-A LITTLE... ABOUT IVEY AND CHISE.
......
YOU'VE LEARNED HOW TO SLIP THROUGH THE SPELL OF SI-LENCE?
YOU DO YOUR HOME-WORK, I'LL GIVE YOU THAT.
YOU TWO KNOW EACH OTHER, THEN?
YES. WE'RE SECOND COUSINS.
HUH?!
WHISPER
THERE'S LOTS OF INTERMARRIAGE IN THE OLD HOUSES LIKE THEIRS, AYE?
THAT BRINGS IN NEW BLOOD AND CEMENTS ALLIANCES AND SUCH.
WE WERE PLAY-MATES AS CHILDREN, BUT... WELL.
W-will it be okay?
Dunno.
I FEAR WE'VE LITTLE CHOICE.
I'D HOPED WE COULD AVOID DOING THIS, BUT EVIDENTLY NOT.
ANY SIGN OF ANYONE--OR ANY-THING--ELSE NOSING AROUND?
No.
ZISS...

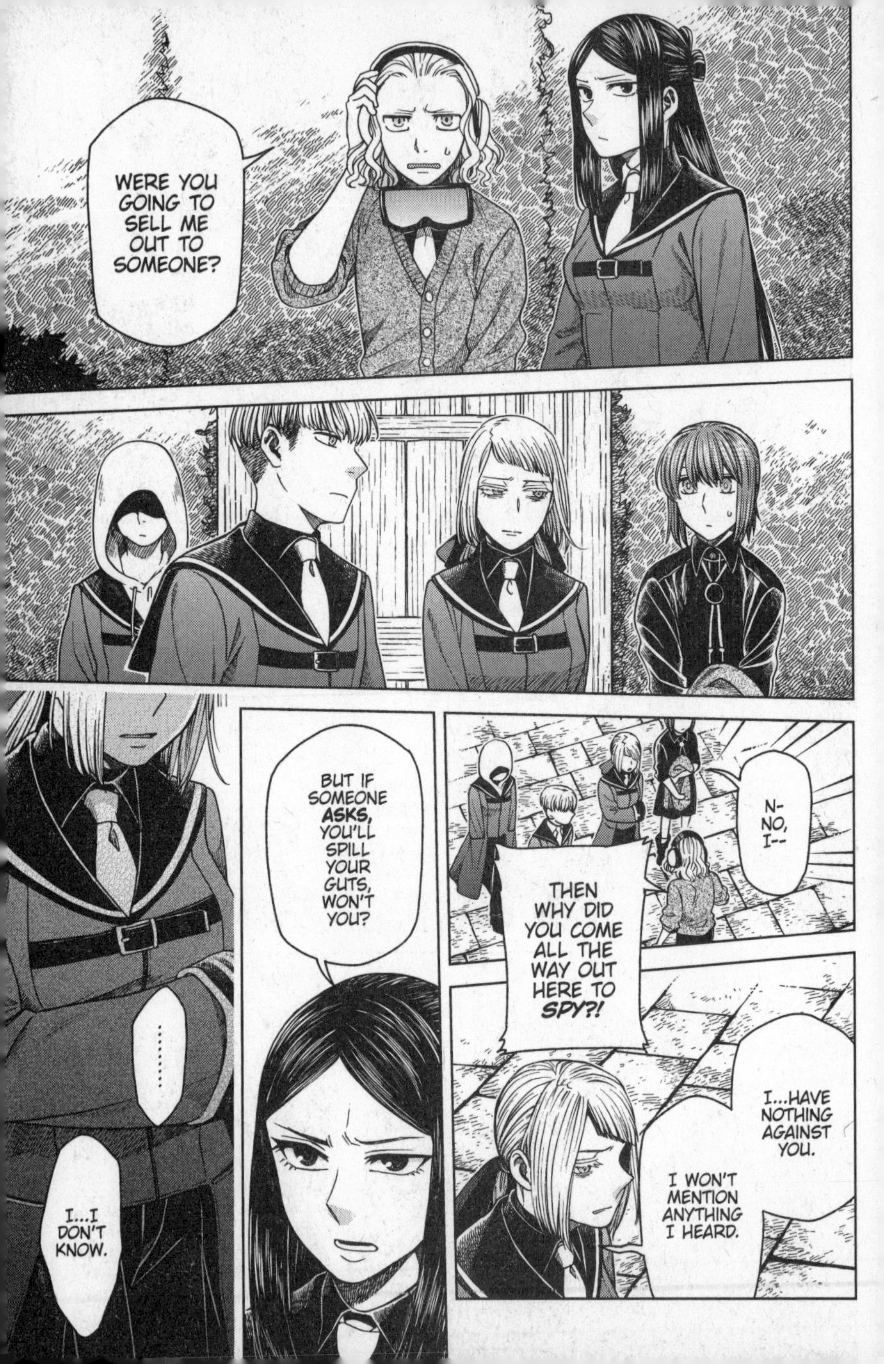
WERE YOU GOING TO SELL ME OUT TO SOMEONE?
N-NO, I--
THEN WHY DID YOU COME ALL THE WAY OUT HERE TO SPY?!
I...HAVE NOTHING AGAINST YOU.
I WON'T MENTION ANYTHING I HEARD.
BUT IF SOMEONE ASKS, YOU'LL SPILL YOUR GUTS, WON'T YOU?
......
I...I DON'T KNOW.

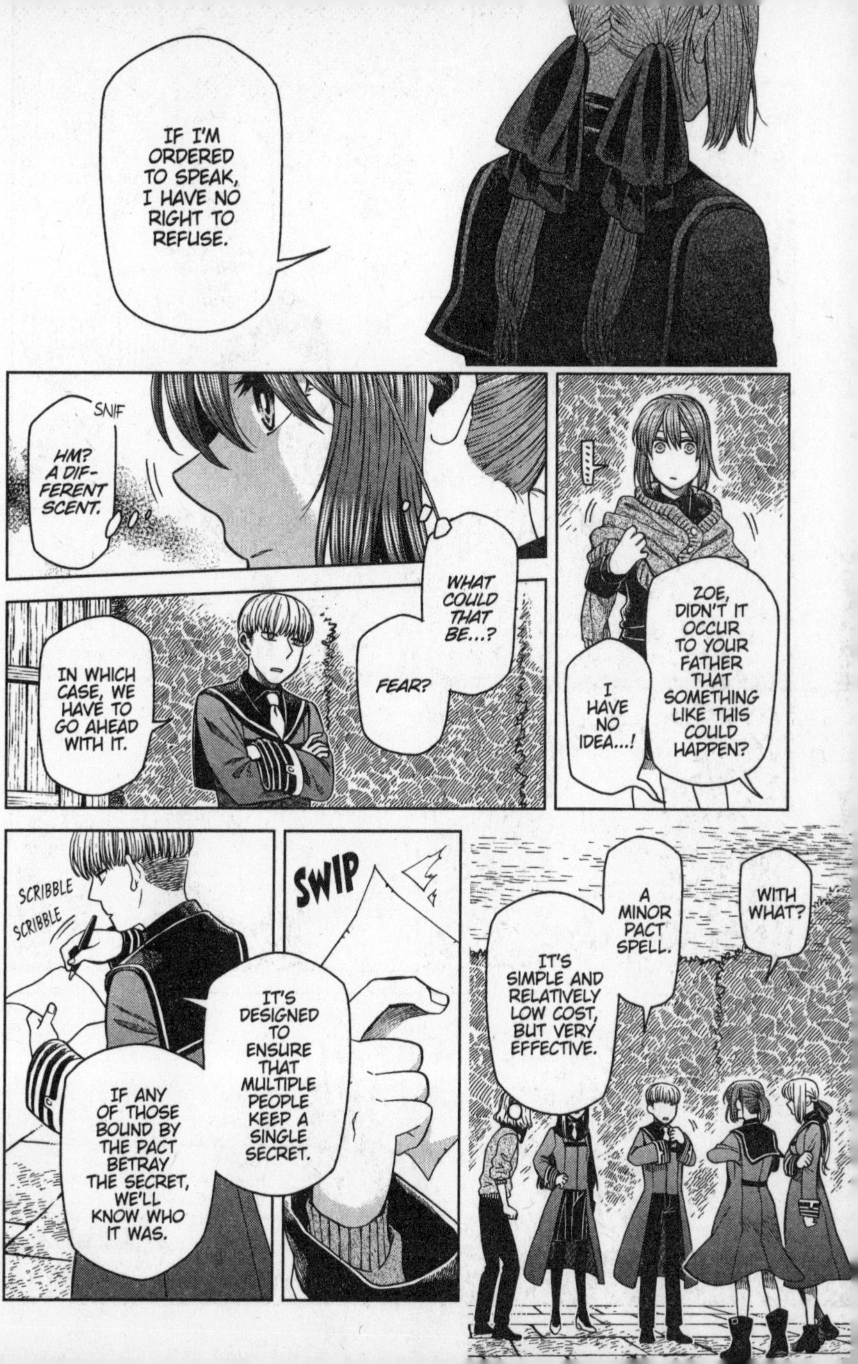
IF I'M ORDERED TO SPEAK, I HAVE NO RIGHT TO REFUSE.
ZOE, DIDN'T IT OCCUR TO YOUR FATHER THAT SOMETHING LIKE THIS COULD HAPPEN?
I HAVE NO IDEA...!
SNIF
HM? A DIFFERENT SCENT.
WHAT COULD THAT BE...?
FEAR?
IN WHICH CASE, WE HAVE TO GO AHEAD WITH IT.
WITH WHAT?
A MINOR PACT SPELL.
IT'S SIMPLE AND RELATIVELY LOW COST, BUT VERY EFFECTIVE.
SWIP
IT'S DESIGNED TO ENSURE THAT MULTIPLE PEOPLE KEEP A SINGLE SECRET.
SCRIBBLE
SCRIBBLE
IF ANY OF THOSE BOUND BY THE PACT BETRAY THE SECRET, WE'LL KNOW WHO IT WAS.

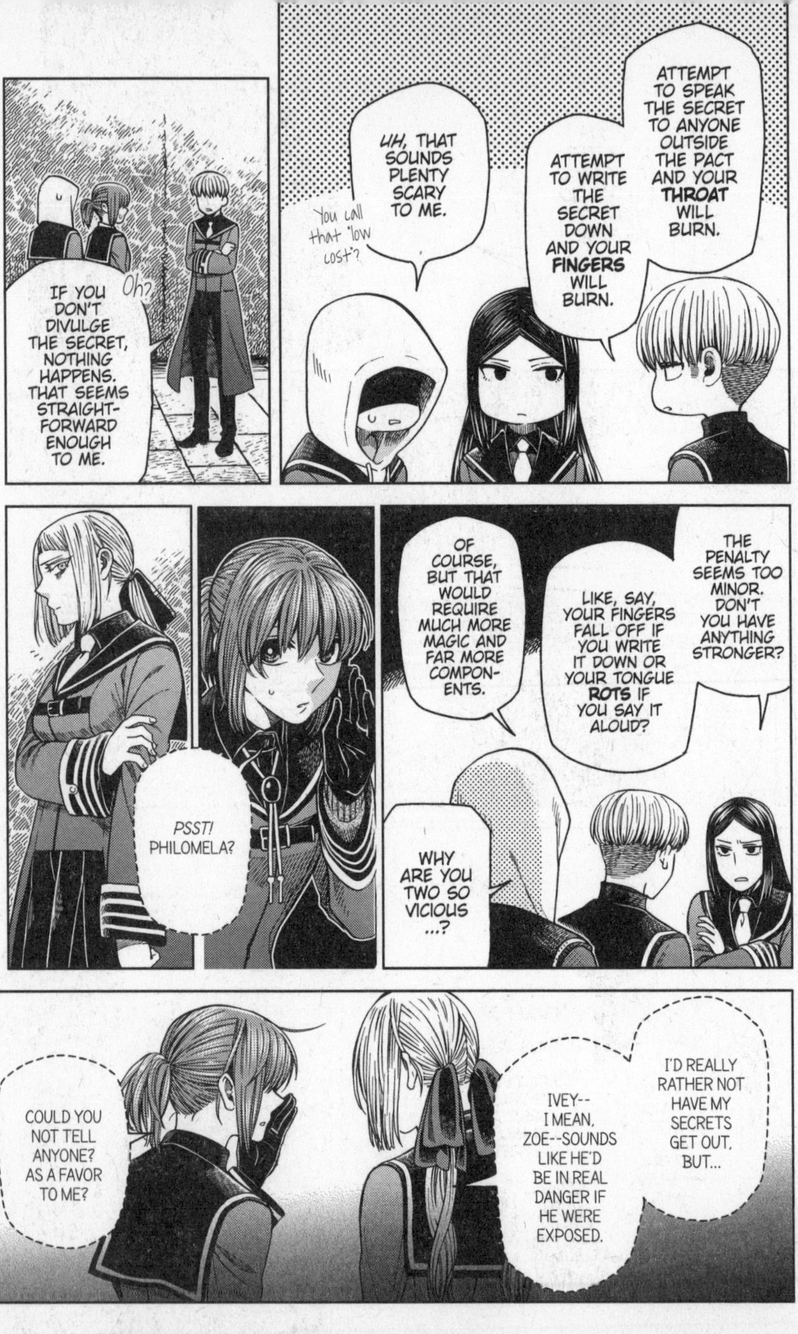
ATTEMPT TO SPEAK THE SECRET TO ANYONE OUTSIDE THE PACT AND YOUR **THROAT** WILL BURN.
ATTEMPT TO WRITE THE SECRET DOWN AND YOUR **FINGERS** WILL BURN.
*UH*, THAT SOUNDS PLENTY SCARY TO ME.
You call that "low cost"?
Oh?
IF YOU DON'T DIVULGE THE SECRET, NOTHING HAPPENS. THAT SEEMS STRAIGHT-FORWARD ENOUGH TO ME.
THE PENALTY SEEMS TOO MINOR. DON'T YOU HAVE ANYTHING STRONGER?
LIKE, SAY, YOUR FINGERS FALL OFF IF YOU WRITE IT DOWN OR YOUR TONGUE **ROTS** IF YOU SAY IT ALOUD?
OF COURSE, BUT THAT WOULD REQUIRE MUCH MORE MAGIC AND FAR MORE COMPON-ENTS.
WHY ARE YOU TWO SO VICIOUS ...?
*PSST!* PHILOMELA?
I'D REALLY RATHER NOT HAVE MY SECRETS GET OUT, BUT...
IVEY-- I MEAN, ZOE--SOUNDS LIKE HE'D BE IN REAL DANGER IF HE WERE EXPOSED.
COULD YOU NOT TELL ANYONE? AS A FAVOR TO ME?

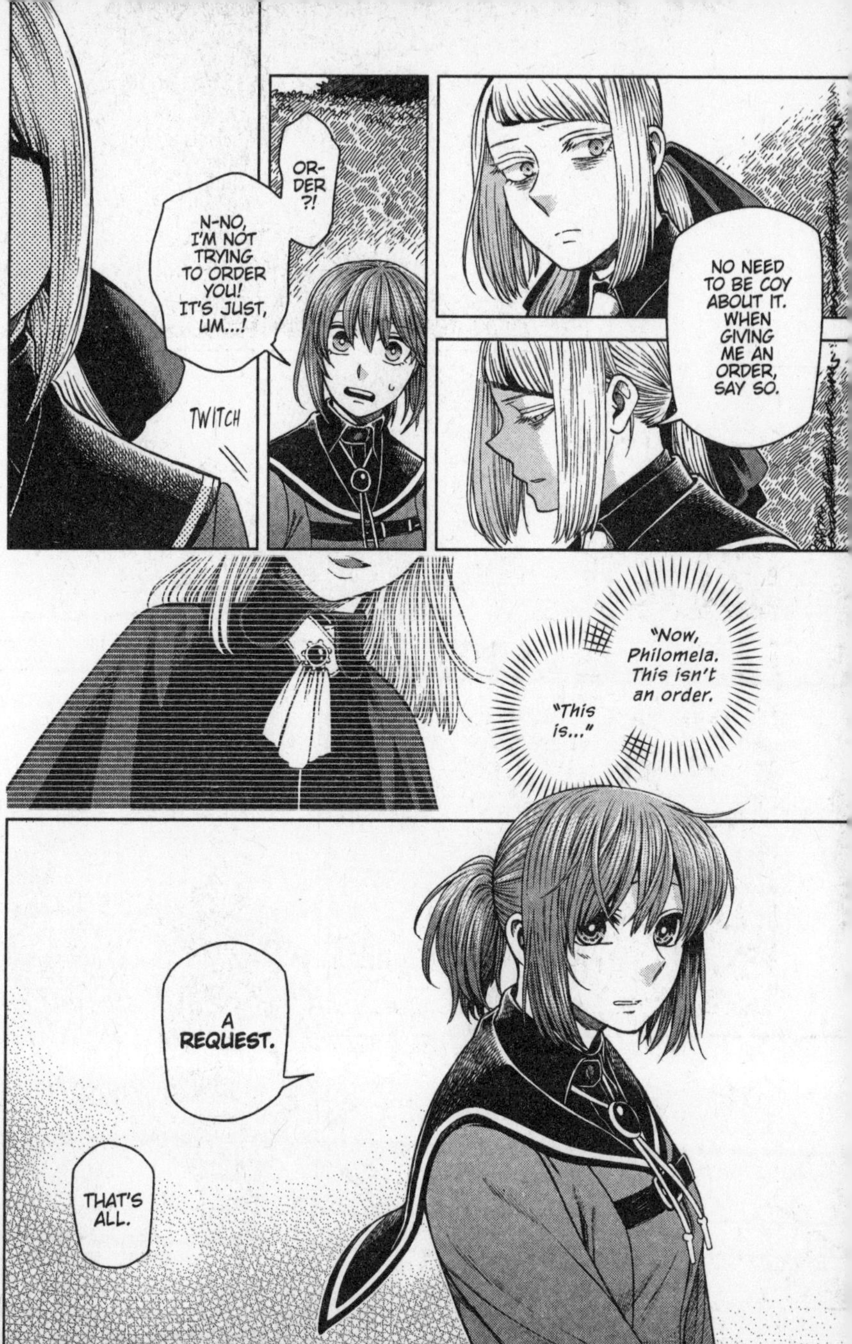
NO NEED TO BE COY ABOUT IT. WHEN GIVING ME AN ORDER, SAY SO.
ORDER?!
N-NO, I'M NOT TRYING TO ORDER YOU! IT'S JUST, UM...!
TWITCH
"Now, Philomela. This isn't an order.
"This is..."
A REQUEST.
THAT'S ALL.

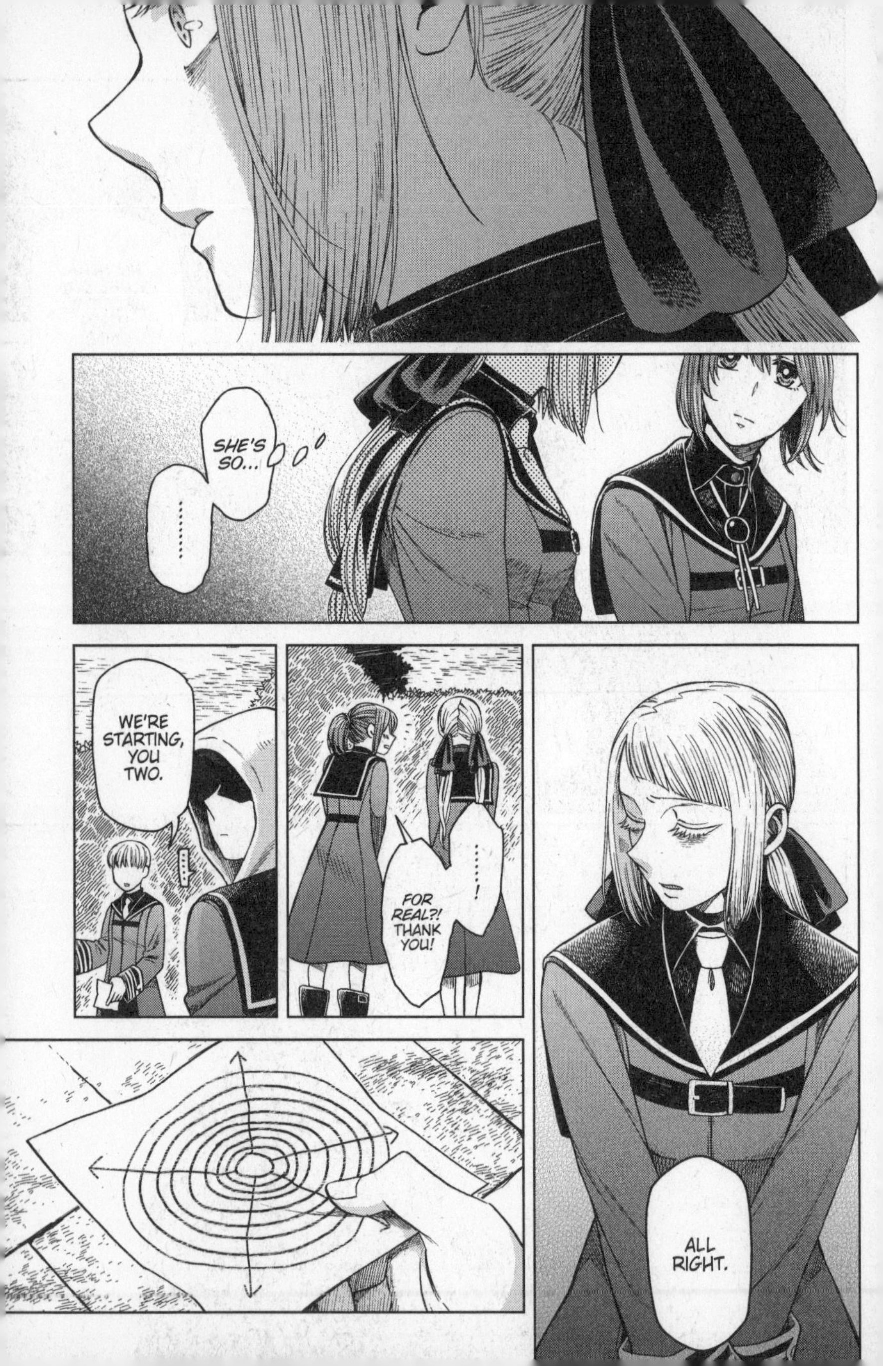
SHE'S SO...
......
ALL RIGHT.
......!
FOR REAL?! THANK YOU!
WE'RE STARTING, YOU TWO.
...

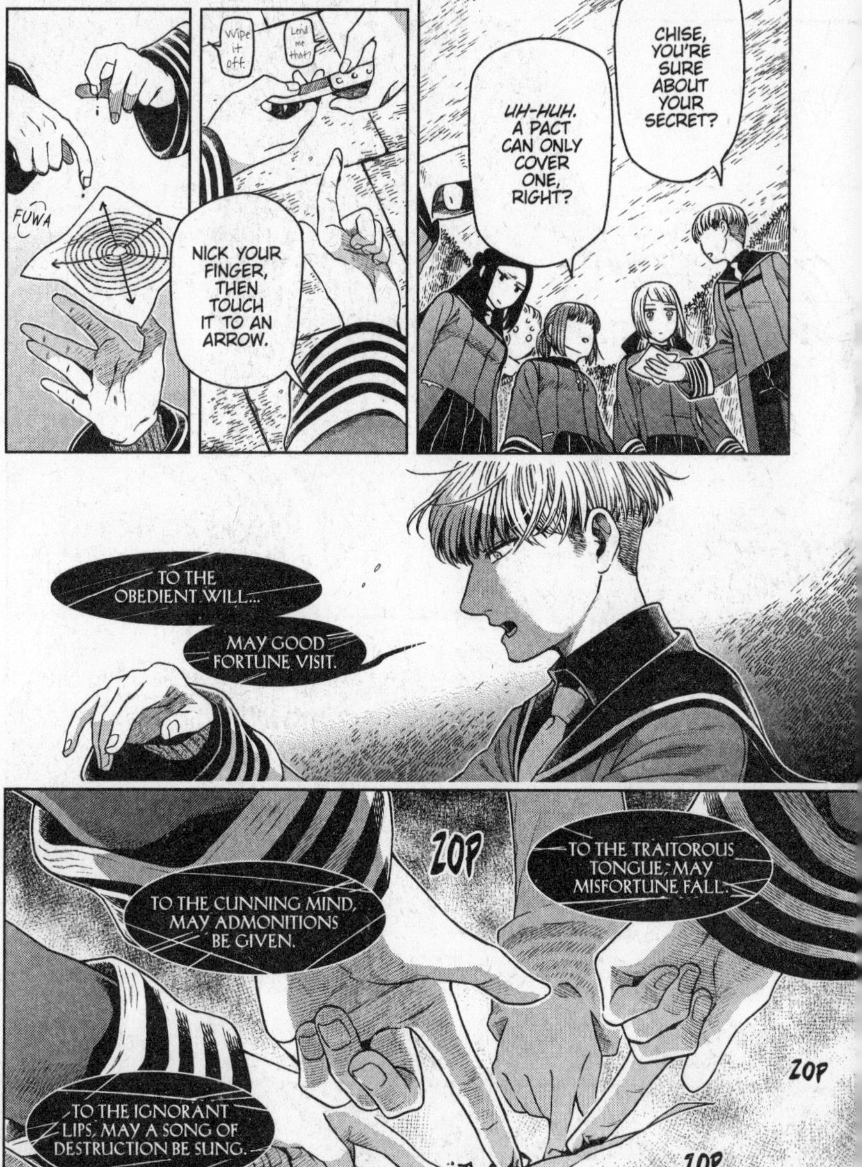
CHISE, YOU'RE SURE ABOUT YOUR SECRET?
UH-HUH. A PACT CAN ONLY COVER ONE, RIGHT?
Lend me that?
Wipe it off.
NICK YOUR FINGER, THEN TOUCH IT TO AN ARROW.
FUWA
TO THE OBEDIENT WILL...
MAY GOOD FORTUNE VISIT.
TO THE TRAITOROUS TONGUE, MAY MISFORTUNE FALL.
ZOP
TO THE CUNNING MIND, MAY ADMONITIONS BE GIVEN.
ZOP
ZOP
TO THE IGNORANT LIPS, MAY A SONG OF DESTRUCTION BE SUNG.

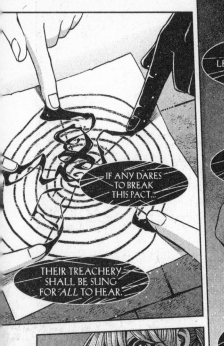

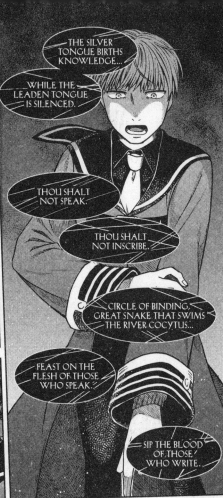

THE SILVER TONGUE BIRTHS KNOWLEDGE...
WHILE THE LEADEN TONGUE IS SILENCED.
THOU SHALT NOT SPEAK.
THOU SHALT NOT INSCRIBE.
CIRCLE OF BINDING, GREAT SNAKE THAT SWIMS THE RIVER COCYTUS...
FEAST ON THE FLESH OF THOSE WHO SPEAK.
SIP THE BLOOD OF THOSE WHO WRITE.
IF ANY DARES TO BREAK THIS PACT...
THEIR TREACHERY SHALL BE SUNG FOR *ALL* TO HEAR.
!
HISSSS!

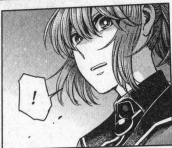

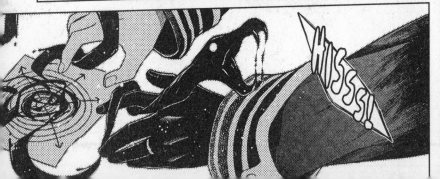

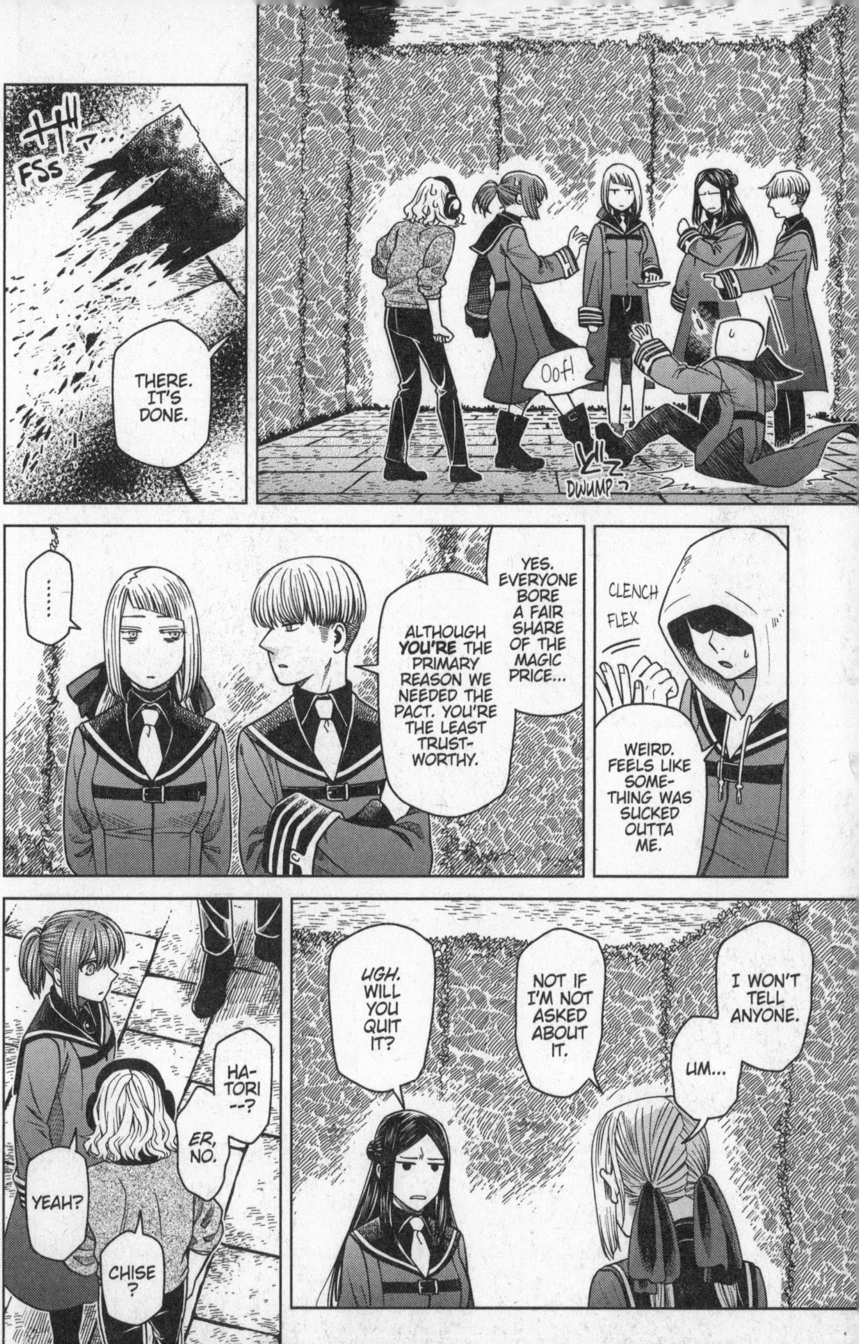
Oof!
DWUMP
FSS
THERE. IT'S DONE.
CLENCH
FLEX
WEIRD. FEELS LIKE SOME-THING WAS SUCKED OUTTA ME.
YES. EVERYONE BORE A FAIR SHARE OF THE MAGIC PRICE...
ALTHOUGH **YOU'RE** THE PRIMARY REASON WE NEEDED THE PACT. YOU'RE THE LEAST TRUST-WORTHY.
......
I WON'T TELL ANYONE.
UM...
NOT IF I'M NOT ASKED ABOUT IT.
UGH. WILL YOU QUIT IT?
HA-TORI--?
ER, NO.
YEAH?
CHISE?

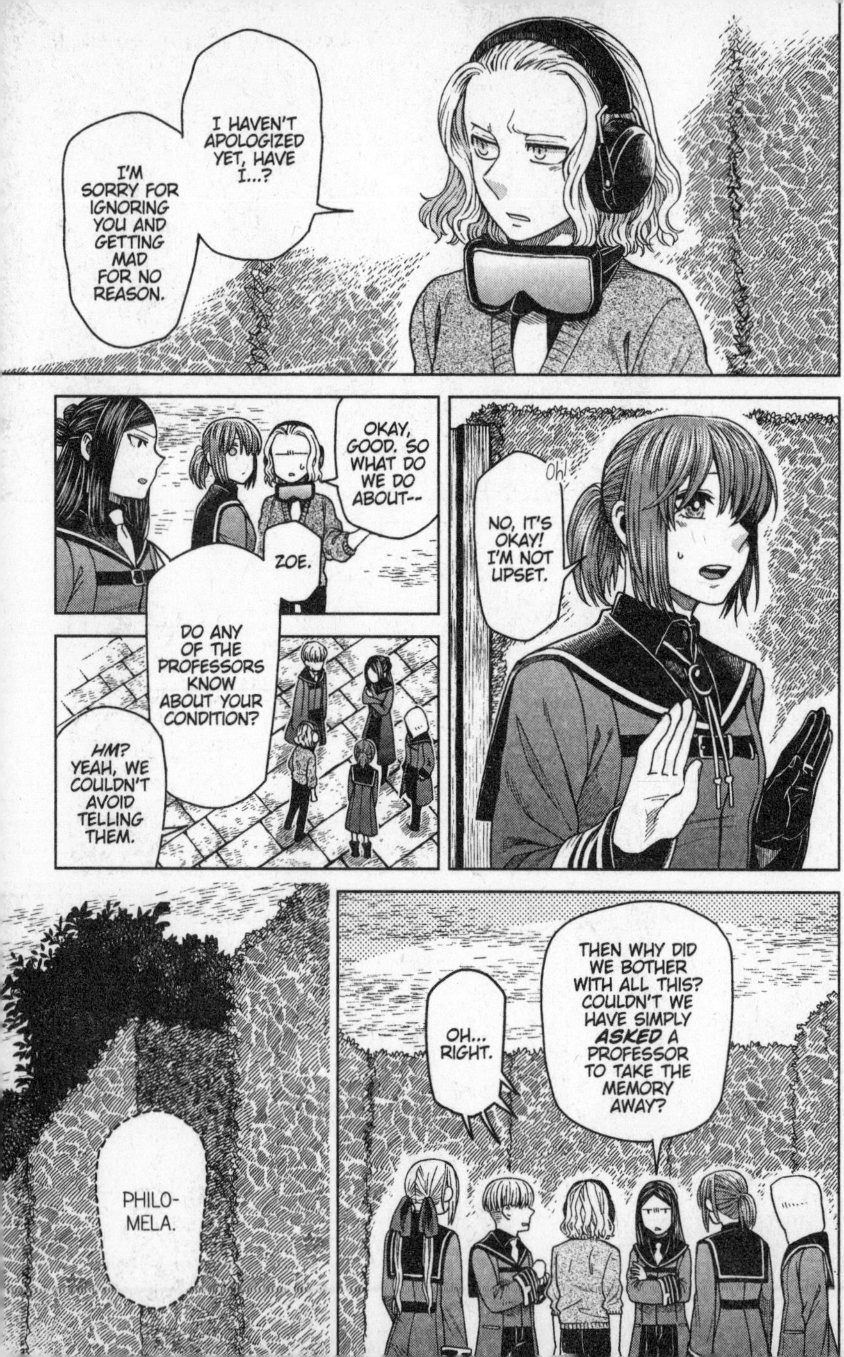
I HAVEN'T APOLOGIZED YET, HAVE I...?
I'M SORRY FOR IGNORING YOU AND GETTING MAD FOR NO REASON.
Oh!
NO, IT'S OKAY! I'M NOT UPSET.
OKAY, GOOD. SO WHAT DO WE DO ABOUT--
ZOE.
DO ANY OF THE PROFESSORS KNOW ABOUT YOUR CONDITION?
HM? YEAH, WE COULDN'T AVOID TELLING THEM.
THEN WHY DID WE BOTHER WITH ALL THIS? COULDN'T WE HAVE SIMPLY ASKED A PROFESSOR TO TAKE THE MEMORY AWAY?
OH... RIGHT.
......
PHILO-MELA.

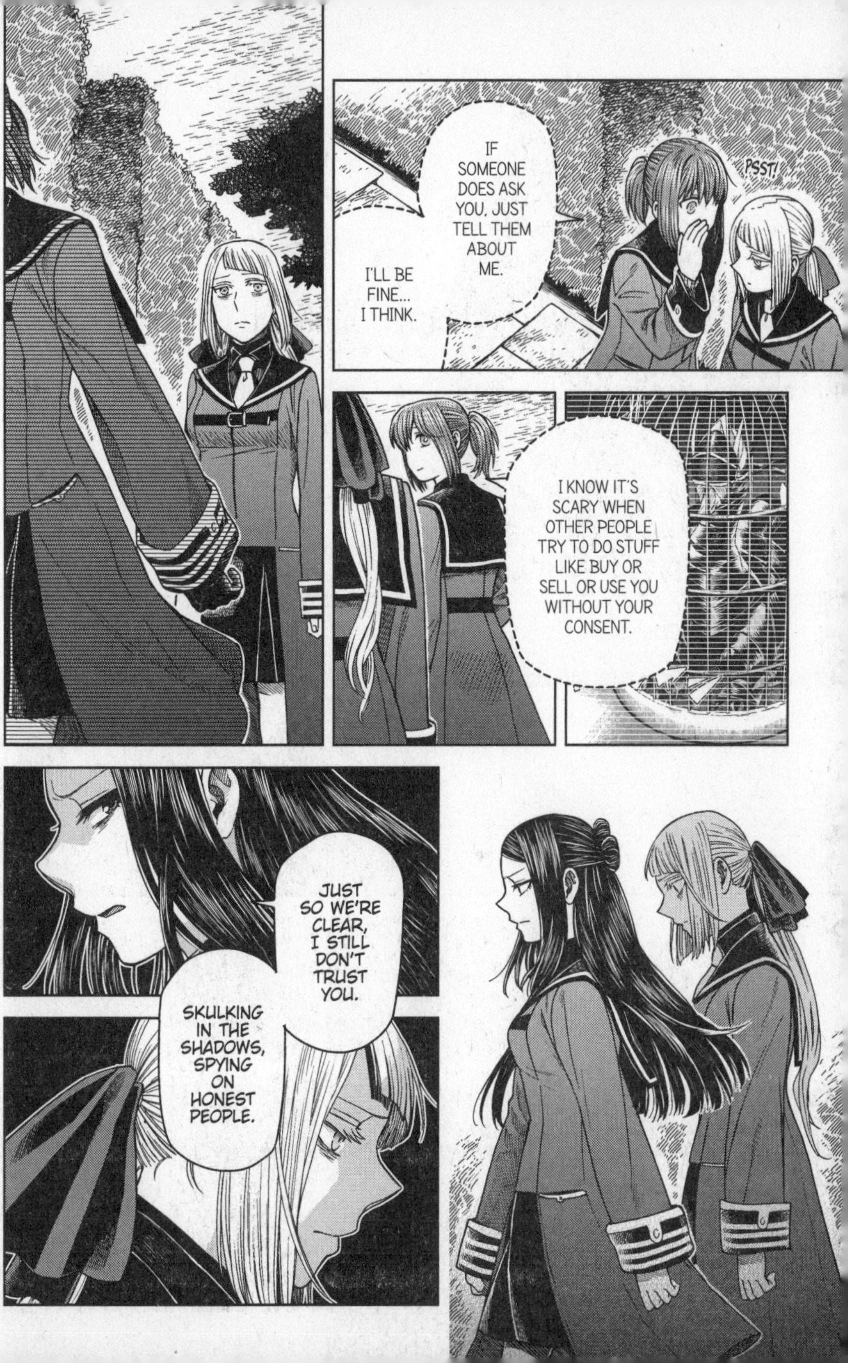
PSST!
IF SOMEONE DOES ASK YOU, JUST TELL THEM ABOUT ME.
I'LL BE FINE... I THINK.
I KNOW IT'S SCARY WHEN OTHER PEOPLE TRY TO DO STUFF LIKE BUY OR SELL OR USE YOU WITHOUT YOUR CONSENT.
JUST SO WE'RE CLEAR, I STILL DON'T TRUST YOU.
SKULKING IN THE SHADOWS, SPYING ON HONEST PEOPLE.

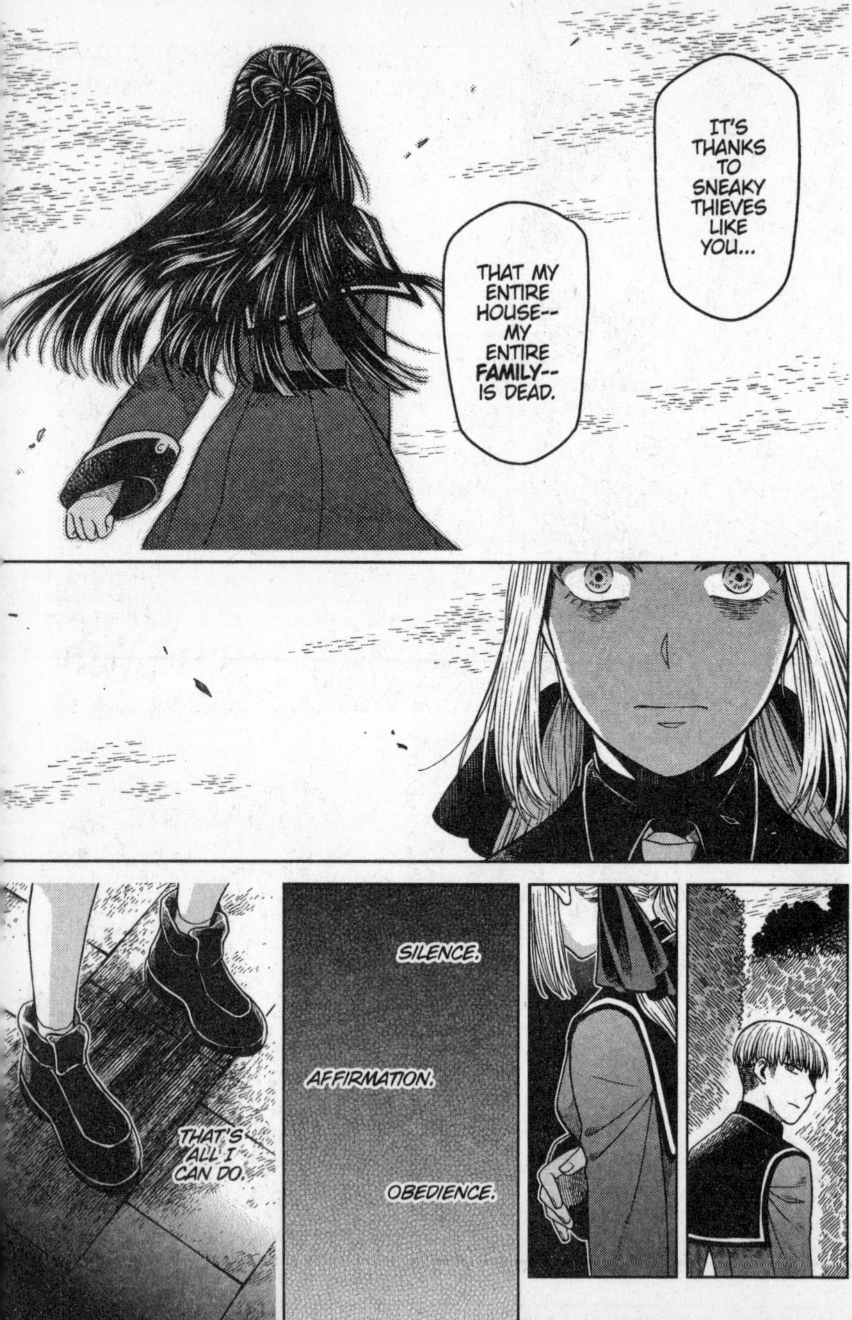
IT'S THANKS TO SNEAKY THIEVES LIKE YOU...
THAT MY ENTIRE HOUSE-- MY ENTIRE FAMILY-- IS DEAD.
SILENCE.
AFFIRMATION.
OBEDIENCE.
THAT'S ALL I CAN DO.

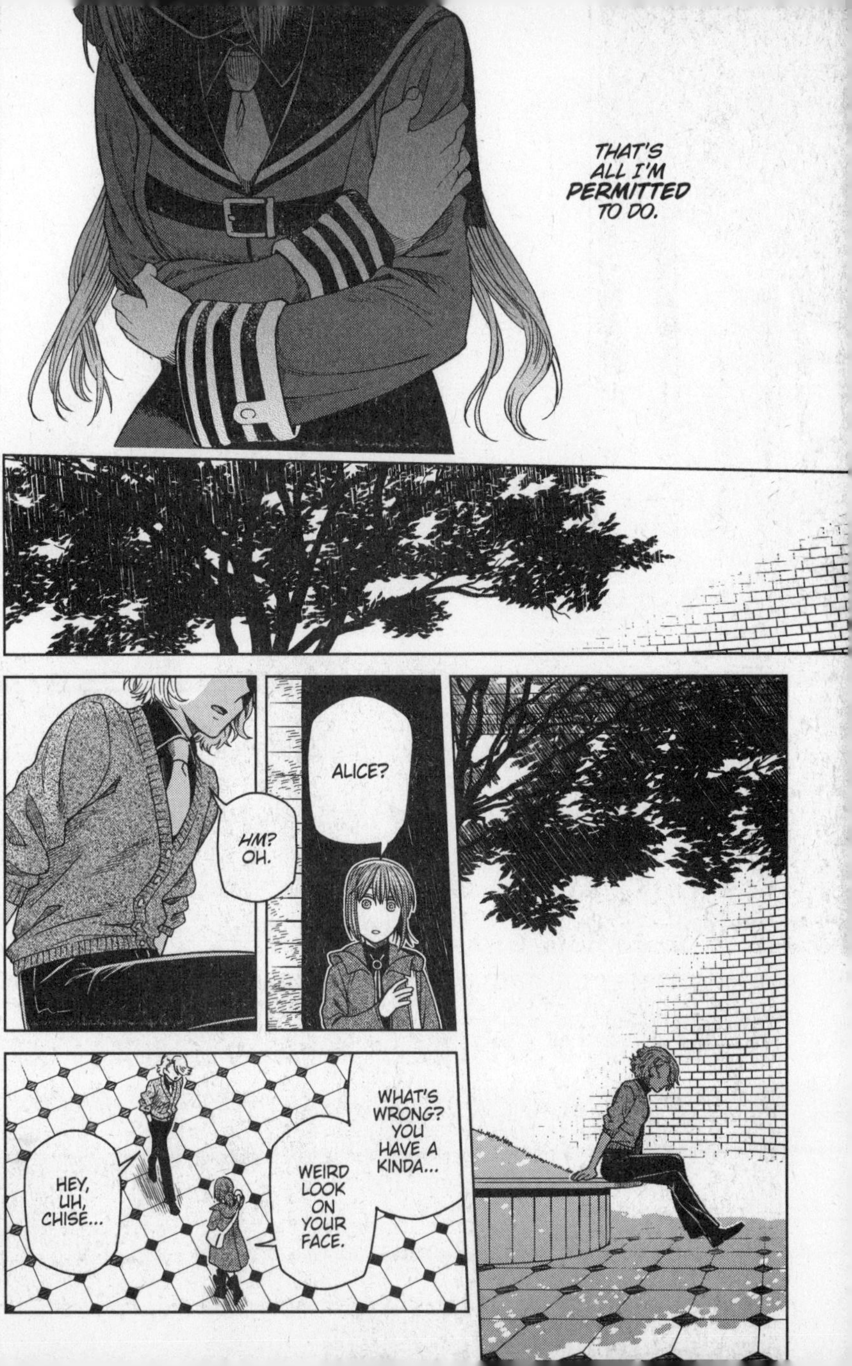
THAT'S ALL I'M PERMITTED TO DO.
ALICE?
HM? OH.
WHAT'S WRONG? YOU HAVE A KINDA...
WEIRD LOOK ON YOUR FACE.
HEY, UH, CHISE...

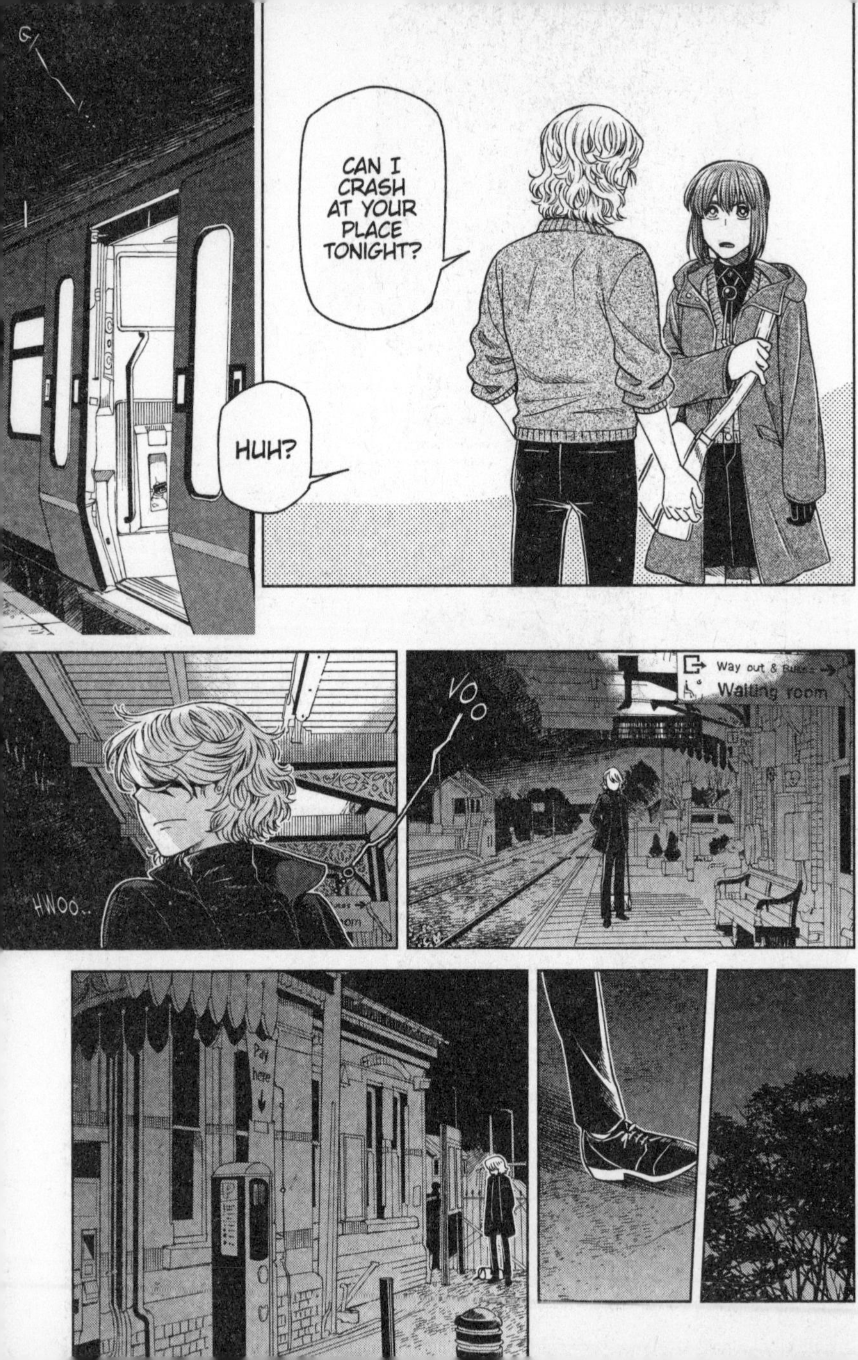
CAN I CRASH AT YOUR PLACE TONIGHT?
HUH?
Waiting room
VOO
HWOO..
Pay here

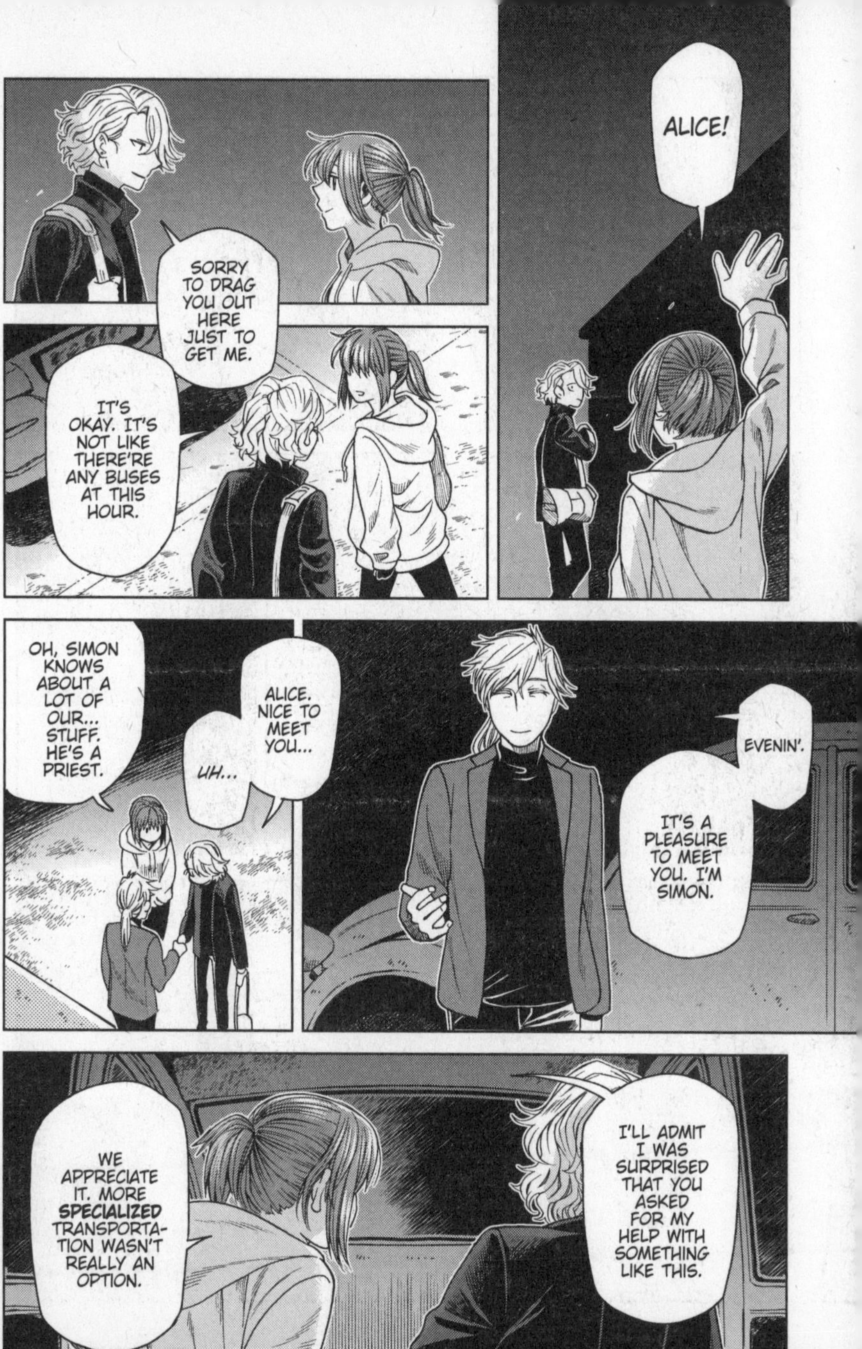
ALICE!
SORRY TO DRAG YOU OUT HERE JUST TO GET ME.
IT'S OKAY. IT'S NOT LIKE THERE'RE ANY BUSES AT THIS HOUR.
EVENIN'.
IT'S A PLEASURE TO MEET YOU. I'M SIMON.
ALICE. NICE TO MEET YOU...
UH...
OH, SIMON KNOWS ABOUT A LOT OF OUR... STUFF. HE'S A PRIEST.
I'LL ADMIT I WAS SURPRISED THAT YOU ASKED FOR MY HELP WITH SOMETHING LIKE THIS.
WE APPRECIATE IT. MORE **SPECIALIZED** TRANSPORTATION WASN'T REALLY AN OPTION.

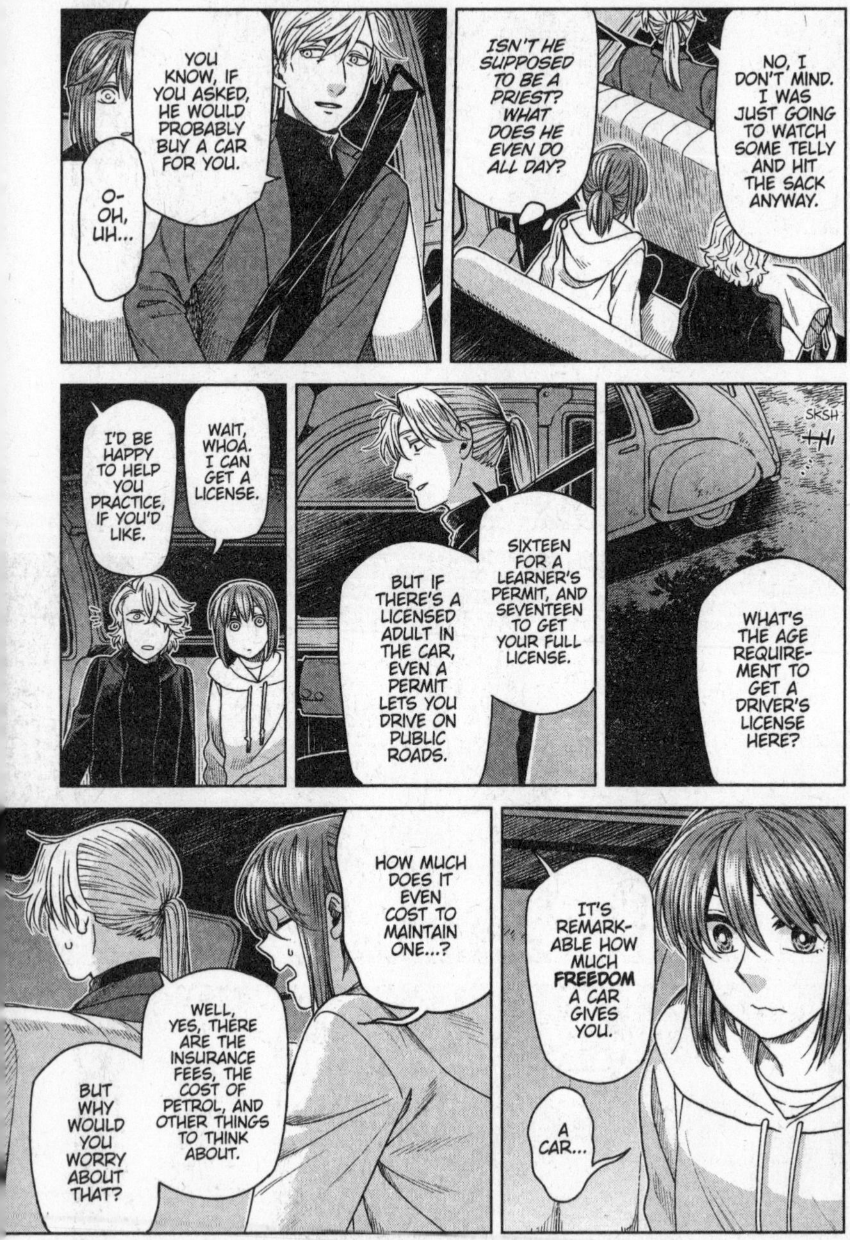
NO, I DON'T MIND. I WAS JUST GOING TO WATCH SOME TELLY AND HIT THE SACK ANYWAY.
ISN'T HE SUPPOSED TO BE A PRIEST? WHAT DOES HE EVEN DO ALL DAY?
YOU KNOW, IF YOU ASKED, HE WOULD PROBABLY BUY A CAR FOR YOU.
O-OH, UH...
SKSH
WHAT'S THE AGE REQUIREMENT TO GET A DRIVER'S LICENSE HERE?
SIXTEEN FOR A LEARNER'S PERMIT, AND SEVENTEEN TO GET YOUR FULL LICENSE.
BUT IF THERE'S A LICENSED ADULT IN THE CAR, EVEN A PERMIT LETS YOU DRIVE ON PUBLIC ROADS.
WAIT, WHOA. I CAN GET A LICENSE.
I'D BE HAPPY TO HELP YOU PRACTICE, IF YOU'D LIKE.
IT'S REMARKABLE HOW MUCH **FREEDOM** A CAR GIVES YOU.
A CAR...
HOW MUCH DOES IT EVEN COST TO MAINTAIN ONE...?
WELL, YES, THERE ARE THE INSURANCE FEES, THE COST OF PETROL, AND OTHER THINGS TO THINK ABOUT.
BUT WHY WOULD YOU WORRY ABOUT THAT?

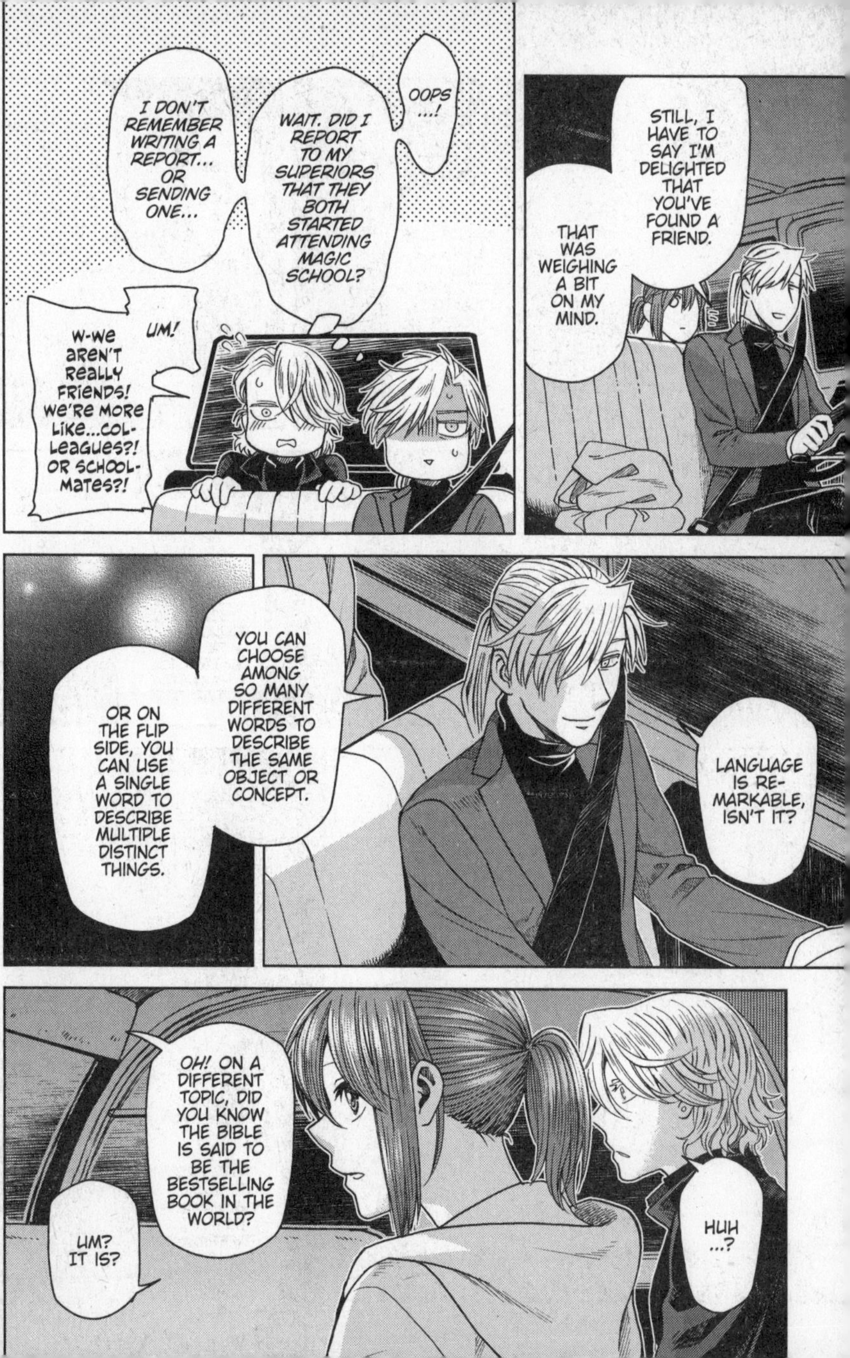
STILL, I HAVE TO SAY I'M DELIGHTED THAT YOU'VE FOUND A FRIEND.
THAT WAS WEIGHING A BIT ON MY MIND.
OOPS ...!
WAIT. DID I REPORT TO MY SUPERIORS THAT THEY BOTH STARTED ATTENDING MAGIC SCHOOL?
I DON'T REMEMBER WRITING A REPORT... OR SENDING ONE...
UM!
W-WE AREN'T REALLY FRIENDS! WE'RE MORE LIKE...COL-LEAGUES?! OR SCHOOL-MATES?!
LANGUAGE IS RE-MARKABLE, ISN'T IT?
YOU CAN CHOOSE AMONG SO MANY DIFFERENT WORDS TO DESCRIBE THE SAME OBJECT OR CONCEPT.
OR ON THE FLIP SIDE, YOU CAN USE A SINGLE WORD TO DESCRIBE MULTIPLE DISTINCT THINGS.
OH! ON A DIFFERENT TOPIC, DID YOU KNOW THE BIBLE IS SAID TO BE THE BESTSELLING BOOK IN THE WORLD?
HUH ...?
UM? IT IS?

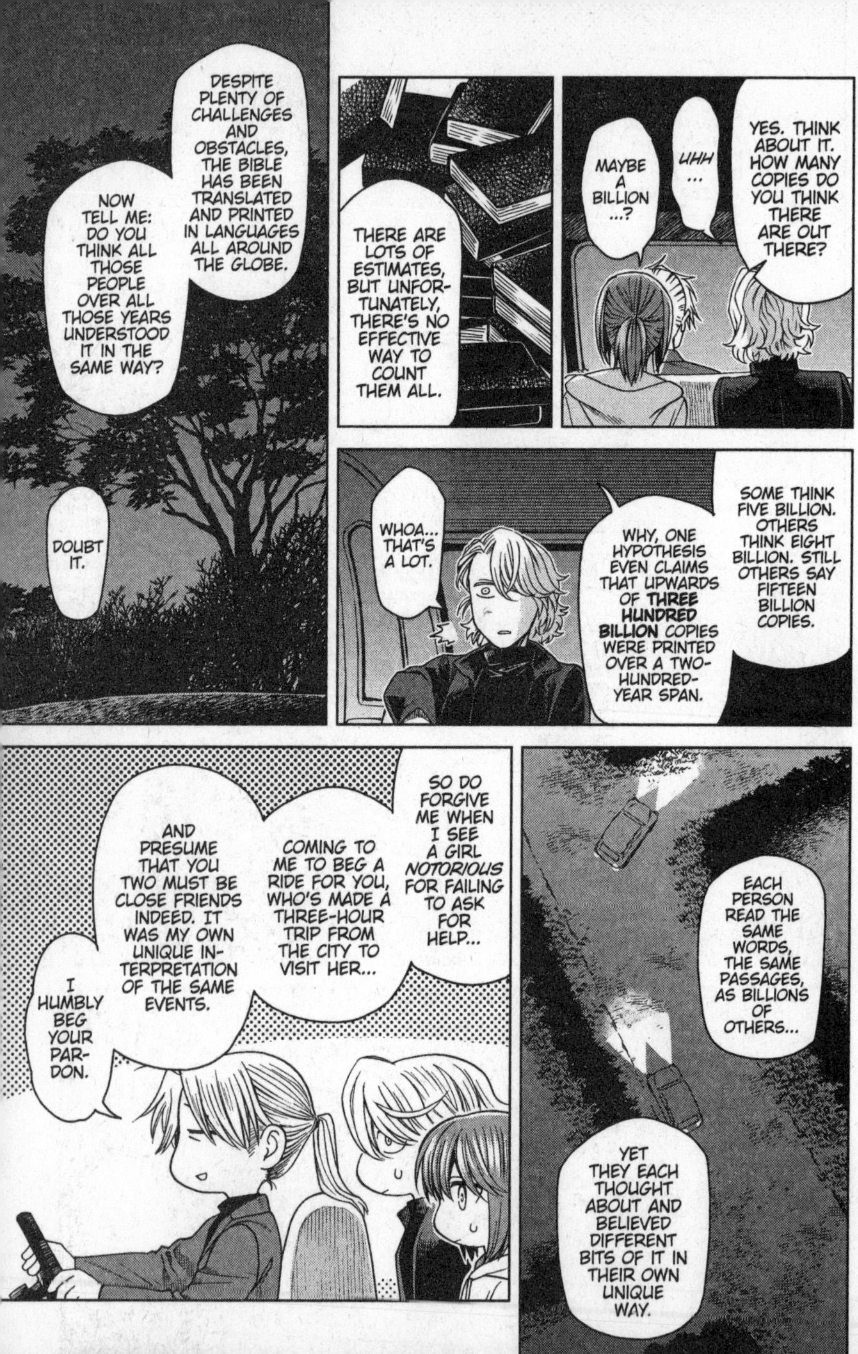
YES. THINK ABOUT IT. HOW MANY COPIES DO YOU THINK THERE ARE OUT THERE?
UHH ...
MAYBE A BILLION ...?
THERE ARE LOTS OF ESTIMATES, BUT UNFOR-TUNATELY, THERE'S NO EFFECTIVE WAY TO COUNT THEM ALL.
SOME THINK FIVE BILLION. OTHERS THINK EIGHT BILLION. STILL OTHERS SAY FIFTEEN BILLION COPIES.
WHY, ONE HYPOTHESIS EVEN CLAIMS THAT UPWARDS OF **THREE HUNDRED BILLION** COPIES WERE PRINTED OVER A TWO-HUNDRED-YEAR SPAN.
WHOA... THAT'S A LOT.
DESPITE PLENTY OF CHALLENGES AND OBSTACLES, THE BIBLE HAS BEEN TRANSLATED AND PRINTED IN LANGUAGES ALL AROUND THE GLOBE.
NOW TELL ME: DO YOU THINK ALL THOSE PEOPLE OVER ALL THOSE YEARS UNDERSTOOD IT IN THE SAME WAY?
DOUBT IT.
EACH PERSON READ THE SAME WORDS, THE SAME PASSAGES, AS BILLIONS OF OTHERS...
YET THEY EACH THOUGHT ABOUT AND BELIEVED DIFFERENT BITS OF IT IN THEIR OWN UNIQUE WAY.
SO DO FORGIVE ME WHEN I SEE A GIRL *NOTORIOUS* FOR FAILING TO ASK FOR HELP...
COMING TO ME TO BEG A RIDE FOR YOU, WHO'S MADE A THREE-HOUR TRIP FROM THE CITY TO VISIT HER...
AND PRESUME THAT YOU TWO MUST BE CLOSE FRIENDS INDEED. IT WAS MY OWN UNIQUE IN-TERPRETATION OF THE SAME EVENTS.
I HUMBLY BEG YOUR PAR-DON.

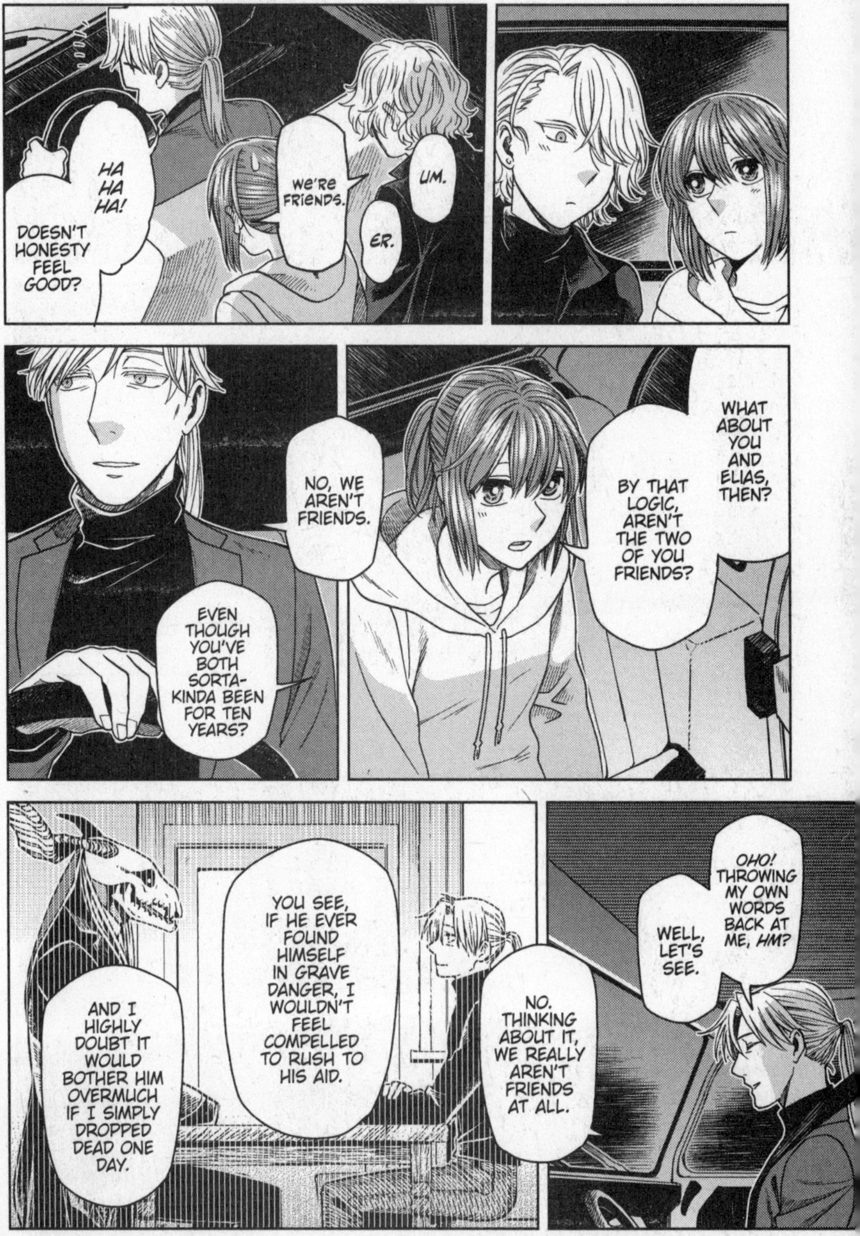
UM.
ER.
WE'RE FRIENDS.
HA HA HA! DOESN'T HONESTY FEEL GOOD?
WHAT ABOUT YOU AND ELIAS, THEN?
BY THAT LOGIC, AREN'T THE TWO OF YOU FRIENDS?
NO, WE AREN'T FRIENDS.
EVEN THOUGH YOU'VE BOTH SORTA-KINDA BEEN FOR TEN YEARS?
OHO! THROWING MY OWN WORDS BACK AT ME, HM?
WELL, LET'S SEE.
NO. THINKING ABOUT IT, WE REALLY AREN'T FRIENDS AT ALL.
YOU SEE, IF HE EVER FOUND HIMSELF IN GRAVE DANGER, I WOULDN'T FEEL COMPELLED TO RUSH TO HIS AID.
AND I HIGHLY DOUBT IT WOULD BOTHER HIM OVERMUCH IF I SIMPLY DROPPED DEAD ONE DAY.

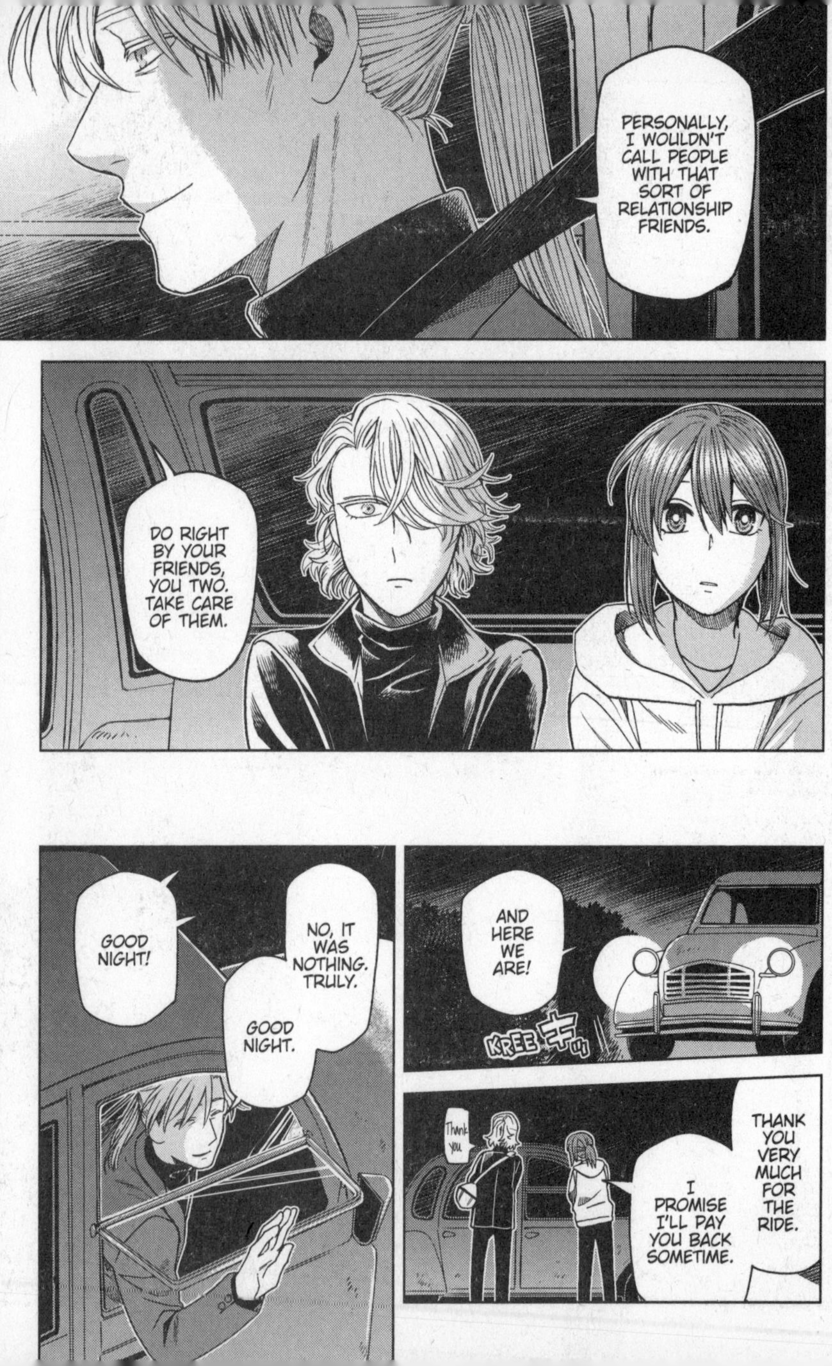
PERSONALLY, I WOULDN'T CALL PEOPLE WITH THAT SORT OF RELATIONSHIP FRIENDS.
DO RIGHT BY YOUR FRIENDS, YOU TWO. TAKE CARE OF THEM.
AND HERE WE ARE!
KREE キュ
THANK YOU VERY MUCH FOR THE RIDE.
I PROMISE I'LL PAY YOU BACK SOMETIME.
Thank you
NO, IT WAS NOTHING. TRULY.
GOOD NIGHT.
GOOD NIGHT!

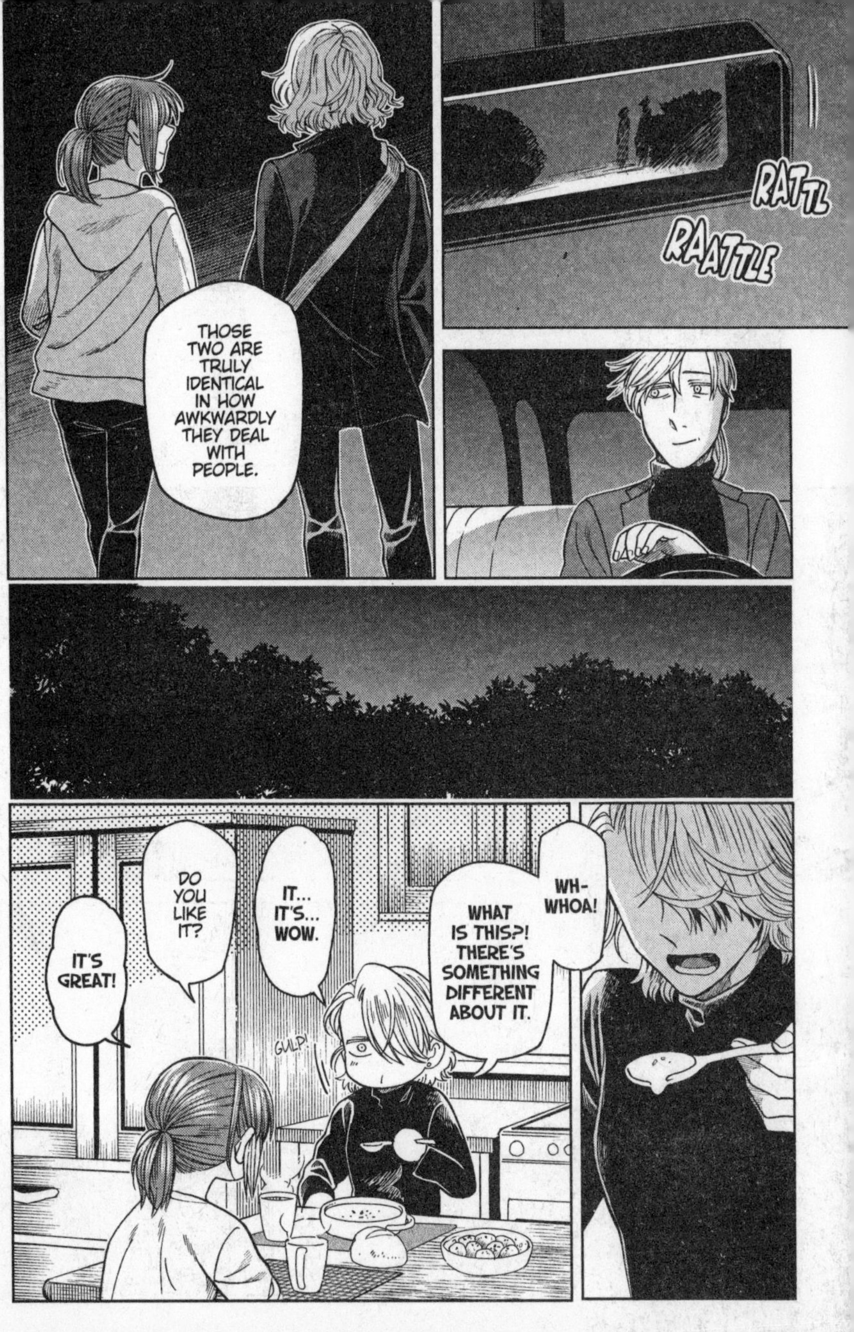
RATTL
RAATTLE
THOSE TWO ARE TRULY IDENTICAL IN HOW AWKWARDLY THEY DEAL WITH PEOPLE.
WH- WHOA!
WHAT IS THIS?! THERE'S SOMETHING DIFFERENT ABOUT IT.
IT... IT'S... WOW.
DO YOU LIKE IT?
IT'S GREAT!
GULP!

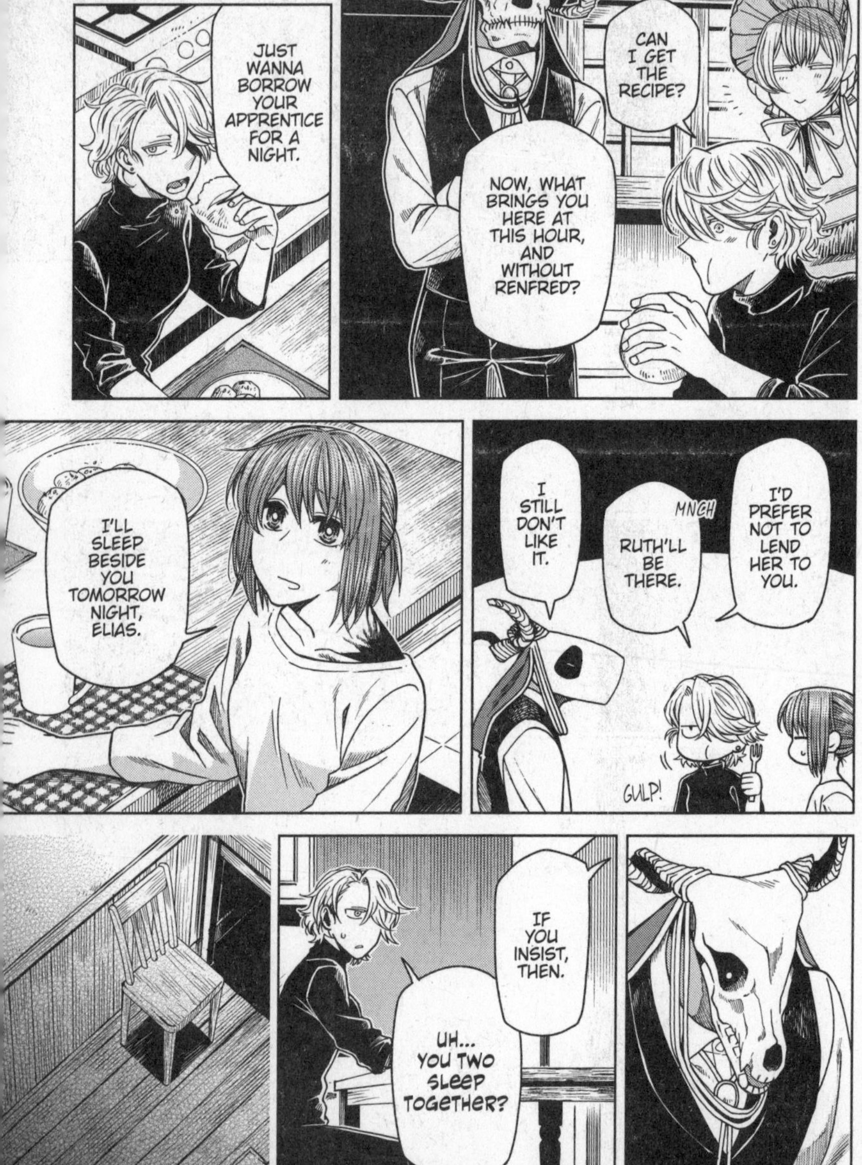
CAN I GET THE RECIPE?
NOW, WHAT BRINGS YOU HERE AT THIS HOUR, AND WITHOUT RENFRED?
JUST WANNA BORROW YOUR APPRENTICE FOR A NIGHT.
I'D PREFER NOT TO LEND HER TO YOU.
MNCH
RUTH'LL BE THERE.
I STILL DON'T LIKE IT.
GULP!
I'LL SLEEP BESIDE YOU TOMORROW NIGHT, ELIAS.
IF YOU INSIST, THEN.
UH... YOU TWO SLEEP TOGETHER?

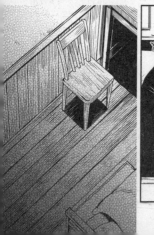

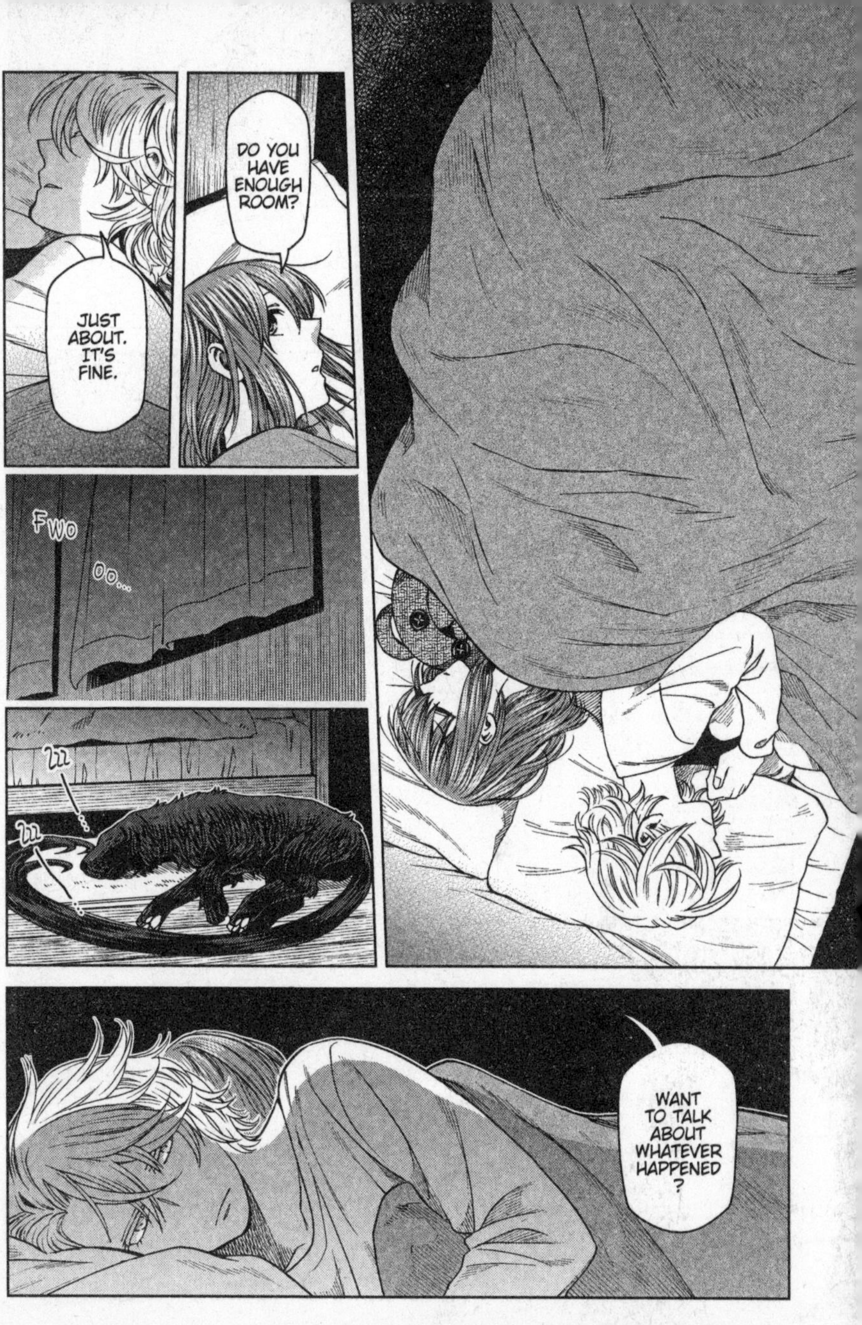
DO YOU HAVE ENOUGH ROOM?
JUST ABOUT. IT'S FINE.
FWOOO...
ZZZ...
ZZZ...
WANT TO TALK ABOUT WHATEVER HAPPENED?

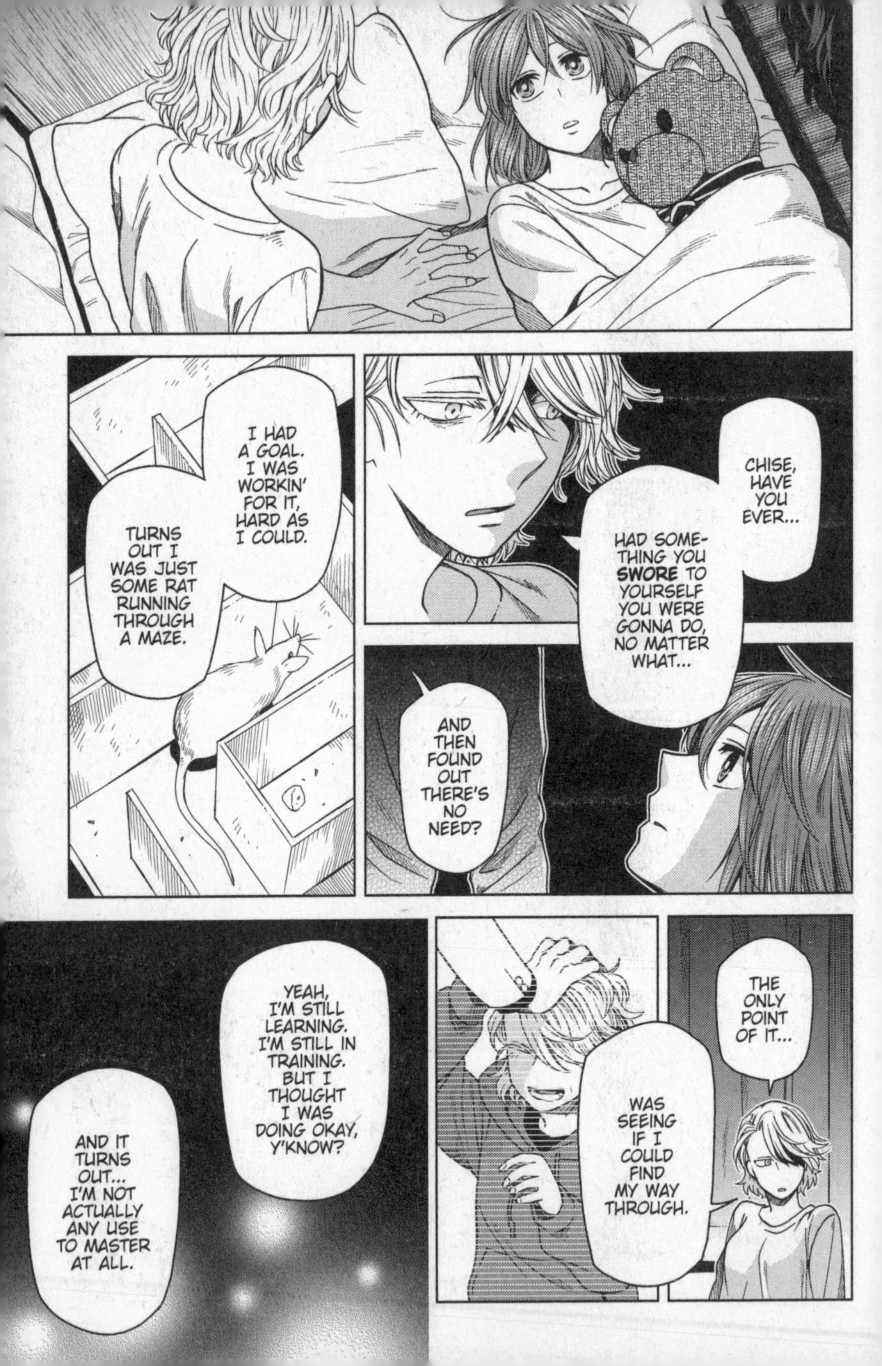
CHISE, HAVE YOU EVER...
HAD SOME-THING YOU **SWORE** TO YOURSELF YOU WERE GONNA DO, NO MATTER WHAT...
AND THEN FOUND OUT THERE'S NO NEED?
I HAD A GOAL. I WAS WORKIN' FOR IT, HARD AS I COULD.
TURNS OUT I WAS JUST SOME RAT RUNNING THROUGH A MAZE.
THE ONLY POINT OF IT...
WAS SEEING IF I COULD FIND MY WAY THROUGH.
YEAH, I'M STILL LEARNING. I'M STILL IN TRAINING. BUT I THOUGHT I WAS DOING OKAY, Y'KNOW?
AND IT TURNS OUT... I'M NOT ACTUALLY ANY USE TO MASTER AT ALL.

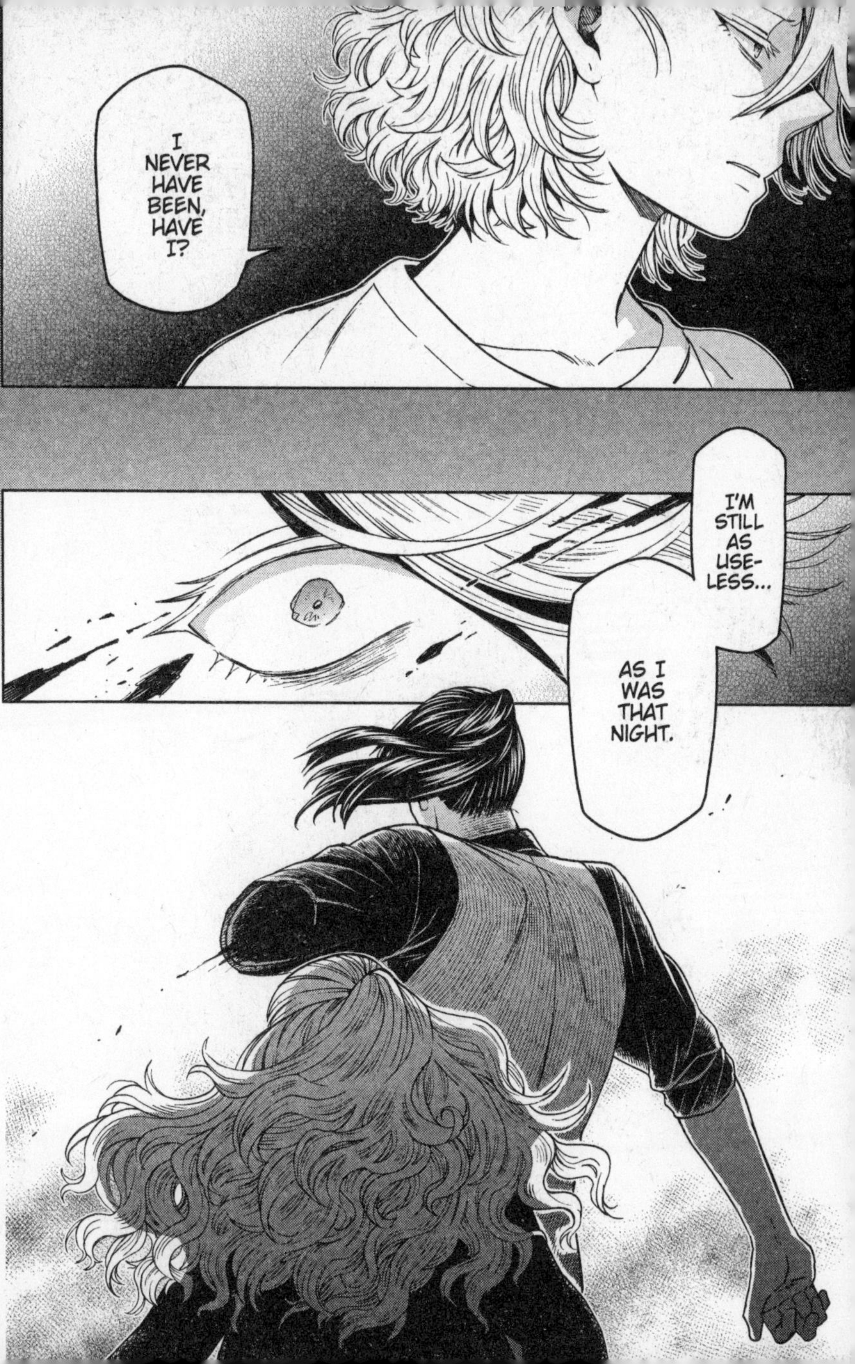
I NEVER HAVE BEEN, HAVE I?
I'M STILL AS USELESS...
AS I WAS THAT NIGHT.

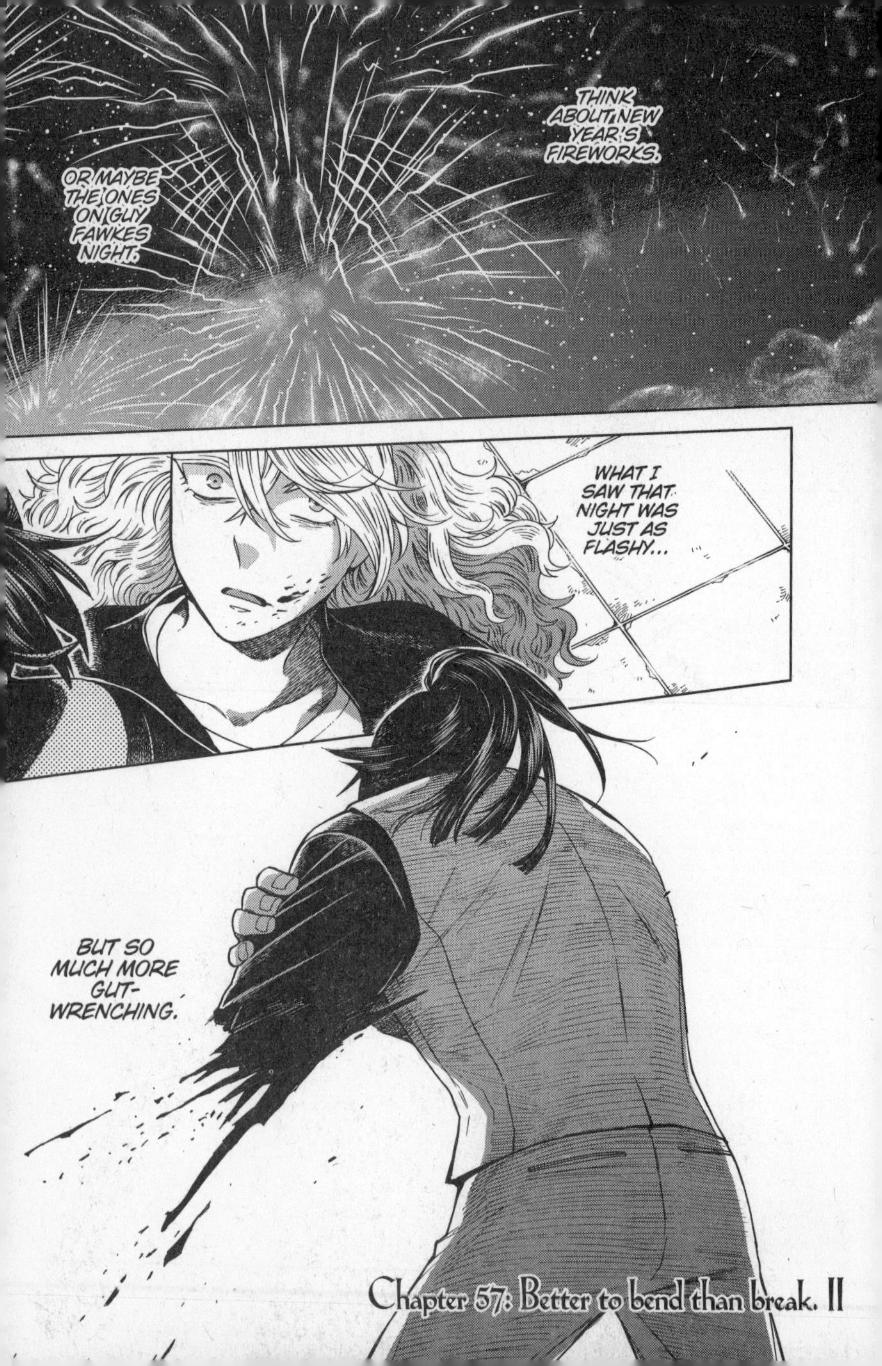
THINK ABOUT NEW YEAR'S FIREWORKS.
OR MAYBE THE ONES ON GUY FAWKES NIGHT.
WHAT I SAW THAT NIGHT WAS JUST AS FLASHY...
BUT SO MUCH MORE GUT-WRENCHING.

# Chapter 57: Better to bend than break. II

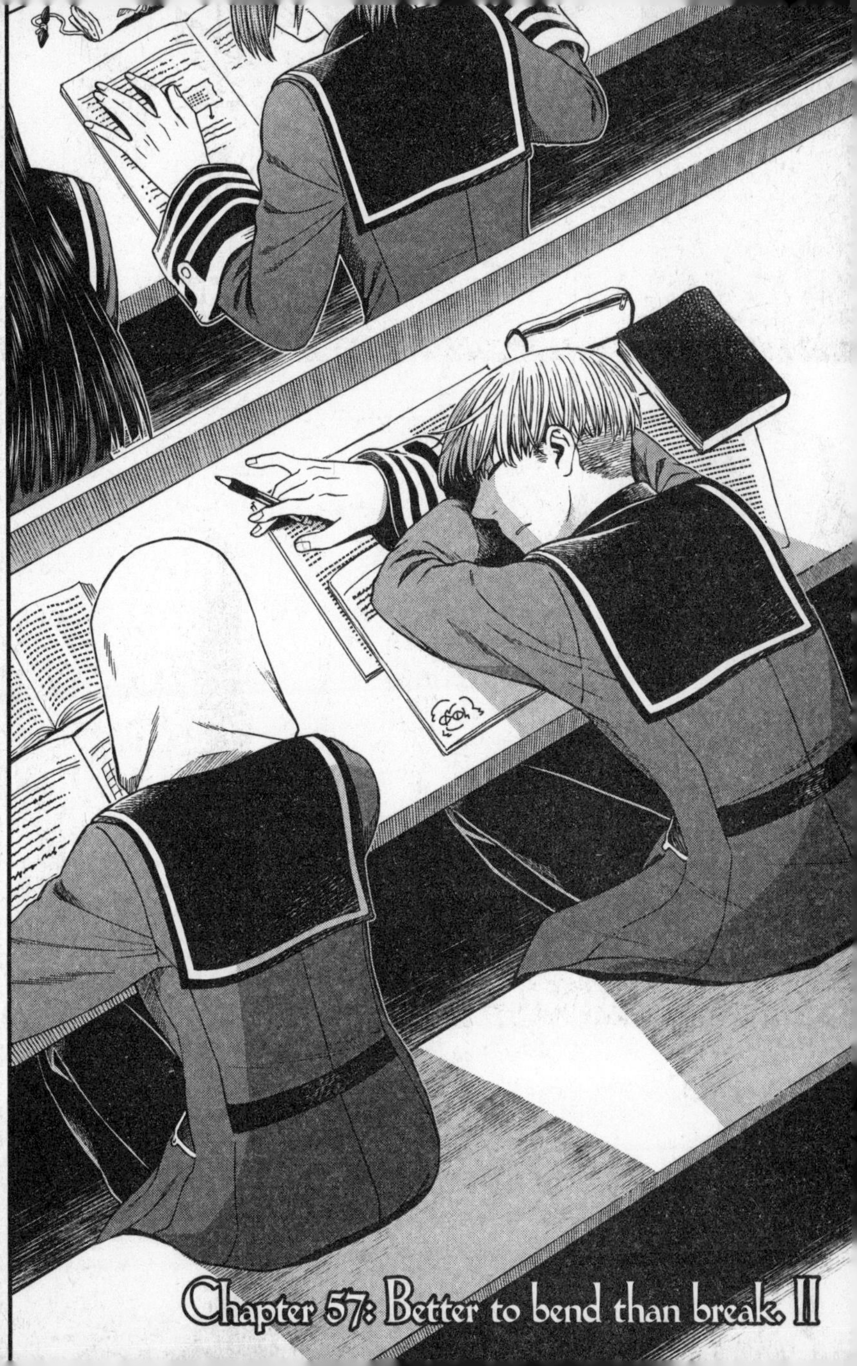

# Chapter 57: Better to bend than break. II

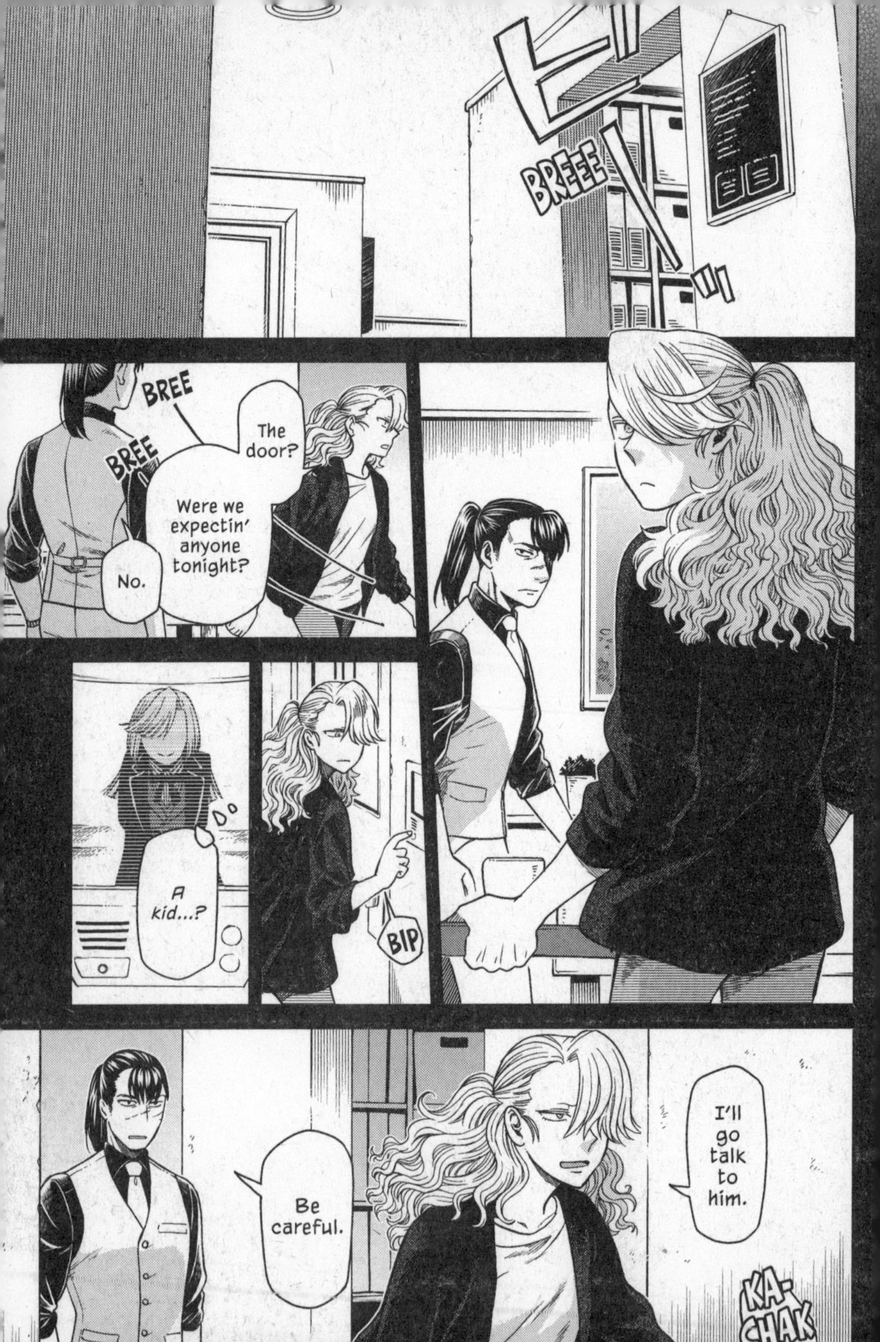
BREEE
The door?
BREE
BREE
Were we expectin' anyone tonight?
No.
BIP
DO
A kid...?
I'll go talk to him.
KA-CHAK
Be careful.

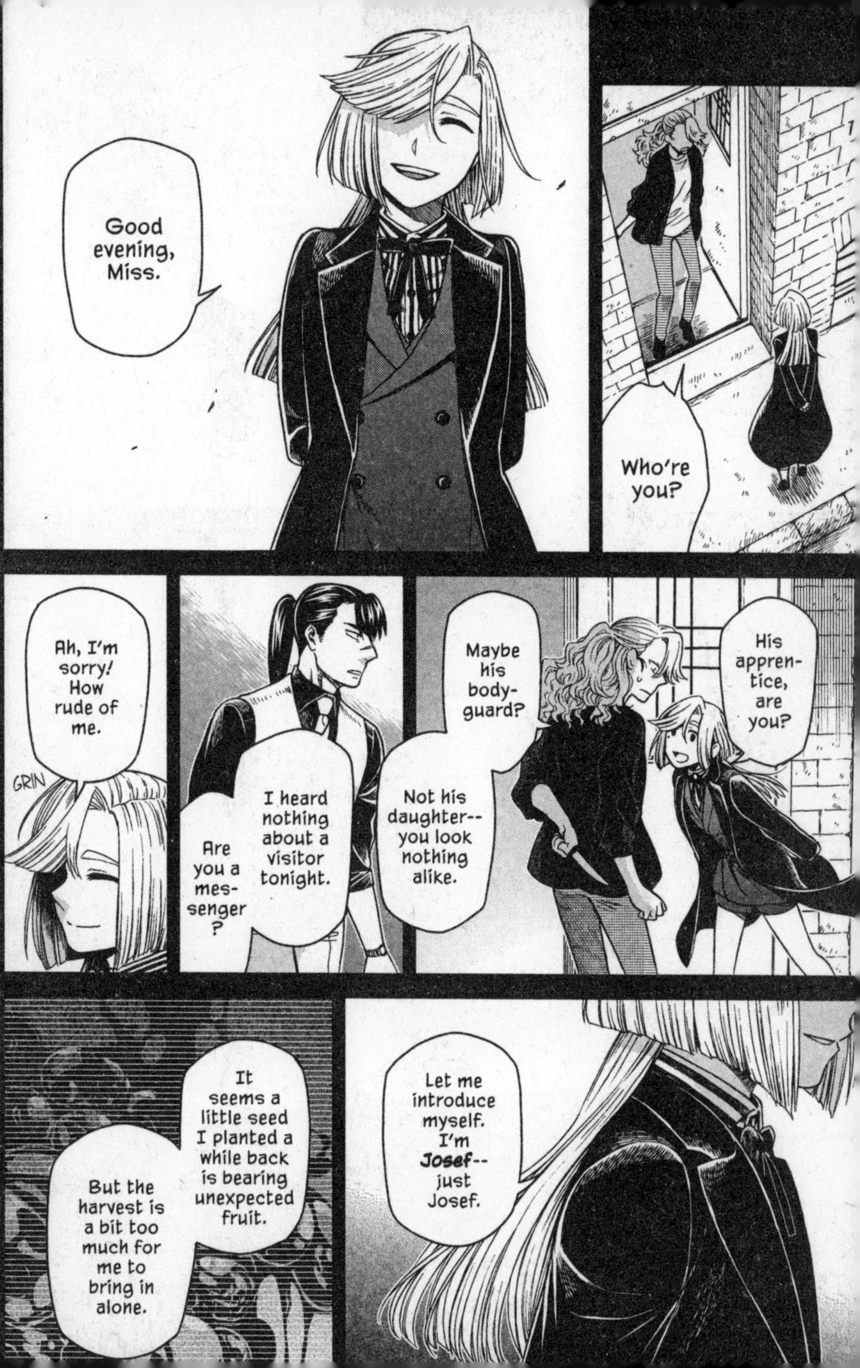
Who're you?
Good evening, Miss.
His apprentice, are you?
Maybe his bodyguard?
Not his daughter-- you look nothing alike.
I heard nothing about a visitor tonight.
Are you a messenger?
Ah, I'm sorry! How rude of me.
GRIN
Let me introduce myself. I'm **Josef**-- just Josef.
It seems a little seed I planted a while back is bearing unexpected fruit.
But the harvest is a bit too much for me to bring in alone.

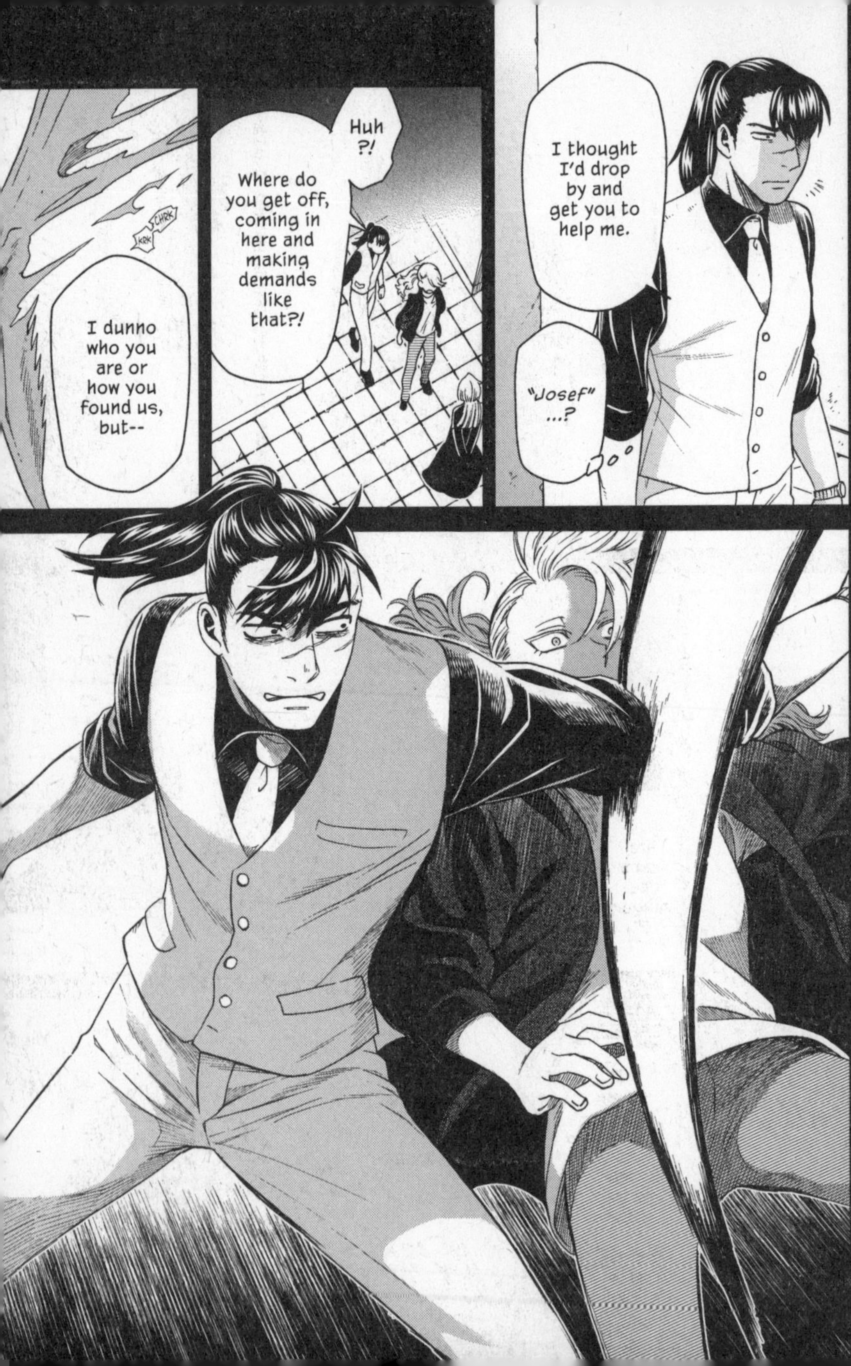
I thought I'd drop by and get you to help me.
"Josef" ...?
Huh ?!
Where do you get off, coming in here and making demands like that?!
CHRK
KRK
I dunno who you are or how you found us, but--

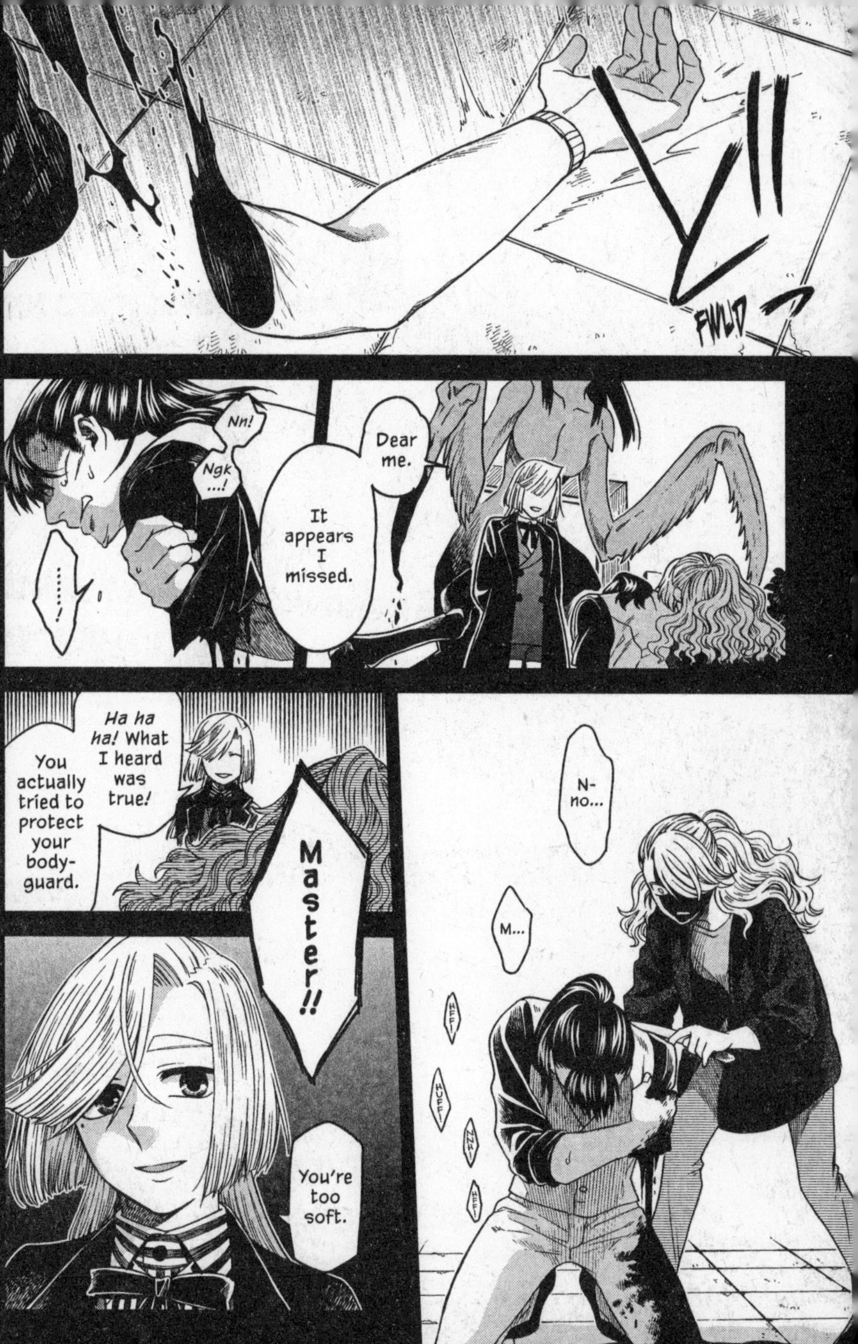
FWUD
Dear me.
It appears I missed.
Nn!
Ngk ...!
......!
N-no...
M...
Master!!
HFF!
HUFF!
NNH!
HFF!
Ha ha ha! What I heard was true!
You actually tried to protect your body-guard.
You're too soft.

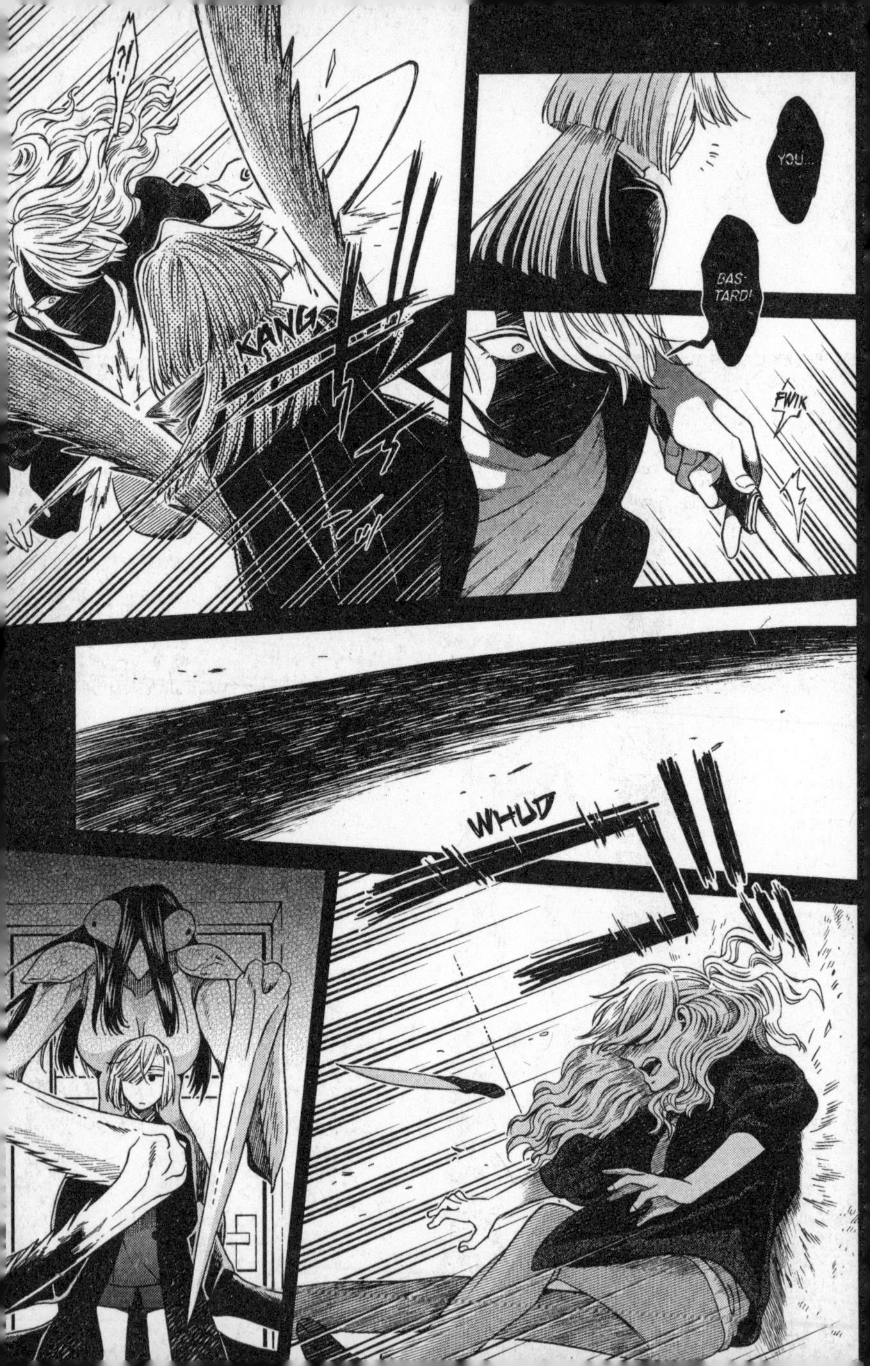
YOU...
BAS-TARD!
FWIK
?!
KANG
WHUD

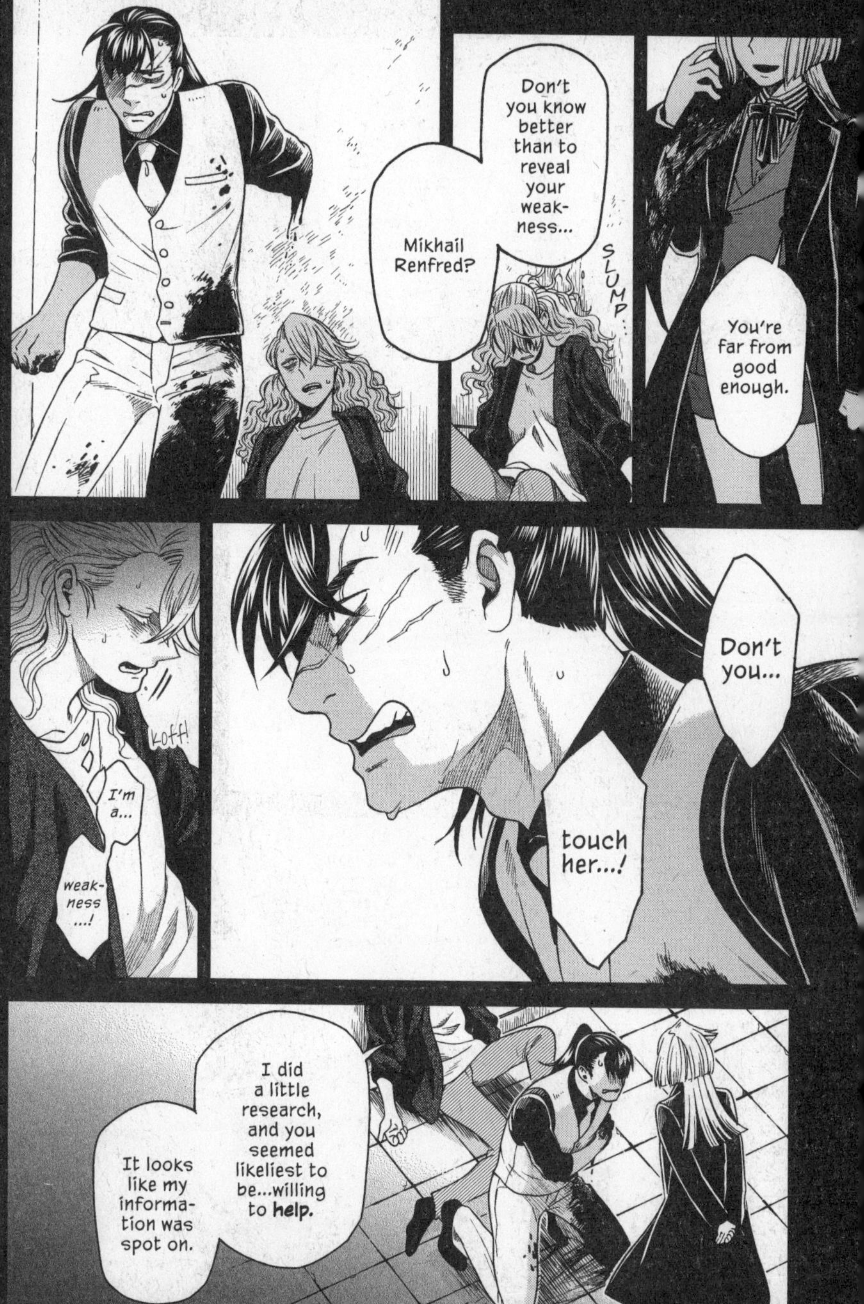
You're far from good enough.
Don't you know better than to reveal your weakness...
Mikhail Renfred?
SLUMP...
Don't you...
touch her...!
koff!
I'm a...
weakness...!
I did a little research, and you seemed likeliest to be...willing to **help.**
It looks like my information was spot on.

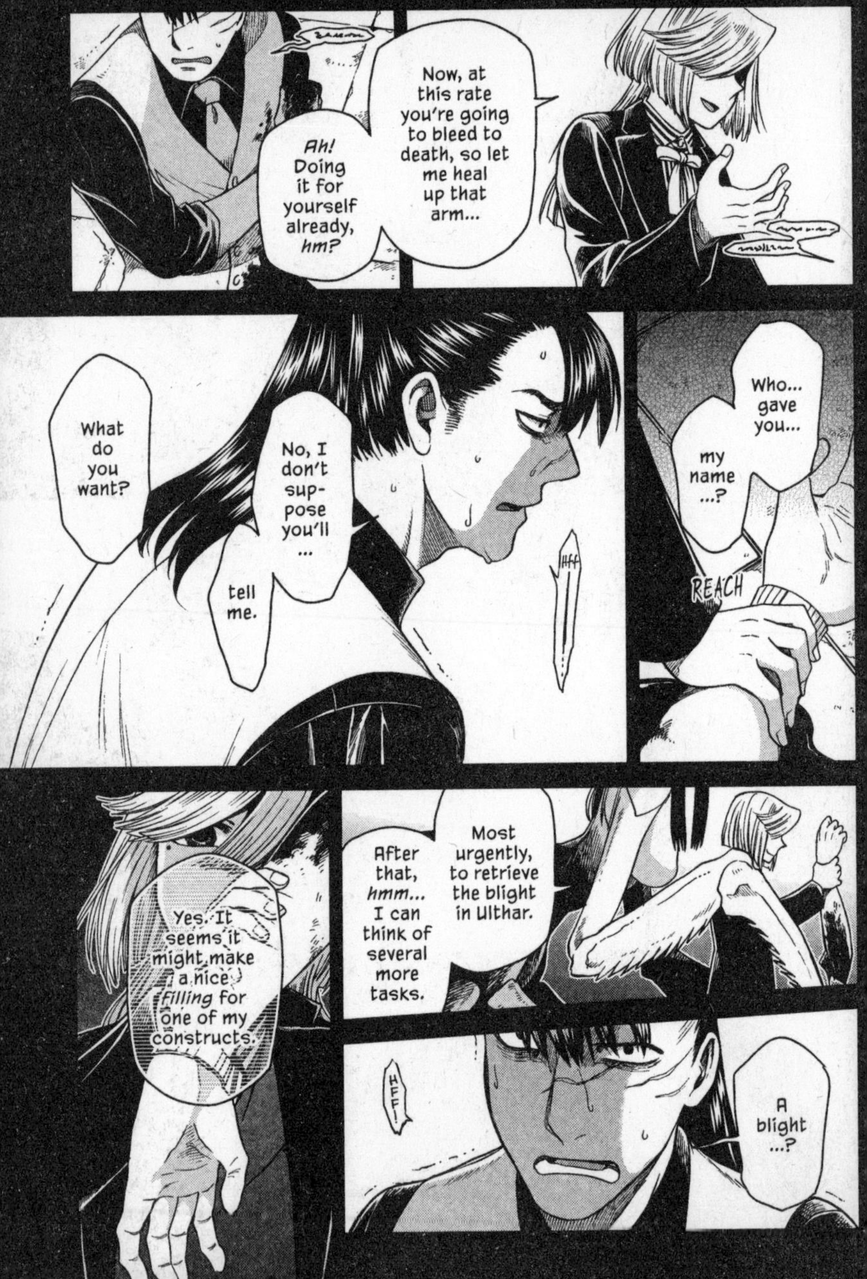
Now, at this rate you're going to bleed to death, so let me heal up that arm...
*Ah!* Doing it for yourself already, *hm?*
Who... gave you... my name ...?
REACH
No, I don't suppose you'll ...
tell me.
HFF
What do you want?
Most urgently, to retrieve the blight in Ulthar.
After that, *hmm...* I can think of several more tasks.
A blight ...?
HFF!
Yes. It seems it might make a nice *filling* for one of my constructs.

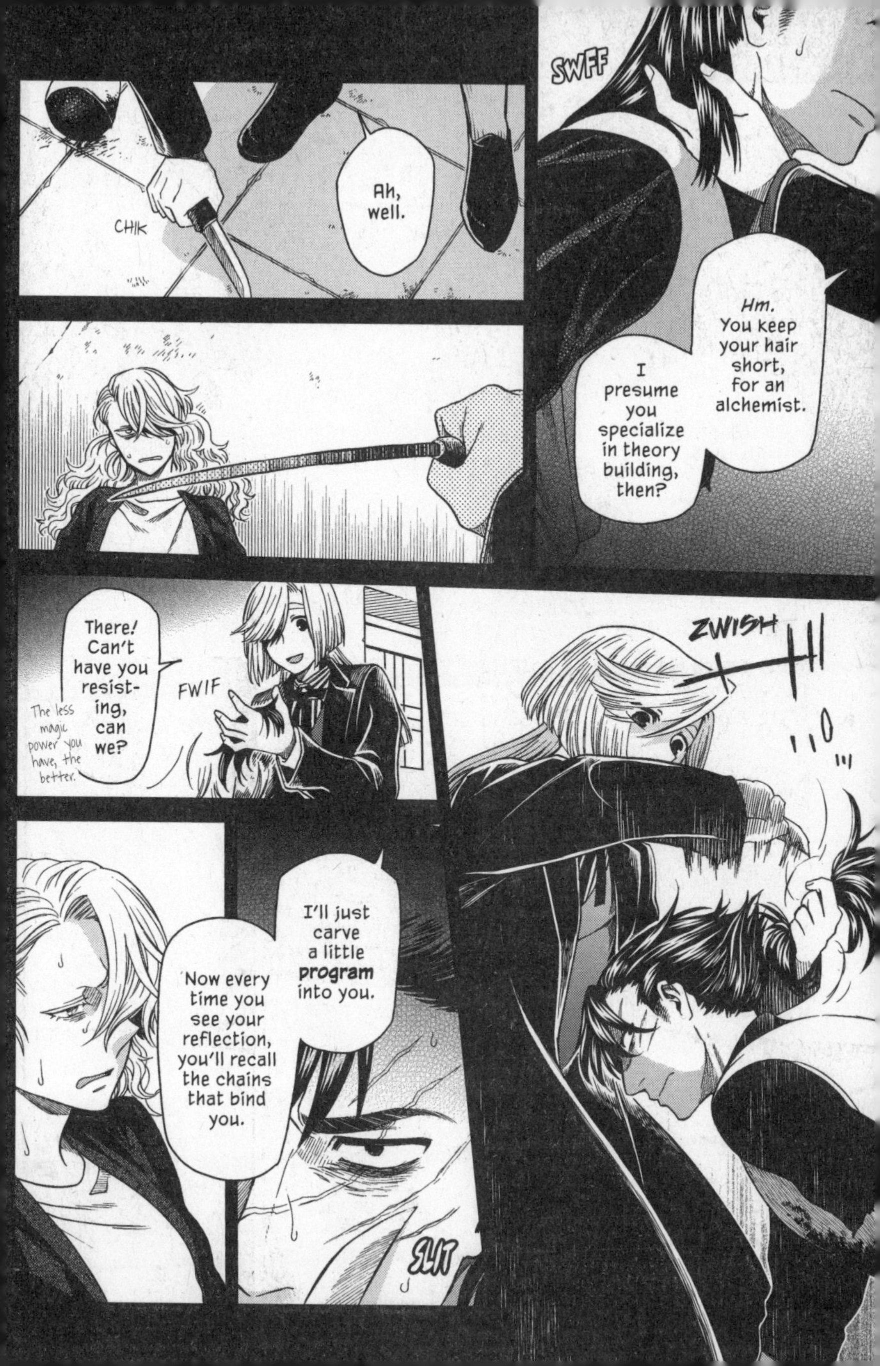
SWFF
Hm. You keep your hair short, for an alchemist.
I presume you specialize in theory building, then?
Ah, well.
CHIK
ZWISH
There! Can't have you resisting, can we?
FWIF
The less magic power you have, the better.
I'll just carve a little **program** into you.
Now every time you see your reflection, you'll recall the chains that bind you.
SLIT

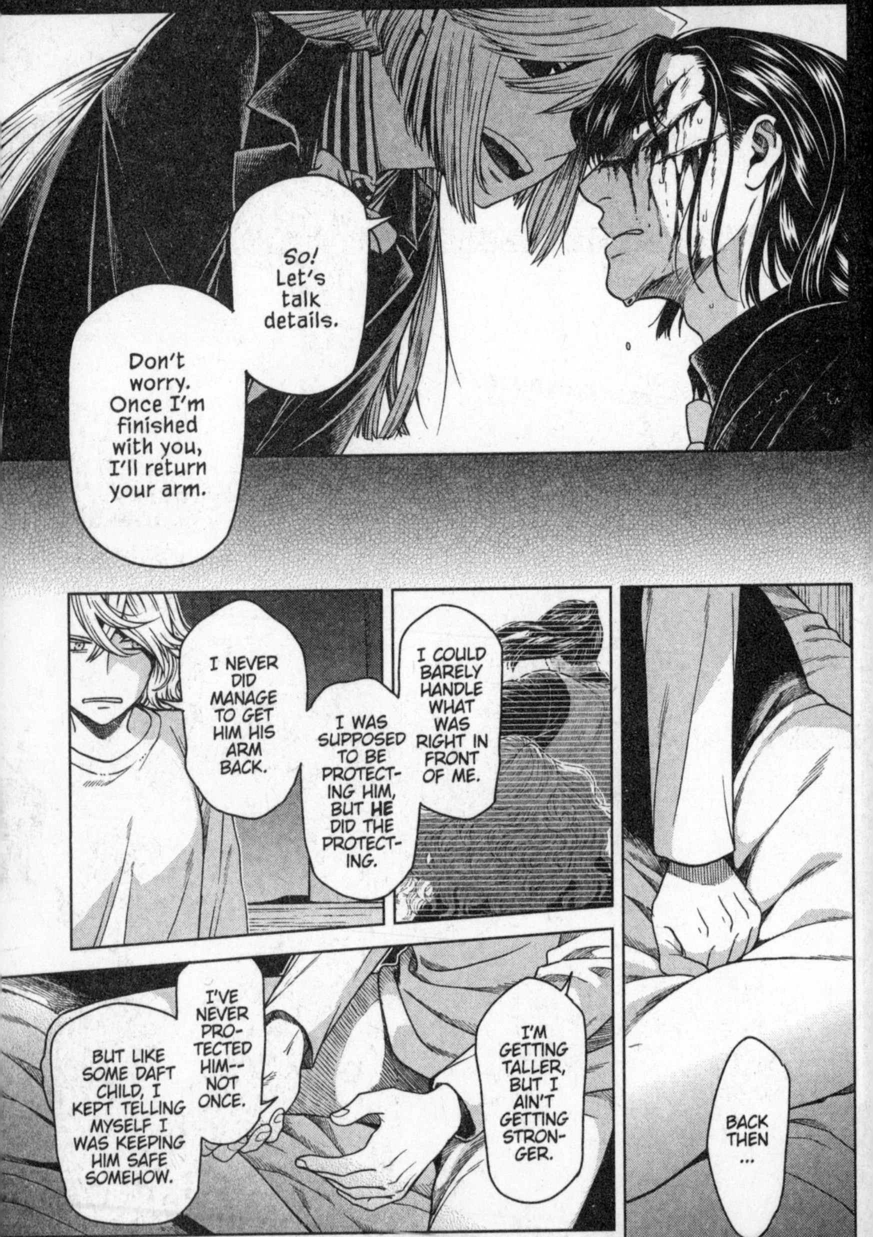
So! Let's talk details.
Don't worry. Once I'm finished with you, I'll return your arm.
BACK THEN ...
I COULD BARELY HANDLE WHAT WAS RIGHT IN FRONT OF ME.
I WAS SUPPOSED TO BE PROTECTING HIM, BUT HE DID THE PROTECTING.
I NEVER DID MANAGE TO GET HIM HIS ARM BACK.
I'M GETTING TALLER, BUT I AIN'T GETTING STRONGER.
I'VE NEVER PROTECTED HIM--NOT ONCE.
BUT LIKE SOME DAFT CHILD, I KEPT TELLING MYSELF I WAS KEEPING HIM SAFE SOMEHOW.

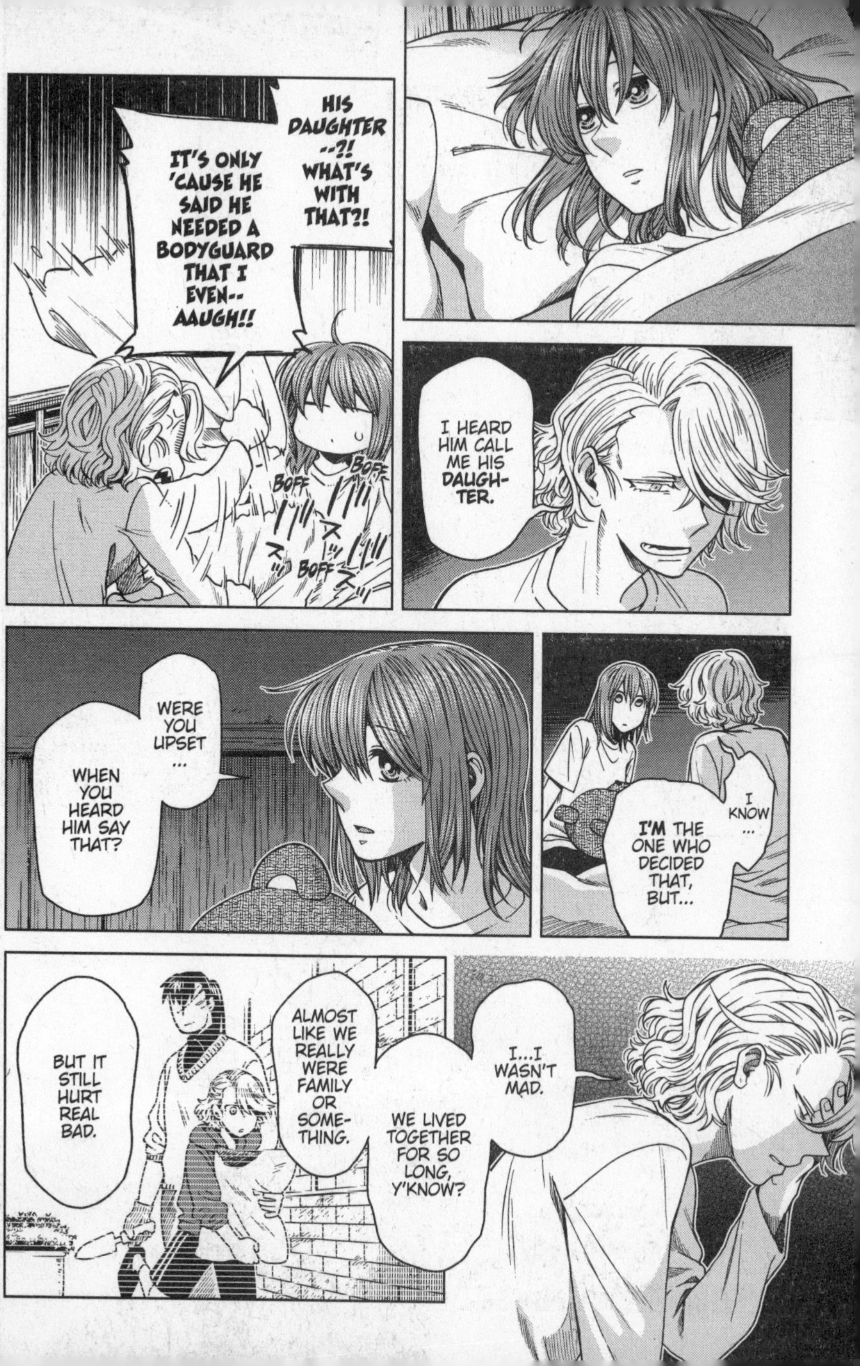
I HEARD HIM CALL ME HIS DAUGHTER.
HIS DAUGHTER--?! WHAT'S WITH THAT?!
IT'S ONLY 'CAUSE HE SAID HE NEEDED A BODYGUARD THAT I EVEN--AAUGH!!
BOFF
BOFF
BOFF
I KNOW...
I'M THE ONE WHO DECIDED THAT, BUT...
WERE YOU UPSET...
WHEN YOU HEARD HIM SAY THAT?
I...I WASN'T MAD.
WE LIVED TOGETHER FOR SO LONG, Y'KNOW?
ALMOST LIKE WE REALLY WERE FAMILY OR SOMETHING.
BUT IT STILL HURT REAL BAD.

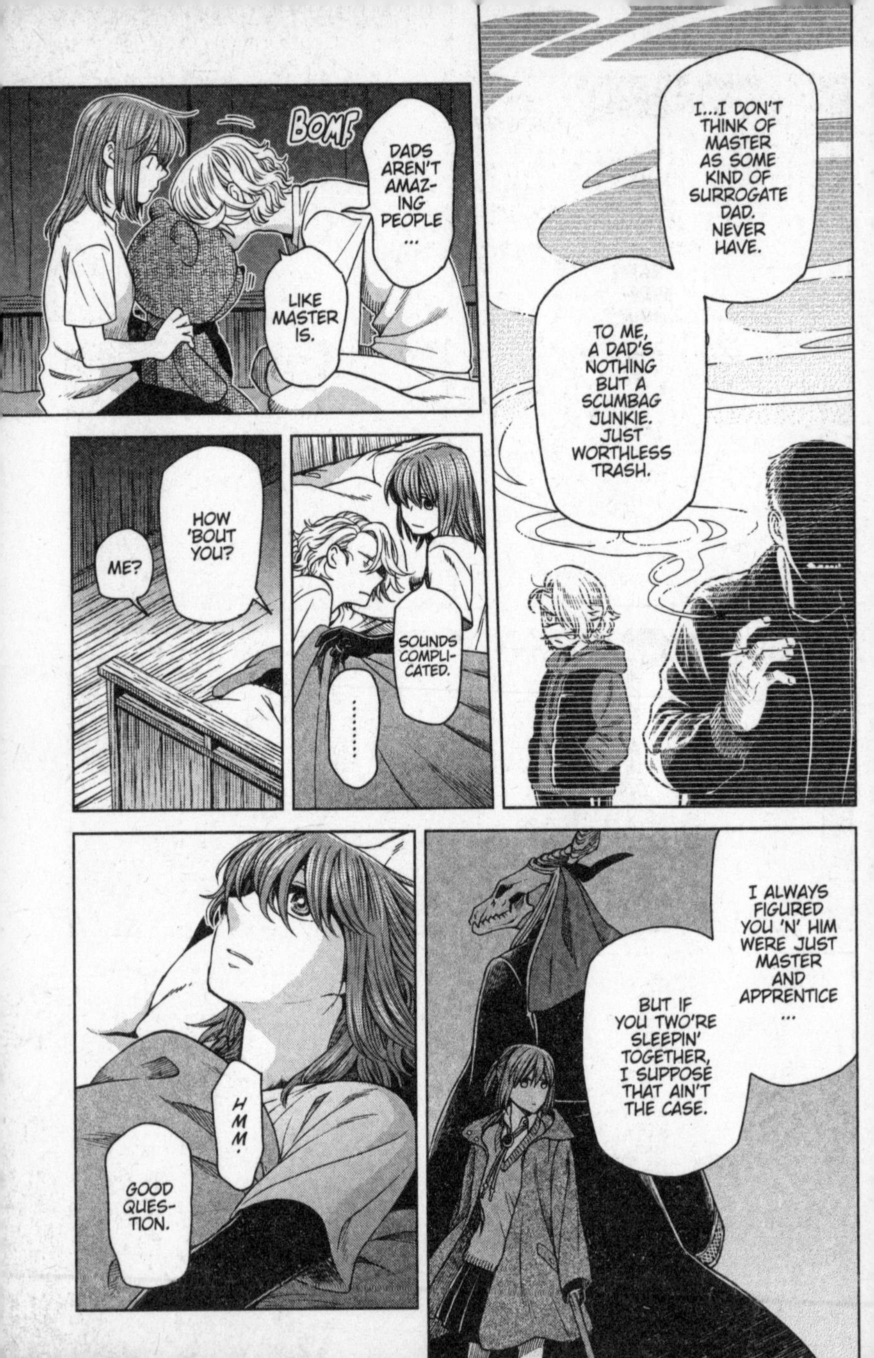
I...I DON'T THINK OF MASTER AS SOME KIND OF SURROGATE DAD. NEVER HAVE.
TO ME, A DAD'S NOTHING BUT A SCUMBAG JUNKIE. JUST WORTHLESS TRASH.
BOMF
DADS AREN'T AMAZ-ING PEOPLE...
LIKE MASTER IS.
SOUNDS COMPLI-CATED.
......
HOW 'BOUT YOU?
ME?
I ALWAYS FIGURED YOU 'N' HIM WERE JUST MASTER AND APPRENTICE...
BUT IF YOU TWO'RE SLEEPIN' TOGETHER, I SUPPOSE THAT AIN'T THE CASE.
HMM.
GOOD QUES-TION.

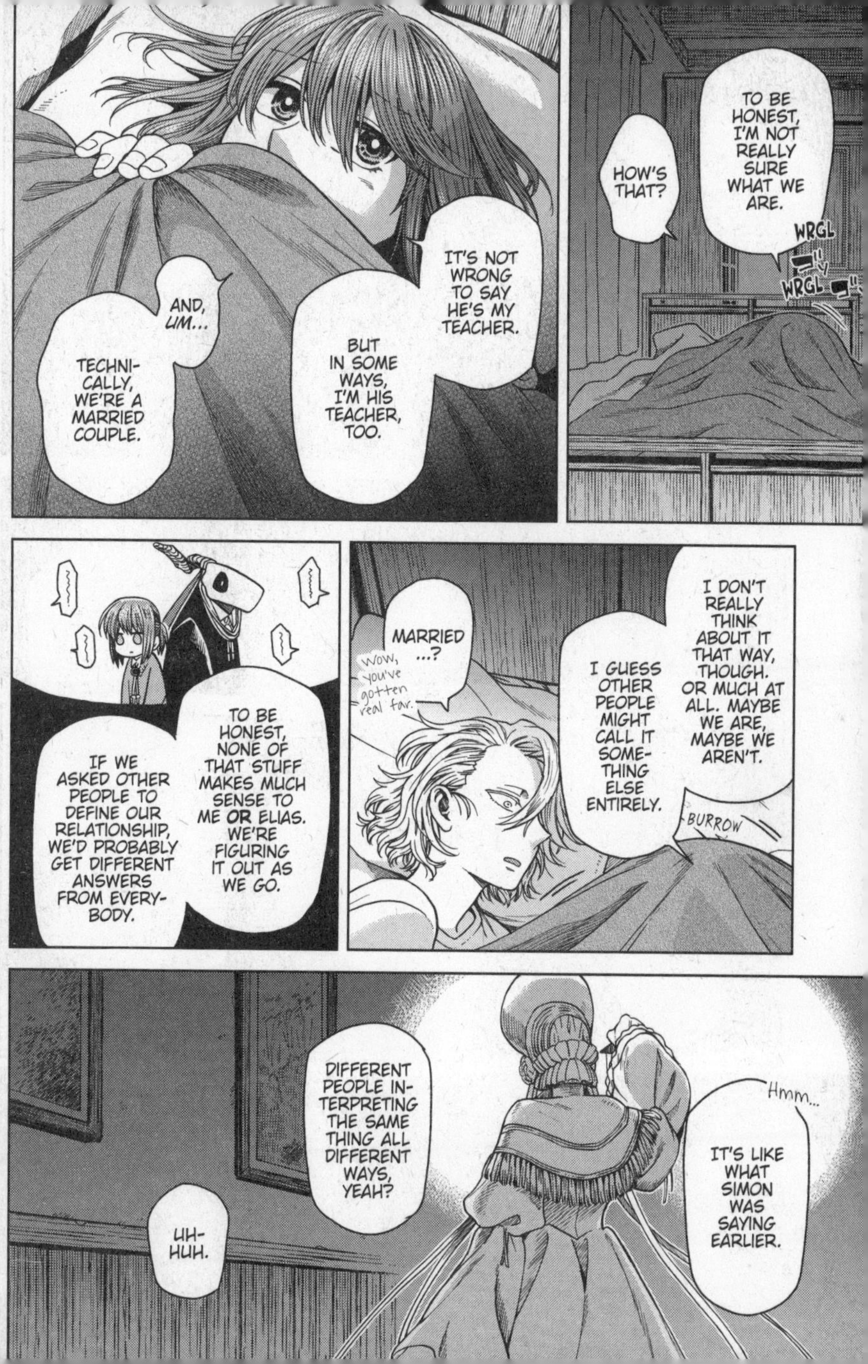
TO BE HONEST, I'M NOT REALLY SURE WHAT WE ARE.
HOW'S THAT?
WRGL
WRGL
IT'S NOT WRONG TO SAY HE'S MY TEACHER.
BUT IN SOME WAYS, I'M HIS TEACHER, TOO.
AND, UM...
TECHNI-CALLY, WE'RE A MARRIED COUPLE.
MARRIED ...?
Wow, you've gotten real far.
I DON'T REALLY THINK ABOUT IT THAT WAY, THOUGH. OR MUCH AT ALL. MAYBE WE ARE, MAYBE WE AREN'T.
I GUESS OTHER PEOPLE MIGHT CALL IT SOME-THING ELSE ENTIRELY.
BURROW
TO BE HONEST, NONE OF THAT STUFF MAKES MUCH SENSE TO ME OR ELIAS. WE'RE FIGURING IT OUT AS WE GO.
IF WE ASKED OTHER PEOPLE TO DEFINE OUR RELATIONSHIP, WE'D PROBABLY GET DIFFERENT ANSWERS FROM EVERY-BODY.
Hmm...
IT'S LIKE WHAT SIMON WAS SAYING EARLIER.
DIFFERENT PEOPLE IN-TERPRETING THE SAME THING ALL DIFFERENT WAYS, YEAH?
UH-HUH.

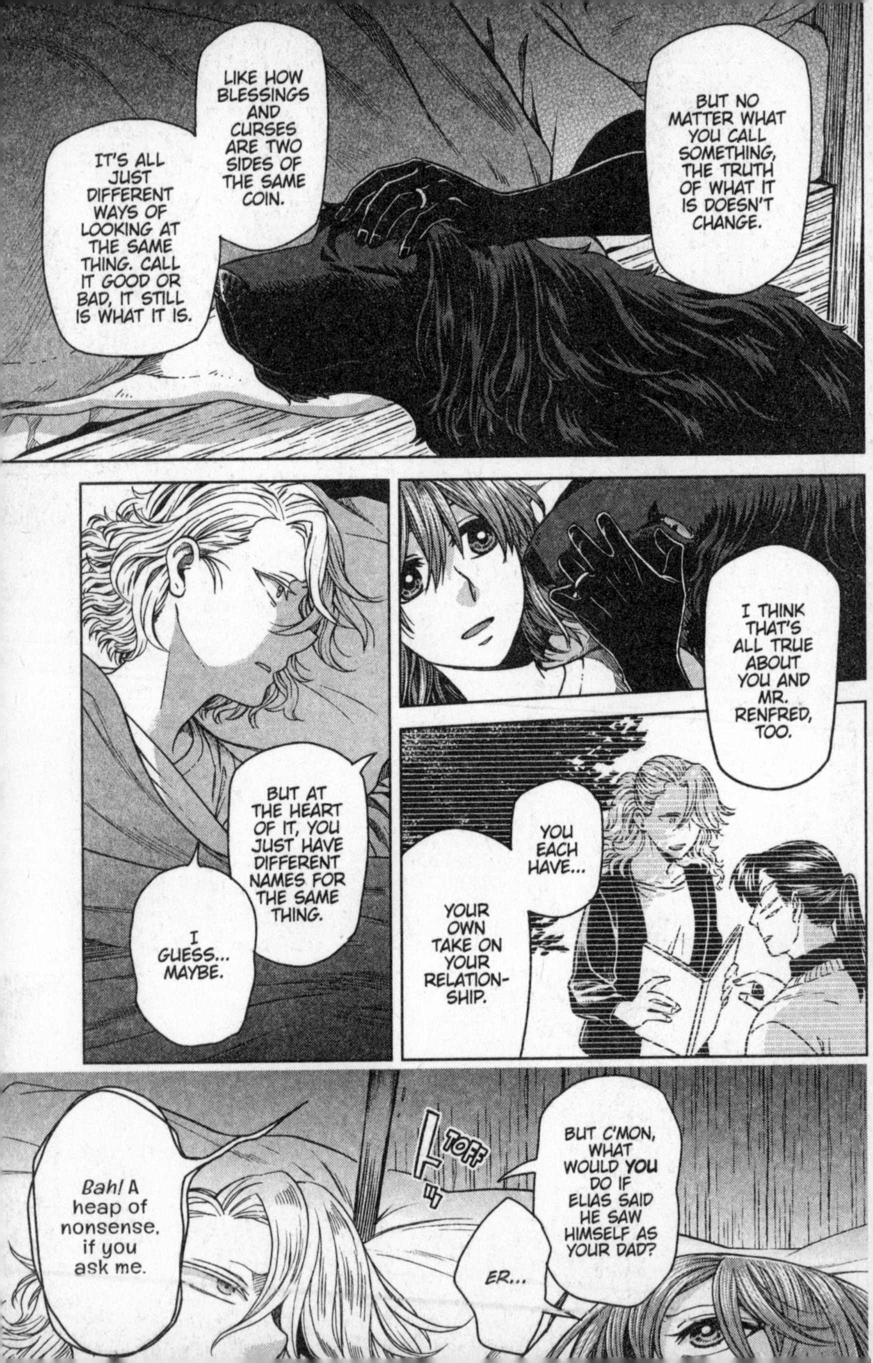
BUT NO MATTER WHAT YOU CALL SOMETHING, THE TRUTH OF WHAT IT IS DOESN'T CHANGE.
LIKE HOW BLESSINGS AND CURSES ARE TWO SIDES OF THE SAME COIN.
IT'S ALL JUST DIFFERENT WAYS OF LOOKING AT THE SAME THING. CALL IT GOOD OR BAD, IT STILL IS WHAT IT IS.
I THINK THAT'S ALL TRUE ABOUT YOU AND MR. RENFRED, TOO.
YOU EACH HAVE...
YOUR OWN TAKE ON YOUR RELATIONSHIP.
BUT AT THE HEART OF IT, YOU JUST HAVE DIFFERENT NAMES FOR THE SAME THING.
I GUESS... MAYBE.
BUT C'MON, WHAT WOULD **YOU** DO IF ELIAS SAID HE SAW HIMSELF AS YOUR DAD?
ER...
TOFF
*Bah!* A heap of nonsense, if you ask me.

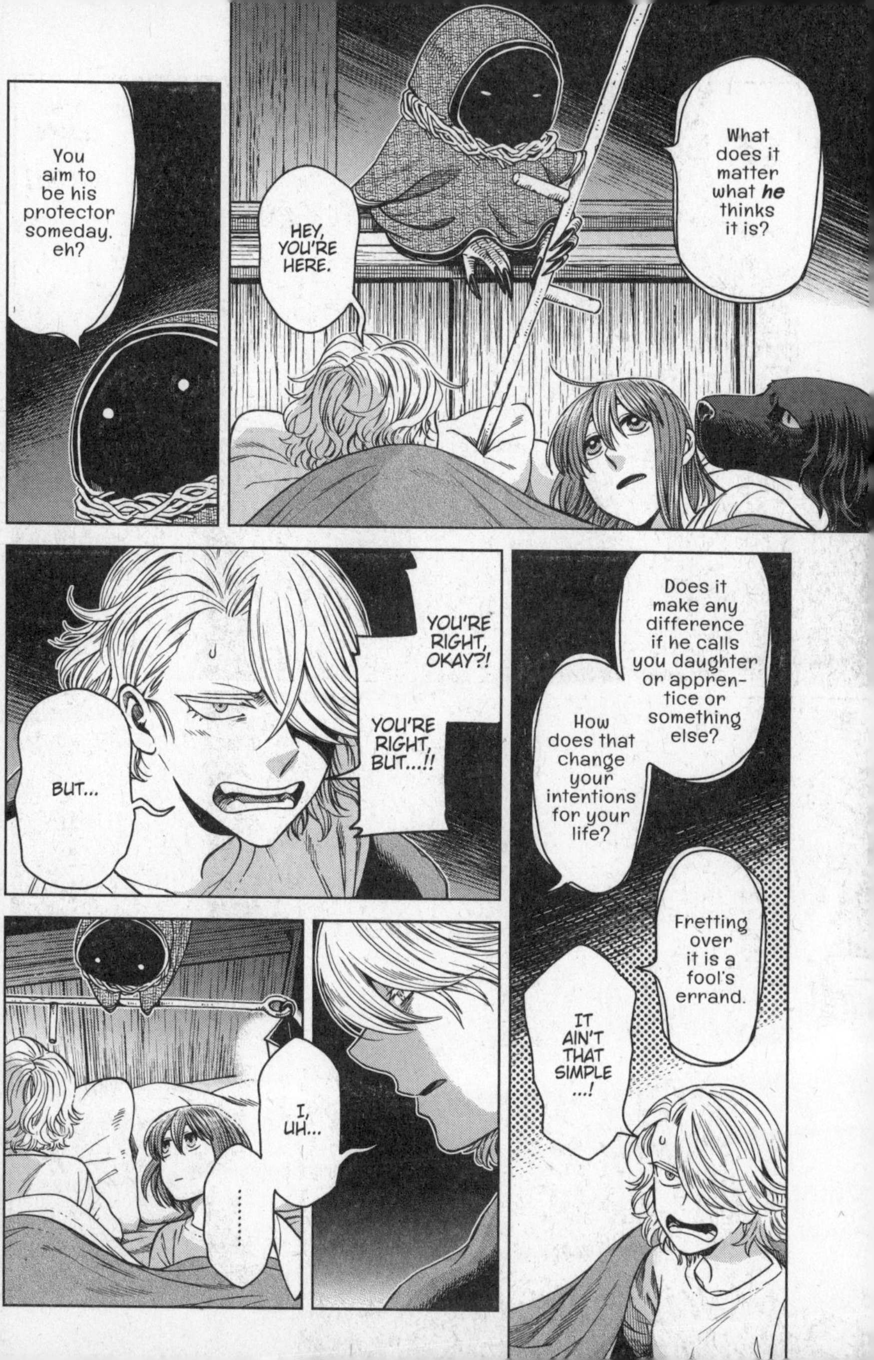

What does it matter what **he** thinks it is?
HEY, YOU'RE HERE.
You aim to be his protector someday, eh?
Does it make any difference if he calls you daughter or apprentice or something else?
How does that change your intentions for your life?
YOU'RE RIGHT, OKAY?!
YOU'RE RIGHT, BUT...!!
BUT...
Fretting over it is a fool's errand.
IT AIN'T THAT SIMPLE ...!
I, UH...
......

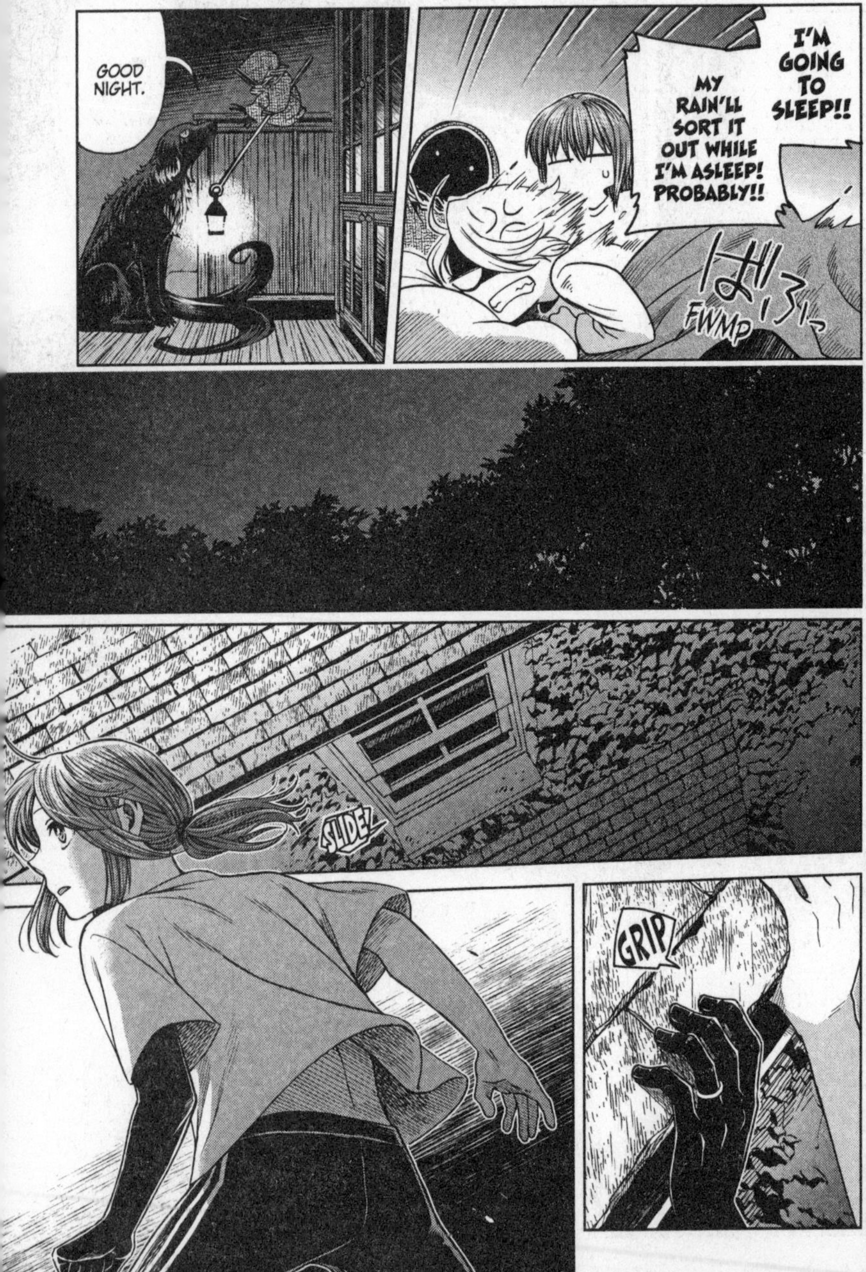
I'M GOING TO SLEEP!!
MY RAIN'LL SORT IT OUT WHILE I'M ASLEEP! PROBABLY!!
ばふっ
FWMP
GOOD NIGHT.
SLIDE
GRIP

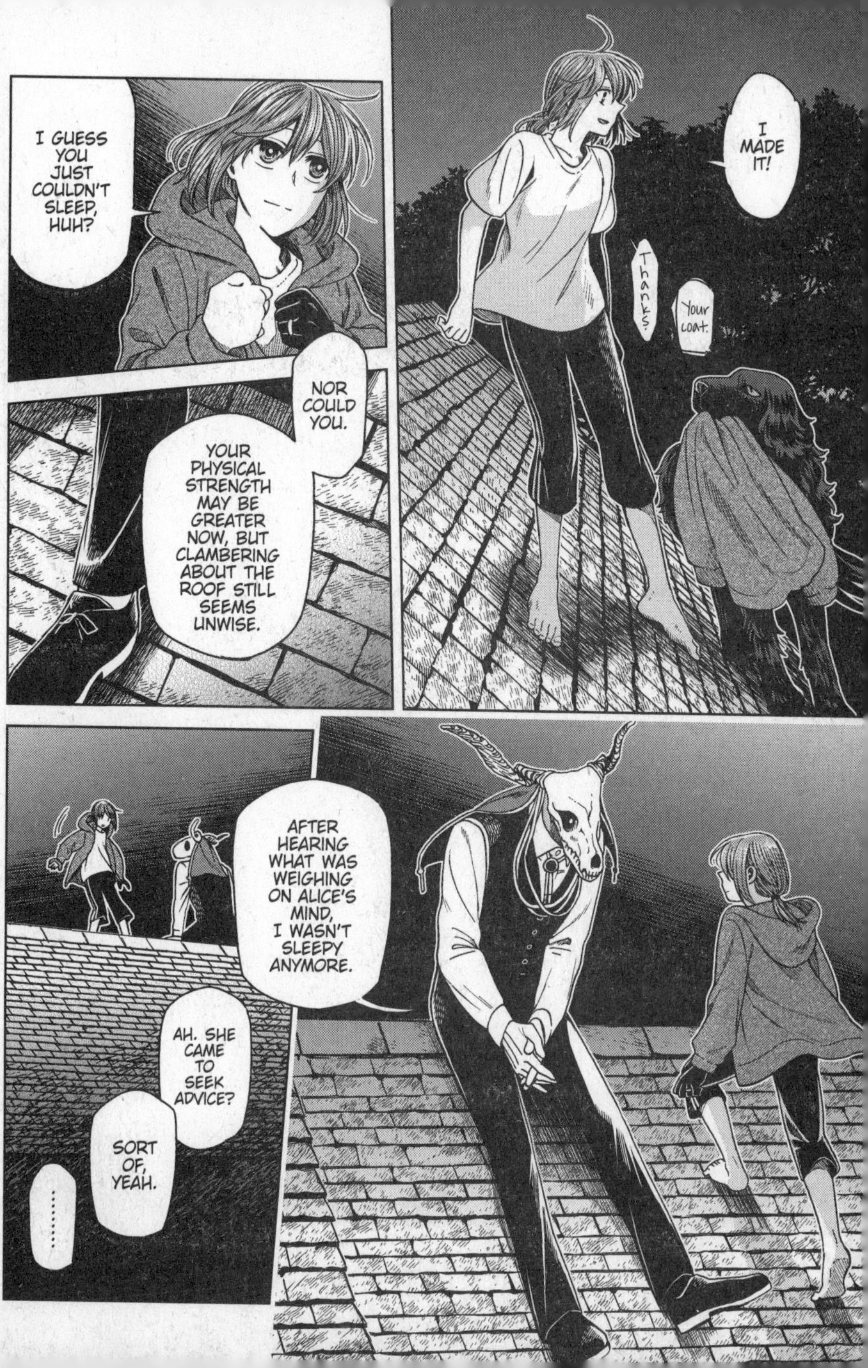
I MADE IT!
Your coat.
Thanks.
I GUESS YOU JUST COULDN'T SLEEP, HUH?
NOR COULD YOU.
YOUR PHYSICAL STRENGTH MAY BE GREATER NOW, BUT CLAMBERING ABOUT THE ROOF STILL SEEMS UNWISE.
AFTER HEARING WHAT WAS WEIGHING ON ALICE'S MIND, I WASN'T SLEEPY ANYMORE.
AH. SHE CAME TO SEEK ADVICE?
SORT OF, YEAH.
......

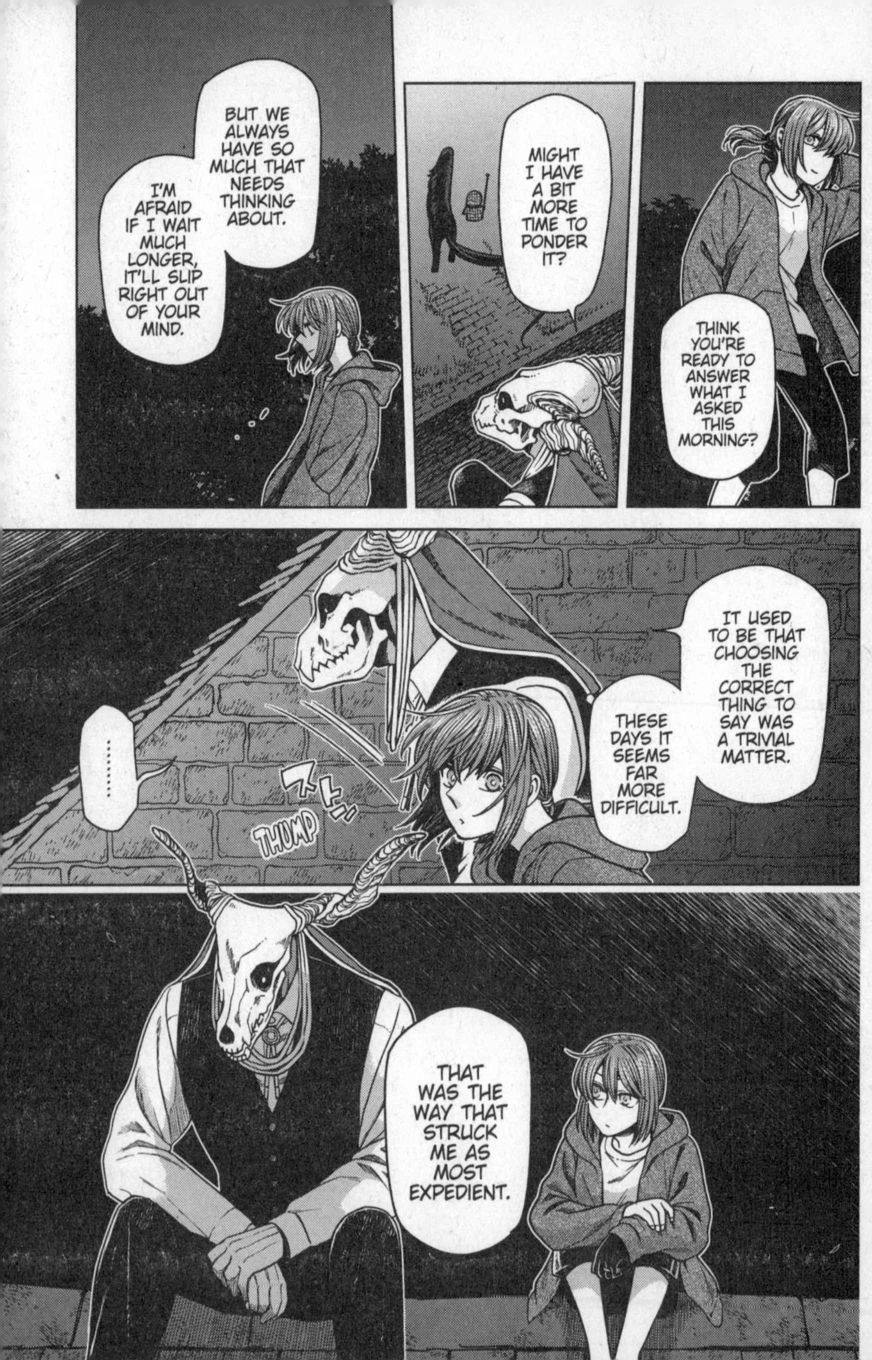
THINK YOU'RE READY TO ANSWER WHAT I ASKED THIS MORNING?
MIGHT I HAVE A BIT MORE TIME TO PONDER IT?
BUT WE ALWAYS HAVE SO MUCH THAT NEEDS THINKING ABOUT.
I'M AFRAID IF I WAIT MUCH LONGER, IT'LL SLIP RIGHT OUT OF YOUR MIND.
IT USED TO BE THAT CHOOSING THE CORRECT THING TO SAY WAS A TRIVIAL MATTER.
THESE DAYS IT SEEMS FAR MORE DIFFICULT.
THUMP
......
THAT WAS THE WAY THAT STRUCK ME AS MOST EXPEDIENT.

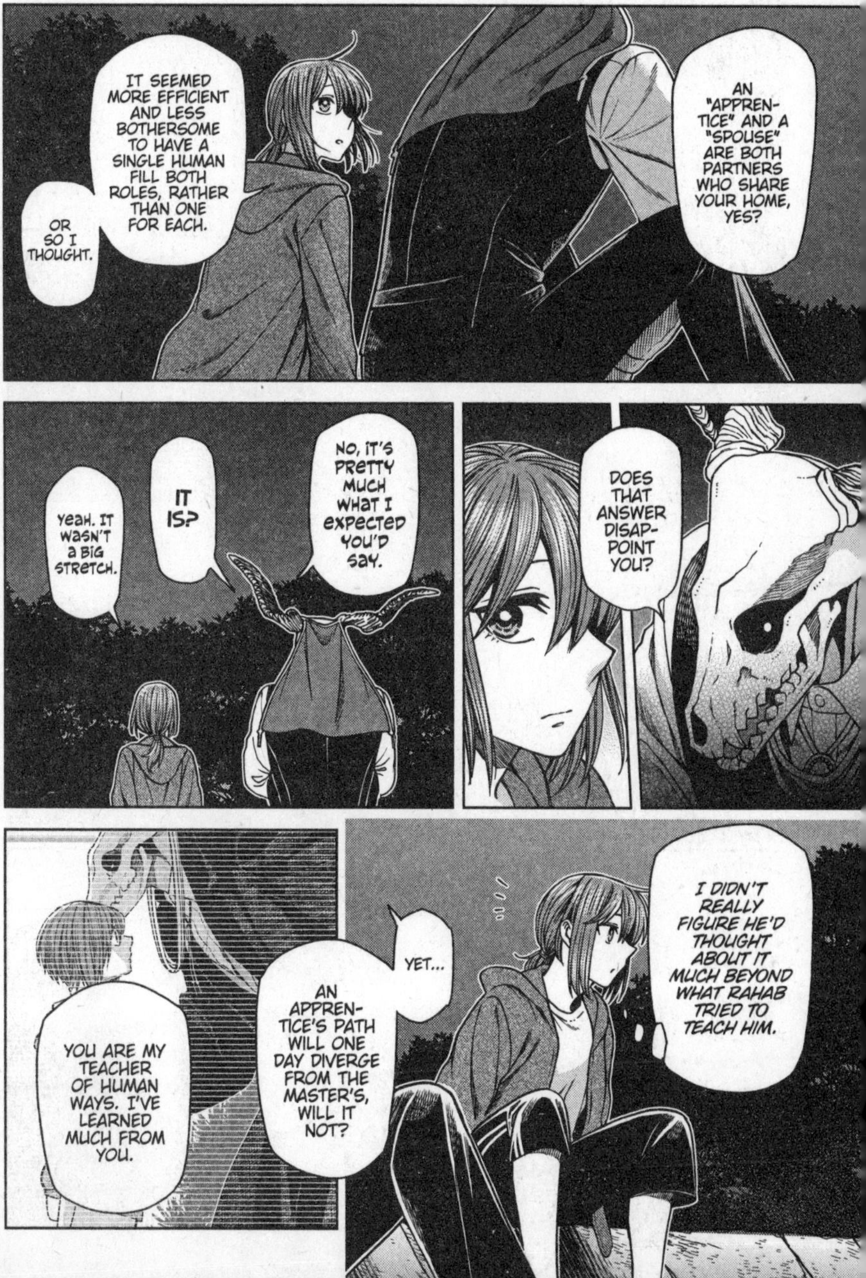
AN "APPREN-TICE" AND A "SPOUSE" ARE BOTH PARTNERS WHO SHARE YOUR HOME, YES?
IT SEEMED MORE EFFICIENT AND LESS BOTHERSOME TO HAVE A SINGLE HUMAN FILL BOTH ROLES, RATHER THAN ONE FOR EACH.
OR SO I THOUGHT.
DOES THAT ANSWER DISAP-POINT YOU?
No, it's pretty much what I expected you'd say.
IT IS?
Yeah. It wasn't a big stretch.
I DIDN'T REALLY FIGURE HE'D THOUGHT ABOUT IT MUCH BEYOND WHAT RAHAB TRIED TO TEACH HIM.
YET...
AN APPREN-TICE'S PATH WILL ONE DAY DIVERGE FROM THE MASTER'S, WILL IT NOT?
YOU ARE MY TEACHER OF HUMAN WAYS. I'VE LEARNED MUCH FROM YOU.

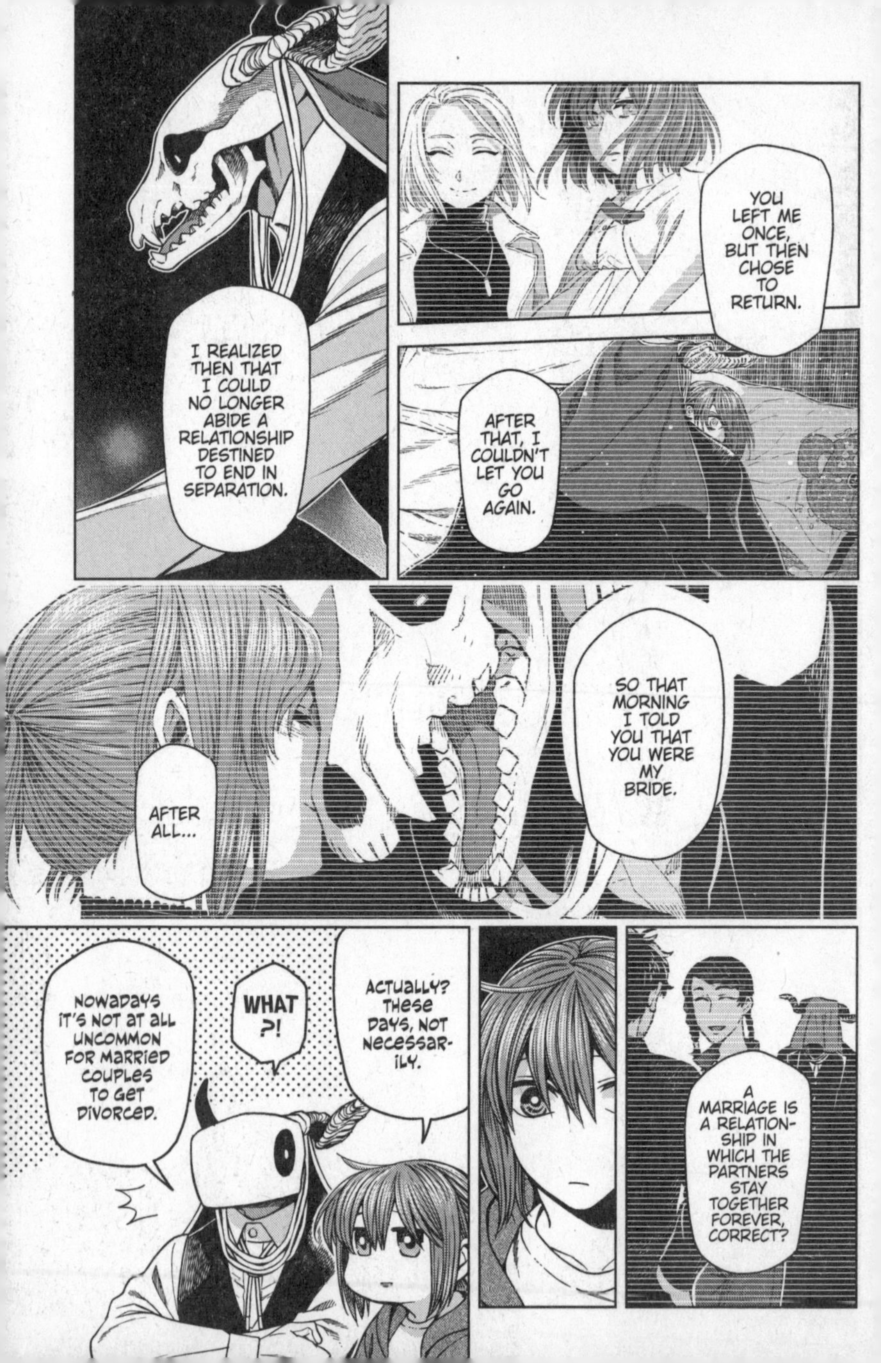
YOU LEFT ME ONCE, BUT THEN CHOSE TO RETURN.
AFTER THAT, I COULDN'T LET YOU GO AGAIN.
I REALIZED THEN THAT I COULD NO LONGER ABIDE A RELATIONSHIP DESTINED TO END IN SEPARATION.
SO THAT MORNING I TOLD YOU THAT YOU WERE MY BRIDE.
AFTER ALL...
A MARRIAGE IS A RELATION-SHIP IN WHICH THE PARTNERS STAY TOGETHER FOREVER, CORRECT?
ACTUALLY? THESE DAYS, NOT NECESSAR-ILY.
WHAT ?!
NOWADAYS IT'S NOT AT ALL UNCOMMON FOR MARRIED COUPLES TO GET DIVORCED.

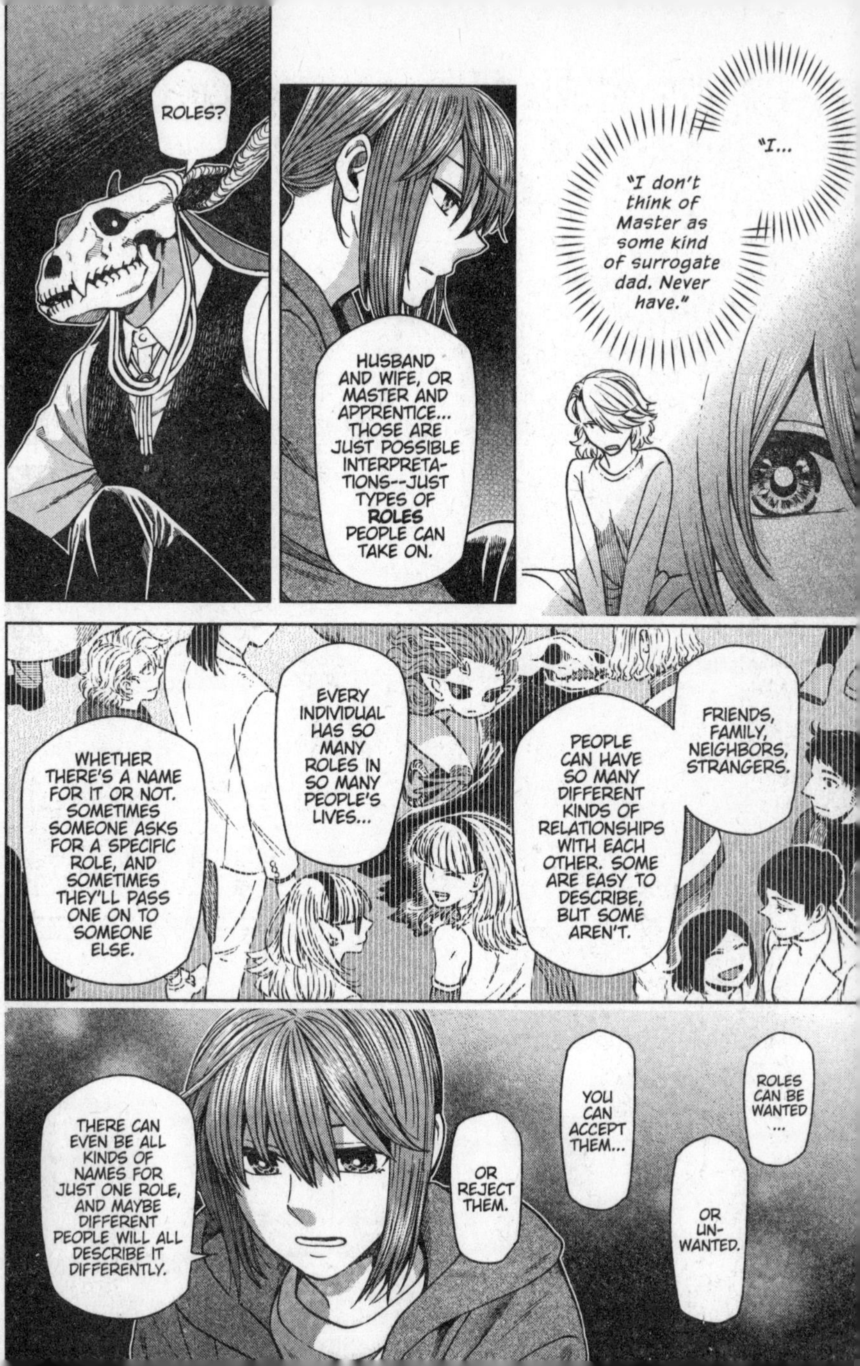
"I...
"I don't think of Master as some kind of surrogate dad. Never have."
HUSBAND AND WIFE, OR MASTER AND APPRENTICE... THOSE ARE JUST POSSIBLE INTERPRETA-TIONS--JUST TYPES OF **ROLES** PEOPLE CAN TAKE ON.
ROLES?
FRIENDS, FAMILY, NEIGHBORS, STRANGERS.
PEOPLE CAN HAVE SO MANY DIFFERENT KINDS OF RELATIONSHIPS WITH EACH OTHER. SOME ARE EASY TO DESCRIBE, BUT SOME AREN'T.
EVERY INDIVIDUAL HAS SO MANY ROLES IN SO MANY PEOPLE'S LIVES...
WHETHER THERE'S A NAME FOR IT OR NOT. SOMETIMES SOMEONE ASKS FOR A SPECIFIC ROLE, AND SOMETIMES THEY'LL PASS ONE ON TO SOMEONE ELSE.
ROLES CAN BE WANTED...
OR UN-WANTED.
YOU CAN ACCEPT THEM...
OR REJECT THEM.
THERE CAN EVEN BE ALL KINDS OF NAMES FOR JUST ONE ROLE, AND MAYBE DIFFERENT PEOPLE WILL ALL DESCRIBE IT DIFFERENTLY.

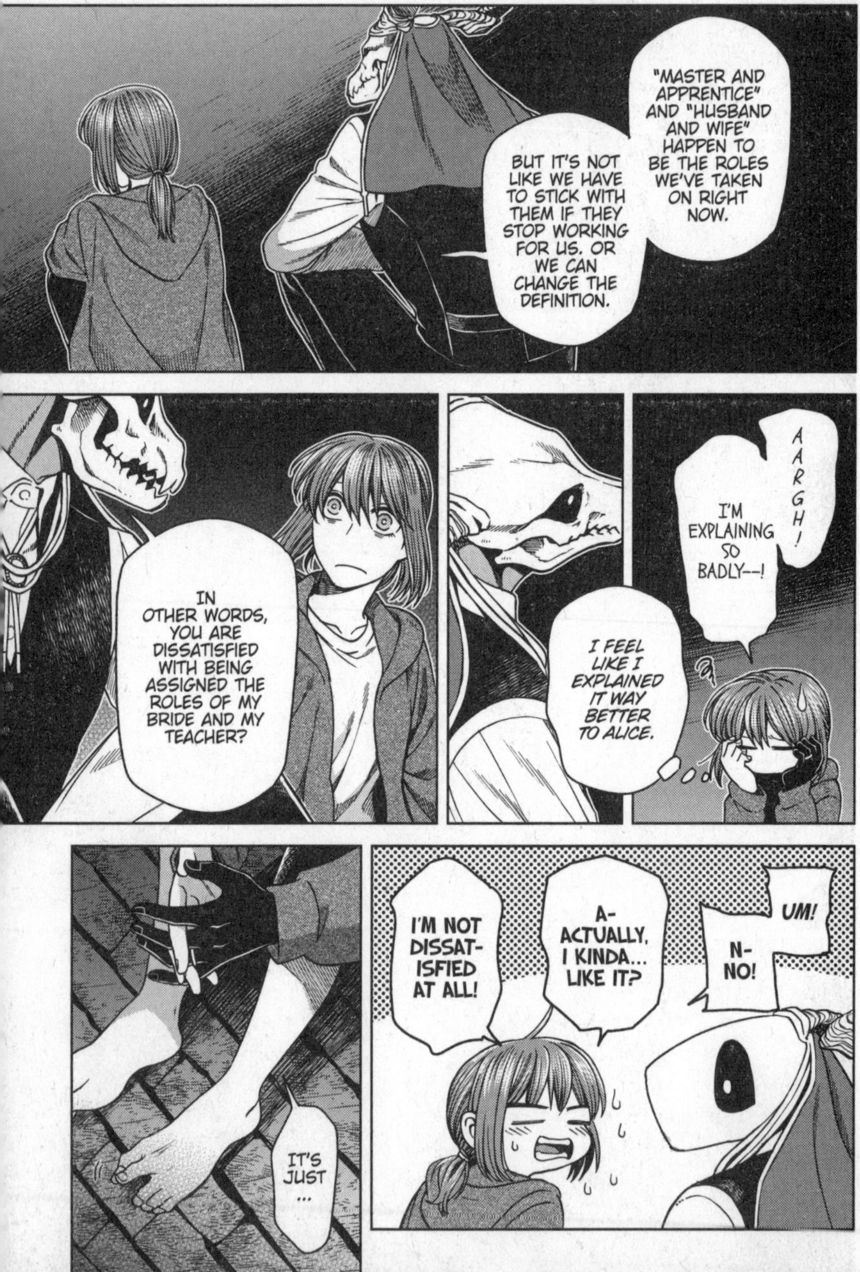
"MASTER AND APPRENTICE" AND "HUSBAND AND WIFE" HAPPEN TO BE THE ROLES WE'VE TAKEN ON RIGHT NOW.
BUT IT'S NOT LIKE WE HAVE TO STICK WITH THEM IF THEY STOP WORKING FOR US. OR WE CAN CHANGE THE DEFINITION.
AARGH!
I'M EXPLAINING SO BADLY--!
I FEEL LIKE I EXPLAINED IT WAY BETTER TO ALICE.
IN OTHER WORDS, YOU ARE DISSATISFIED WITH BEING ASSIGNED THE ROLES OF MY BRIDE AND MY TEACHER?
UM!
N-NO!
A-ACTUALLY, I KINDA... LIKE IT?
I'M NOT DISSATISFIED AT ALL!
IT'S JUST ...

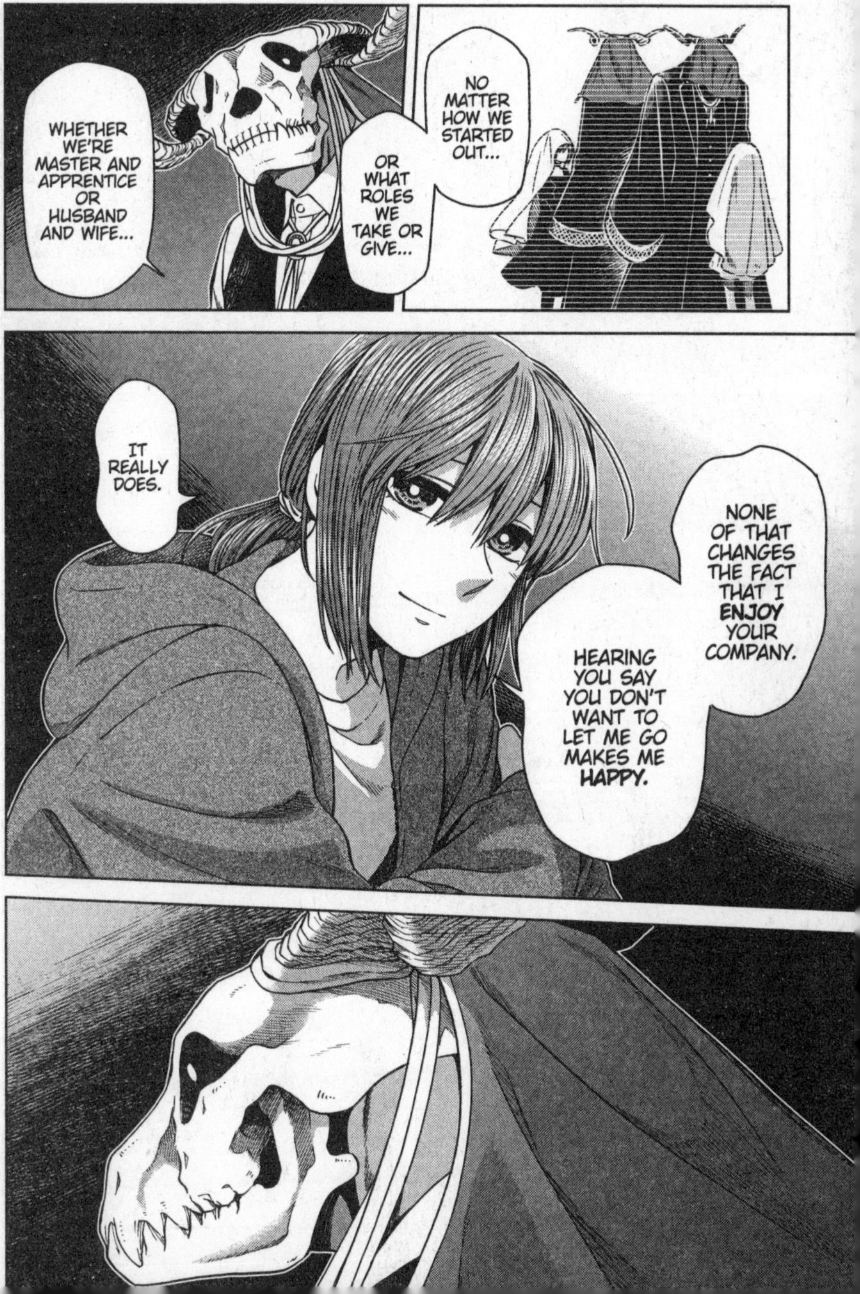
NO MATTER HOW WE STARTED OUT...
OR WHAT ROLES WE TAKE OR GIVE...
WHETHER WE'RE MASTER AND APPRENTICE OR HUSBAND AND WIFE...
NONE OF THAT CHANGES THE FACT THAT I **ENJOY** YOUR COMPANY.
HEARING YOU SAY YOU DON'T WANT TO LET ME GO MAKES ME **HAPPY.**
IT REALLY DOES.

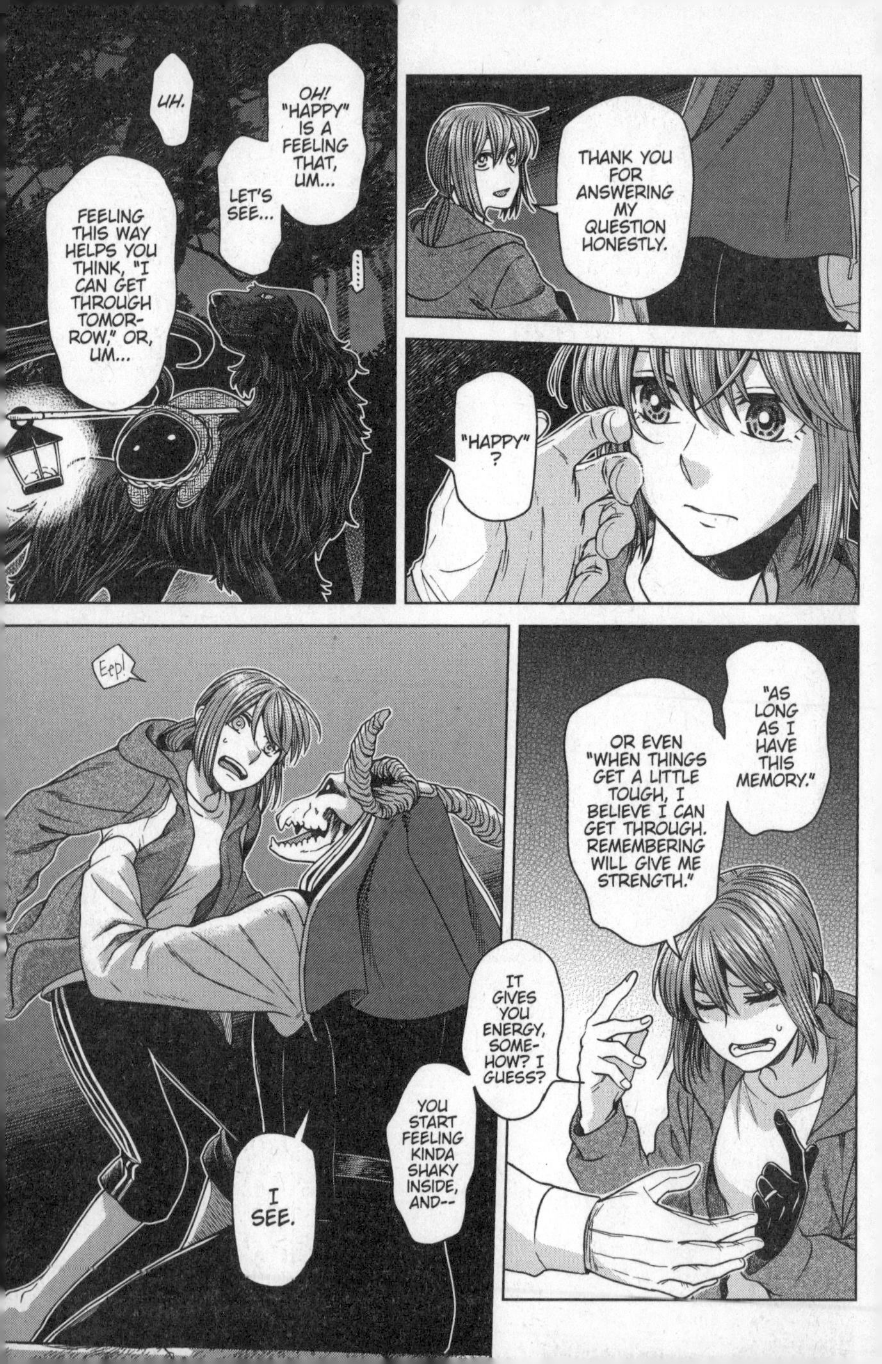
THANK YOU FOR ANSWERING MY QUESTION HONESTLY.
"HAPPY"?
OH! "HAPPY" IS A FEELING THAT, UM...
LET'S SEE...
UH.
......
FEELING THIS WAY HELPS YOU THINK, "I CAN GET THROUGH TOMORROW," OR, UM...
"AS LONG AS I HAVE THIS MEMORY."
OR EVEN "WHEN THINGS GET A LITTLE TOUGH, I BELIEVE I CAN GET THROUGH. REMEMBERING WILL GIVE ME STRENGTH."
IT GIVES YOU ENERGY, SOMEHOW? I GUESS?
YOU START FEELING KINDA SHAKY INSIDE, AND--
Eep!
I SEE.

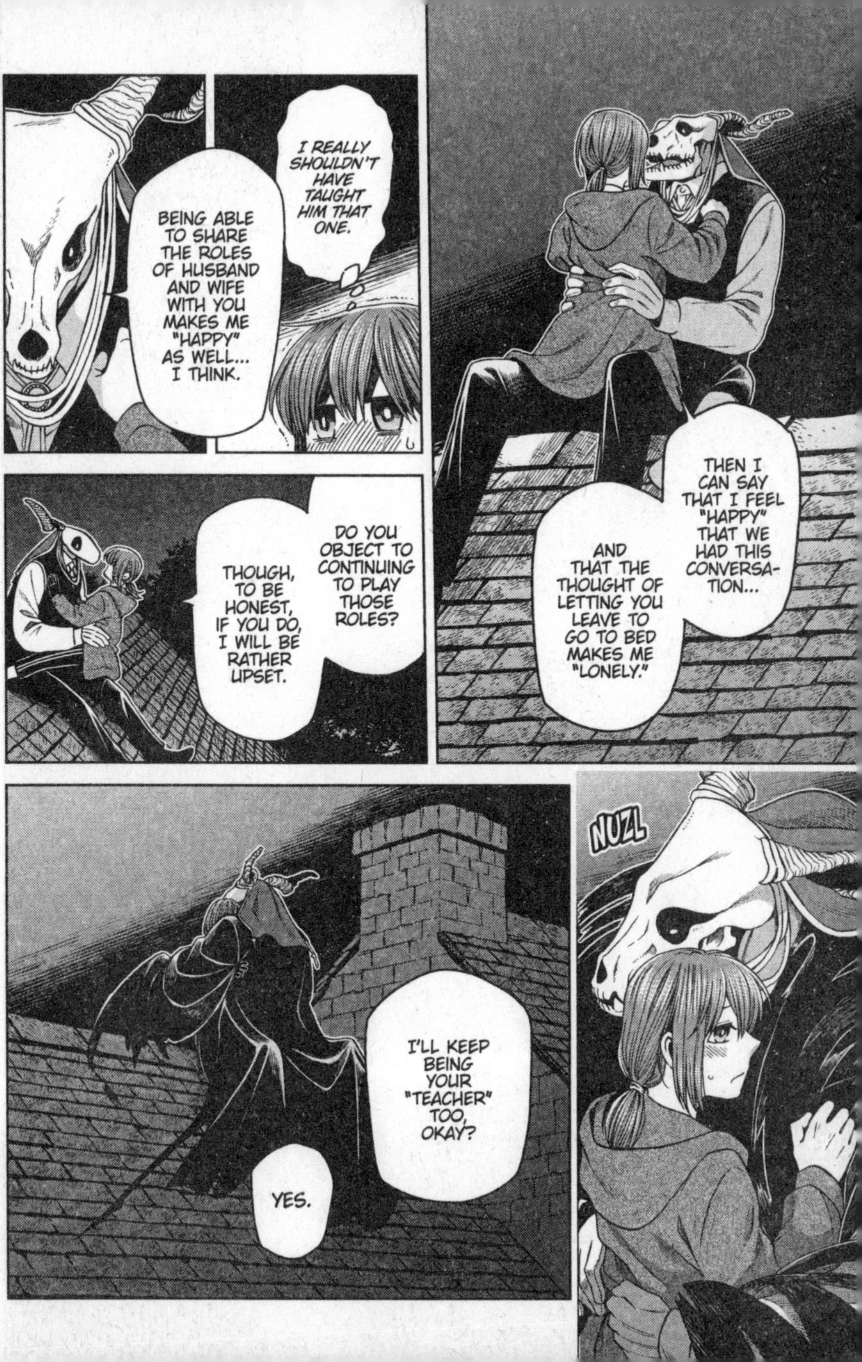
THEN I CAN SAY THAT I FEEL "HAPPY" THAT WE HAD THIS CONVERSA-TION...
AND THAT THE THOUGHT OF LETTING YOU LEAVE TO GO TO BED MAKES ME "LONELY."
I REALLY SHOULDN'T HAVE TAUGHT HIM THAT ONE.
BEING ABLE TO SHARE THE ROLES OF HUSBAND AND WIFE WITH YOU MAKES ME "HAPPY" AS WELL... I THINK.
DO YOU OBJECT TO CONTINUING TO PLAY THOSE ROLES?
THOUGH, TO BE HONEST, IF YOU DO, I WILL BE RATHER UPSET.
NUZL
I'LL KEEP BEING YOUR "TEACHER" TOO, OKAY?
YES.

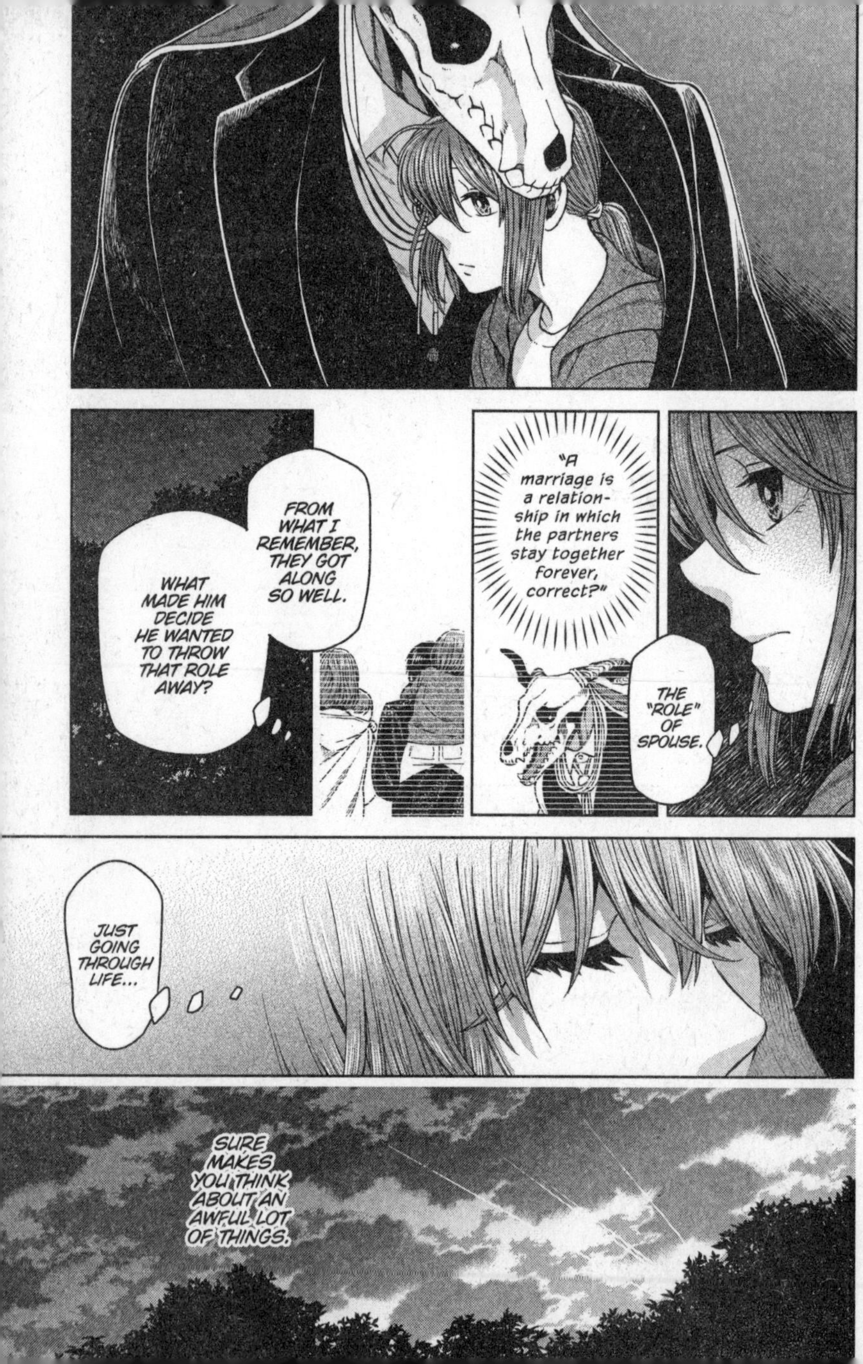
THE "ROLE" OF SPOUSE.
"A marriage is a relationship in which the partners stay together forever, correct?"
FROM WHAT I REMEMBER, THEY GOT ALONG SO WELL.
WHAT MADE HIM DECIDE HE WANTED TO THROW THAT ROLE AWAY?
JUST GOING THROUGH LIFE...
SURE MAKES YOU THINK ABOUT AN AWFUL LOT OF THINGS.

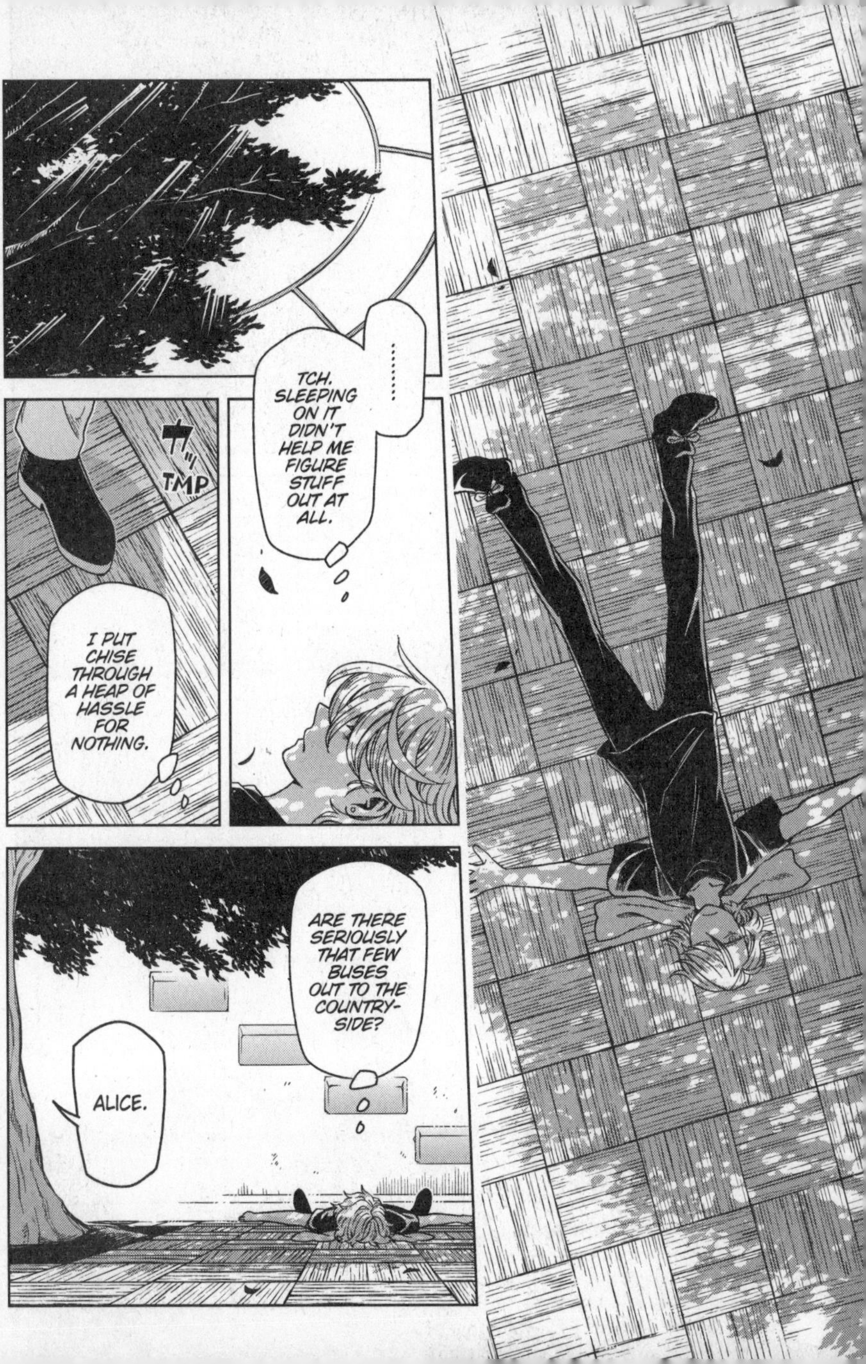
……
TCH. SLEEPING ON IT DIDN'T HELP ME FIGURE STUFF OUT AT ALL.
TMP
I PUT CHISE THROUGH A HEAP OF HASSLE FOR NOTHING.
ARE THERE SERIOUSLY THAT FEW BUSES OUT TO THE COUNTRY-SIDE?
ALICE.

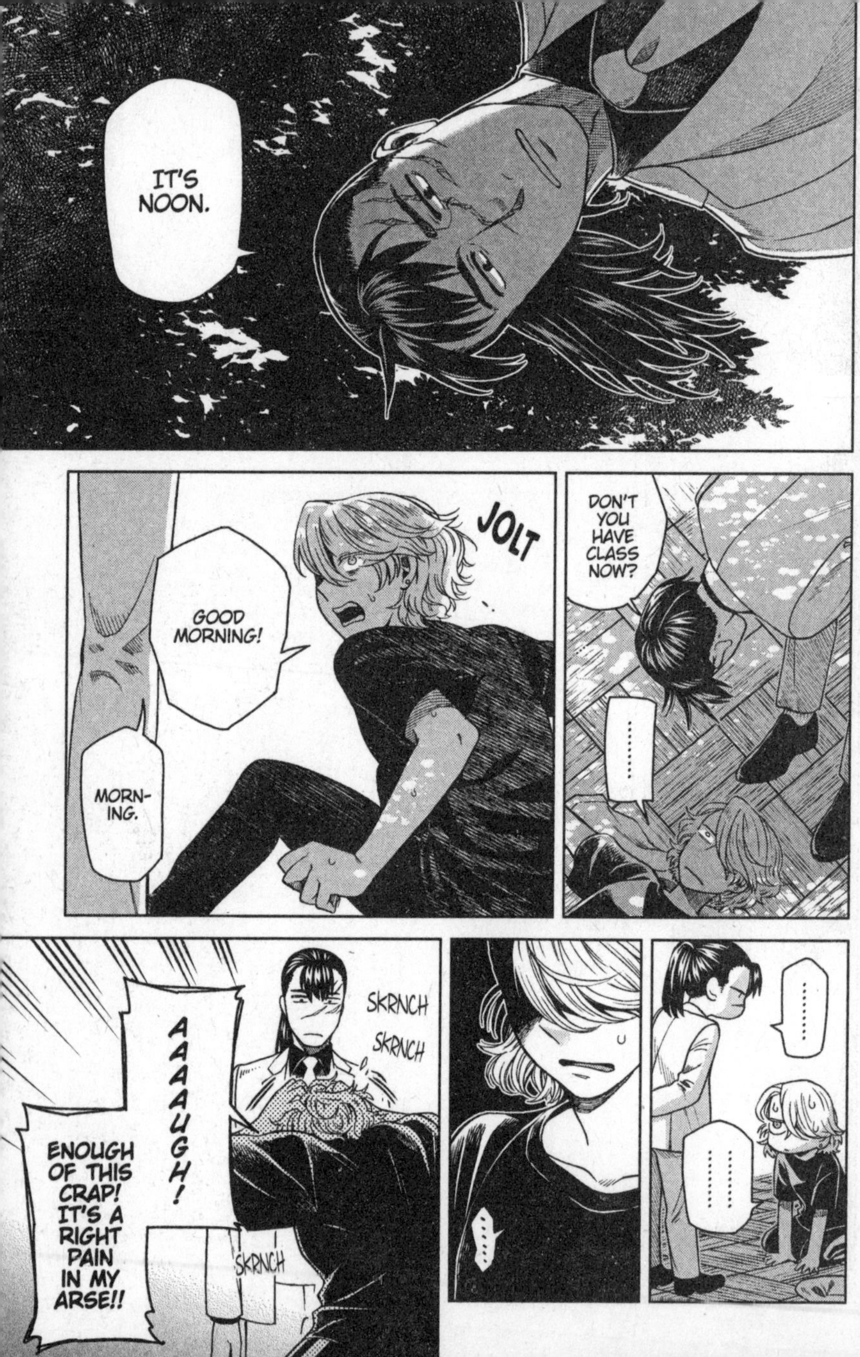
IT'S NOON.
DON'T YOU HAVE CLASS NOW?
......
JOLT
GOOD MORNING!
MORN-ING.
......
......
......
SKRNCH
SKRNCH
AAAAAUGH!
ENOUGH OF THIS CRAP! IT'S A RIGHT PAIN IN MY ARSE!!
SKRNCH

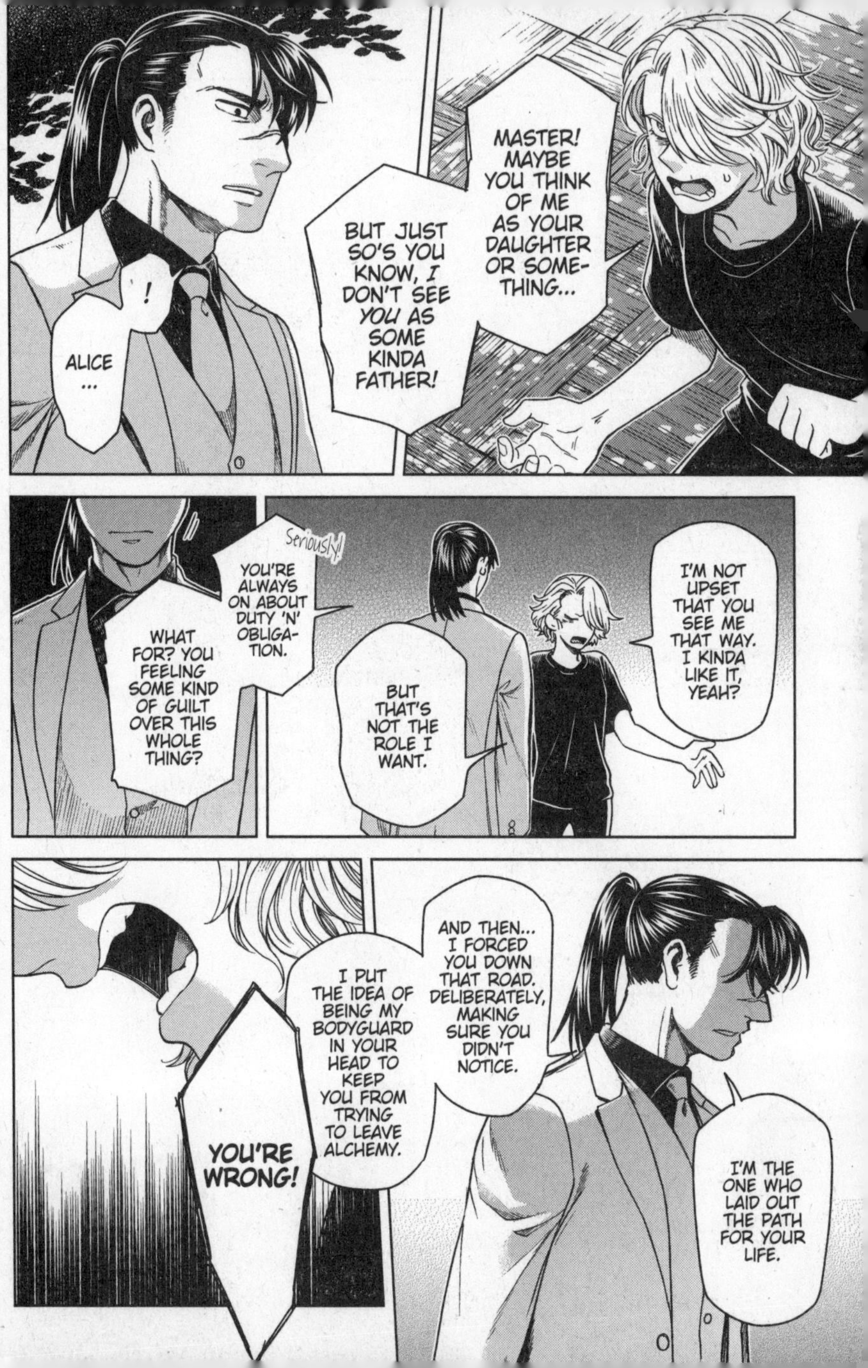
MASTER! MAYBE YOU THINK OF ME AS YOUR DAUGHTER OR SOME-THING...
BUT JUST SO'S YOU KNOW, *I* DON'T SEE *YOU* AS SOME KINDA FATHER!
!
ALICE...
I'M NOT UPSET THAT YOU SEE ME THAT WAY. I KINDA LIKE IT, YEAH?
BUT THAT'S NOT THE ROLE I WANT.
Seriously!
YOU'RE ALWAYS ON ABOUT DUTY 'N' OBLIGATION.
WHAT FOR? YOU FEELING SOME KIND OF GUILT OVER THIS WHOLE THING?
I'M THE ONE WHO LAID OUT THE PATH FOR YOUR LIFE.
AND THEN... I FORCED YOU DOWN THAT ROAD. DELIBERATELY, MAKING SURE YOU DIDN'T NOTICE.
I PUT THE IDEA OF BEING MY BODYGUARD IN YOUR HEAD TO KEEP YOU FROM TRYING TO LEAVE ALCHEMY.
YOU'RE WRONG!

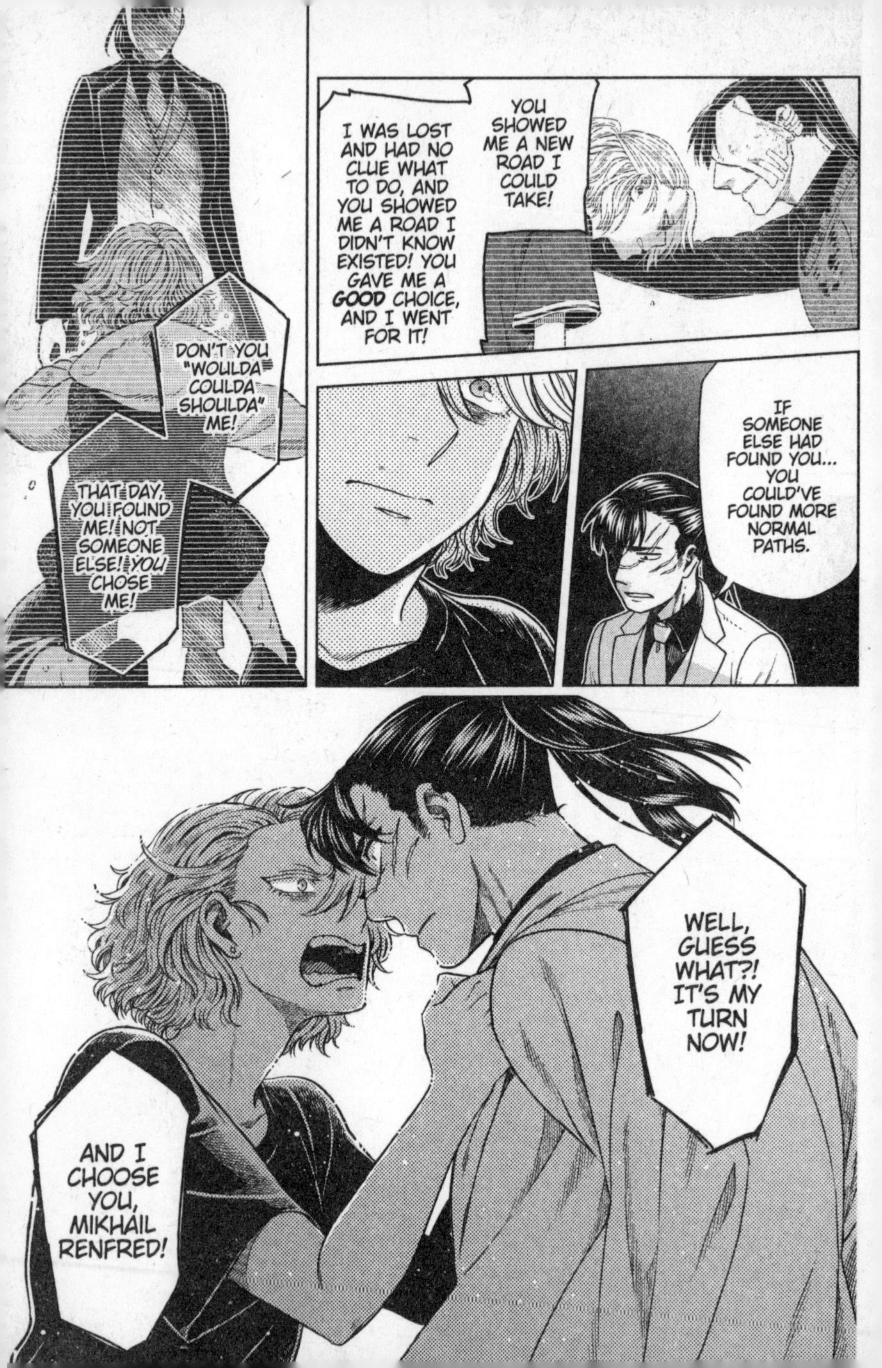
YOU SHOWED ME A NEW ROAD I COULD TAKE!
I WAS LOST AND HAD NO CLUE WHAT TO DO, AND YOU SHOWED ME A ROAD I DIDN'T KNOW EXISTED! YOU GAVE ME A **GOOD** CHOICE, AND I WENT FOR IT!
IF SOMEONE ELSE HAD FOUND YOU... YOU COULD'VE FOUND MORE NORMAL PATHS.
DON'T YOU "WOULDA COULDA SHOULDA" ME!
THAT DAY, YOU FOUND ME! NOT SOMEONE ELSE! *YOU* CHOSE ME!
WELL, GUESS WHAT?! IT'S MY TURN NOW!
AND I CHOOSE YOU, MIKHAIL RENFRED!

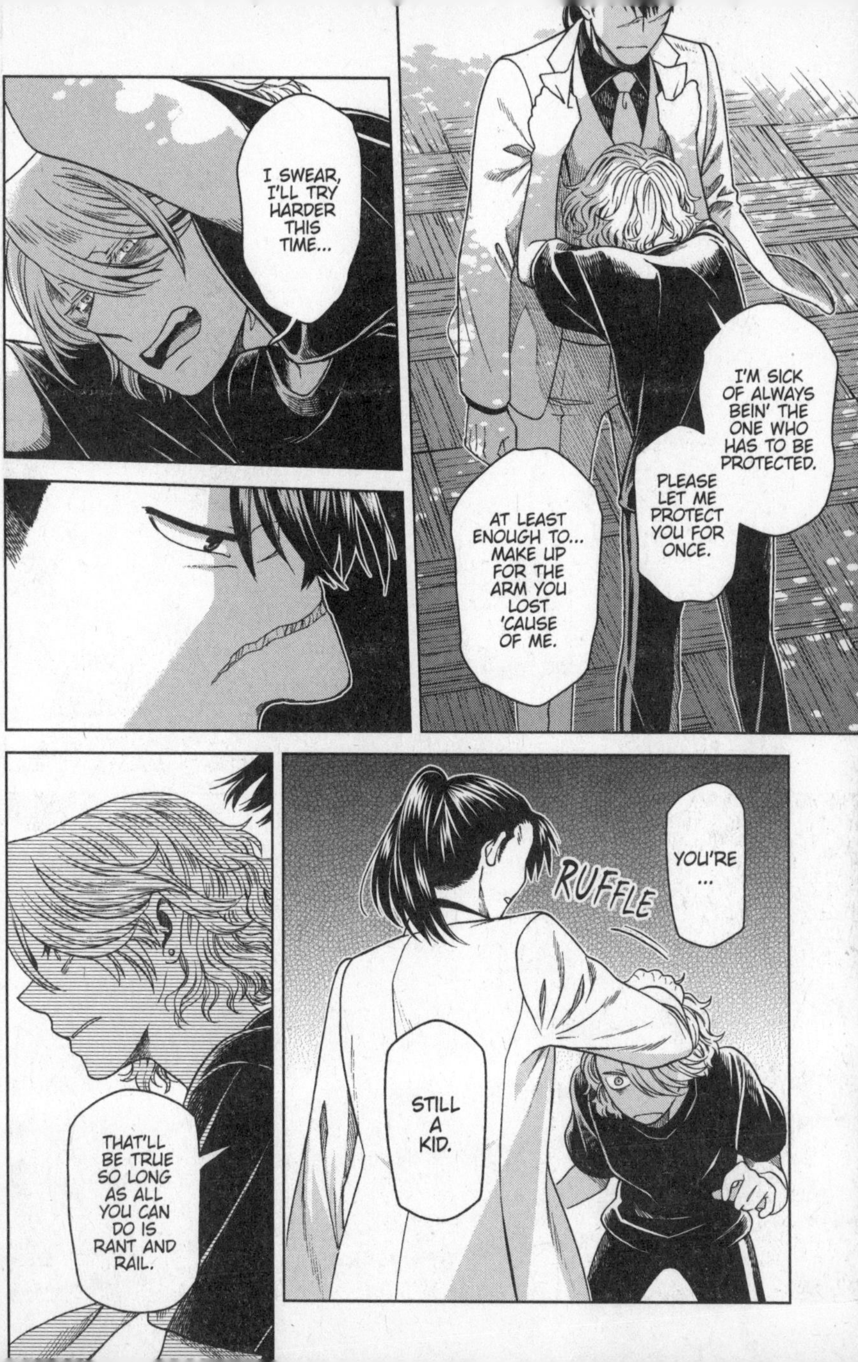
I'M SICK OF ALWAYS BEIN' THE ONE WHO HAS TO BE PROTECTED.
PLEASE LET ME PROTECT YOU FOR ONCE.
AT LEAST ENOUGH TO... MAKE UP FOR THE ARM YOU LOST 'CAUSE OF ME.
I SWEAR, I'LL TRY HARDER THIS TIME...
YOU'RE ...
RUFFLE
STILL A KID.
THAT'LL BE TRUE SO LONG AS ALL YOU CAN DO IS RANT AND RAIL.

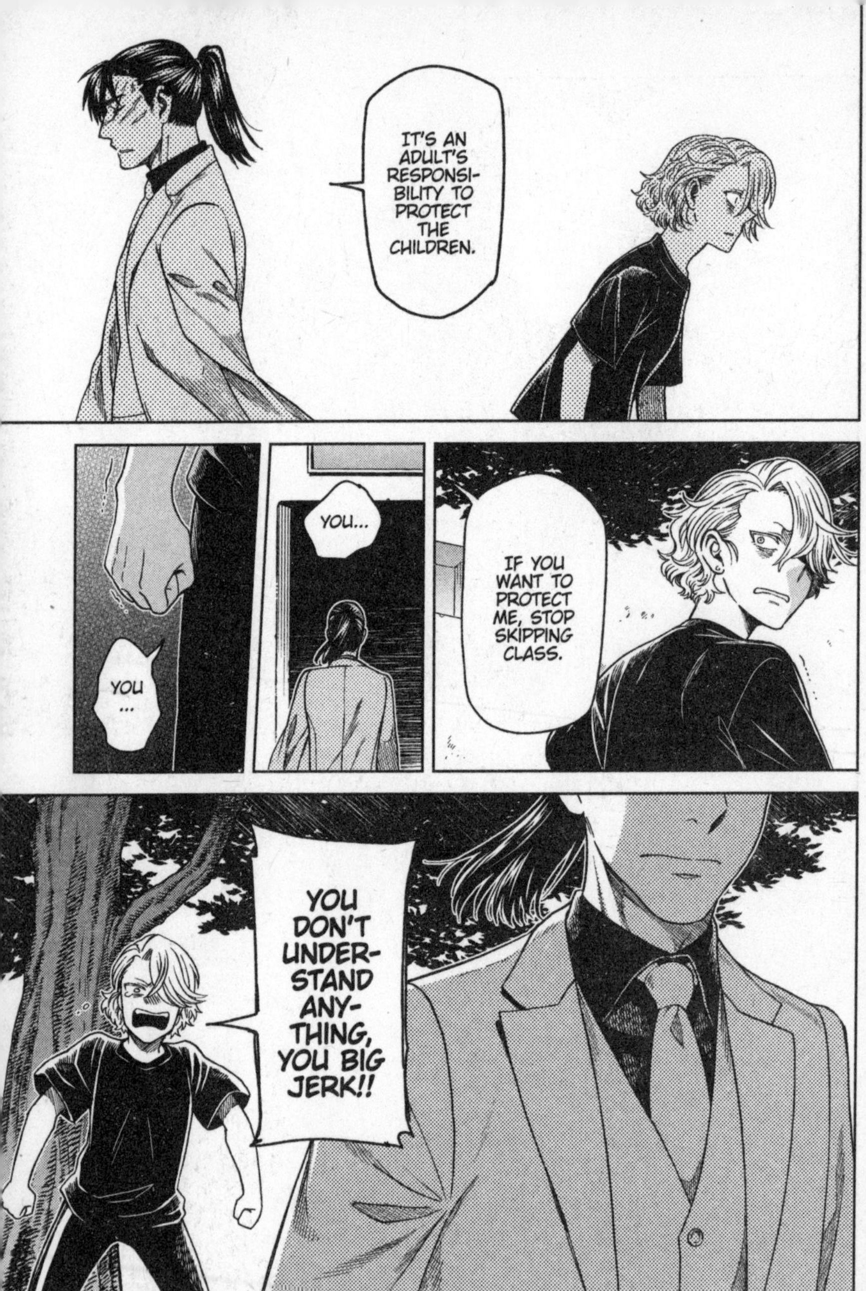
IT'S AN ADULT'S RESPONSIBILITY TO PROTECT THE CHILDREN.
IF YOU WANT TO PROTECT ME, STOP SKIPPING CLASS.
YOU...
YOU ...
YOU DON'T UNDERSTAND ANYTHING, YOU BIG JERK!!

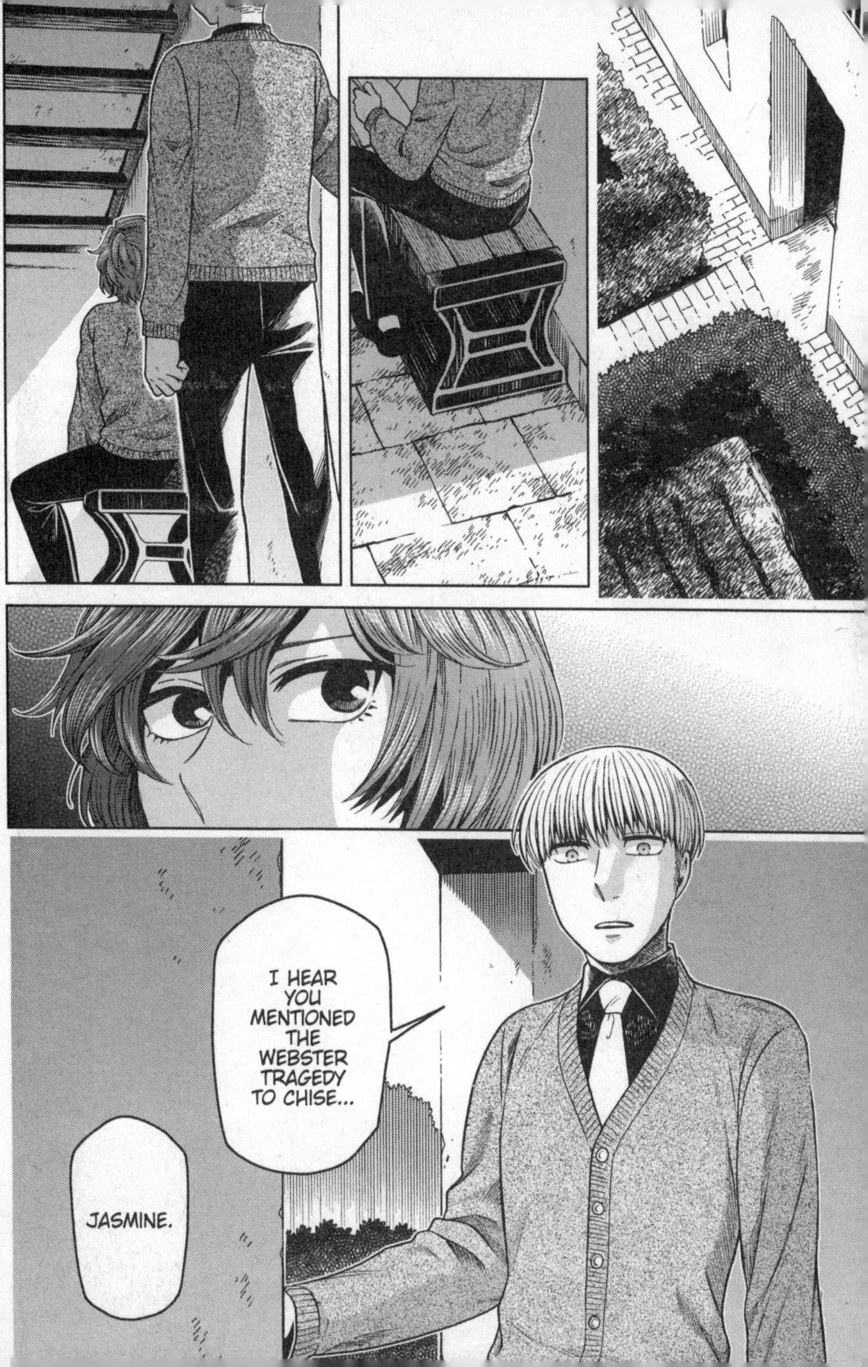
I HEAR YOU MENTIONED THE WEBSTER TRAGEDY TO CHISE...
JASMINE.

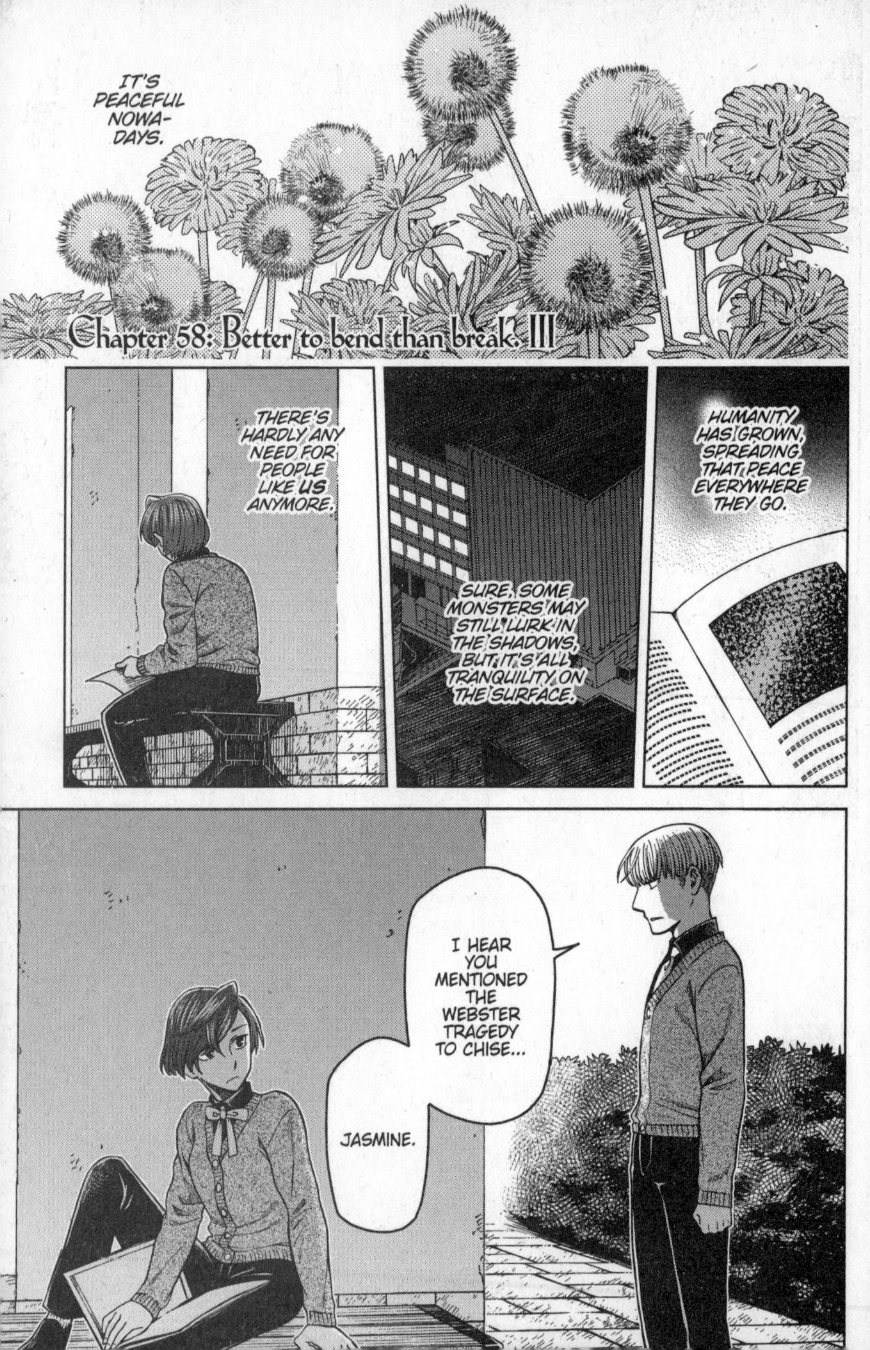
IT'S PEACEFUL NOWA-DAYS.
Chapter 58: Better to bend than break. III
HUMANITY HAS GROWN, SPREADING THAT PEACE EVERYWHERE THEY GO.
SURE, SOME MONSTERS MAY STILL LURK IN THE SHADOWS, BUT IT'S ALL TRANQUILITY ON THE SURFACE.
THERE'S HARDLY ANY NEED FOR PEOPLE LIKE US ANYMORE.
I HEAR YOU MENTIONED THE WEBSTER TRAGEDY TO CHISE...
JASMINE.

# Chapter 58: Better to bend than break. III

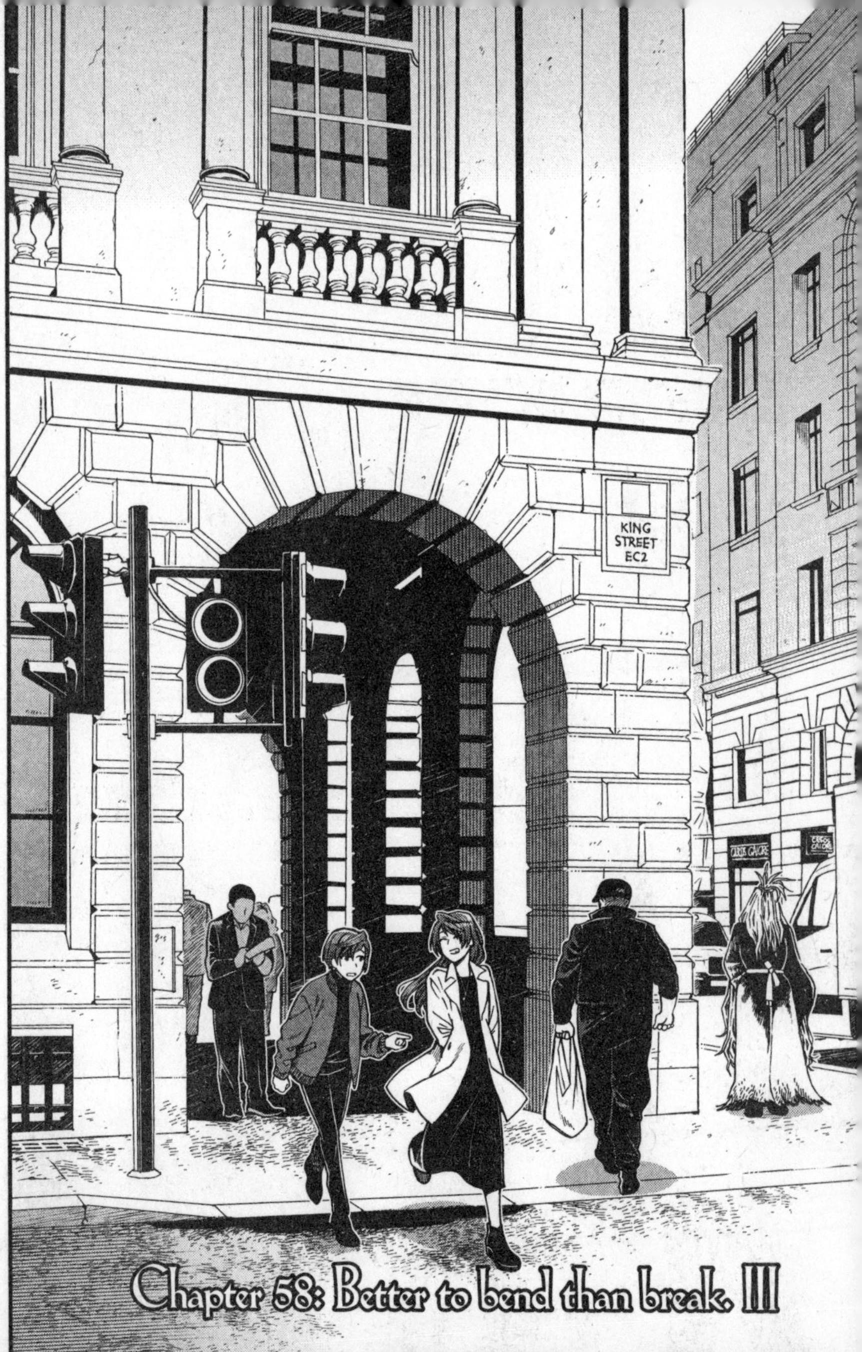
KING
STREET
EC2

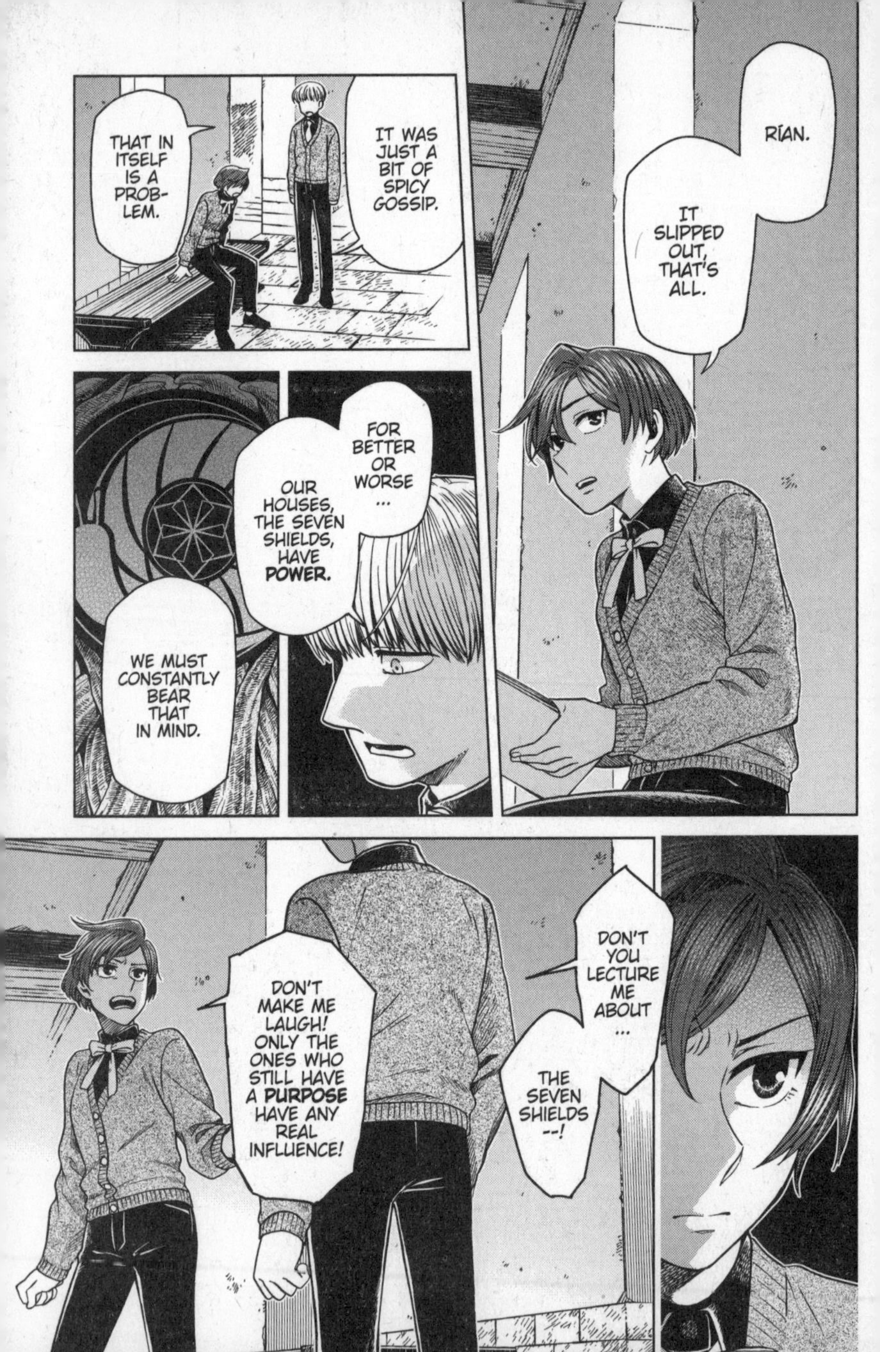
RÍAN.
IT SLIPPED OUT, THAT'S ALL.
IT WAS JUST A BIT OF SPICY GOSSIP.
THAT IN ITSELF IS A PROB-LEM.
FOR BETTER OR WORSE ...
OUR HOUSES, THE SEVEN SHIELDS, HAVE **POWER.**
WE MUST CONSTANTLY BEAR THAT IN MIND.
DON'T YOU LECTURE ME ABOUT ...
THE SEVEN SHIELDS --!
DON'T MAKE ME LAUGH! ONLY THE ONES WHO STILL HAVE A **PURPOSE** HAVE ANY REAL INFLUENCE!

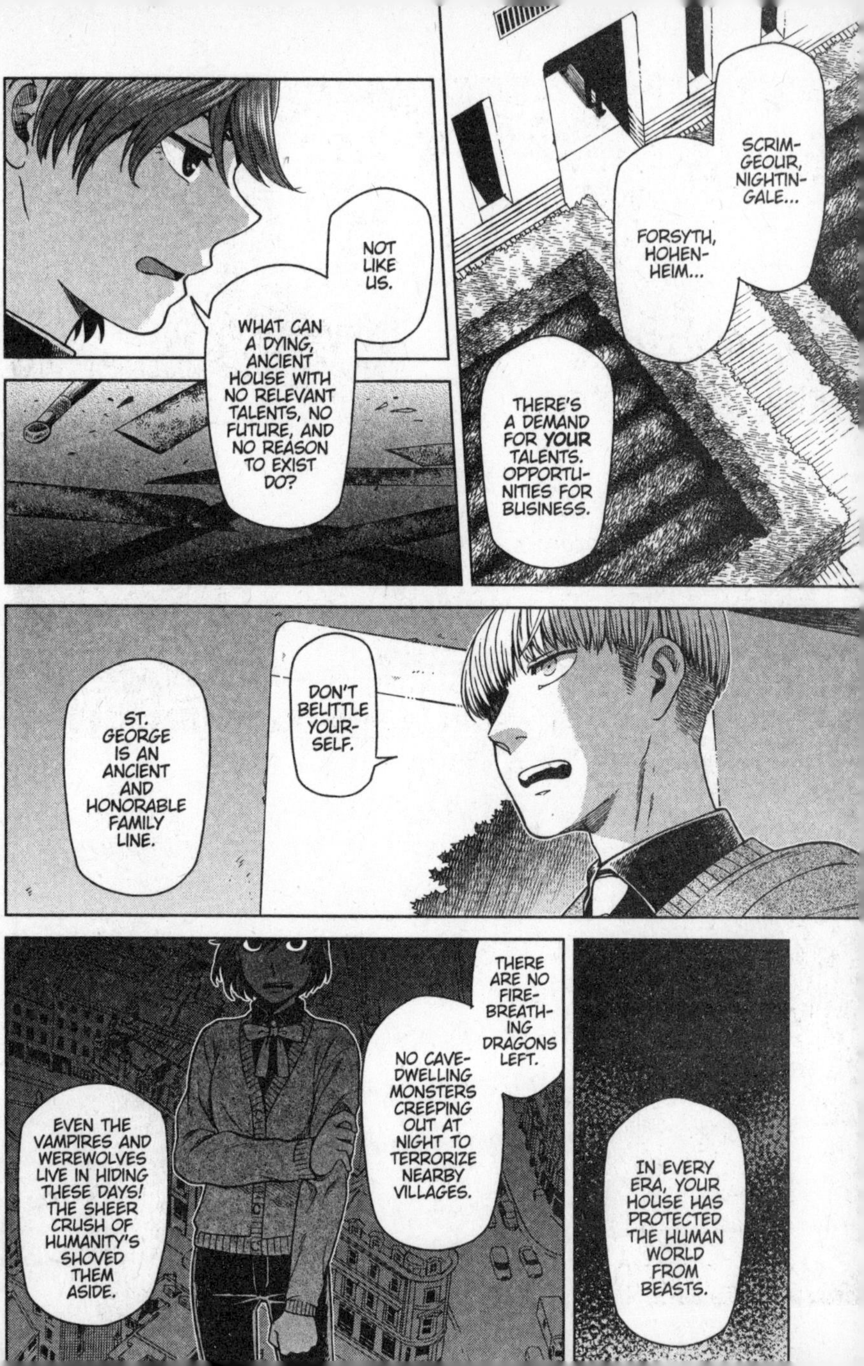
SCRIMGEOUR, NIGHTINGALE...
FORSYTH, HOHENHEIM...
THERE'S A DEMAND FOR **YOUR** TALENTS. OPPORTUNITIES FOR BUSINESS.
NOT LIKE US.
WHAT CAN A DYING, ANCIENT HOUSE WITH NO RELEVANT TALENTS, NO FUTURE, AND NO REASON TO EXIST DO?
DON'T BELITTLE YOURSELF.
ST. GEORGE IS AN ANCIENT AND HONORABLE FAMILY LINE.
IN EVERY ERA, YOUR HOUSE HAS PROTECTED THE HUMAN WORLD FROM BEASTS.
THERE ARE NO FIRE-BREATHING DRAGONS LEFT.
NO CAVE-DWELLING MONSTERS CREEPING OUT AT NIGHT TO TERRORIZE NEARBY VILLAGES.
EVEN THE VAMPIRES AND WEREWOLVES LIVE IN HIDING THESE DAYS! THE SHEER CRUSH OF HUMANITY'S SHOVED THEM ASIDE.

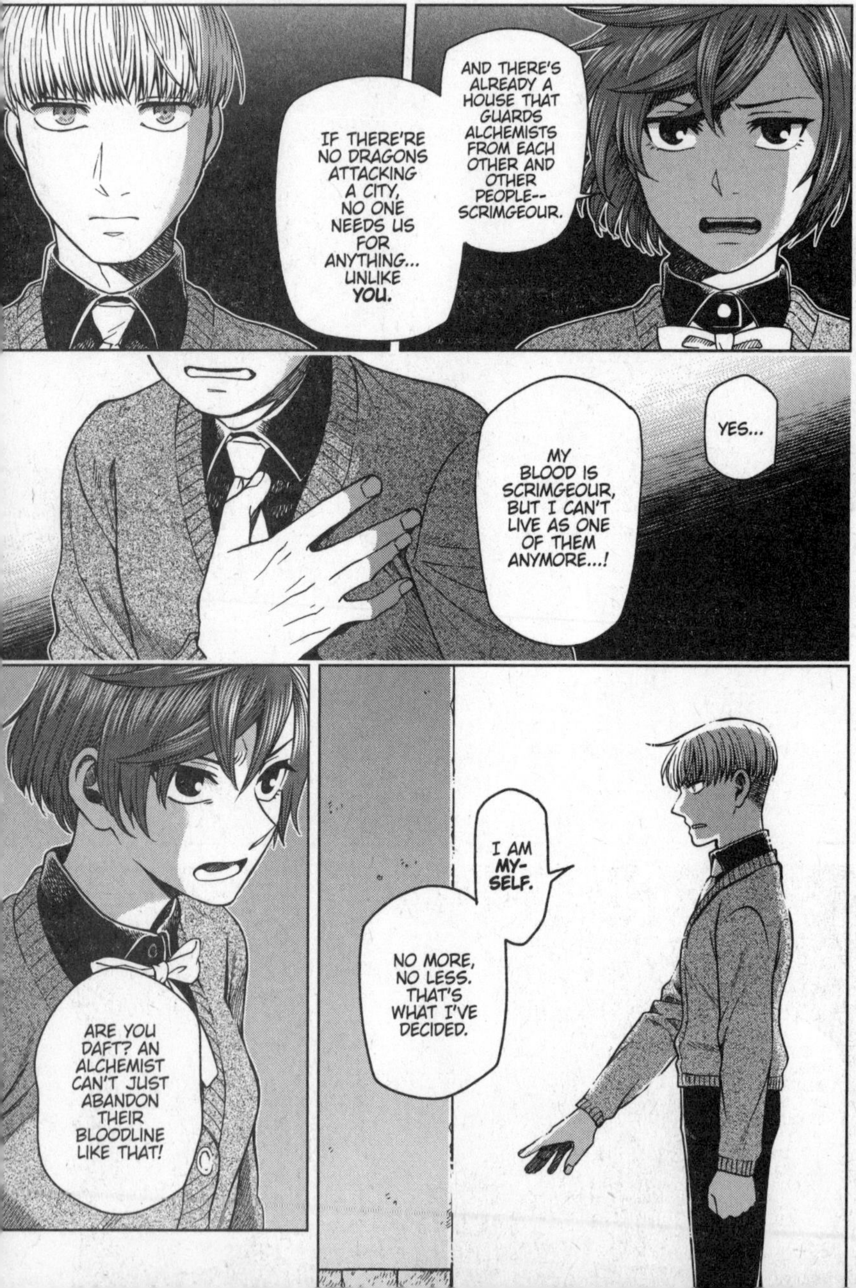
IF THERE'RE NO DRAGONS ATTACKING A CITY, NO ONE NEEDS US FOR ANYTHING... UNLIKE **YOU.**
AND THERE'S ALREADY A HOUSE THAT GUARDS ALCHEMISTS FROM EACH OTHER AND OTHER PEOPLE-- SCRIMGEOUR.
YES...
MY BLOOD IS SCRIMGEOUR, BUT I CAN'T LIVE AS ONE OF THEM ANYMORE...!
I AM **MY-SELF.**
NO MORE, NO LESS. THAT'S WHAT I'VE DECIDED.
ARE YOU DAFT? AN ALCHEMIST CAN'T JUST ABANDON THEIR BLOODLINE LIKE THAT!

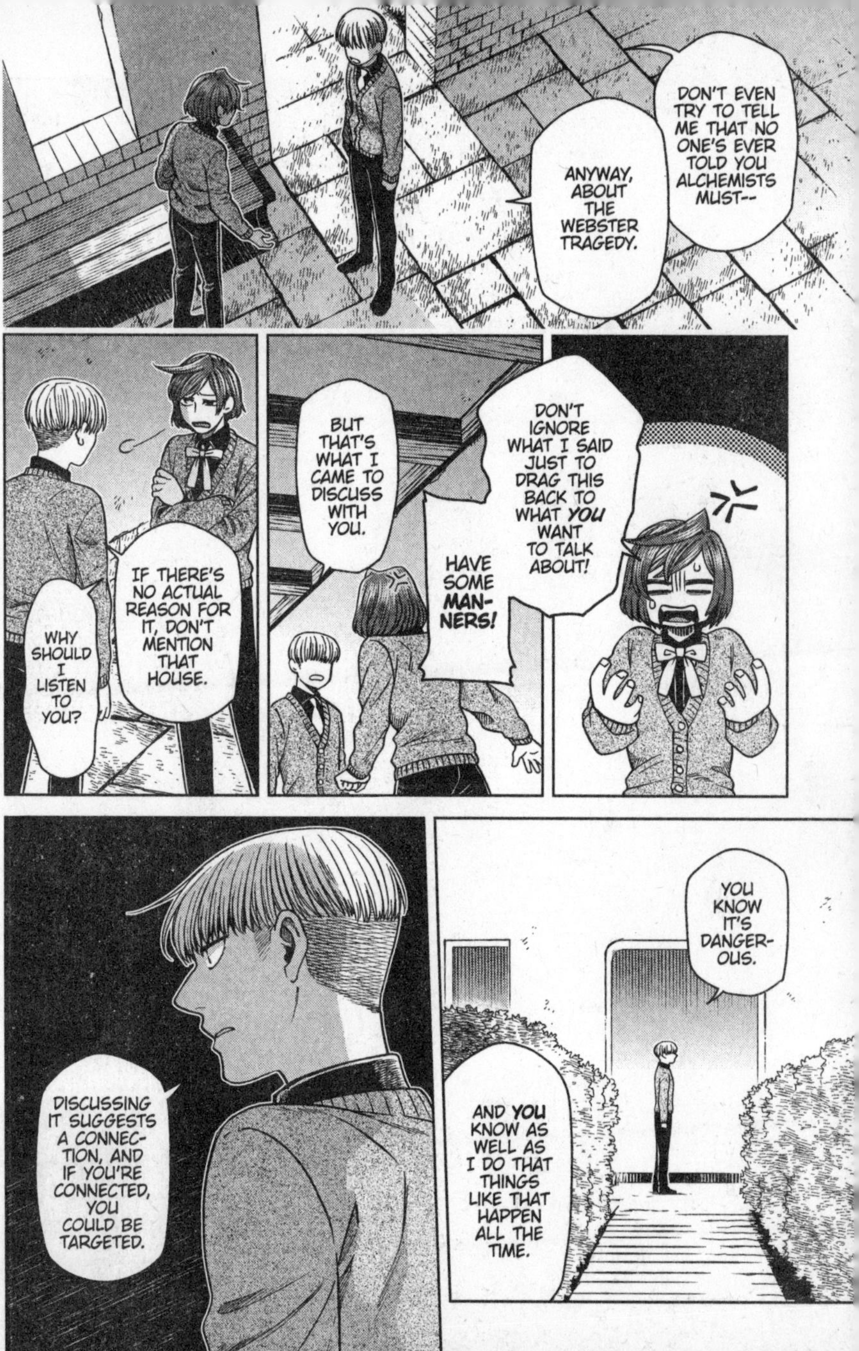
DON'T EVEN TRY TO TELL ME THAT NO ONE'S EVER TOLD YOU ALCHEMISTS MUST--
ANYWAY, ABOUT THE WEBSTER TRAGEDY.
DON'T IGNORE WHAT I SAID JUST TO DRAG THIS BACK TO WHAT **YOU** WANT TO TALK ABOUT!
HAVE SOME **MANNERS!**
BUT THAT'S WHAT I CAME TO DISCUSS WITH YOU.
IF THERE'S NO ACTUAL REASON FOR IT, DON'T MENTION THAT HOUSE.
WHY SHOULD I LISTEN TO YOU?
YOU KNOW IT'S DANGEROUS.
AND **YOU** KNOW AS WELL AS I DO THAT THINGS LIKE THAT HAPPEN ALL THE TIME.
DISCUSSING IT SUGGESTS A CONNECTION, AND IF YOU'RE CONNECTED, YOU COULD BE TARGETED.

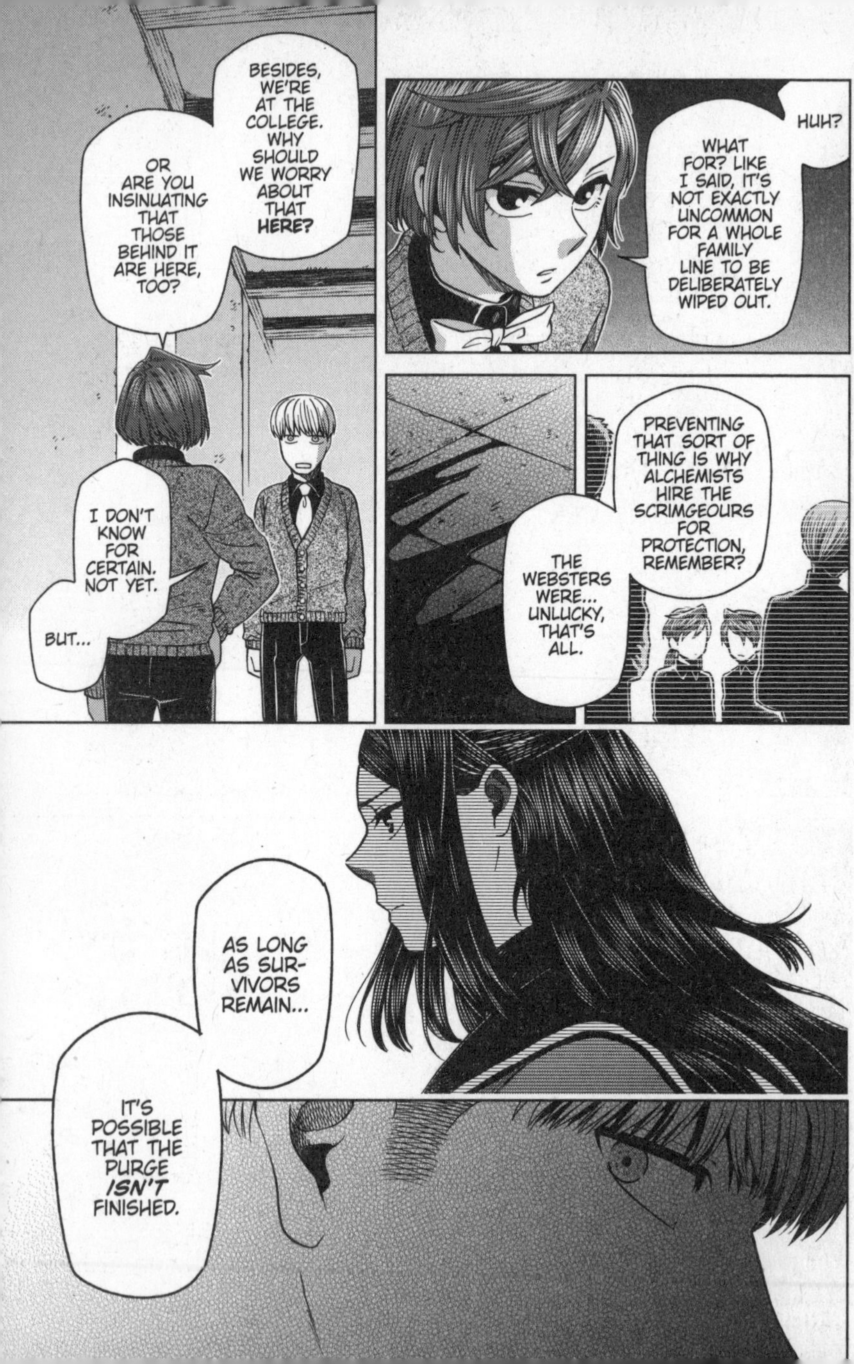
HUH?
WHAT FOR? LIKE I SAID, IT'S NOT EXACTLY UNCOMMON FOR A WHOLE FAMILY LINE TO BE DELIBERATELY WIPED OUT.
PREVENTING THAT SORT OF THING IS WHY ALCHEMISTS HIRE THE SCRIMGEOURS FOR PROTECTION, REMEMBER?
THE WEBSTERS WERE... UNLUCKY, THAT'S ALL.
BESIDES, WE'RE AT THE COLLEGE. WHY SHOULD WE WORRY ABOUT THAT **HERE?**
OR ARE YOU INSINUATING THAT THOSE BEHIND IT ARE HERE, TOO?
I DON'T KNOW FOR CERTAIN. NOT YET.
BUT...
AS LONG AS SUR-VIVORS REMAIN...
IT'S POSSIBLE THAT THE PURGE ***ISN'T*** FINISHED.

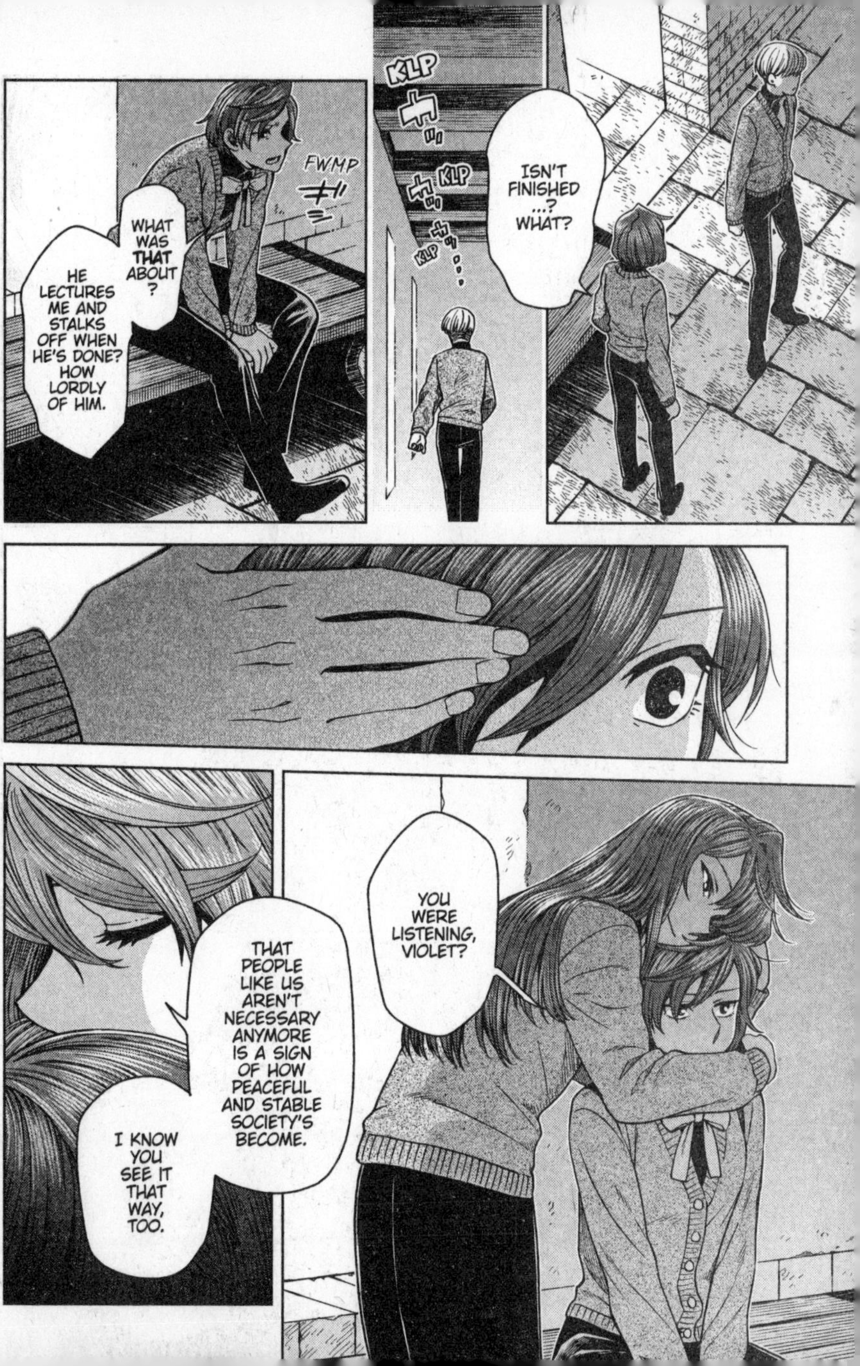
ISN'T FINISHED ...? WHAT?
KLP
KLP
KLP
FWMP
WHAT WAS THAT ABOUT?
HE LECTURES ME AND STALKS OFF WHEN HE'S DONE? HOW LORDLY OF HIM.
YOU WERE LISTENING, VIOLET?
THAT PEOPLE LIKE US AREN'T NECESSARY ANYMORE IS A SIGN OF HOW PEACEFUL AND STABLE SOCIETY'S BECOME.
I KNOW YOU SEE IT THAT WAY, TOO.

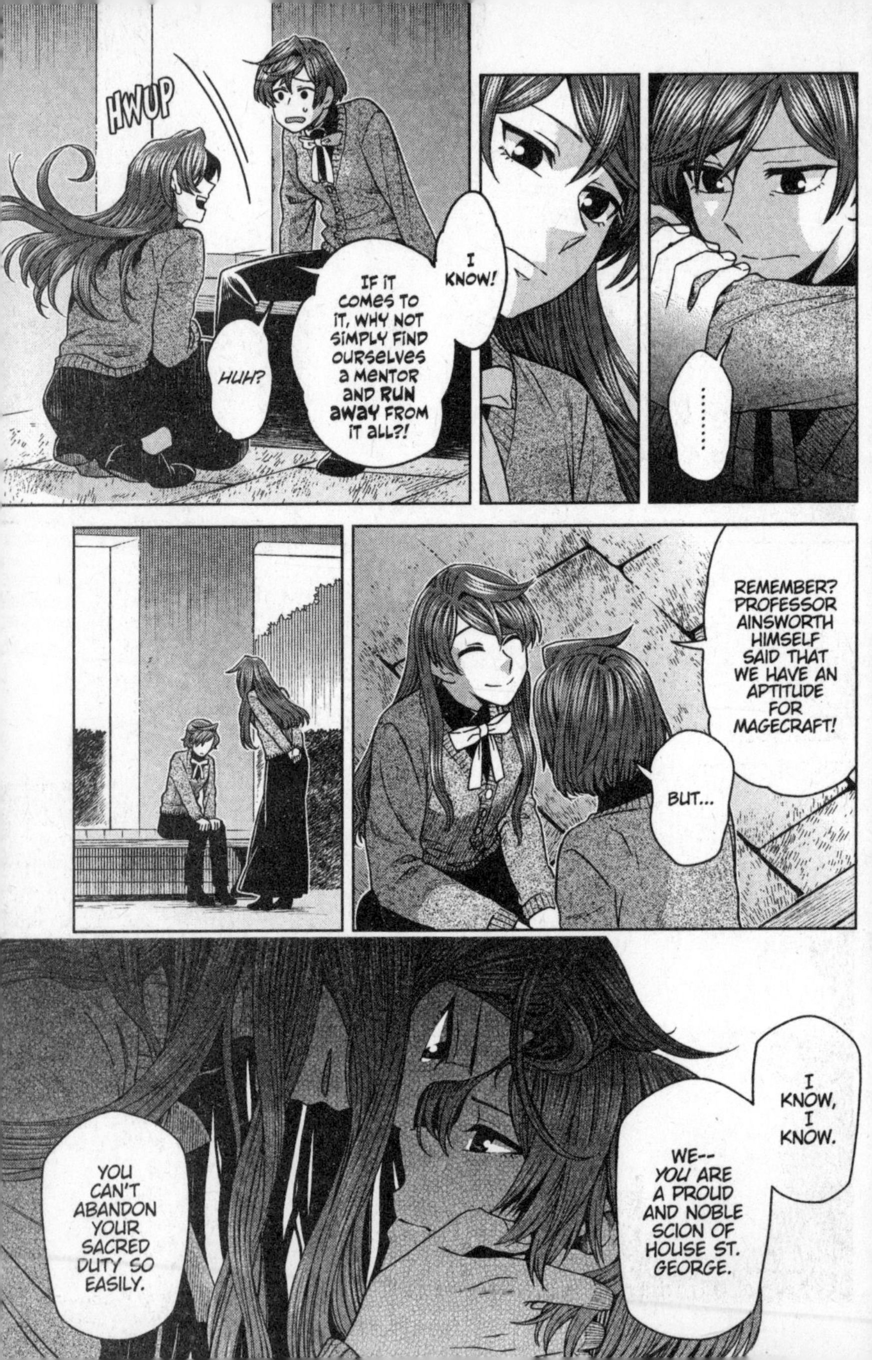
......
I KNOW!
HWUP
IF IT COMES TO IT, WHY NOT SIMPLY FIND OURSELVES A MENTOR AND RUN AWAY FROM IT ALL?!
HUH?
REMEMBER? PROFESSOR AINSWORTH HIMSELF SAID THAT WE HAVE AN APTITUDE FOR MAGECRAFT!
BUT...
I KNOW, I KNOW.
WE-- *YOU* ARE A PROUD AND NOBLE SCION OF HOUSE ST. GEORGE.
YOU CAN'T ABANDON YOUR SACRED DUTY SO EASILY.

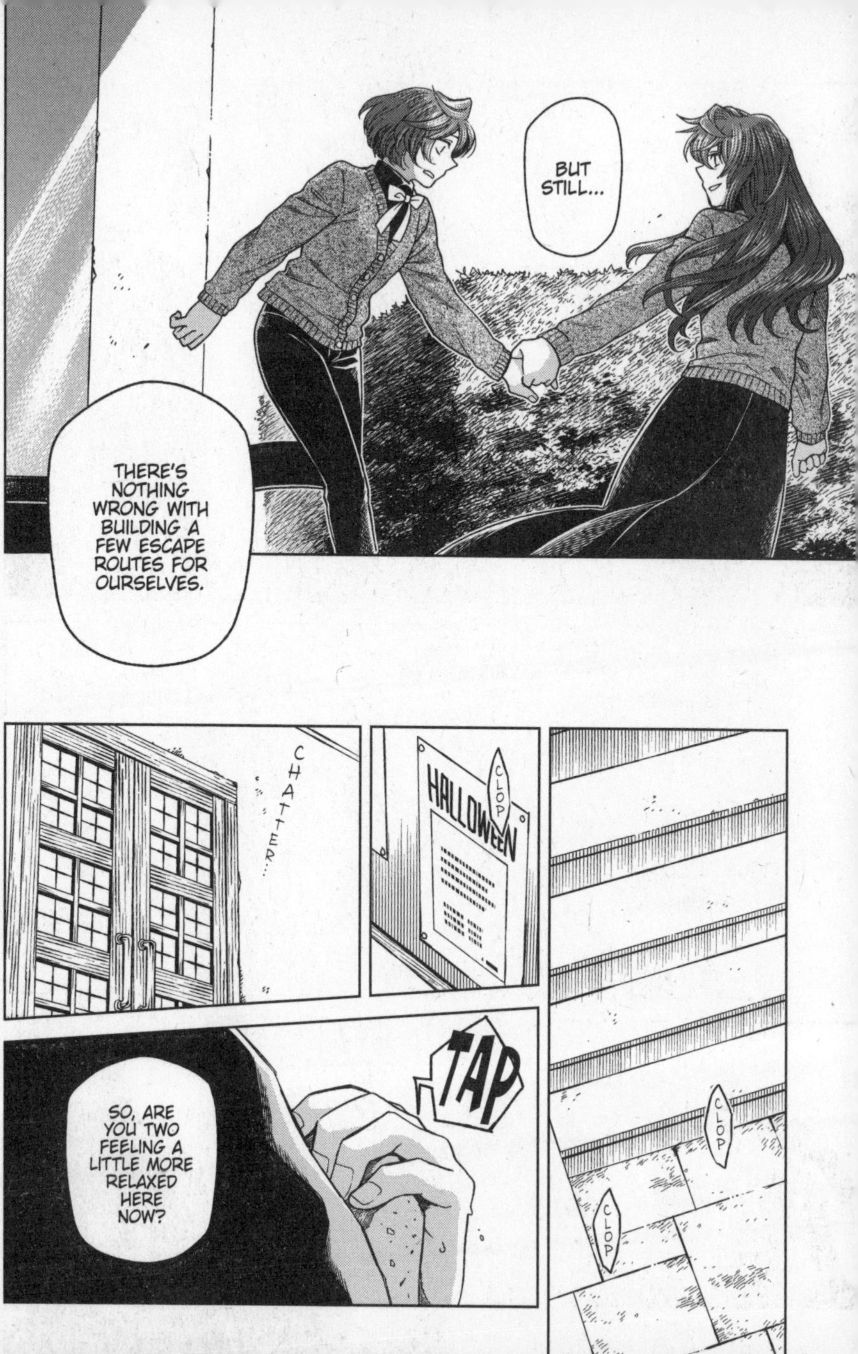
BUT STILL...
THERE'S NOTHING WRONG WITH BUILDING A FEW ESCAPE ROUTES FOR OURSELVES.
CLOP
CLOP
HALLOWEEN
CLOP
CHATTER...
TAP
SO, ARE YOU TWO FEELING A LITTLE MORE RELAXED HERE NOW?

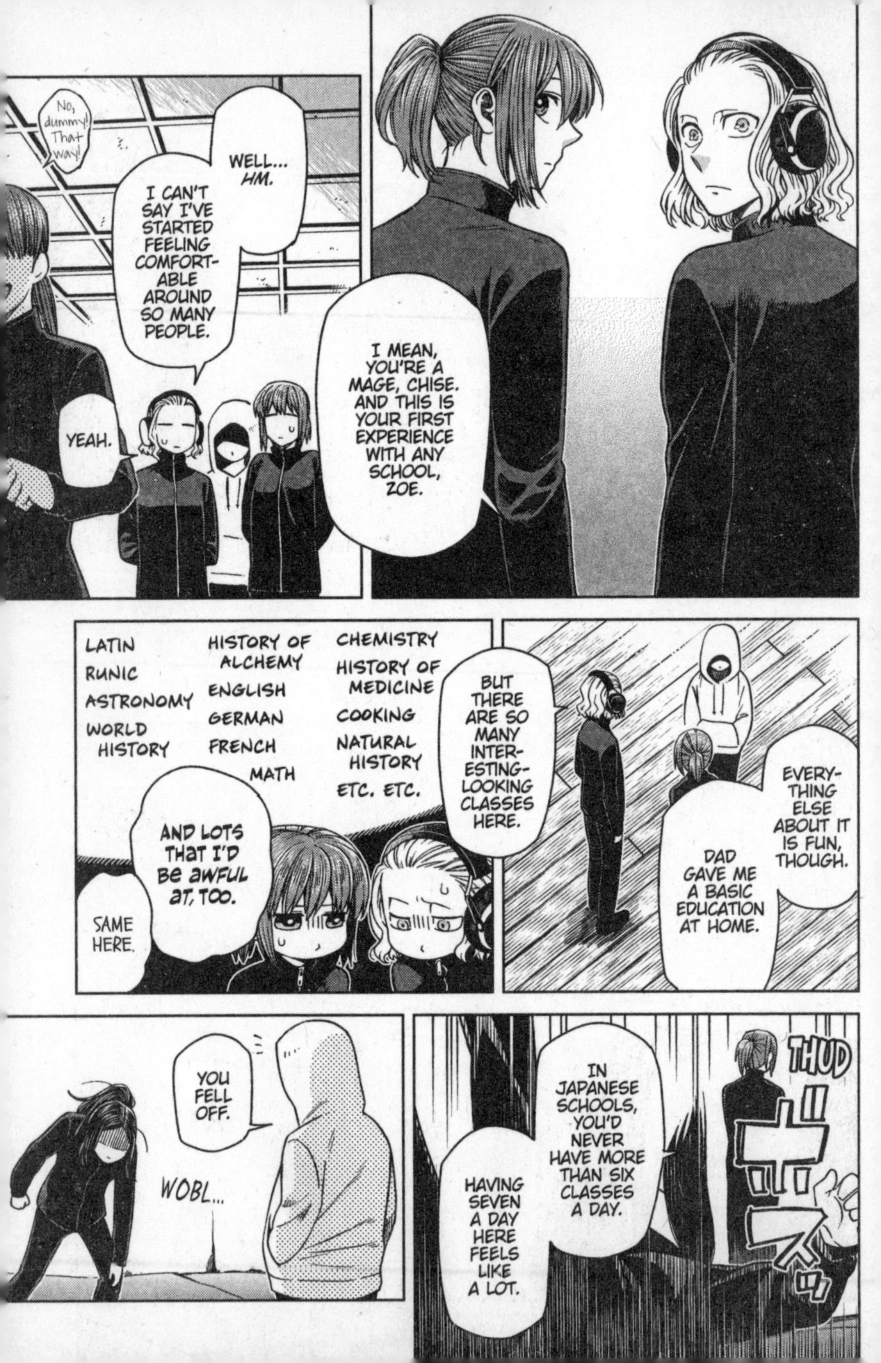
I MEAN, YOU'RE A MAGE, CHISE. AND THIS IS YOUR FIRST EXPERIENCE WITH ANY SCHOOL, ZOE.
WELL... HM.
I CAN'T SAY I'VE STARTED FEELING COMFORTABLE AROUND SO MANY PEOPLE.
No, dummy!! That way!
YEAH.
EVERYTHING ELSE ABOUT IT IS FUN, THOUGH.
DAD GAVE ME A BASIC EDUCATION AT HOME.
BUT THERE ARE SO MANY INTERESTING-LOOKING CLASSES HERE.
CHEMISTRY
HISTORY OF MEDICINE
COOKING
NATURAL HISTORY
ETC. ETC.
HISTORY OF ALCHEMY
ENGLISH
GERMAN
FRENCH
MATH
LATIN
RUNIC
ASTRONOMY
WORLD HISTORY
AND LOTS THAT I'D BE AWFUL AT, TOO.
SAME HERE.
THUD
IN JAPANESE SCHOOLS, YOU'D NEVER HAVE MORE THAN SIX CLASSES A DAY.
HAVING SEVEN A DAY HERE FEELS LIKE A LOT.
YOU FELL OFF.
WOBL...

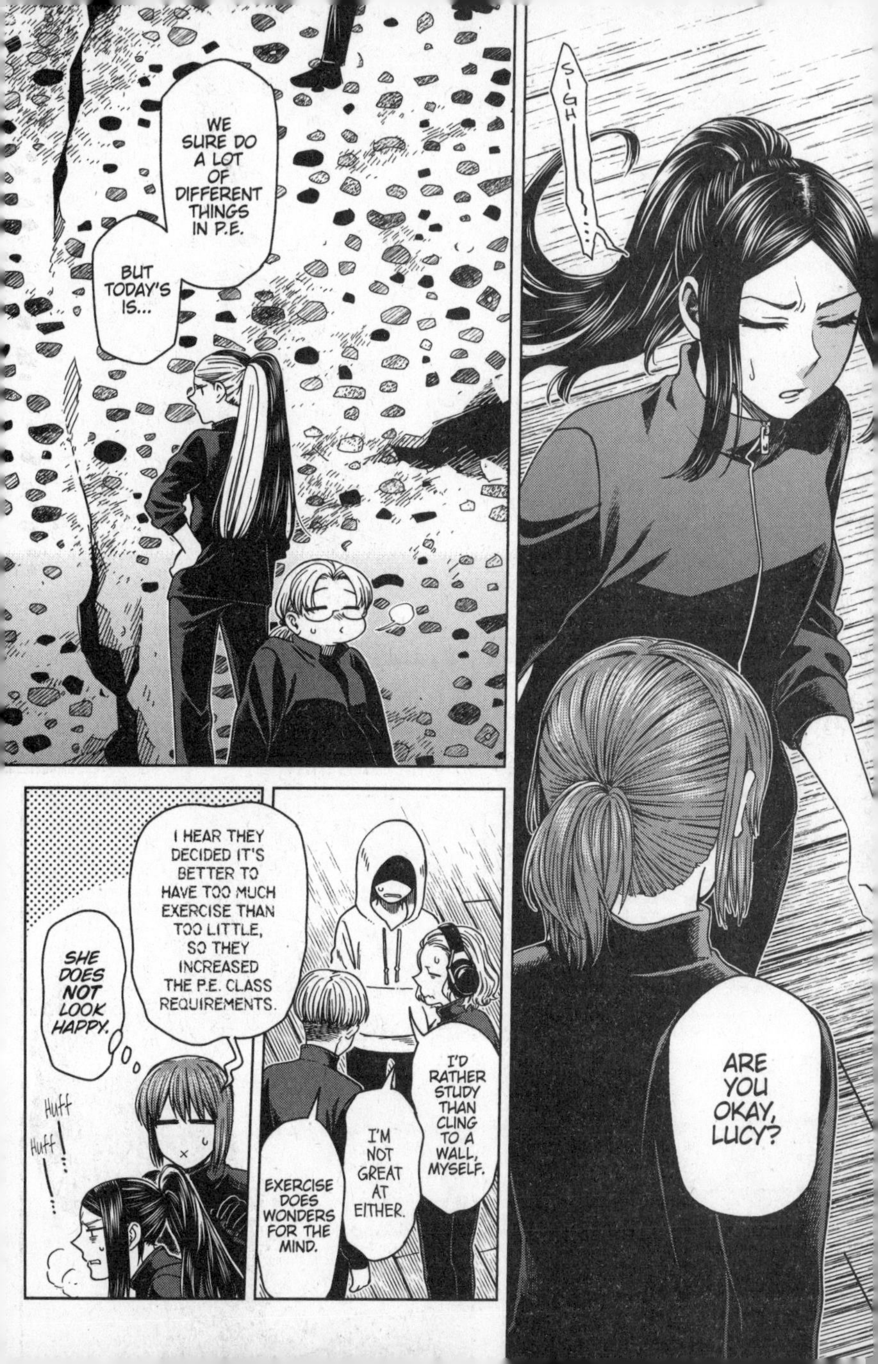
SIGH...
ARE YOU OKAY, LUCY?
WE SURE DO A LOT OF DIFFERENT THINGS IN P.E.
BUT TODAY'S IS...
I'D RATHER STUDY THAN CLING TO A WALL, MYSELF.
I'M NOT GREAT AT EITHER.
EXERCISE DOES WONDERS FOR THE MIND.
I HEAR THEY DECIDED IT'S BETTER TO HAVE TOO MUCH EXERCISE THAN TOO LITTLE, SO THEY INCREASED THE P.E. CLASS REQUIREMENTS.
SHE DOES NOT LOOK HAPPY.
Huff
Huff

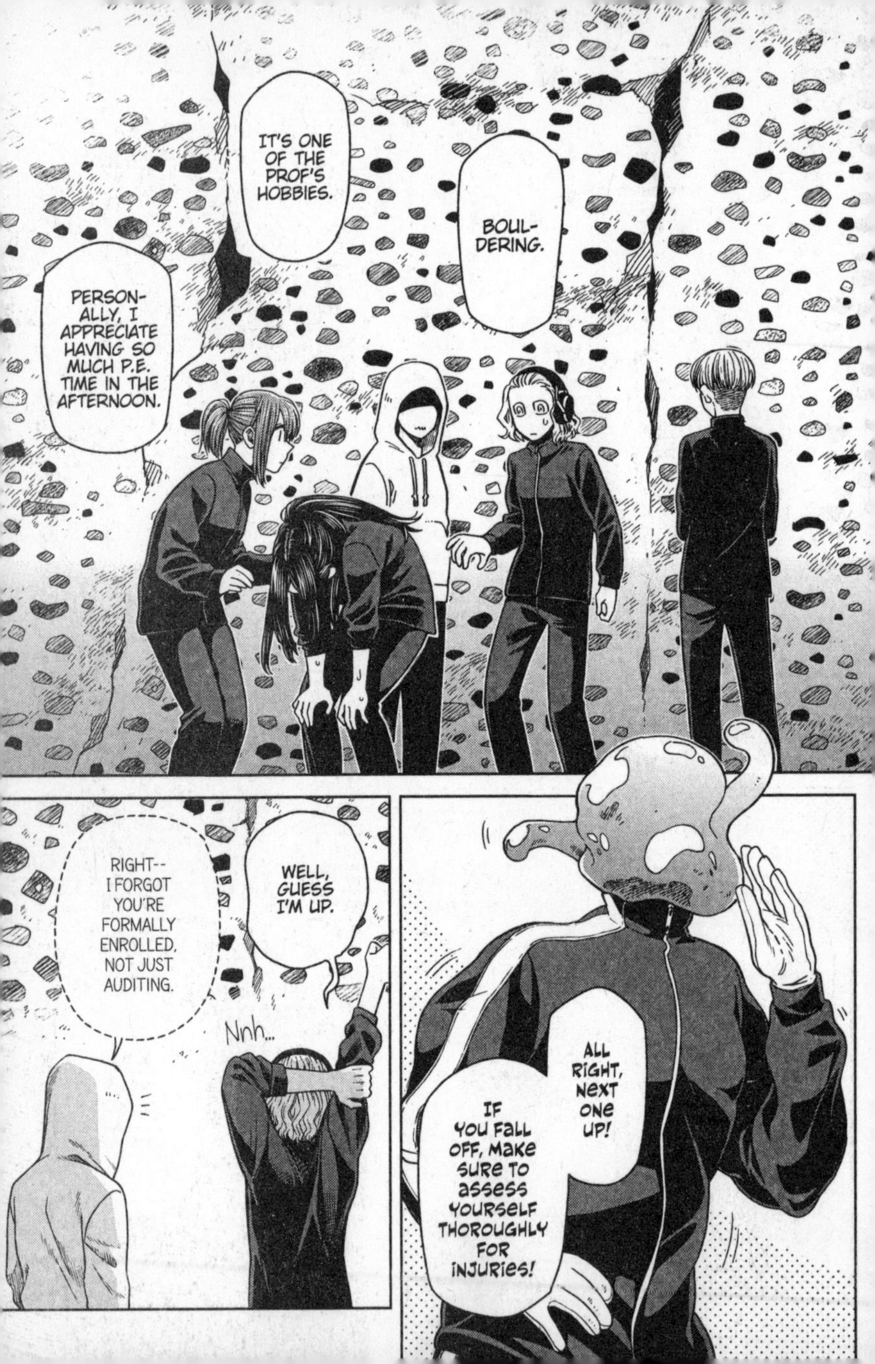
BOULDERING.
IT'S ONE OF THE PROF'S HOBBIES.
PERSONALLY, I APPRECIATE HAVING SO MUCH P.E. TIME IN THE AFTERNOON.
ALL RIGHT, NEXT ONE UP!
IF YOU FALL OFF, MAKE SURE TO ASSESS YOURSELF THOROUGHLY FOR INJURIES!
WELL, GUESS I'M UP.
RIGHT-- I FORGOT YOU'RE FORMALLY ENROLLED, NOT JUST AUDITING.
Nnh...
...

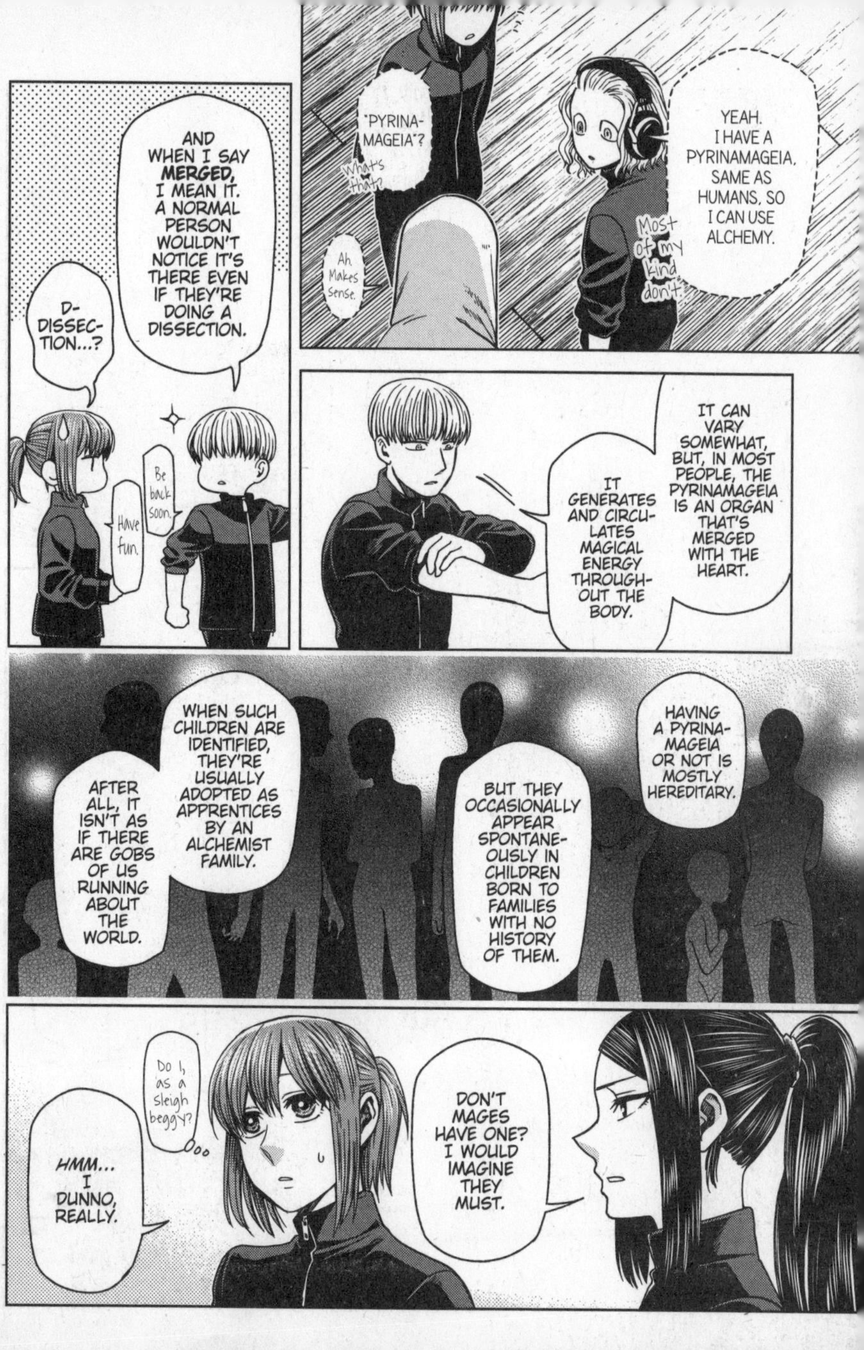
YEAH. I HAVE A PYRINAMAGEIA, SAME AS HUMANS, SO I CAN USE ALCHEMY.
Most of my kind don't.
"PYRINA-MAGEIA"?
What's that?
Ah. Makes sense.
IT CAN VARY SOMEWHAT, BUT, IN MOST PEOPLE, THE PYRINAMAGEIA IS AN ORGAN THAT'S MERGED WITH THE HEART.
IT GENERATES AND CIRCULATES MAGICAL ENERGY THROUGHOUT THE BODY.
AND WHEN I SAY **MERGED**, I MEAN IT. A NORMAL PERSON WOULDN'T NOTICE IT'S THERE EVEN IF THEY'RE DOING A DISSECTION.
D-DISSECTION...?
Be back soon.
Have fun.
HAVING A PYRINAMAGEIA OR NOT IS MOSTLY HEREDITARY.
BUT THEY OCCASIONALLY APPEAR SPONTANEOUSLY IN CHILDREN BORN TO FAMILIES WITH NO HISTORY OF THEM.
WHEN SUCH CHILDREN ARE IDENTIFIED, THEY'RE USUALLY ADOPTED AS APPRENTICES BY AN ALCHEMIST FAMILY.
AFTER ALL, IT ISN'T AS IF THERE ARE GOBS OF US RUNNING ABOUT THE WORLD.
DON'T MAGES HAVE ONE? I WOULD IMAGINE THEY MUST.
Do I, as a sleigh beggy?
*HMM...* I DUNNO, REALLY.

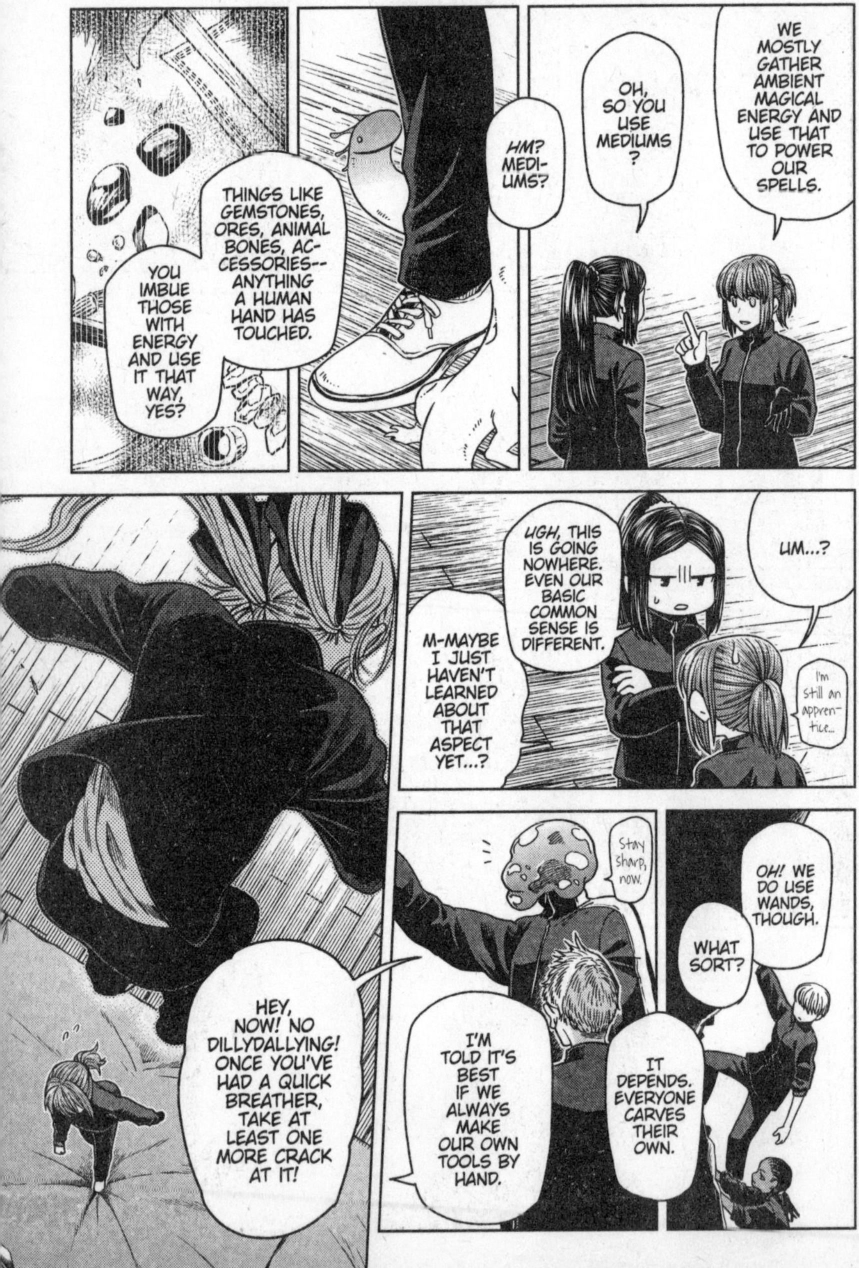
WE MOSTLY GATHER AMBIENT MAGICAL ENERGY AND USE THAT TO POWER OUR SPELLS.
OH, SO YOU USE MEDIUMS?
HM? MEDI-UMS?
THINGS LIKE GEMSTONES, ORES, ANIMAL BONES, AC-CESSORIES-- ANYTHING A HUMAN HAND HAS TOUCHED.
YOU IMBUE THOSE WITH ENERGY AND USE IT THAT WAY, YES?
UM...?
I'm still an appren-tice...
UGH, THIS IS GOING NOWHERE. EVEN OUR BASIC COMMON SENSE IS DIFFERENT.
M-MAYBE I JUST HAVEN'T LEARNED ABOUT THAT ASPECT YET...?
OH! WE DO USE WANDS, THOUGH.
WHAT SORT?
IT DEPENDS. EVERYONE CARVES THEIR OWN.
Stay sharp, now.
I'M TOLD IT'S BEST IF WE ALWAYS MAKE OUR OWN TOOLS BY HAND.
HEY, NOW! NO DILLYDALLYING! ONCE YOU'VE HAD A QUICK BREATHER, TAKE AT LEAST ONE MORE CRACK AT IT!

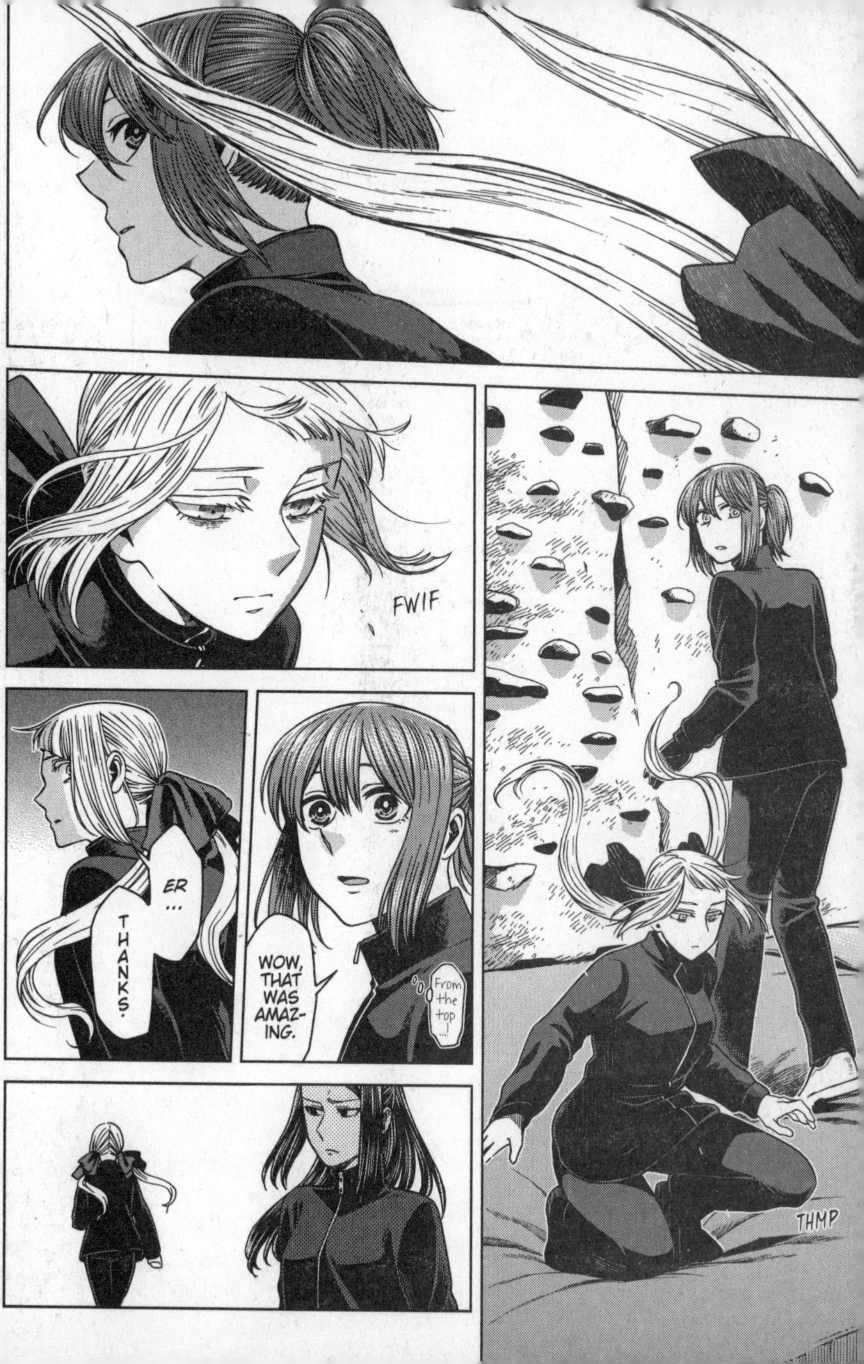
THMP
FWIF
WOW, THAT WAS AMAZ-ING.
From the top...!
ER... THANKS.

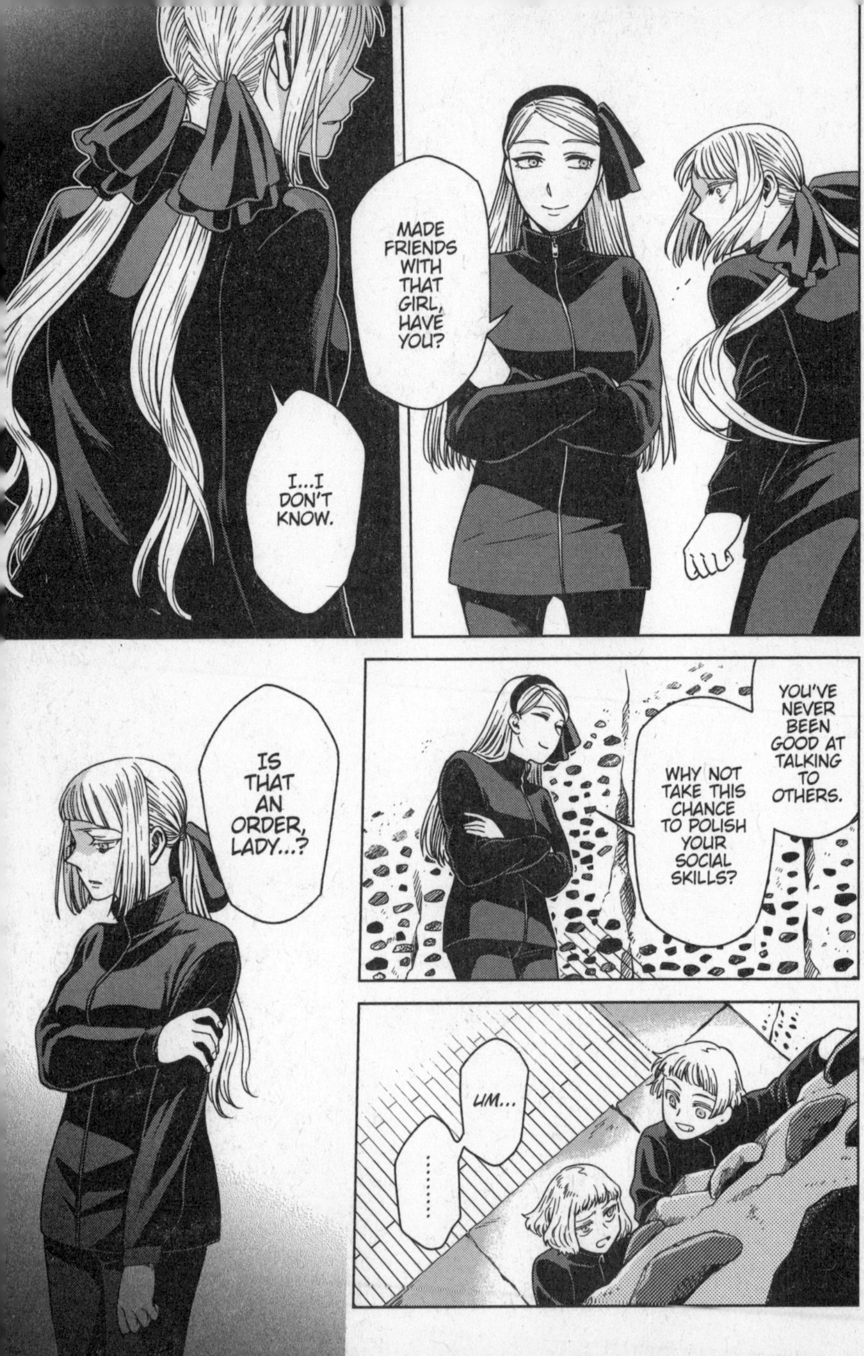
MADE FRIENDS WITH THAT GIRL, HAVE YOU?
I...I DON'T KNOW.
YOU'VE NEVER BEEN GOOD AT TALKING TO OTHERS.
WHY NOT TAKE THIS CHANCE TO POLISH YOUR SOCIAL SKILLS?
UM...
......
IS THAT AN ORDER, LADY...?

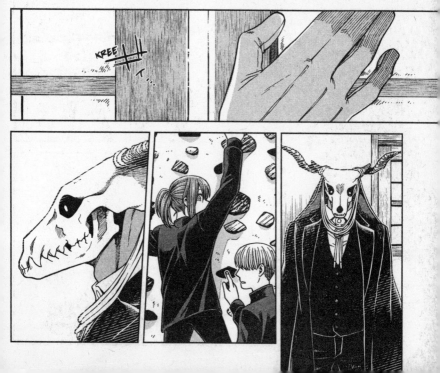

KREE

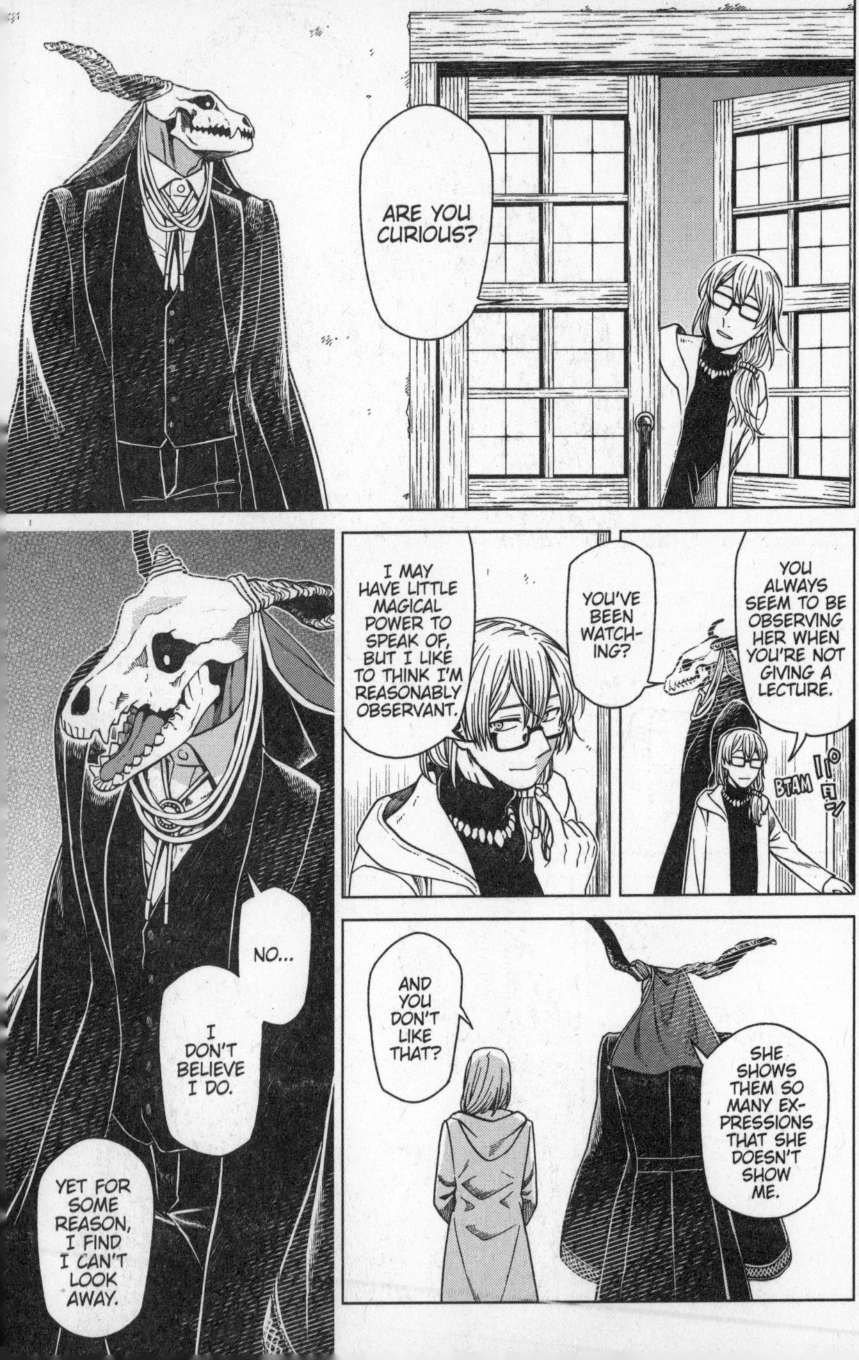
ARE YOU CURIOUS?
YOU ALWAYS SEEM TO BE OBSERVING HER WHEN YOU'RE NOT GIVING A LECTURE.
BTAM
YOU'VE BEEN WATCH-ING?
I MAY HAVE LITTLE MAGICAL POWER TO SPEAK OF, BUT I LIKE TO THINK I'M REASONABLY OBSERVANT.
SHE SHOWS THEM SO MANY EX-PRESSIONS THAT SHE DOESN'T SHOW ME.
AND YOU DON'T LIKE THAT?
NO...
I DON'T BELIEVE I DO.
YET FOR SOME REASON, I FIND I CAN'T LOOK AWAY.

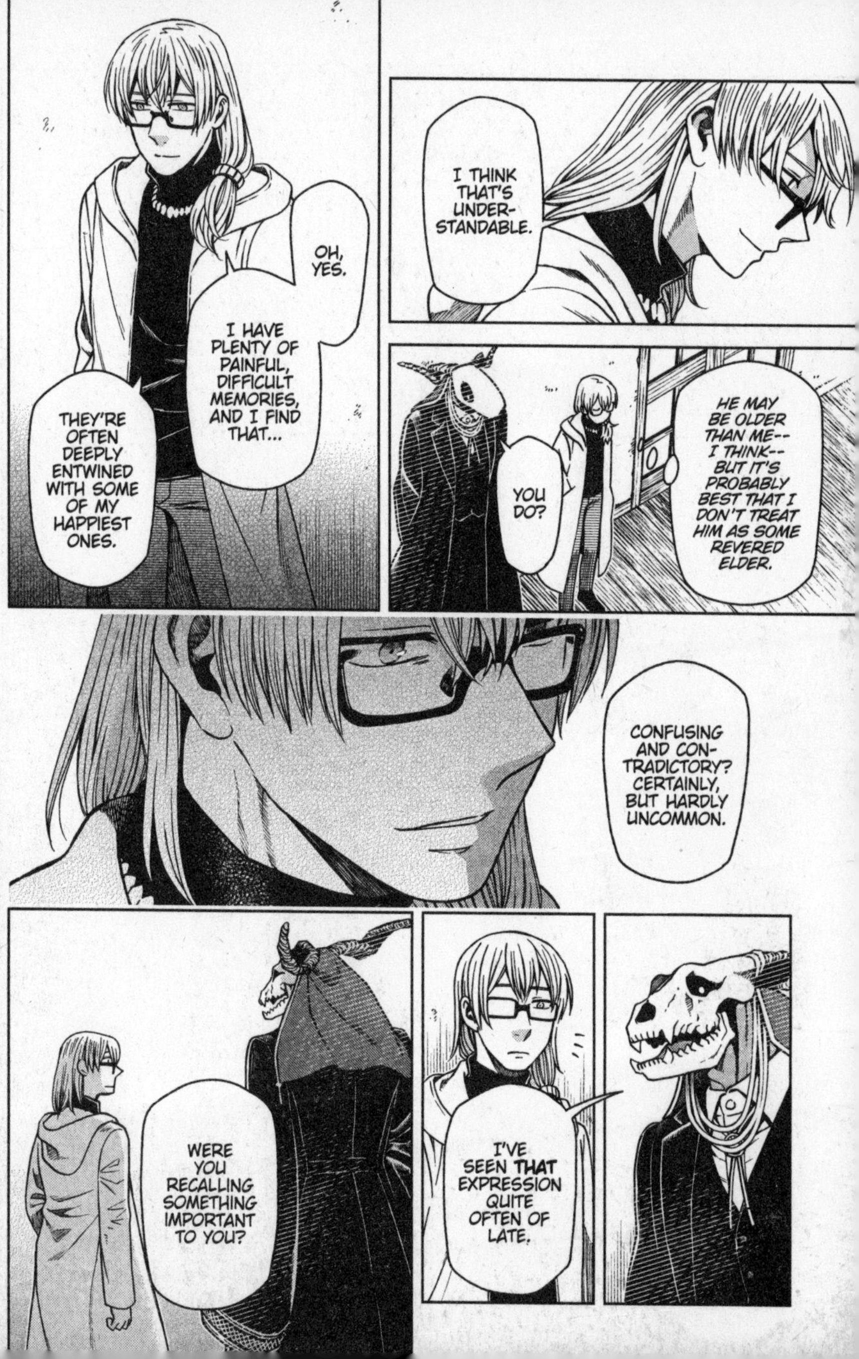
I THINK THAT'S UNDER-STANDABLE.
HE MAY BE OLDER THAN ME-- I THINK-- BUT IT'S PROBABLY BEST THAT I DON'T TREAT HIM AS SOME REVERED ELDER.
YOU DO?
OH, YES.
I HAVE PLENTY OF PAINFUL, DIFFICULT MEMORIES, AND I FIND THAT...
THEY'RE OFTEN DEEPLY ENTWINED WITH SOME OF MY HAPPIEST ONES.
CONFUSING AND CON-TRADICTORY? CERTAINLY, BUT HARDLY UNCOMMON.
I'VE SEEN THAT EXPRESSION QUITE OFTEN OF LATE.
WERE YOU RECALLING SOMETHING IMPORTANT TO YOU?

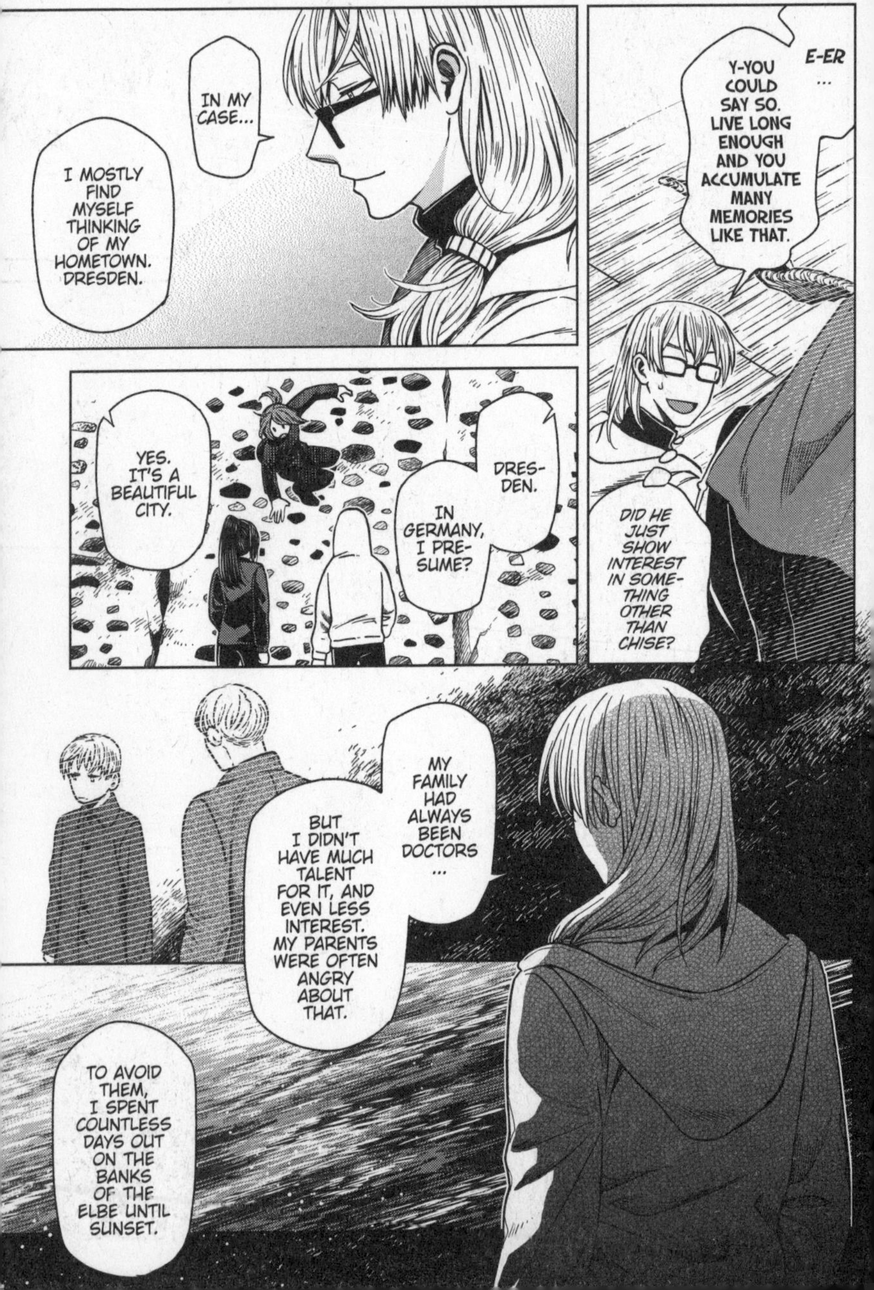
E-ER ...
Y-YOU COULD SAY SO. LIVE LONG ENOUGH AND YOU ACCUMULATE MANY MEMORIES LIKE THAT.
DID HE JUST SHOW INTEREST IN SOME-THING OTHER THAN CHISE?
IN MY CASE...
I MOSTLY FIND MYSELF THINKING OF MY HOMETOWN. DRESDEN.
DRES-DEN.
IN GERMANY, I PRE-SUME?
YES. IT'S A BEAUTIFUL CITY.
MY FAMILY HAD ALWAYS BEEN DOCTORS ...
BUT I DIDN'T HAVE MUCH TALENT FOR IT, AND EVEN LESS INTEREST. MY PARENTS WERE OFTEN ANGRY ABOUT THAT.
TO AVOID THEM, I SPENT COUNTLESS DAYS OUT ON THE BANKS OF THE ELBE UNTIL SUNSET.

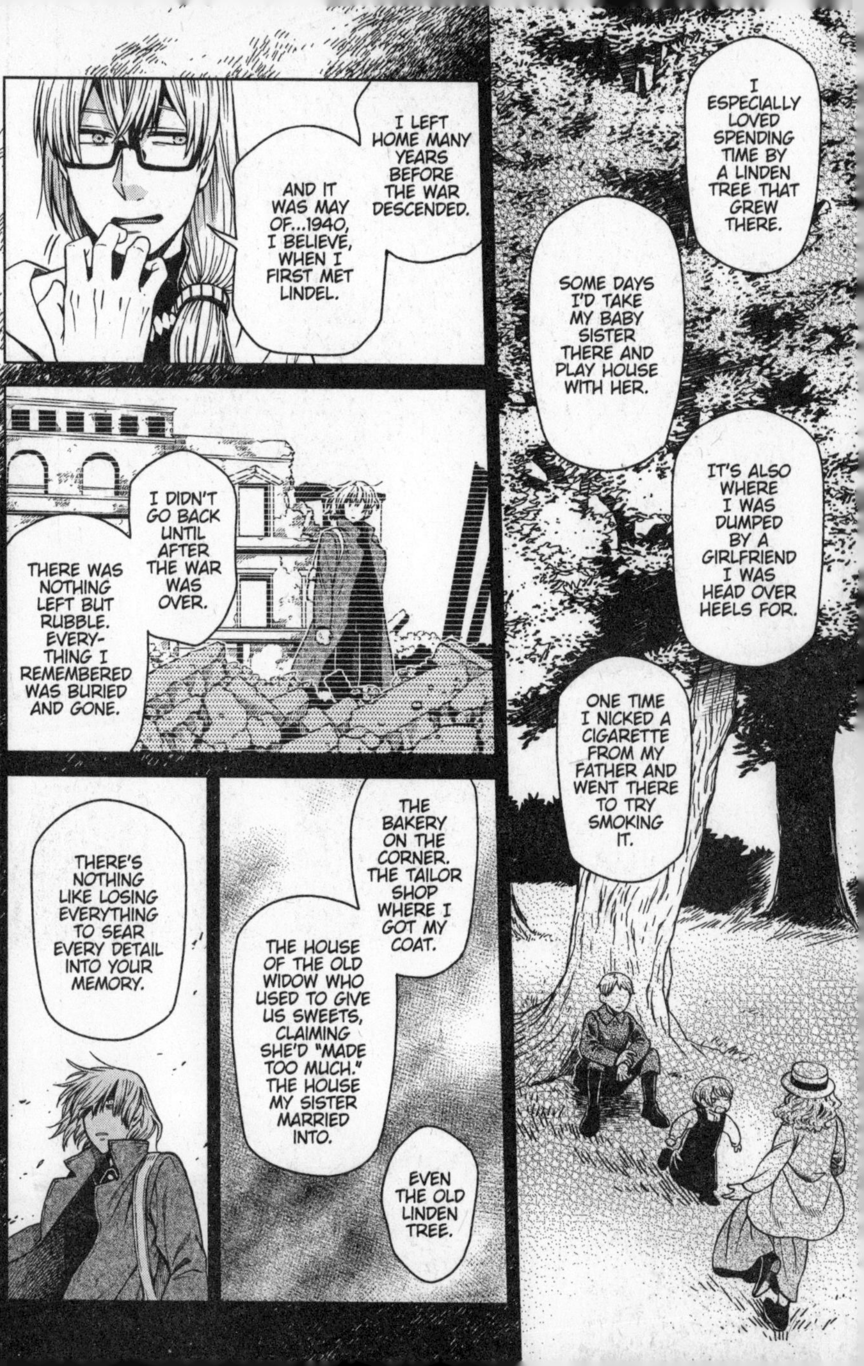
I ESPECIALLY LOVED SPENDING TIME BY A LINDEN TREE THAT GREW THERE.
SOME DAYS I'D TAKE MY BABY SISTER THERE AND PLAY HOUSE WITH HER.
IT'S ALSO WHERE I WAS DUMPED BY A GIRLFRIEND I WAS HEAD OVER HEELS FOR.
ONE TIME I NICKED A CIGARETTE FROM MY FATHER AND WENT THERE TO TRY SMOKING IT.
I LEFT HOME MANY YEARS BEFORE THE WAR DESCENDED.
AND IT WAS MAY OF...1940, I BELIEVE, WHEN I FIRST MET LINDEL.
I DIDN'T GO BACK UNTIL AFTER THE WAR WAS OVER.
THERE WAS NOTHING LEFT BUT RUBBLE. EVERY-THING I REMEMBERED WAS BURIED AND GONE.
THE BAKERY ON THE CORNER. THE TAILOR SHOP WHERE I GOT MY COAT.
THE HOUSE OF THE OLD WIDOW WHO USED TO GIVE US SWEETS, CLAIMING SHE'D "MADE TOO MUCH." THE HOUSE MY SISTER MARRIED INTO.
EVEN THE OLD LINDEN TREE.
THERE'S NOTHING LIKE LOSING EVERYTHING TO SEAR EVERY DETAIL INTO YOUR MEMORY.

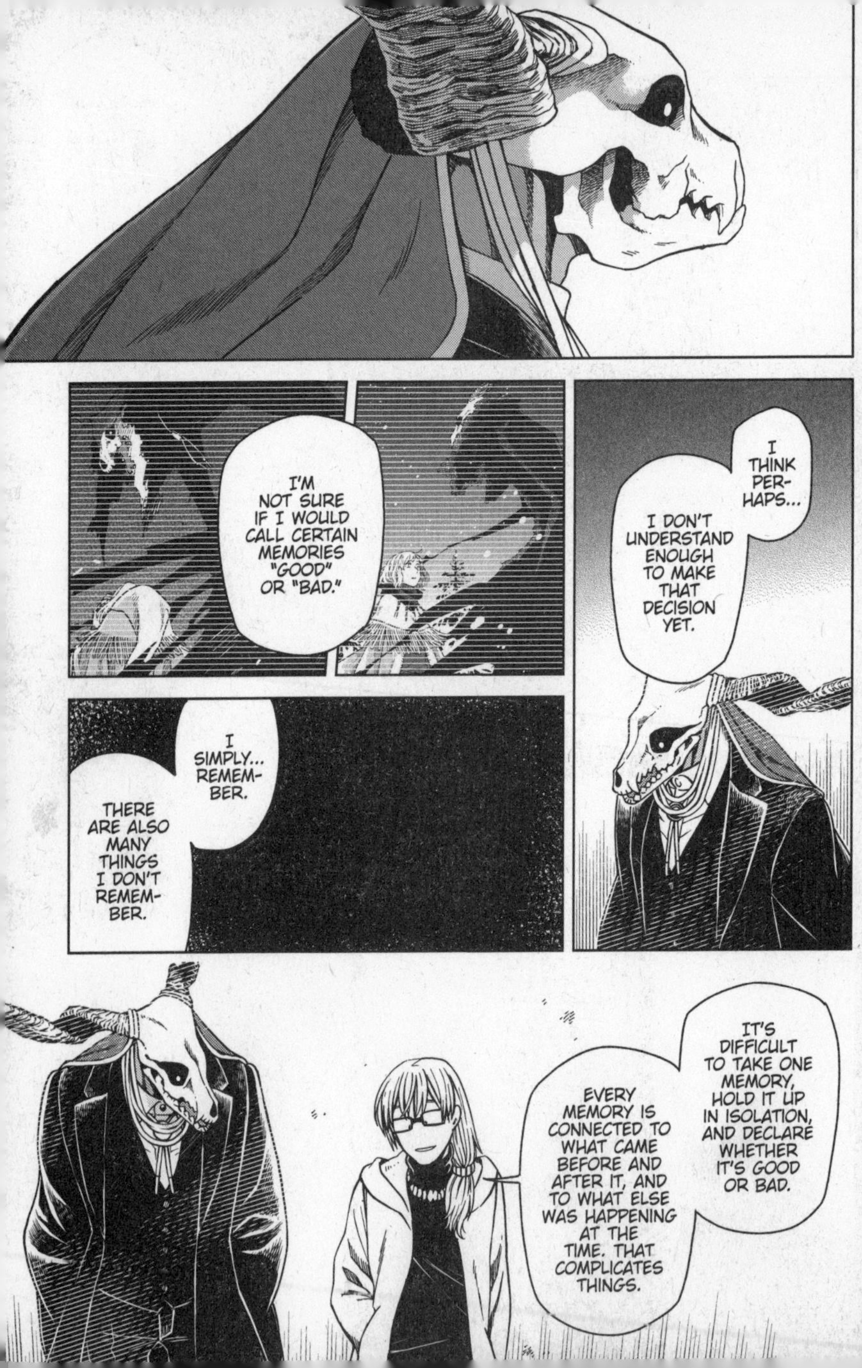
I THINK PERHAPS...
I DON'T UNDERSTAND ENOUGH TO MAKE THAT DECISION YET.
I'M NOT SURE IF I WOULD CALL CERTAIN MEMORIES "GOOD" OR "BAD."
I SIMPLY... REMEMBER.
THERE ARE ALSO MANY THINGS I DON'T REMEMBER.
IT'S DIFFICULT TO TAKE ONE MEMORY, HOLD IT UP IN ISOLATION, AND DECLARE WHETHER IT'S GOOD OR BAD.
EVERY MEMORY IS CONNECTED TO WHAT CAME BEFORE AND AFTER IT, AND TO WHAT ELSE WAS HAPPENING AT THE TIME. THAT COMPLICATES THINGS.

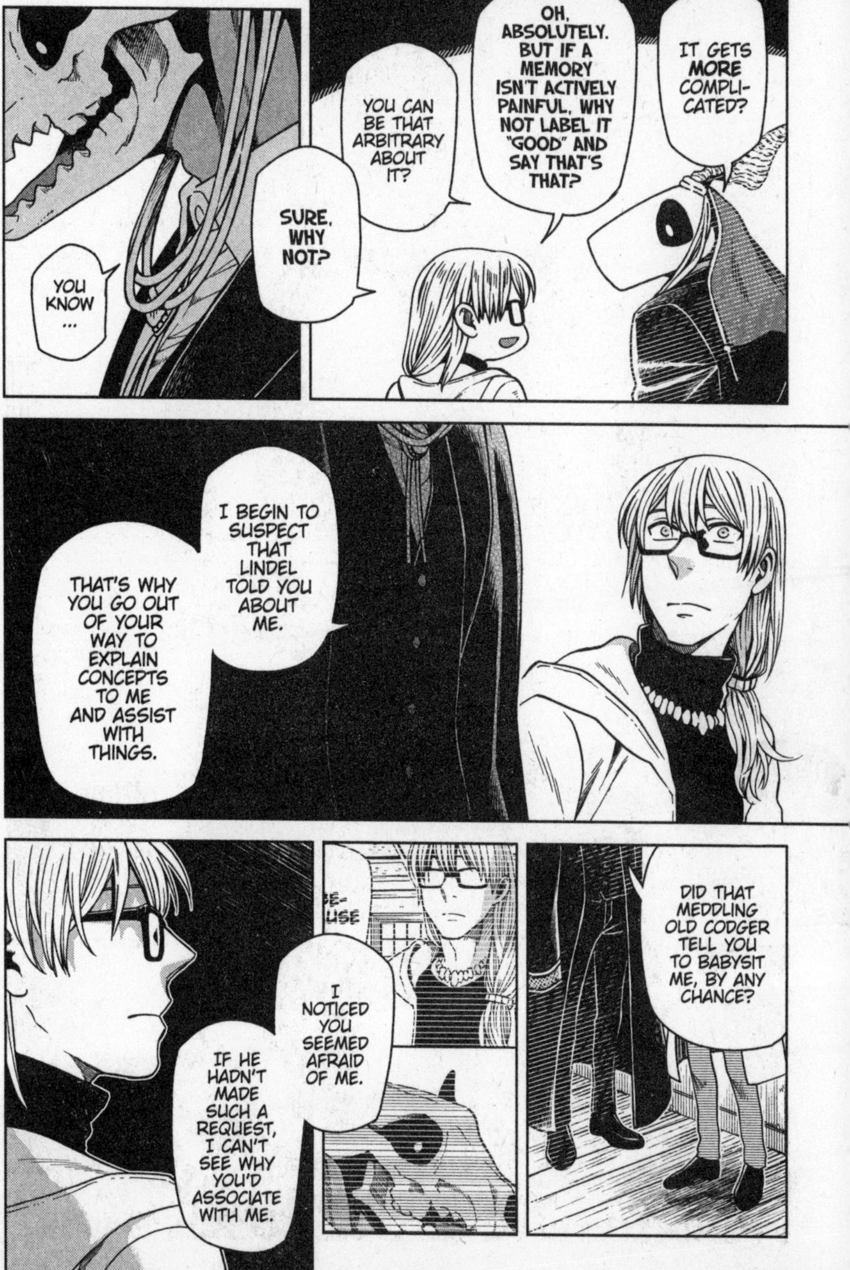
IT GETS MORE COMPLICATED?
OH, ABSOLUTELY. BUT IF A MEMORY ISN'T ACTIVELY PAINFUL, WHY NOT LABEL IT "GOOD" AND SAY THAT'S THAT?
YOU CAN BE THAT ARBITRARY ABOUT IT?
SURE. WHY NOT?
YOU KNOW ...
I BEGIN TO SUSPECT THAT LINDEL TOLD YOU ABOUT ME.
THAT'S WHY YOU GO OUT OF YOUR WAY TO EXPLAIN CONCEPTS TO ME AND ASSIST WITH THINGS.
DID THAT MEDDLING OLD CODGER TELL YOU TO BABYSIT ME, BY ANY CHANCE?
I NOTICED YOU SEEMED AFRAID OF ME.
IF HE HADN'T MADE SUCH A REQUEST, I CAN'T SEE WHY YOU'D ASSOCIATE WITH ME.

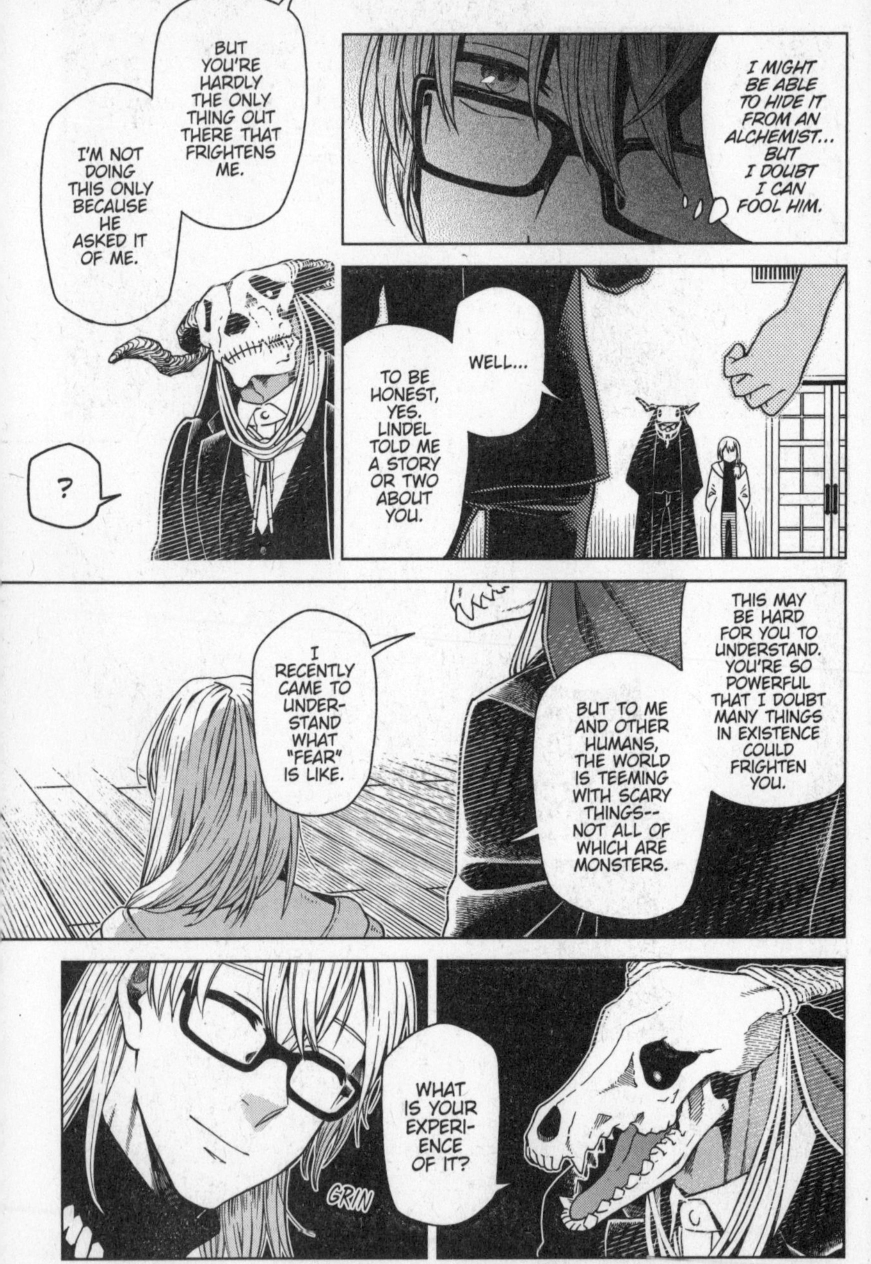
I MIGHT BE ABLE TO HIDE IT FROM AN ALCHEMIST... BUT I DOUBT I CAN FOOL HIM.
BUT YOU'RE HARDLY THE ONLY THING OUT THERE THAT FRIGHTENS ME.
I'M NOT DOING THIS ONLY BECAUSE HE ASKED IT OF ME.
WELL...
TO BE HONEST, YES. LINDEL TOLD ME A STORY OR TWO ABOUT YOU.
?
THIS MAY BE HARD FOR YOU TO UNDERSTAND. YOU'RE SO POWERFUL THAT I DOUBT MANY THINGS IN EXISTENCE COULD FRIGHTEN YOU.
BUT TO ME AND OTHER HUMANS, THE WORLD IS TEEMING WITH SCARY THINGS-- NOT ALL OF WHICH ARE MONSTERS.
I RECENTLY CAME TO UNDER-STAND WHAT "FEAR" IS LIKE.
WHAT IS YOUR EXPERI-ENCE OF IT?
GRIN

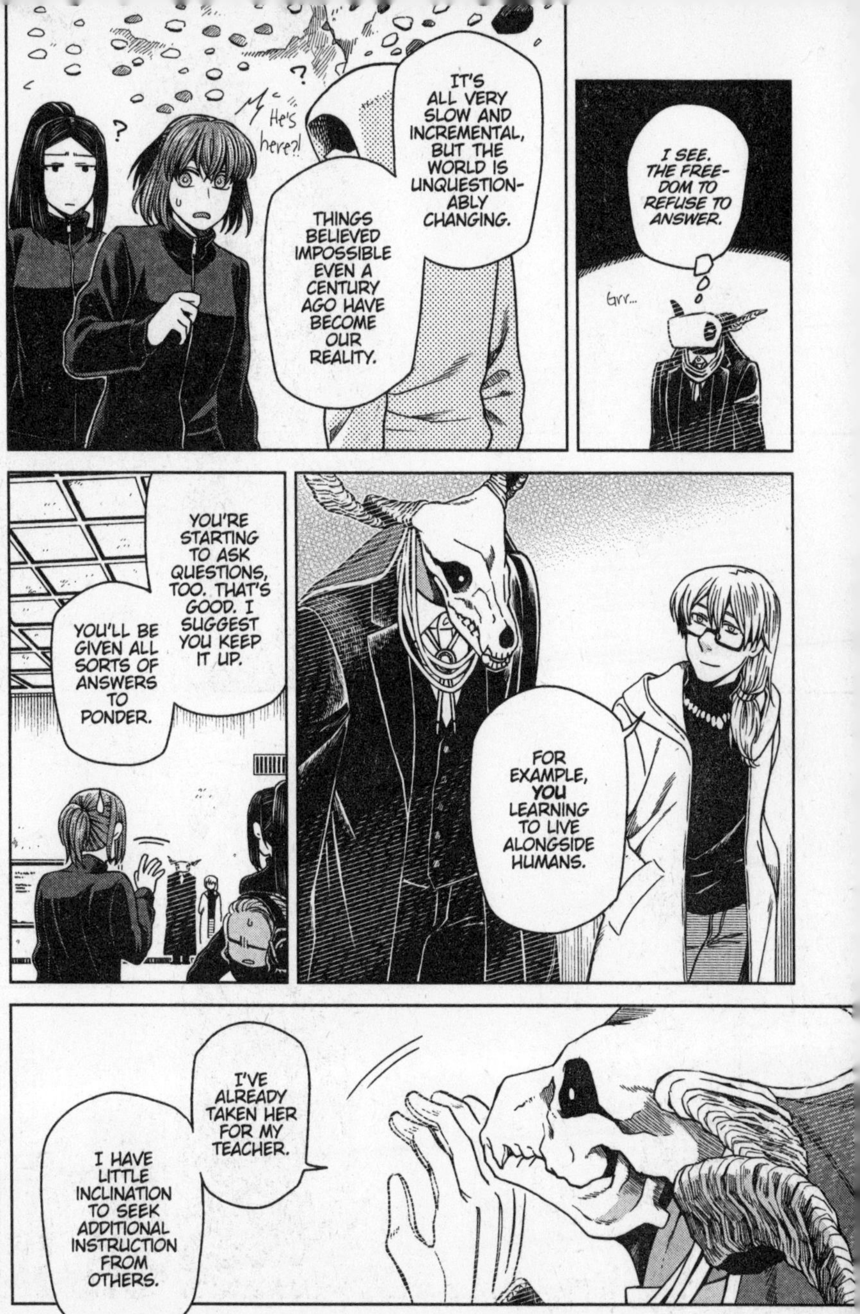
I SEE. THE FREE-DOM TO REFUSE TO ANSWER.
Grr...
IT'S ALL VERY SLOW AND INCREMENTAL, BUT THE WORLD IS UNQUESTION-ABLY CHANGING.
THINGS BELIEVED IMPOSSIBLE EVEN A CENTURY AGO HAVE BECOME OUR REALITY.
He's here?!
?
FOR EXAMPLE, YOU LEARNING TO LIVE ALONGSIDE HUMANS.
YOU'RE STARTING TO ASK QUESTIONS, TOO. THAT'S GOOD. I SUGGEST YOU KEEP IT UP.
YOU'LL BE GIVEN ALL SORTS OF ANSWERS TO PONDER.
I'VE ALREADY TAKEN HER FOR MY TEACHER.
I HAVE LITTLE INCLINATION TO SEEK ADDITIONAL INSTRUCTION FROM OTHERS.

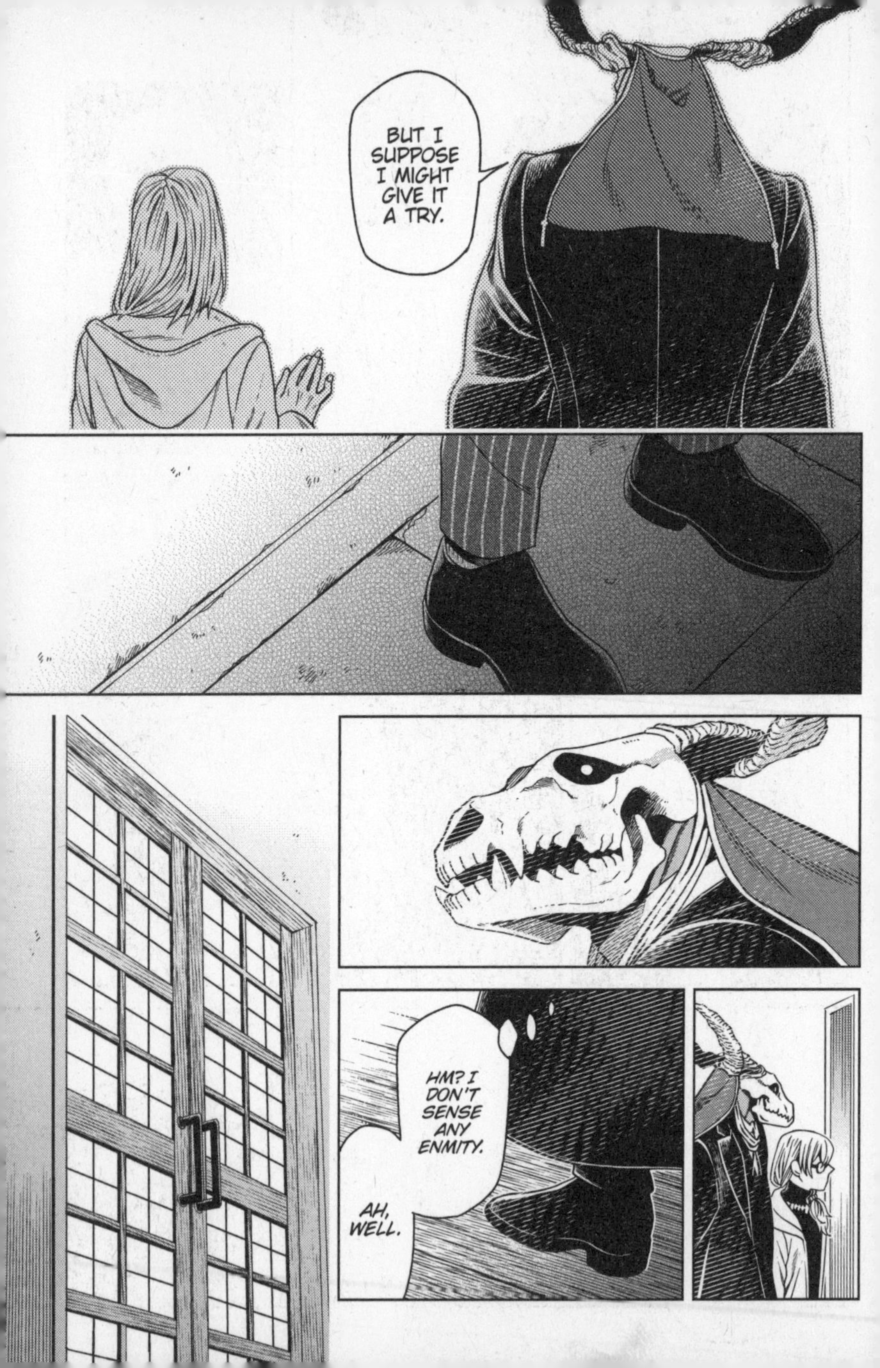
BUT I SUPPOSE I MIGHT GIVE IT A TRY.
HM? I DON'T SENSE ANY ENMITY.
AH, WELL.

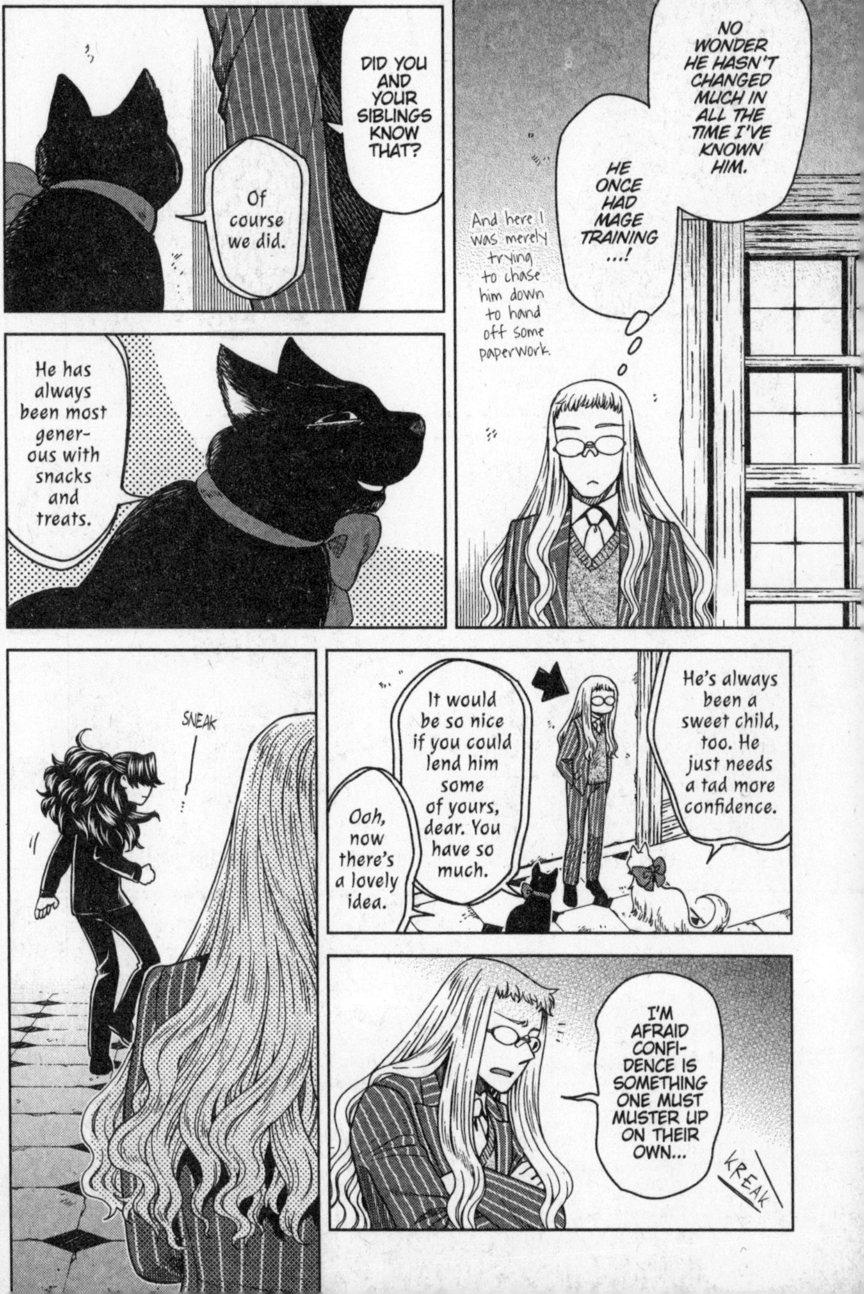
NO WONDER HE HASN'T CHANGED MUCH IN ALL THE TIME I'VE KNOWN HIM.
HE ONCE HAD MAGE TRAINING...!
And here I was merely trying to chase him down to hand off some paperwork.
DID YOU AND YOUR SIBLINGS KNOW THAT?
Of course we did.
He has always been most gener-ous with snacks and treats.
He's always been a sweet child, too. He just needs a tad more confidence.
It would be so nice if you could lend him some of yours, dear. You have so much.
Ooh, now there's a lovely idea.
I'M AFRAID CONFI-DENCE IS SOMETHING ONE MUST MUSTER UP ON THEIR OWN...
KREAK
SNEAK

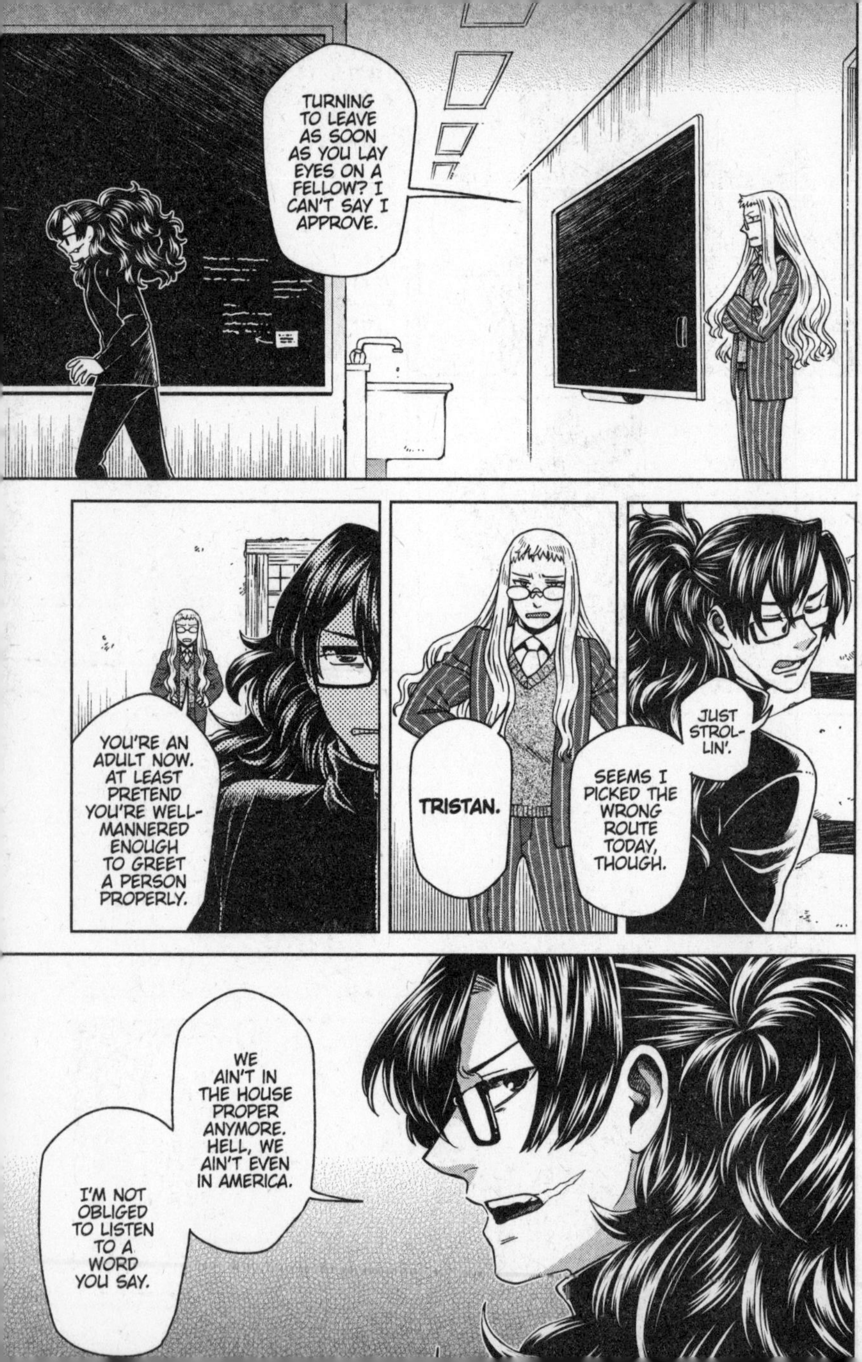
TURNING TO LEAVE AS SOON AS YOU LAY EYES ON A FELLOW? I CAN'T SAY I APPROVE.
JUST STROLLIN'.
SEEMS I PICKED THE WRONG ROUTE TODAY, THOUGH.
TRISTAN.
YOU'RE AN ADULT NOW. AT LEAST PRETEND YOU'RE WELL-MANNERED ENOUGH TO GREET A PERSON PROPERLY.
WE AIN'T IN THE HOUSE PROPER ANYMORE. HELL, WE AIN'T EVEN IN AMERICA.
I'M NOT OBLIGED TO LISTEN TO A WORD YOU SAY.

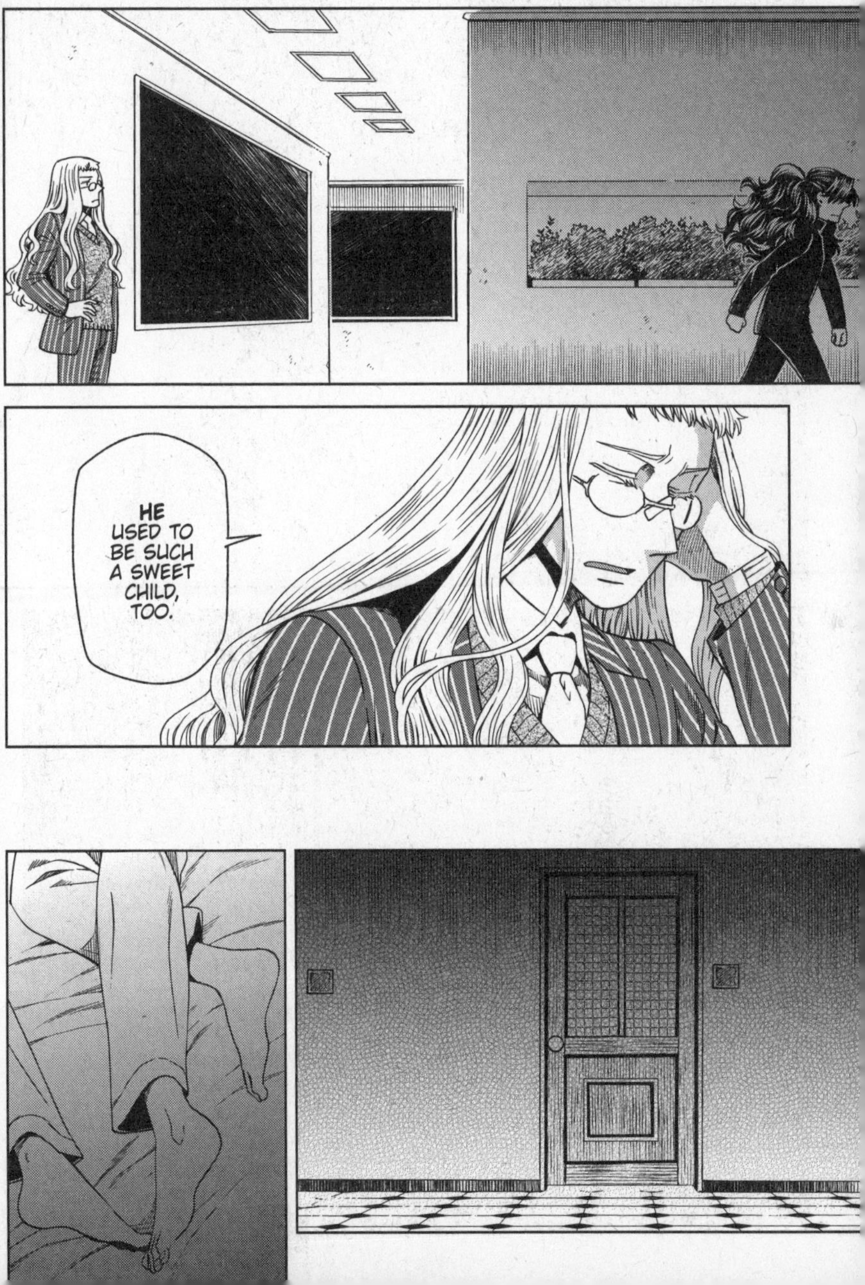
HE USED TO BE SUCH A SWEET CHILD, TOO.

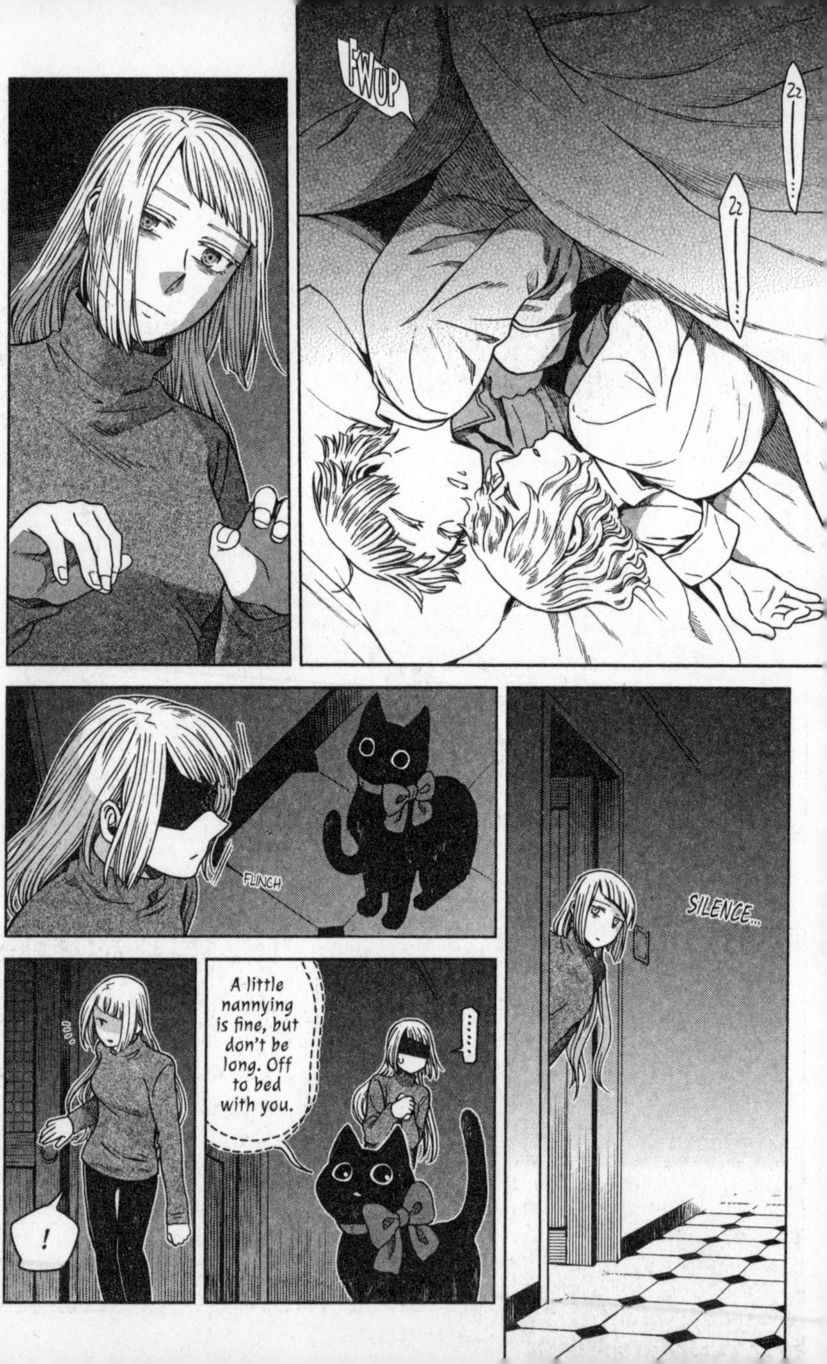
FWOP
zz......
zz......
SILENCE...
FLINCH
......
A little nannying is fine, but don't be long. Off to bed with you.
!

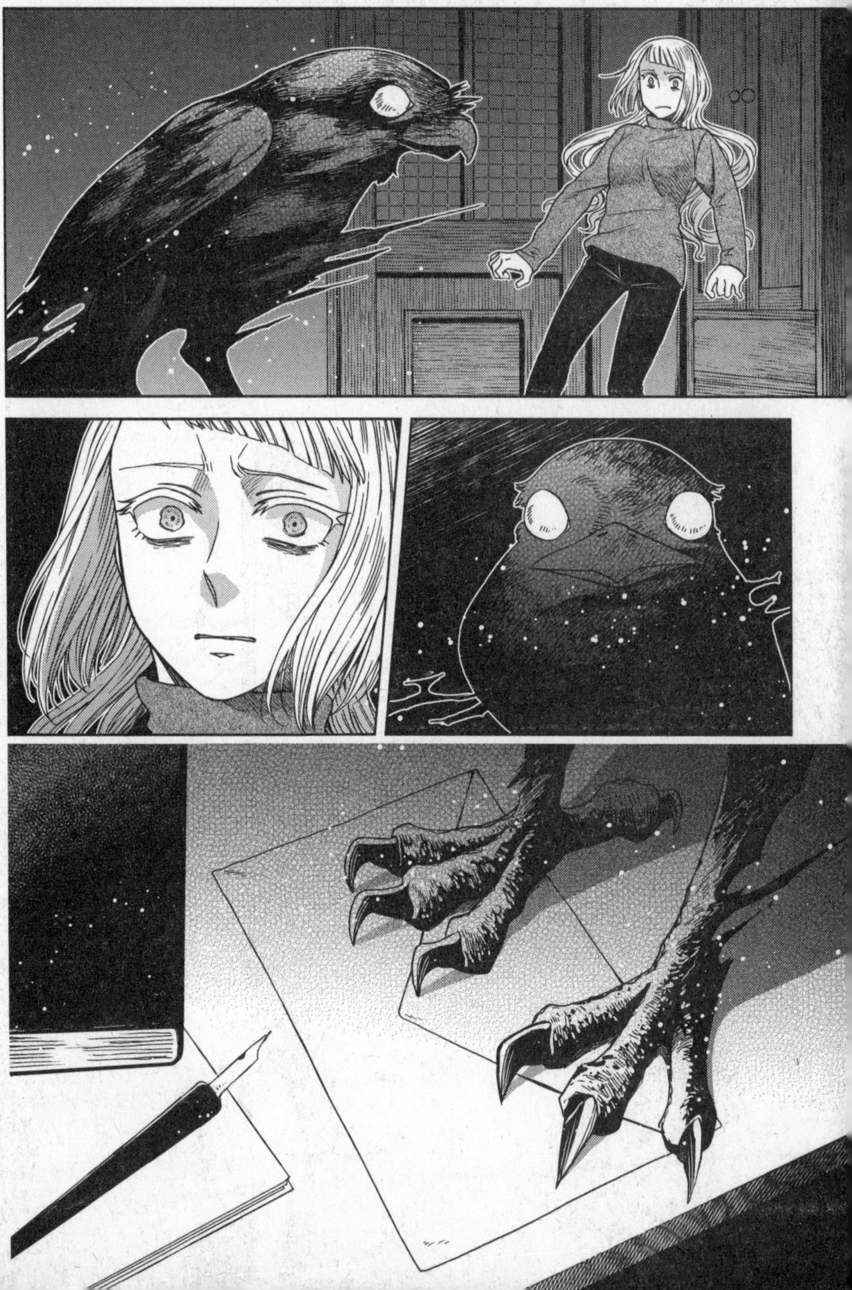

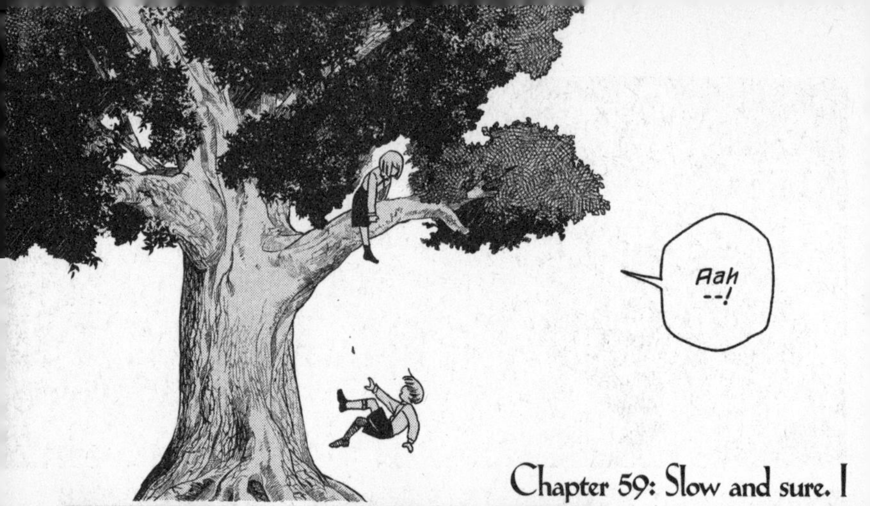
Aah --!

# Chapter 59: Slow and sure. I

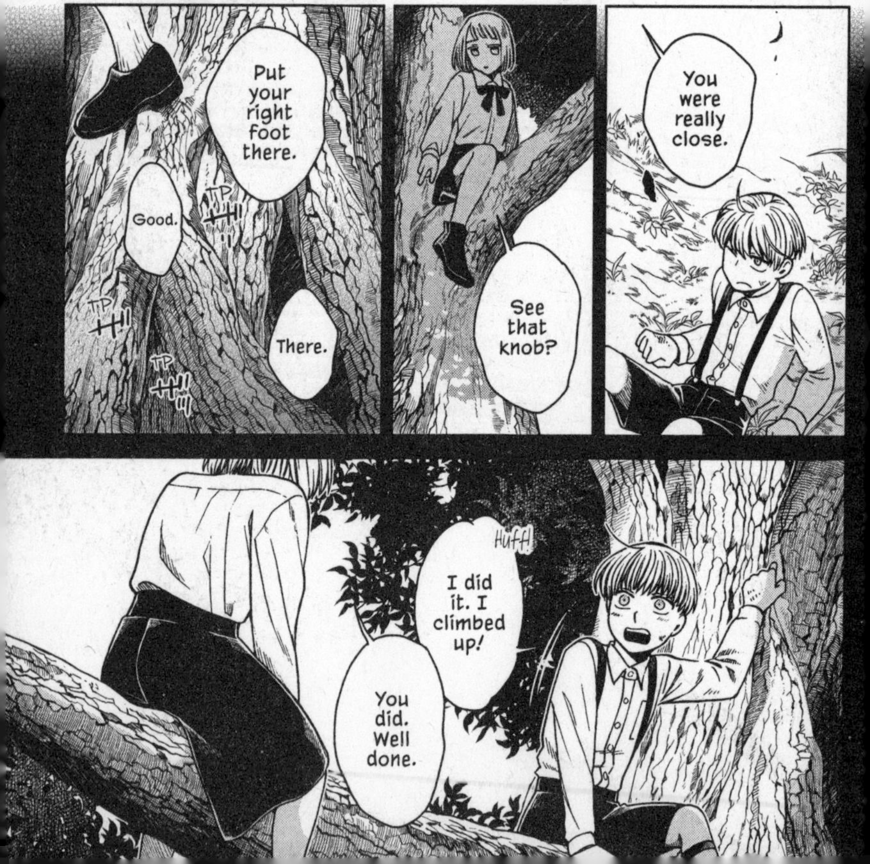
You were really close.
See that knob?
Put your right foot there.
Good.
There.
Huff!
I did it. I climbed up!
You did. Well done.

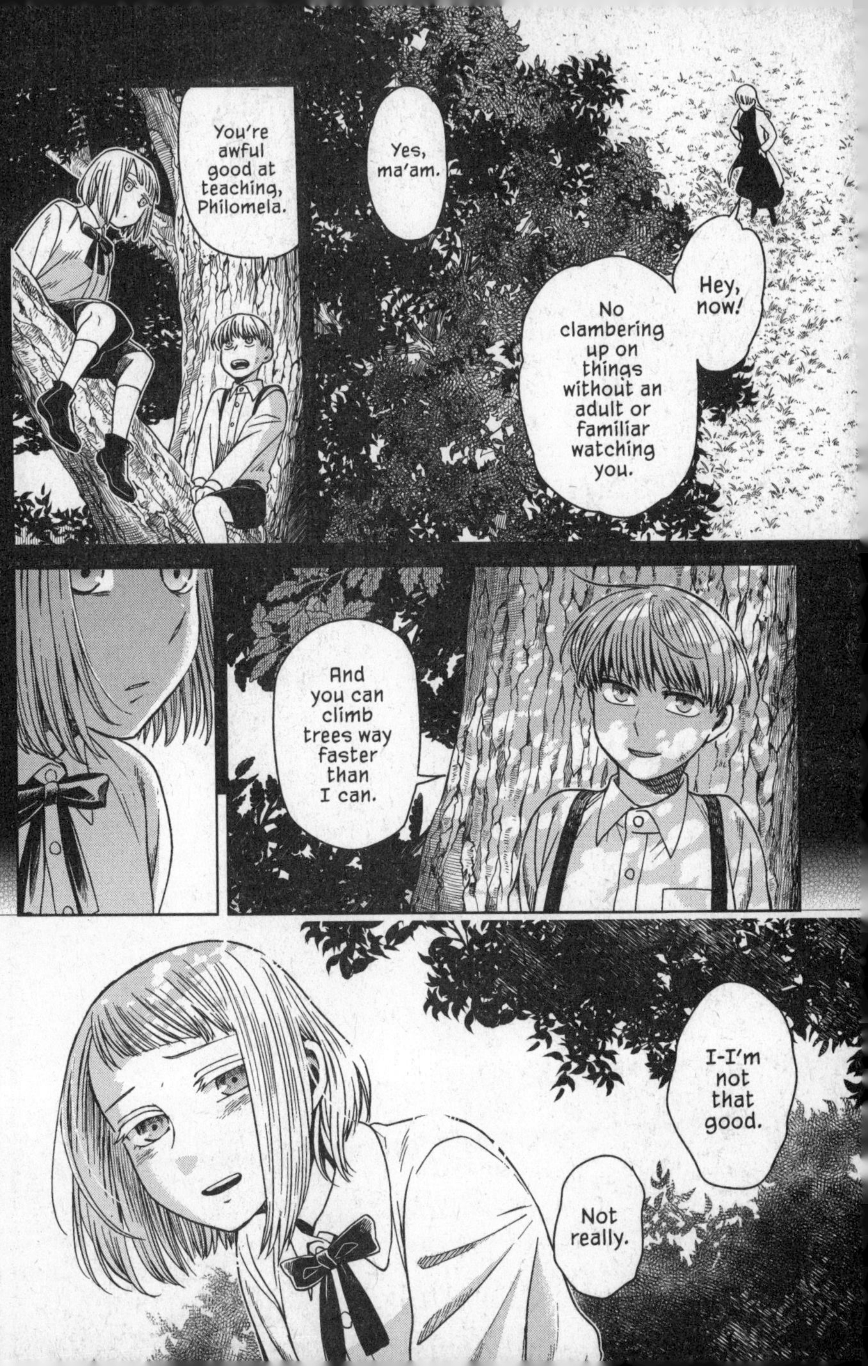
Hey, now!
No clambering up on things without an adult or familiar watching you.
Yes, ma'am.
You're awful good at teaching, Philomela.
And you can climb trees way faster than I can.
I-I'm not that good.
Not really.

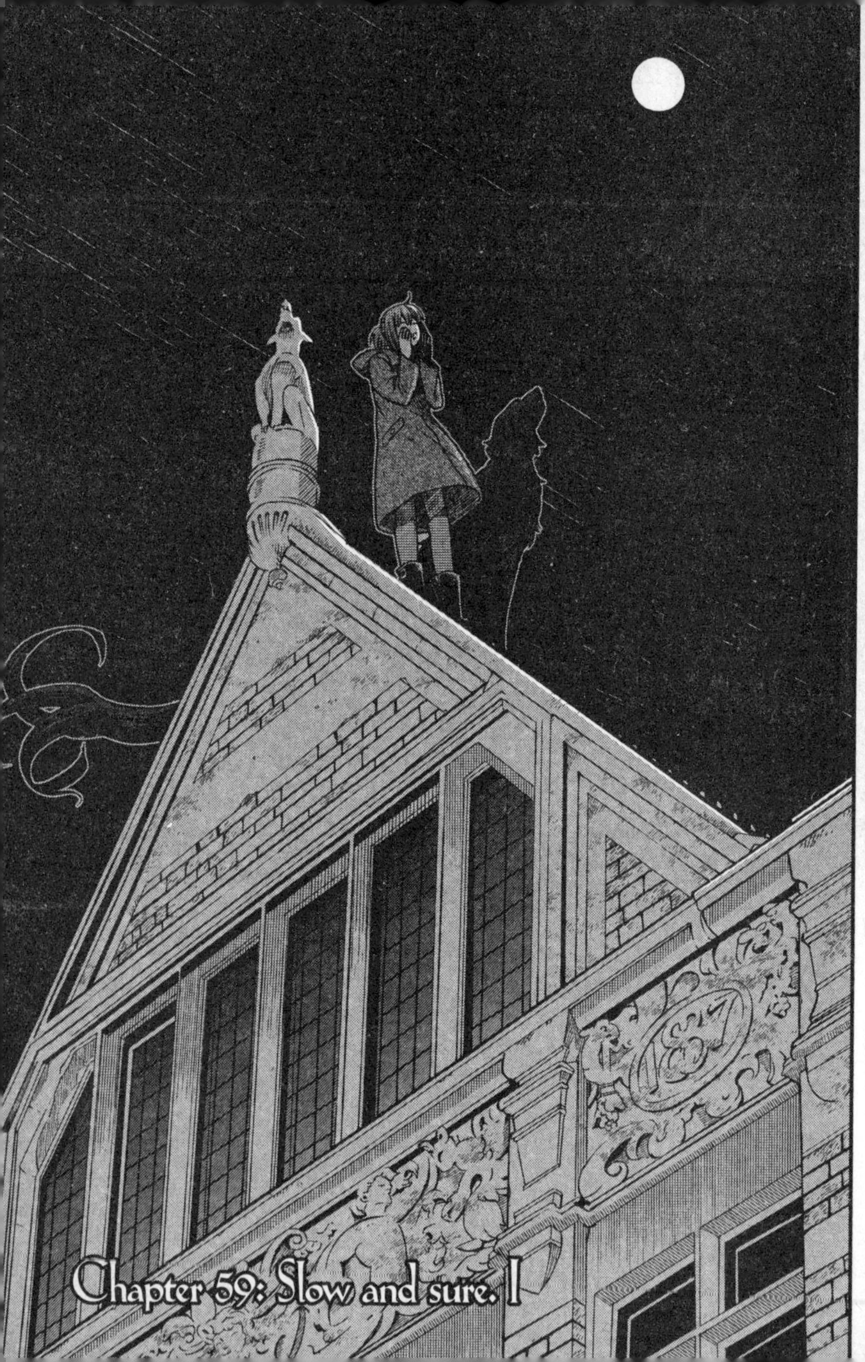
Chapter 59: Slow and sure. 1

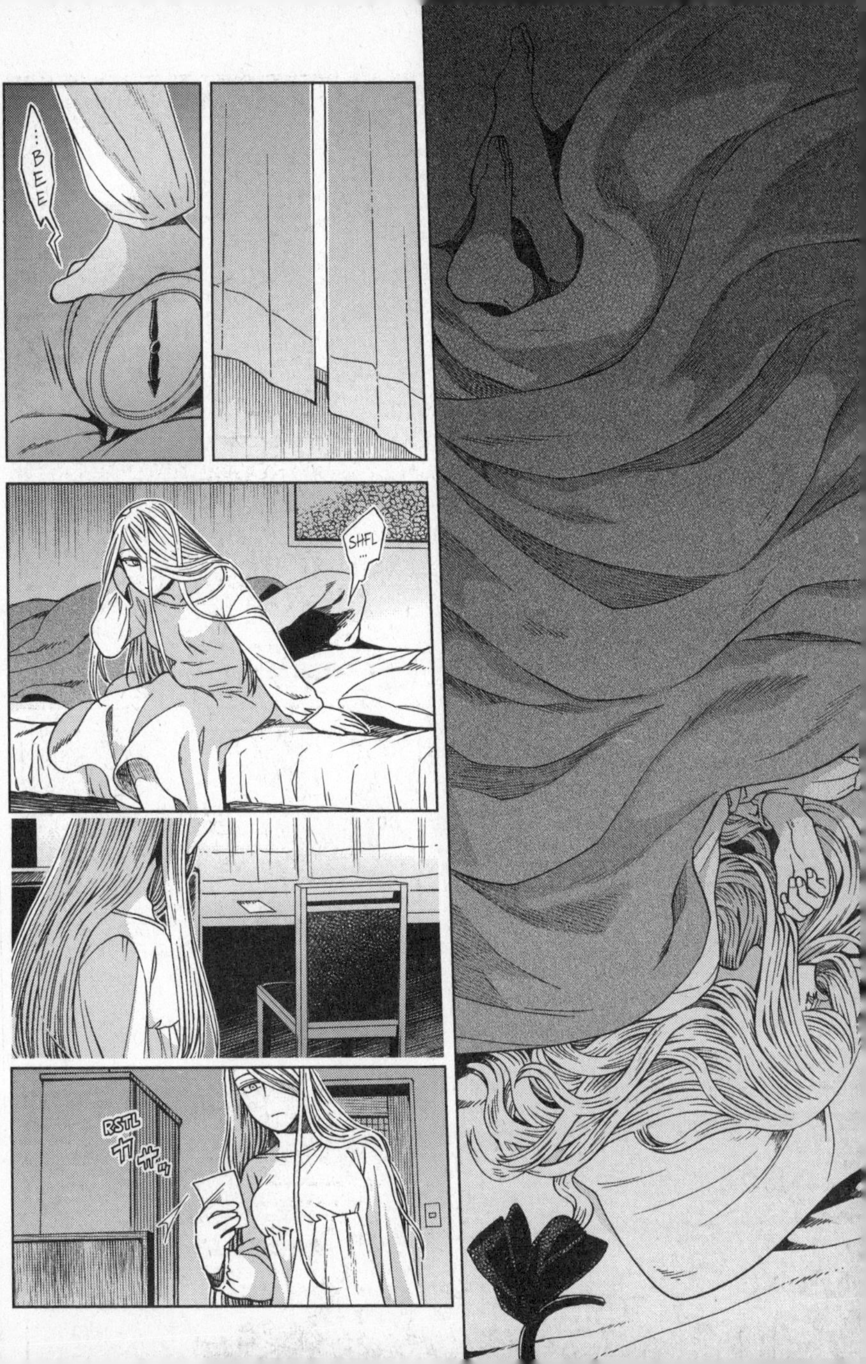
...BEE
SHFL...
RSTL
ガサッ

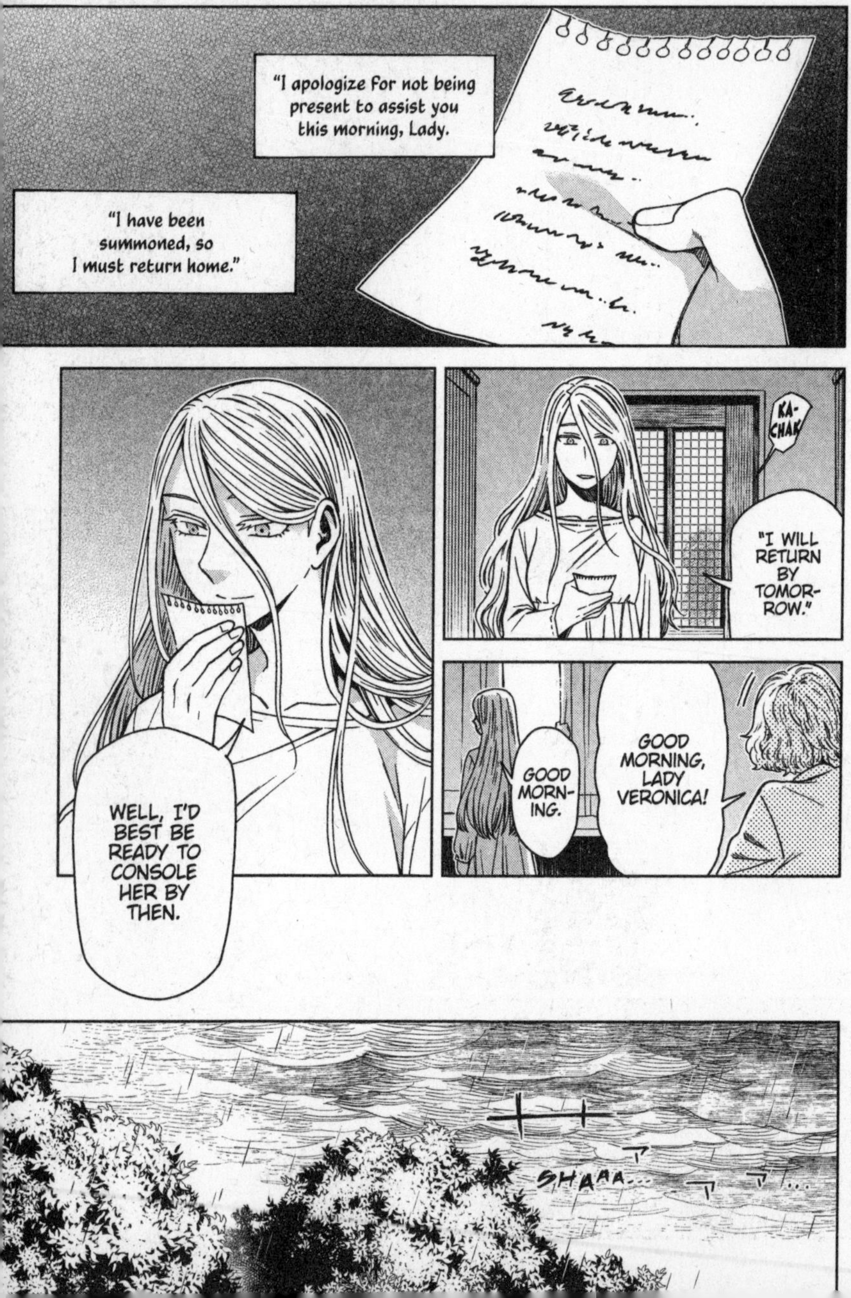
"I apologize for not being present to assist you this morning, Lady.
"I have been summoned, so I must return home."
KA-CHAK
"I WILL RETURN BY TOMORROW."
GOOD MORNING, LADY VERONICA!
GOOD MORNING.
WELL, I'D BEST BE READY TO CONSOLE HER BY THEN.
SHAAA...

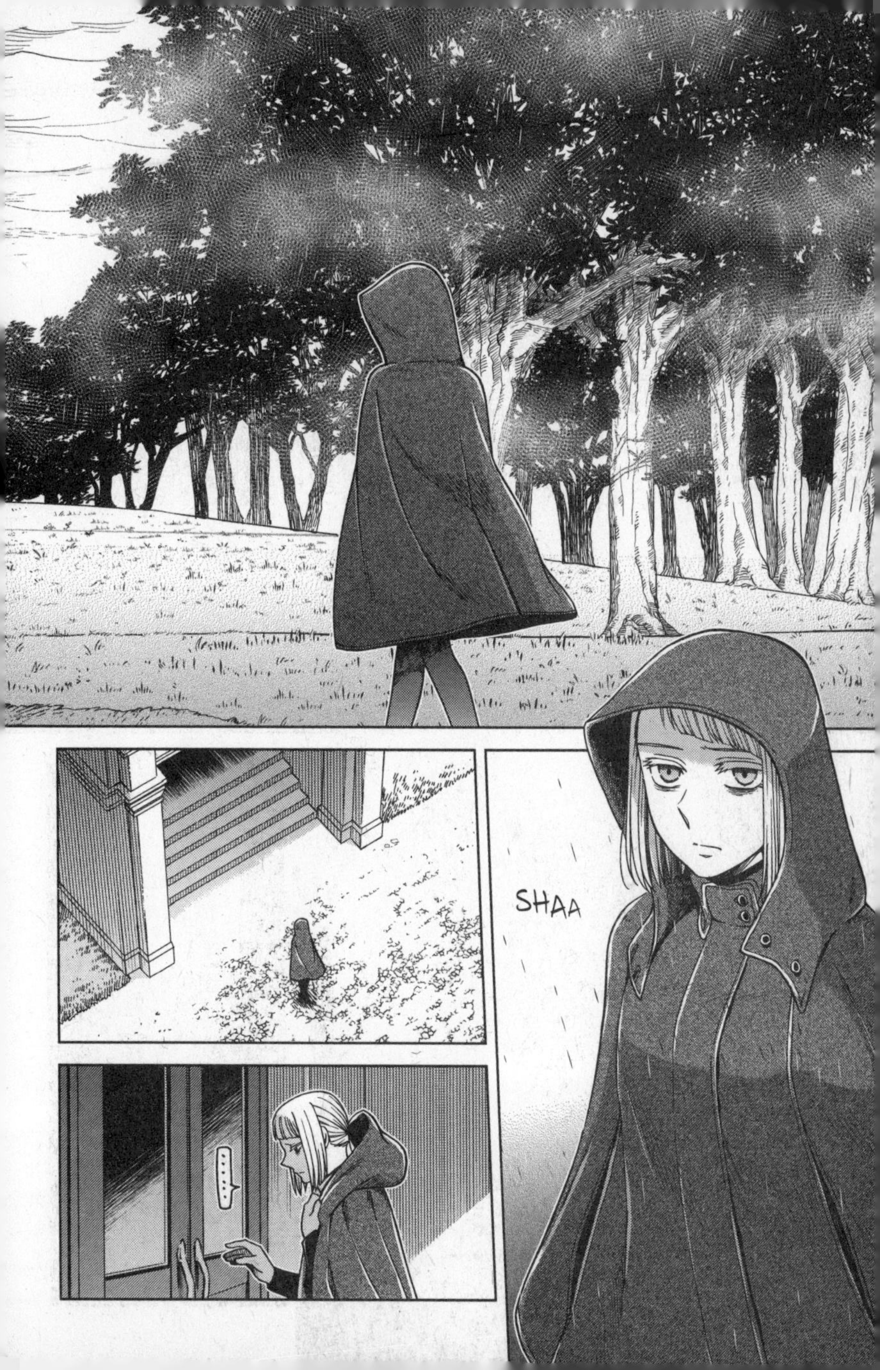
SHAA
......

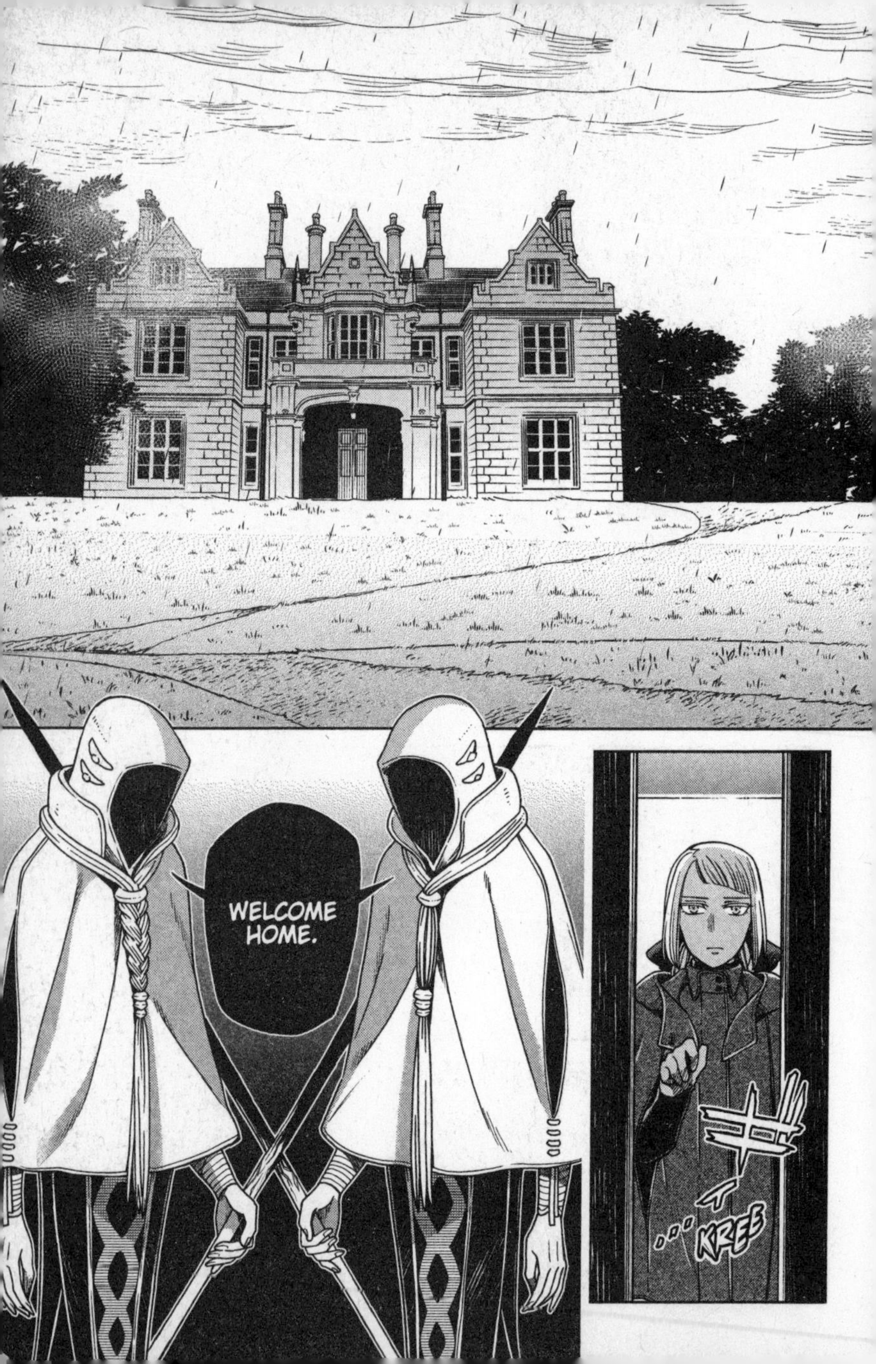
KREE
...
WELCOME HOME.

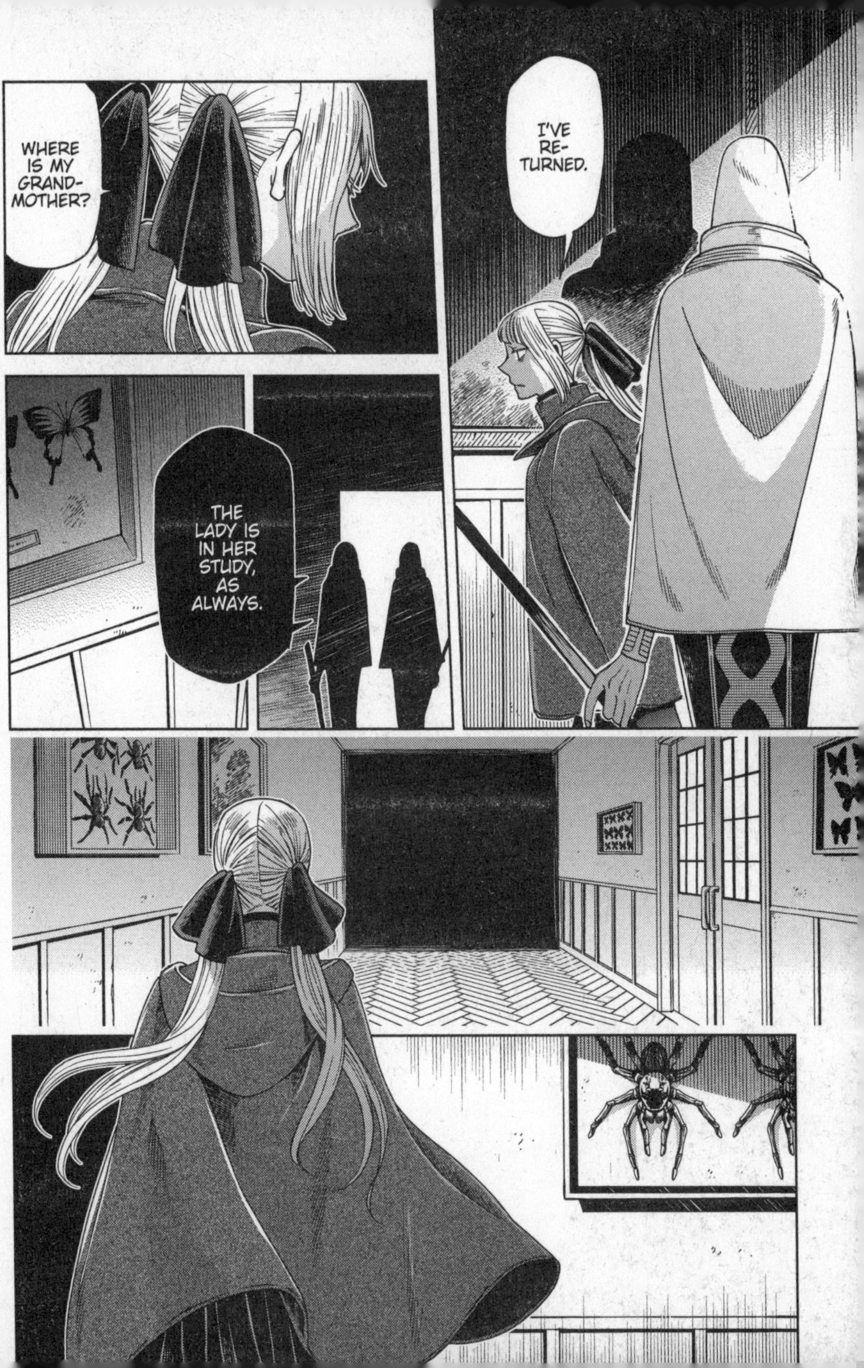
I'VE RE-TURNED.
WHERE IS MY GRAND-MOTHER?
THE LADY IS IN HER STUDY, AS ALWAYS.

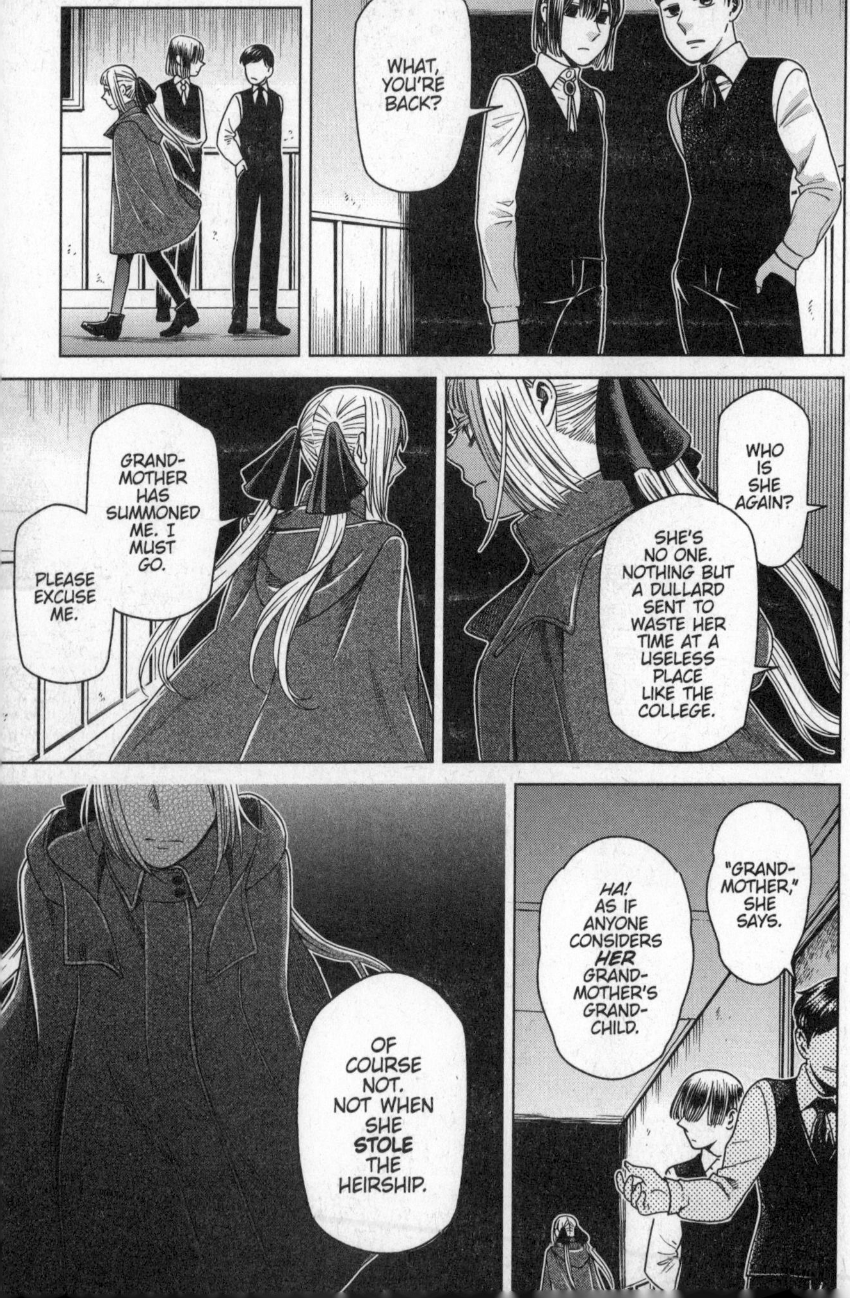
WHAT, YOU'RE BACK?
WHO IS SHE AGAIN?
SHE'S NO ONE. NOTHING BUT A DULLARD SENT TO WASTE HER TIME AT A USELESS PLACE LIKE THE COLLEGE.
GRAND-MOTHER HAS SUMMONED ME. I MUST GO.
PLEASE EXCUSE ME.
"GRAND-MOTHER," SHE SAYS.
HA! AS IF ANYONE CONSIDERS *HER* GRAND-MOTHER'S GRAND-CHILD.
OF COURSE NOT. NOT WHEN SHE **STOLE** THE HEIRSHIP.

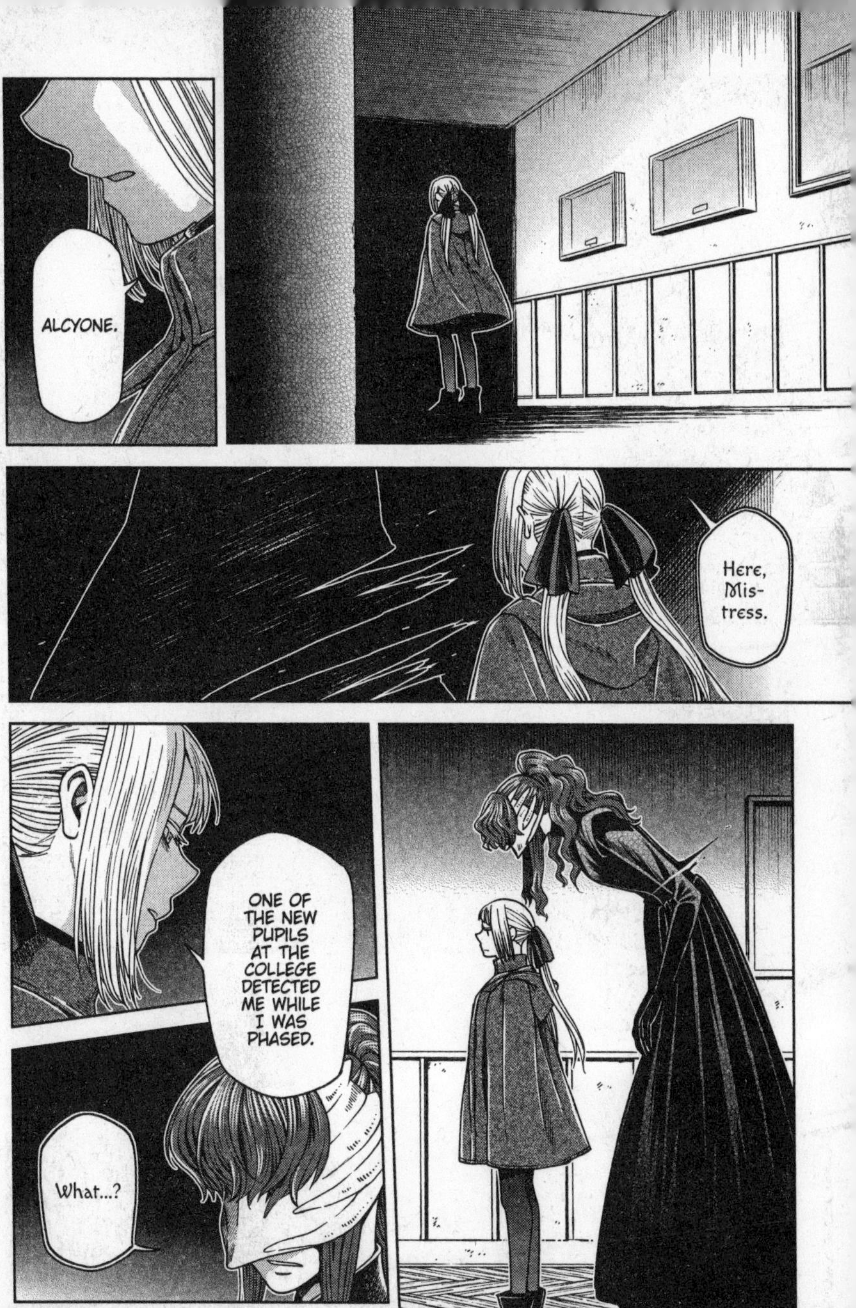
ALCYONE.
Here, Mis-tress.
ONE OF THE NEW PUPILS AT THE COLLEGE DETECTED ME WHILE I WAS PHASED.
What...?

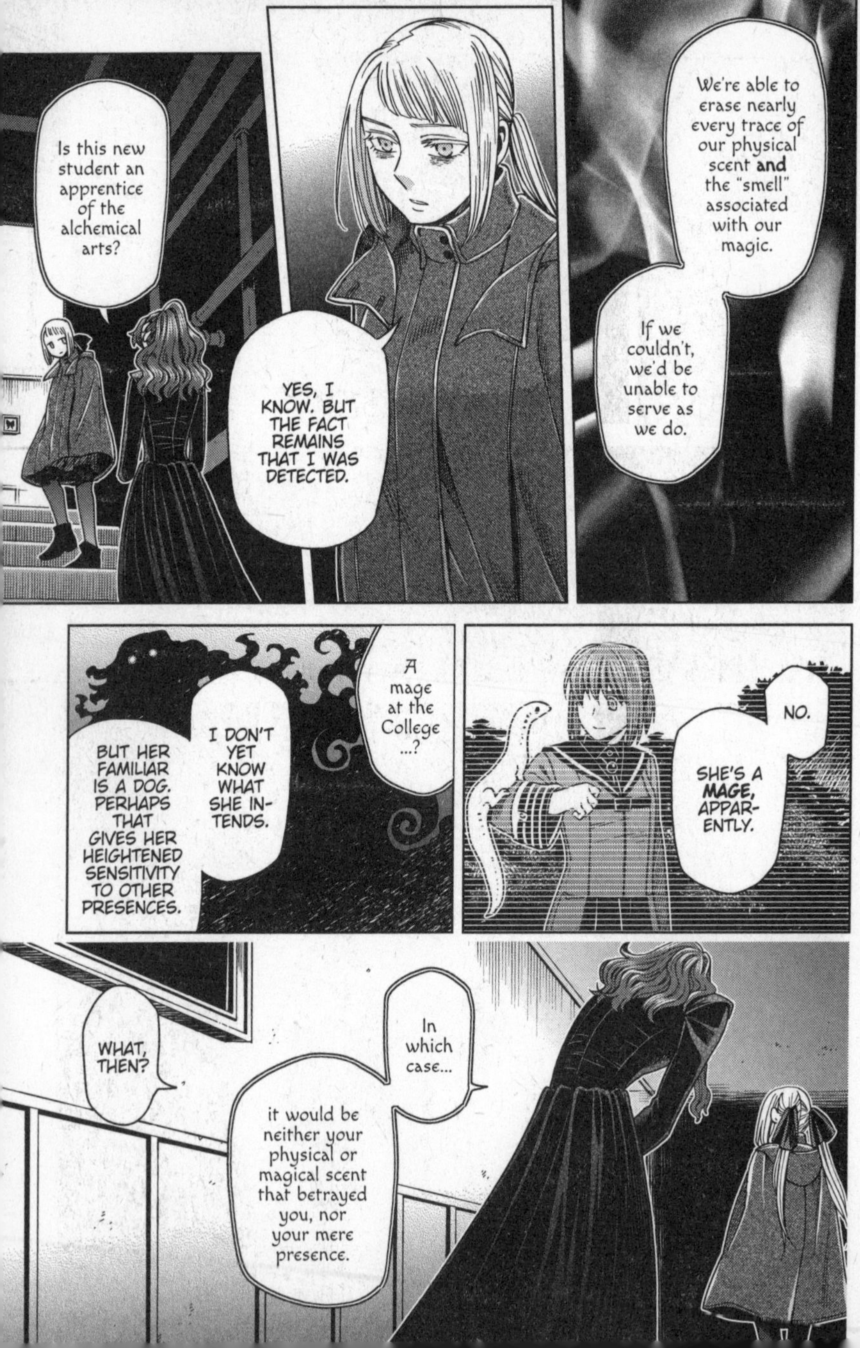

We're able to erase nearly every trace of our physical scent **and** the "smell" associated with our magic.
If we couldn't, we'd be unable to serve as we do.
YES, I KNOW. BUT THE FACT REMAINS THAT I WAS DETECTED.
Is this new student an apprentice of the alchemical arts?
NO.
SHE'S A **MAGE,** APPARENTLY.
A mage at the College ...?
I DON'T YET KNOW WHAT SHE INTENDS.
BUT HER FAMILIAR IS A DOG. PERHAPS THAT GIVES HER HEIGHTENED SENSITIVITY TO OTHER PRESENCES.
In which case...
it would be neither your physical or magical scent that betrayed you, nor your mere presence.
WHAT, THEN?

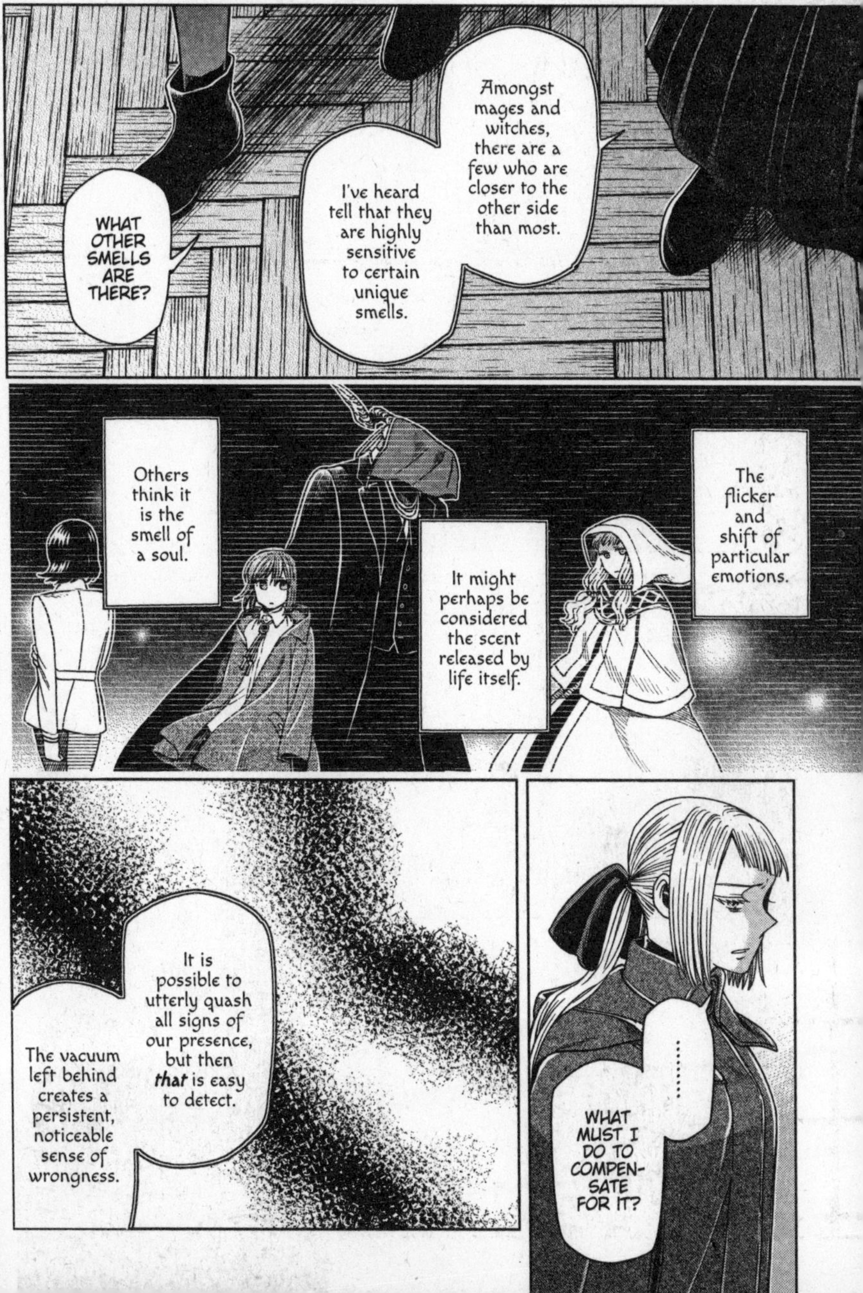

Amongst mages and witches, there are a few who are closer to the other side than most.
I've heard tell that they are highly sensitive to certain unique smells.
WHAT OTHER SMELLS ARE THERE?
The flicker and shift of particular emotions.
It might perhaps be considered the scent released by life itself.
Others think it is the smell of a soul.
......
WHAT MUST I DO TO COMPEN-SATE FOR IT?
It is possible to utterly quash all signs of our presence, but then *that* is easy to detect.
The vacuum left behind creates a persistent, noticeable sense of wrongness.

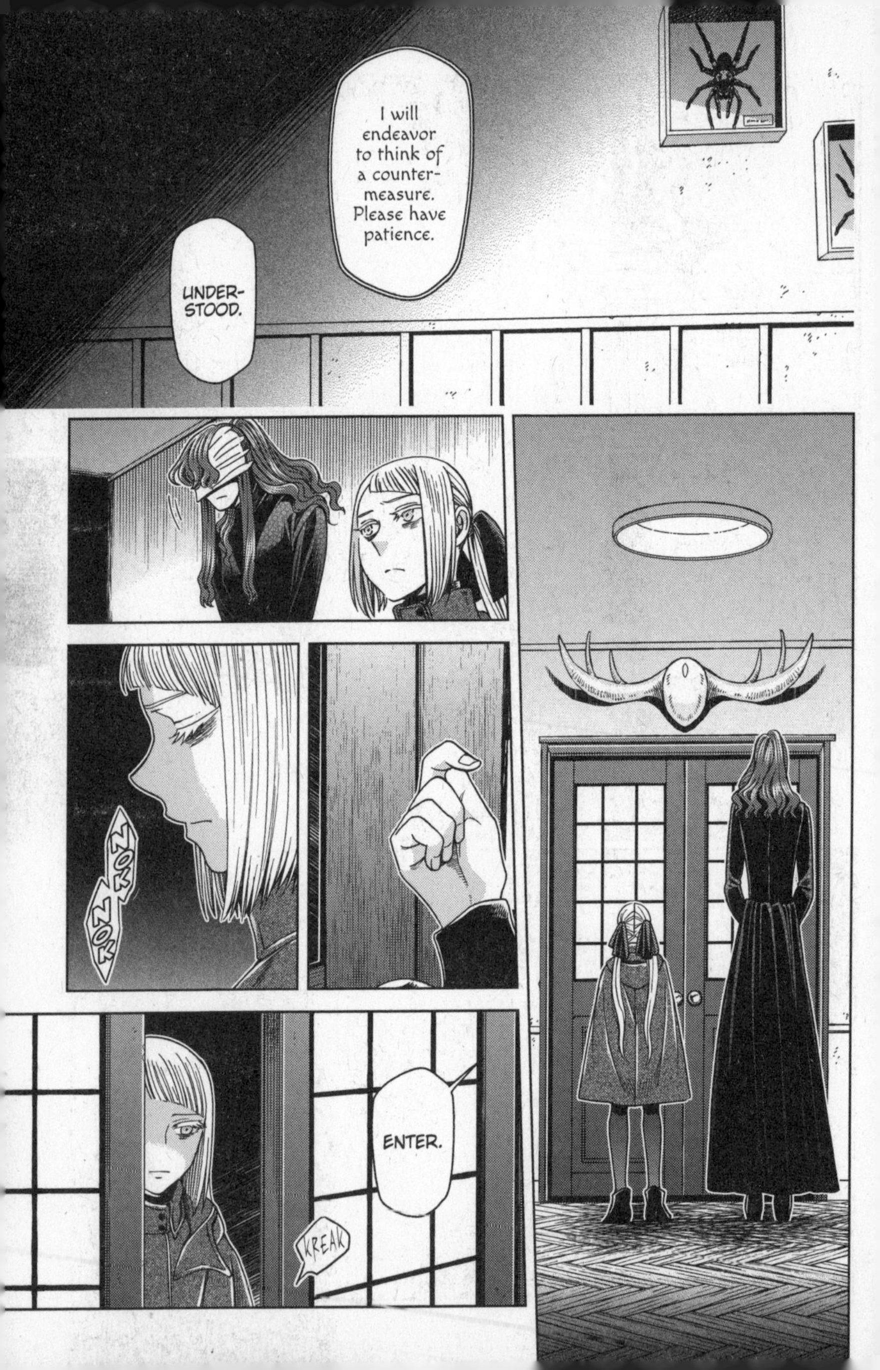
I will endeavor to think of a counter-measure. Please have patience.
UNDER-STOOD.
NOK NOK
ENTER.
KREAK

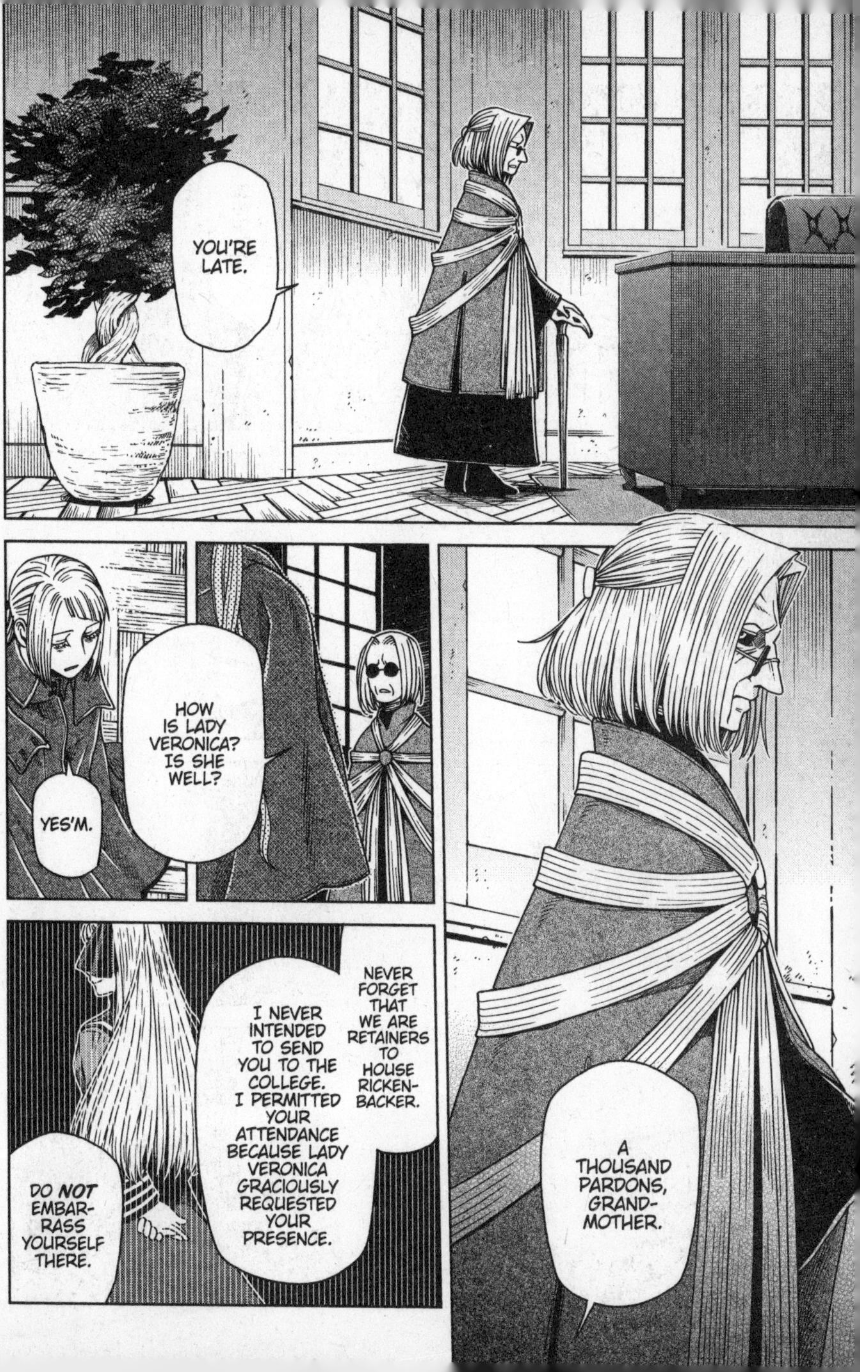
YOU'RE LATE.
A THOUSAND PARDONS, GRAND-MOTHER.
HOW IS LADY VERONICA? IS SHE WELL?
YES'M.
NEVER FORGET THAT WE ARE RETAINERS TO HOUSE RICKEN-BACKER.
I NEVER INTENDED TO SEND YOU TO THE COLLEGE. I PERMITTED YOUR ATTENDANCE BECAUSE LADY VERONICA GRACIOUSLY REQUESTED YOUR PRESENCE.
DO *NOT* EMBAR-RASS YOURSELF THERE.

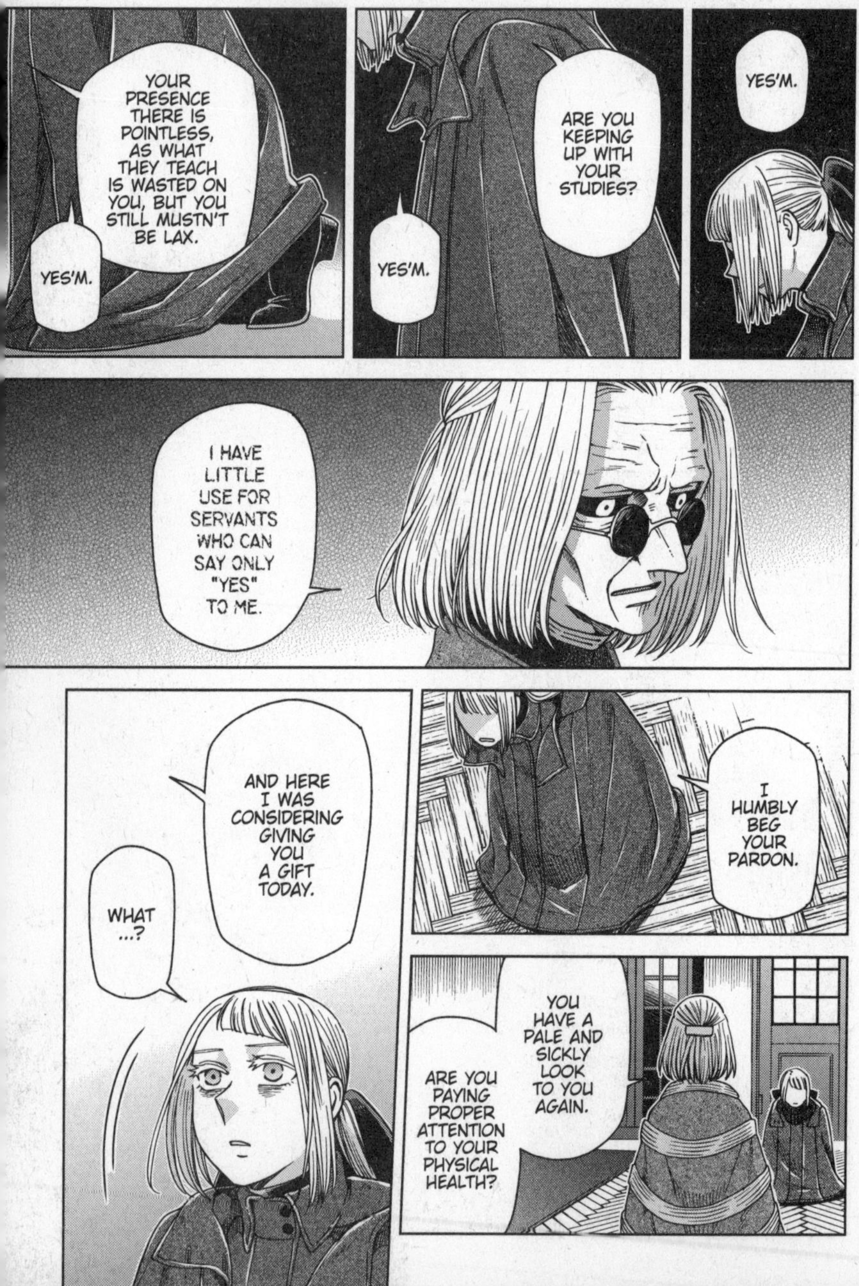
YES'M.
ARE YOU KEEPING UP WITH YOUR STUDIES?
YES'M.
YOUR PRESENCE THERE IS POINTLESS, AS WHAT THEY TEACH IS WASTED ON YOU, BUT YOU STILL MUSTN'T BE LAX.
YES'M.
I HAVE LITTLE USE FOR SERVANTS WHO CAN SAY ONLY "YES" TO ME.
I HUMBLY BEG YOUR PARDON.
YOU HAVE A PALE AND SICKLY LOOK TO YOU AGAIN.
ARE YOU PAYING PROPER ATTENTION TO YOUR PHYSICAL HEALTH?
AND HERE I WAS CONSIDERING GIVING YOU A GIFT TODAY.
WHAT ...?

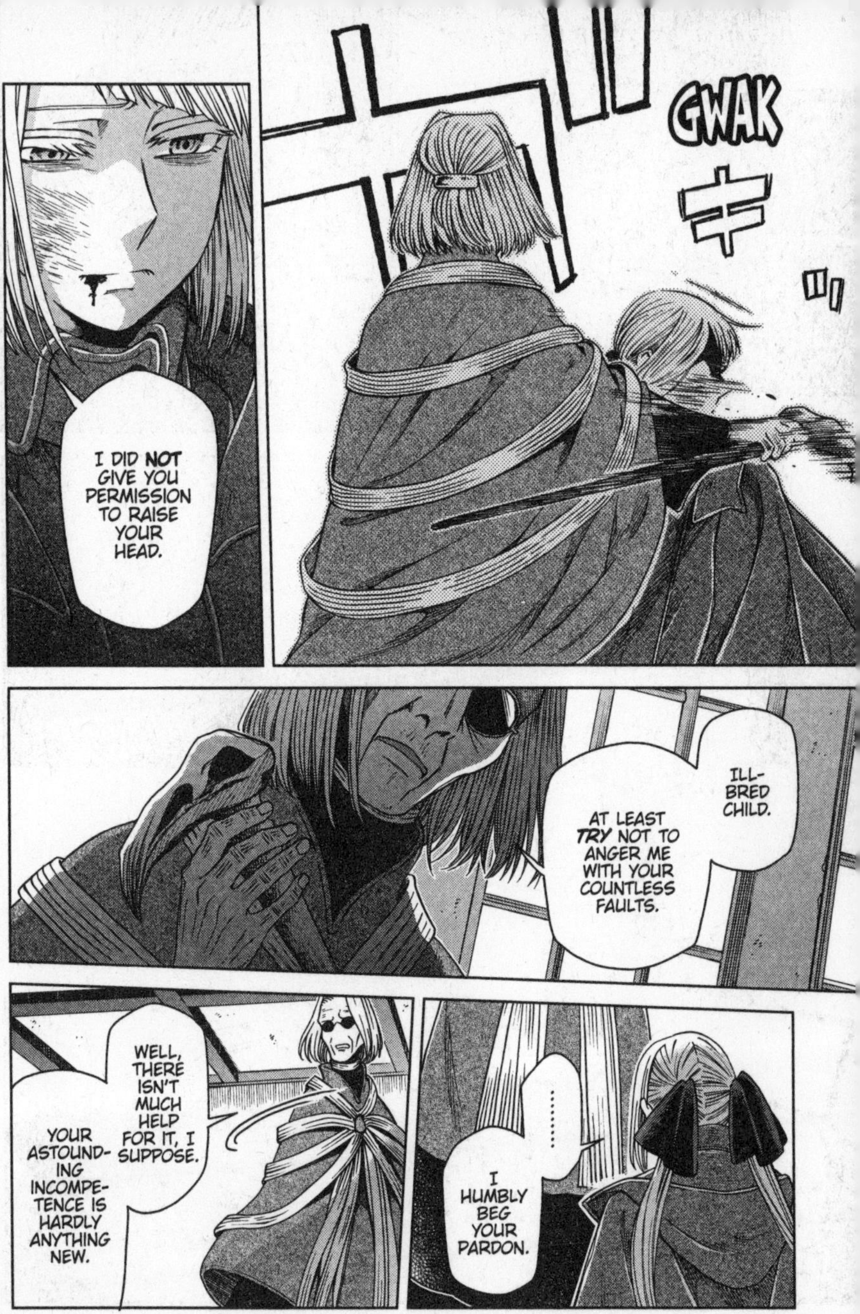
GWAK
I DID **NOT** GIVE YOU PERMISSION TO RAISE YOUR HEAD.
ILL-BRED CHILD.
AT LEAST ***TRY*** NOT TO ANGER ME WITH YOUR COUNTLESS FAULTS.
......
I HUMBLY BEG YOUR PARDON.
WELL, THERE ISN'T MUCH HELP FOR IT, I SUPPOSE.
YOUR ASTOUND-ING INCOMPE-TENCE IS HARDLY ANYTHING NEW.

BE SEATED OVER THERE.

I SUMMONED YOU TODAY FOR A REASON.

I TRUST YOU HAVEN'T FORGOTTEN?

CHOK

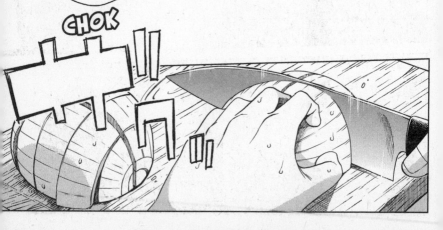

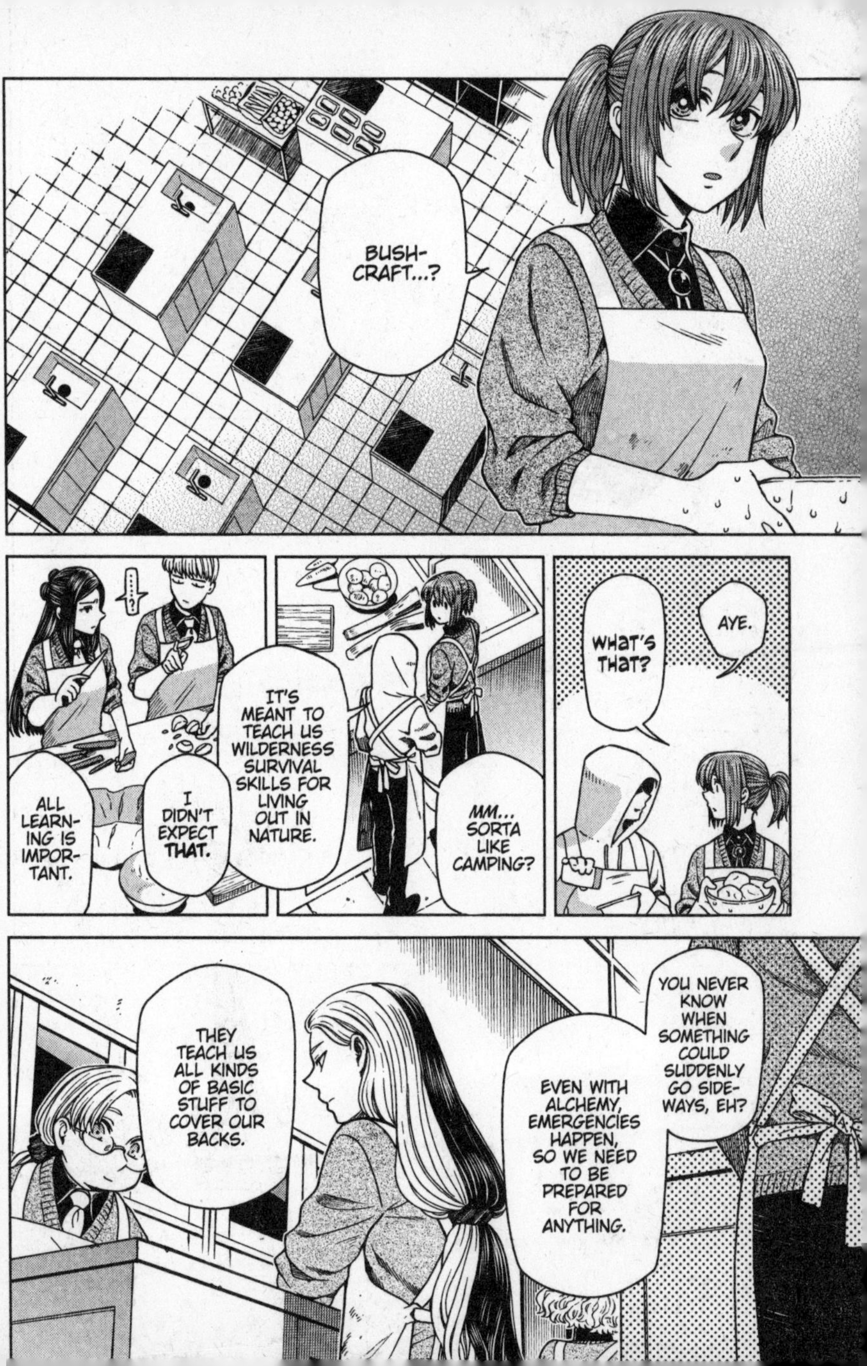
BUSH-CRAFT...?
AYE.
WHAT'S THAT?
IT'S MEANT TO TEACH US WILDERNESS SURVIVAL SKILLS FOR LIVING OUT IN NATURE.
MM... SORTA LIKE CAMPING?
...?
I DIDN'T EXPECT **THAT.**
ALL LEARNING IS IMPORTANT.
YOU NEVER KNOW WHEN SOMETHING COULD SUDDENLY GO SIDEWAYS, EH?
EVEN WITH ALCHEMY, EMERGENCIES HAPPEN, SO WE NEED TO BE PREPARED FOR ANYTHING.
THEY TEACH US ALL KINDS OF BASIC STUFF TO COVER OUR BACKS.

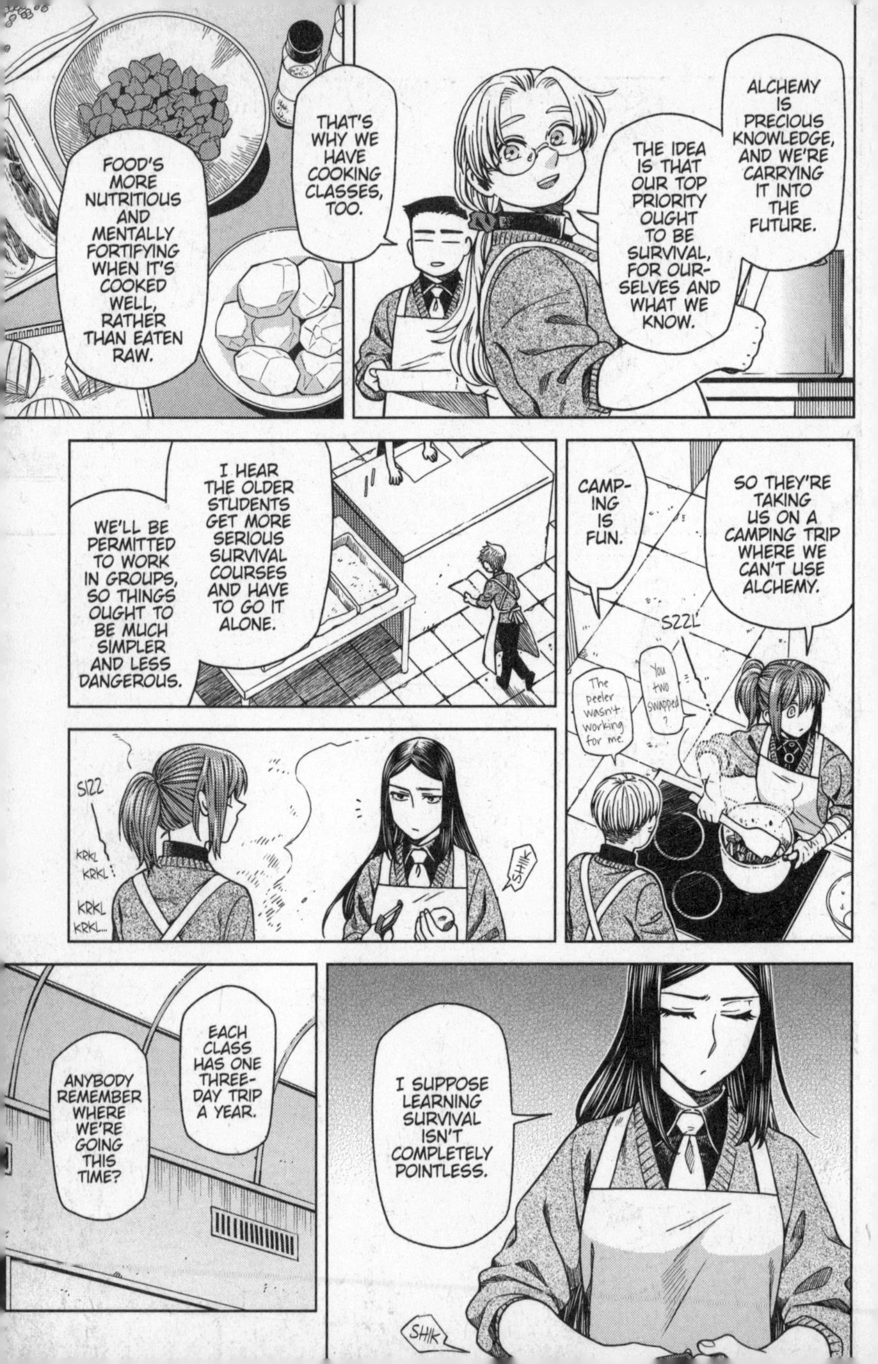
ALCHEMY IS PRECIOUS KNOWLEDGE, AND WE'RE CARRYING IT INTO THE FUTURE.
THE IDEA IS THAT OUR TOP PRIORITY OUGHT TO BE SURVIVAL, FOR OURSELVES AND WHAT WE KNOW.
THAT'S WHY WE HAVE COOKING CLASSES, TOO.
FOOD'S MORE NUTRITIOUS AND MENTALLY FORTIFYING WHEN IT'S COOKED WELL, RATHER THAN EATEN RAW.
SO THEY'RE TAKING US ON A CAMPING TRIP WHERE WE CAN'T USE ALCHEMY.
CAMPING IS FUN.
SZZL
You two swapped?
The peeler wasn't working for me.
I HEAR THE OLDER STUDENTS GET MORE SERIOUS SURVIVAL COURSES AND HAVE TO GO IT ALONE.
WE'LL BE PERMITTED TO WORK IN GROUPS, SO THINGS OUGHT TO BE MUCH SIMPLER AND LESS DANGEROUS.
SHIK
SIZZ
KRKL KRKL KRKL KRKL...
I SUPPOSE LEARNING SURVIVAL ISN'T COMPLETELY POINTLESS.
SHIK
EACH CLASS HAS ONE THREE-DAY TRIP A YEAR.
ANYBODY REMEMBER WHERE WE'RE GOING THIS TIME?

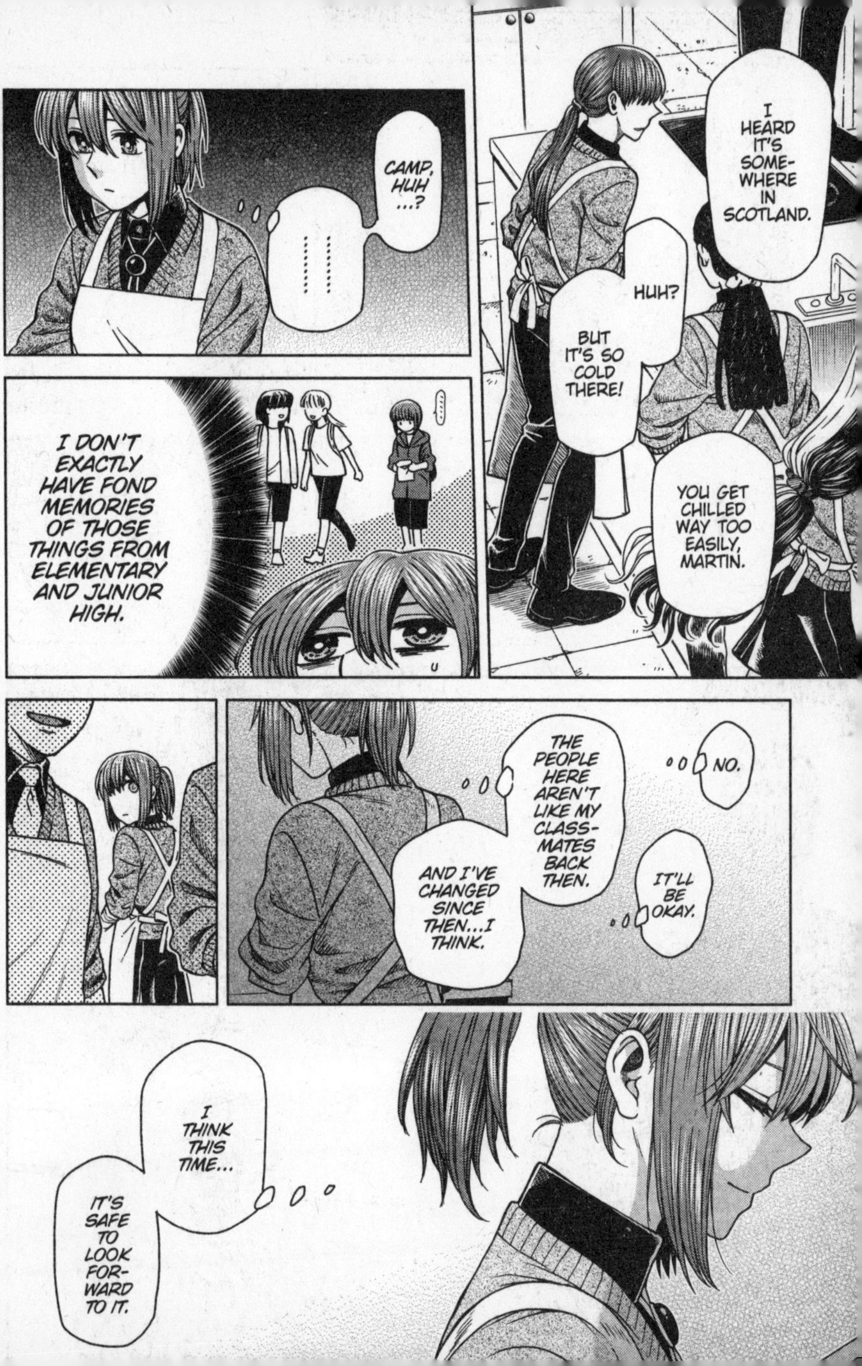
I HEARD IT'S SOME-WHERE IN SCOTLAND.
HUH?
BUT IT'S SO COLD THERE!
YOU GET CHILLED WAY TOO EASILY, MARTIN.
CAMP, HUH ...?
......
I DON'T EXACTLY HAVE FOND MEMORIES OF THOSE THINGS FROM ELEMENTARY AND JUNIOR HIGH.
NO.
THE PEOPLE HERE AREN'T LIKE MY CLASS-MATES BACK THEN.
AND I'VE CHANGED SINCE THEN...I THINK.
IT'LL BE OKAY.
I THINK THIS TIME...
IT'S SAFE TO LOOK FOR-WARD TO IT.

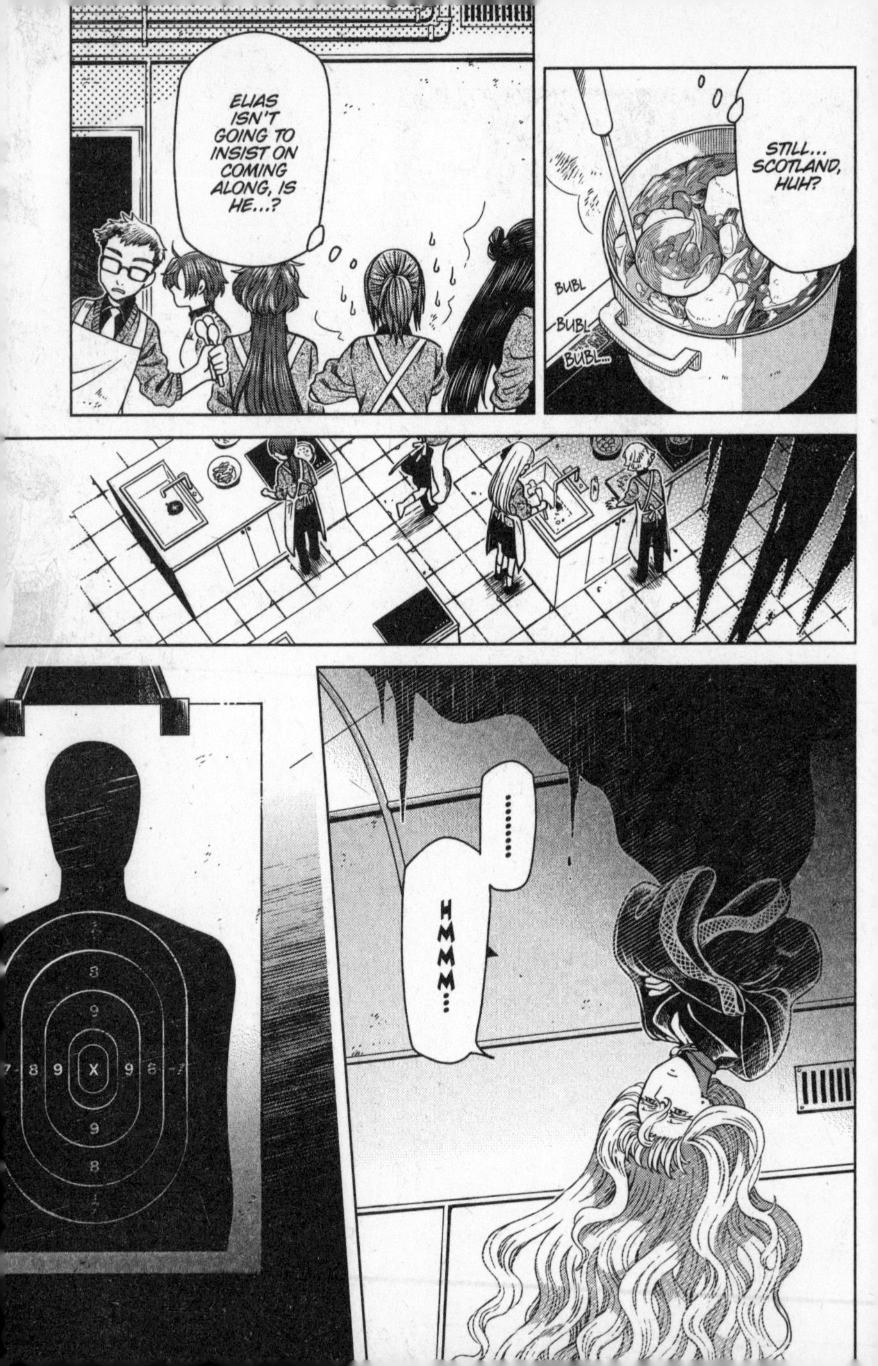
STILL... SCOTLAND, HUH?
BUBL
BUBL
BUBL...
ELIAS ISN'T GOING TO INSIST ON COMING ALONG, IS HE...?
........
HMMM...

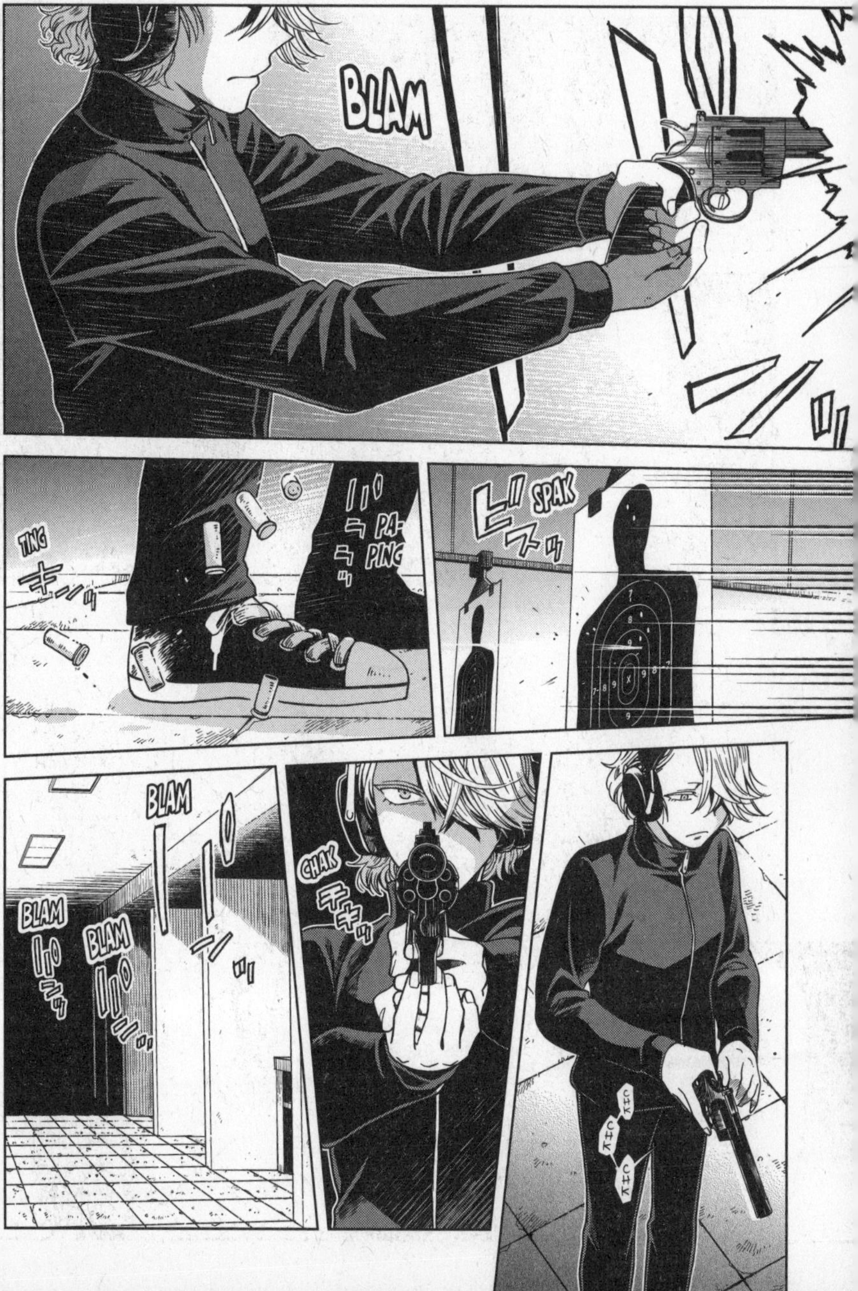
BLAM
SPAK
PA-PING
TING
CHK
CHK
CHK
CHAK
BLAM
BLAM
BLAM

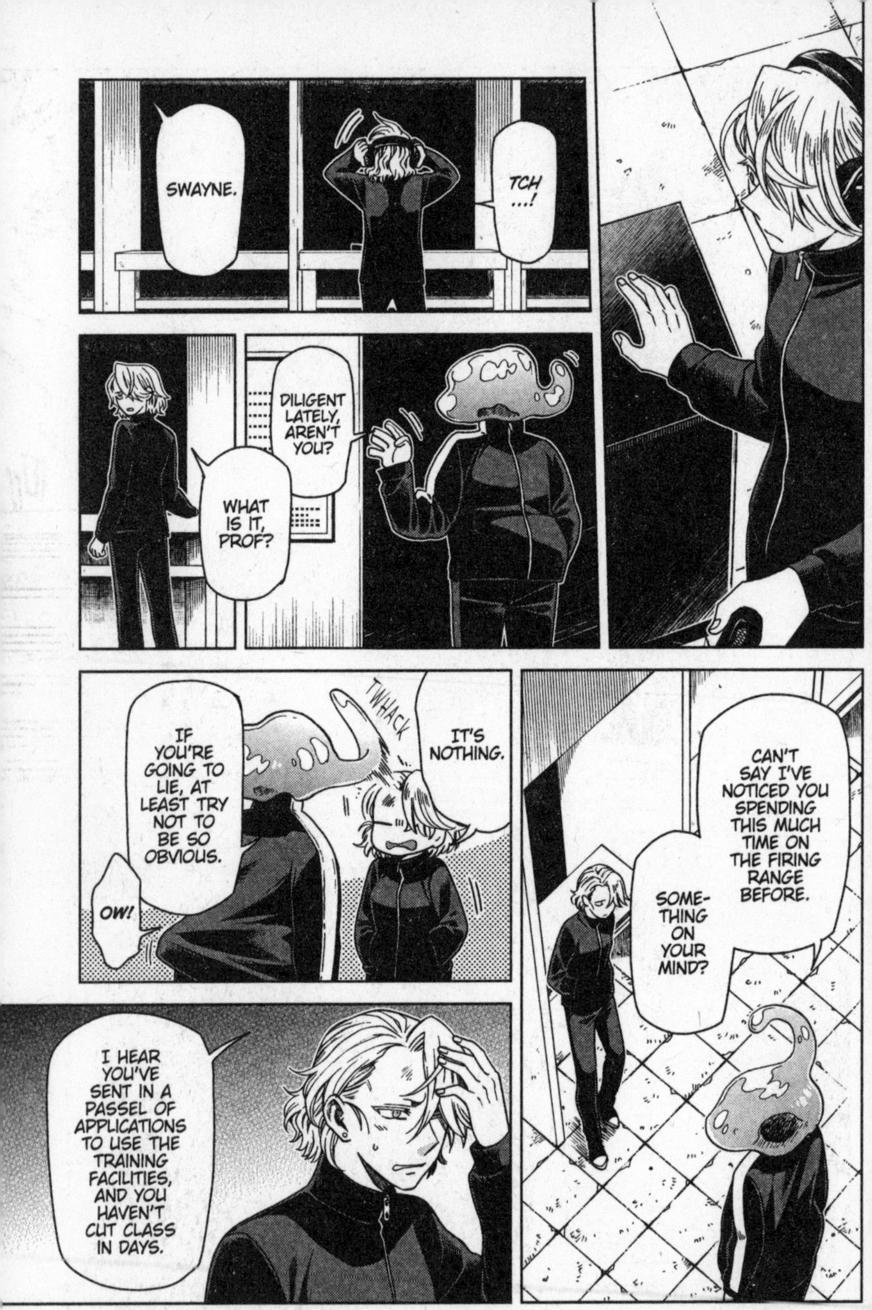
TCH ...!
SWAYNE.
DILIGENT LATELY, AREN'T YOU?
WHAT IS IT, PROF?
CAN'T SAY I'VE NOTICED YOU SPENDING THIS MUCH TIME ON THE FIRING RANGE BEFORE.
SOME-THING ON YOUR MIND?
IT'S NOTHING.
TWHACK
IF YOU'RE GOING TO LIE, AT LEAST TRY NOT TO BE SO OBVIOUS.
OW!
I HEAR YOU'VE SENT IN A PASSEL OF APPLICATIONS TO USE THE TRAINING FACILITIES, AND YOU HAVEN'T CUT CLASS IN DAYS.

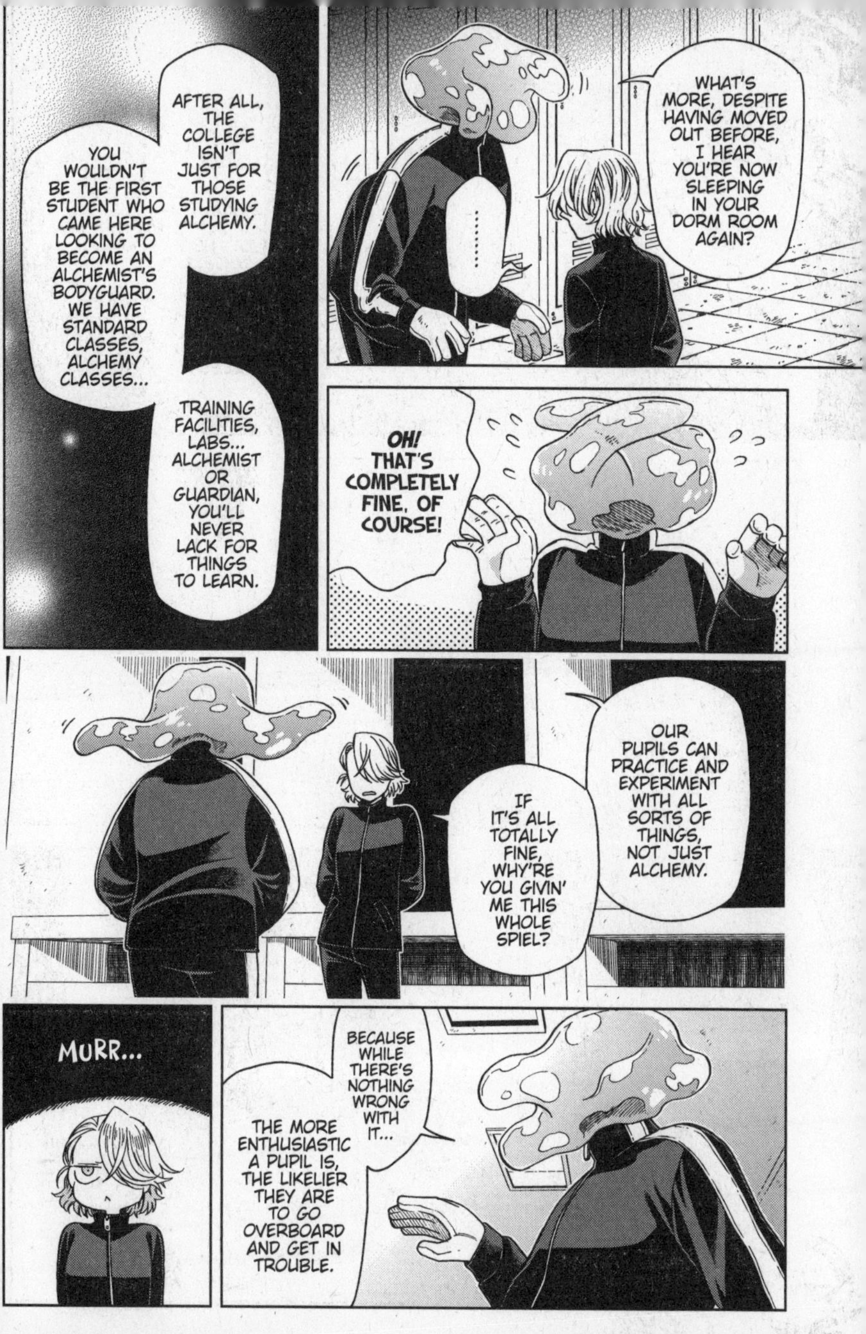
WHAT'S MORE, DESPITE HAVING MOVED OUT BEFORE, I HEAR YOU'RE NOW SLEEPING IN YOUR DORM ROOM AGAIN?
......
OH! THAT'S COMPLETELY FINE, OF COURSE!
AFTER ALL, THE COLLEGE ISN'T JUST FOR THOSE STUDYING ALCHEMY.
YOU WOULDN'T BE THE FIRST STUDENT WHO CAME HERE LOOKING TO BECOME AN ALCHEMIST'S BODYGUARD. WE HAVE STANDARD CLASSES, ALCHEMY CLASSES...
TRAINING FACILITIES, LABS... ALCHEMIST OR GUARDIAN, YOU'LL NEVER LACK FOR THINGS TO LEARN.
OUR PUPILS CAN PRACTICE AND EXPERIMENT WITH ALL SORTS OF THINGS, NOT JUST ALCHEMY.
IF IT'S ALL TOTALLY FINE, WHY'RE YOU GIVIN' ME THIS WHOLE SPIEL?
BECAUSE WHILE THERE'S NOTHING WRONG WITH IT...
THE MORE ENTHUSIASTIC A PUPIL IS, THE LIKELIER THEY ARE TO GO OVERBOARD AND GET IN TROUBLE.
MURR...

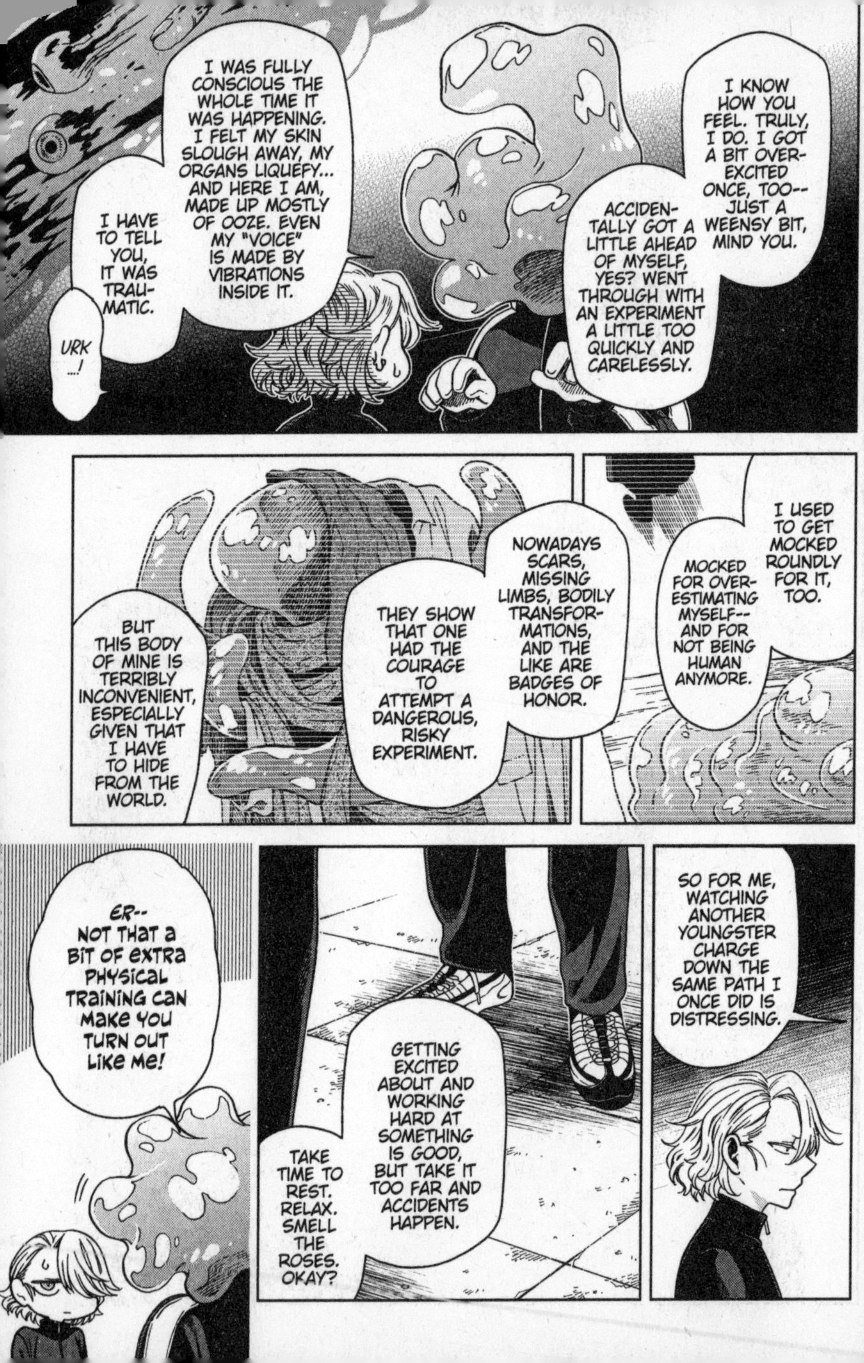
I KNOW HOW YOU FEEL. TRULY, I DO. I GOT A BIT OVER-EXCITED ONCE, TOO-- JUST A WEENSY BIT, MIND YOU.
ACCIDENTALLY GOT A LITTLE AHEAD OF MYSELF, YES? WENT THROUGH WITH AN EXPERIMENT A LITTLE TOO QUICKLY AND CARELESSLY.
I WAS FULLY CONSCIOUS THE WHOLE TIME IT WAS HAPPENING. I FELT MY SKIN SLOUGH AWAY, MY ORGANS LIQUEFY... AND HERE I AM, MADE UP MOSTLY OF OOZE. EVEN MY "VOICE" IS MADE BY VIBRATIONS INSIDE IT.
I HAVE TO TELL YOU, IT WAS TRAUMATIC.
URK ...!
I USED TO GET MOCKED ROUNDLY FOR IT, TOO.
MOCKED FOR OVERESTIMATING MYSELF-- AND FOR NOT BEING HUMAN ANYMORE.
NOWADAYS SCARS, MISSING LIMBS, BODILY TRANSFORMATIONS, AND THE LIKE ARE BADGES OF HONOR.
THEY SHOW THAT ONE HAD THE COURAGE TO ATTEMPT A DANGEROUS, RISKY EXPERIMENT.
BUT THIS BODY OF MINE IS TERRIBLY INCONVENIENT, ESPECIALLY GIVEN THAT I HAVE TO HIDE FROM THE WORLD.
SO FOR ME, WATCHING ANOTHER YOUNGSTER CHARGE DOWN THE SAME PATH I ONCE DID IS DISTRESSING.
GETTING EXCITED ABOUT AND WORKING HARD AT SOMETHING IS GOOD, BUT TAKE IT TOO FAR AND ACCIDENTS HAPPEN.
TAKE TIME TO REST. RELAX. SMELL THE ROSES. OKAY?
ER-- NOT THAT A BIT OF EXTRA PHYSICAL TRAINING CAN MAKE YOU TURN OUT LIKE ME!

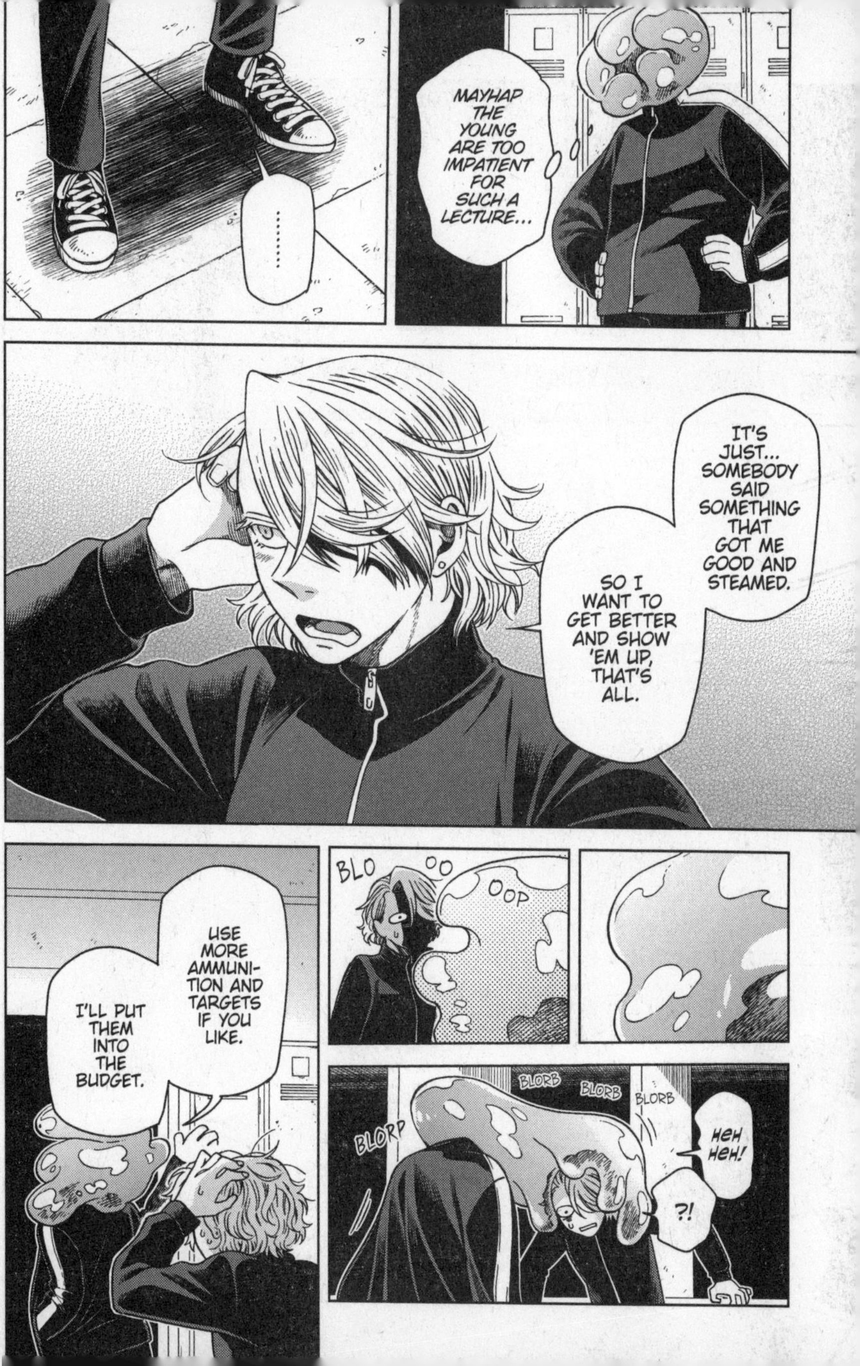
MAYHAP THE YOUNG ARE TOO IMPATIENT FOR SUCH A LECTURE...
......
IT'S JUST... SOMEBODY SAID SOMETHING THAT GOT ME GOOD AND STEAMED.
SO I WANT TO GET BETTER AND SHOW 'EM UP, THAT'S ALL.
BLO OO OOP
BLORB
HEH HEH!
BLORB
BLORB
?!
BLORP
USE MORE AMMUNI-TION AND TARGETS IF YOU LIKE.
I'LL PUT THEM INTO THE BUDGET.

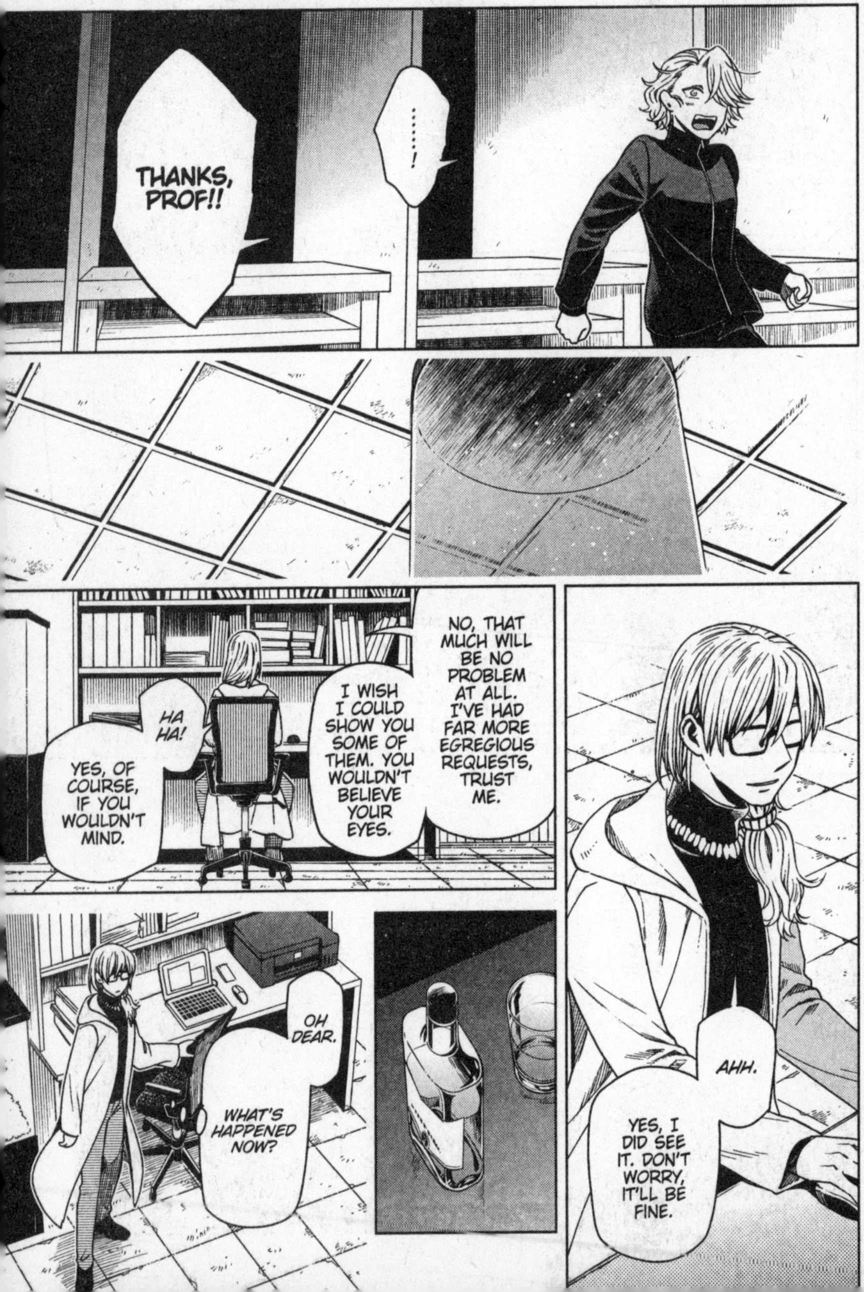
......!
THANKS, PROF!!
AHH.
YES, I DID SEE IT. DON'T WORRY, IT'LL BE FINE.
NO, THAT MUCH WILL BE NO PROBLEM AT ALL. I'VE HAD FAR MORE EGREGIOUS REQUESTS, TRUST ME.
I WISH I COULD SHOW YOU SOME OF THEM. YOU WOULDN'T BELIEVE YOUR EYES.
HA HA!
YES, OF COURSE, IF YOU WOULDN'T MIND.
OH DEAR.
WHAT'S HAPPENED NOW?

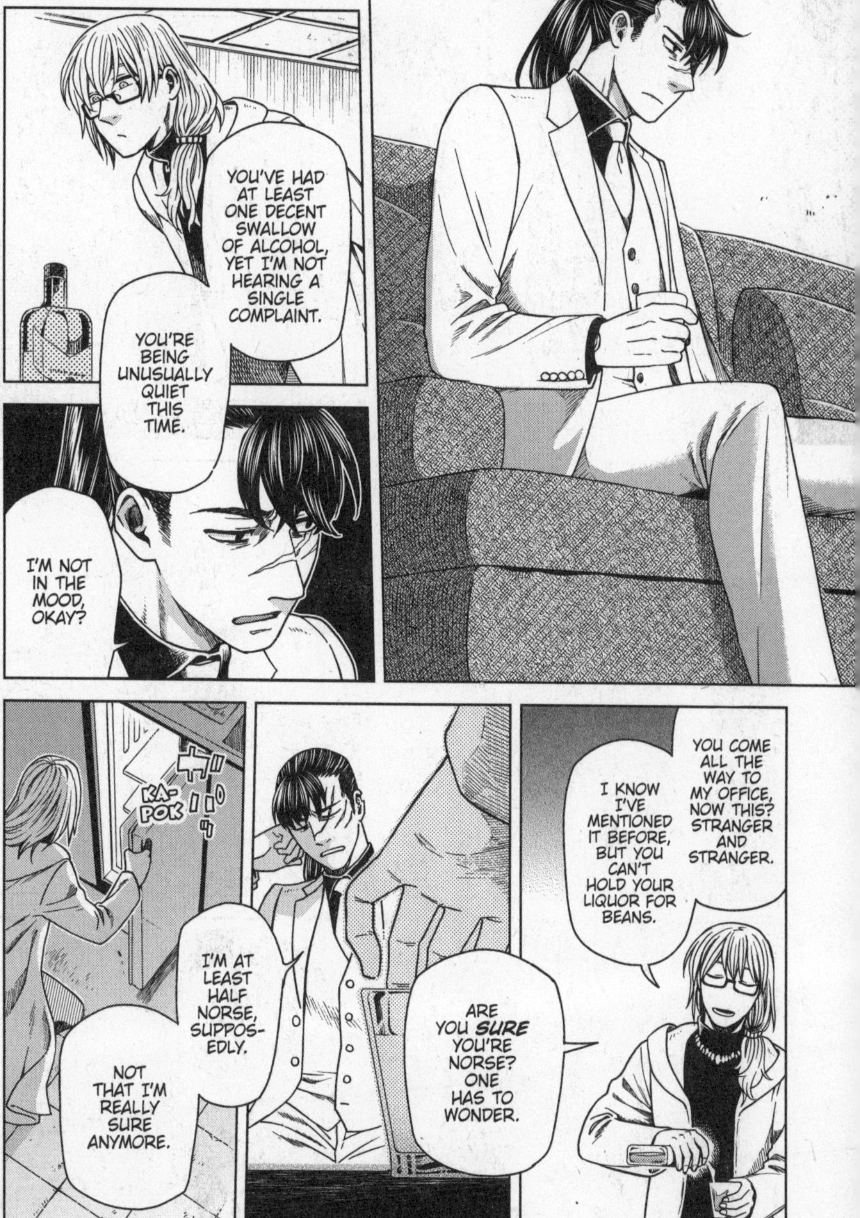
YOU'VE HAD AT LEAST ONE DECENT SWALLOW OF ALCOHOL, YET I'M NOT HEARING A SINGLE COMPLAINT.
YOU'RE BEING UNUSUALLY QUIET THIS TIME.
I'M NOT IN THE MOOD, OKAY?
YOU COME ALL THE WAY TO MY OFFICE, NOW THIS? STRANGER AND STRANGER.
I KNOW I'VE MENTIONED IT BEFORE, BUT YOU CAN'T HOLD YOUR LIQUOR FOR BEANS.
ARE YOU *SURE* YOU'RE NORSE? ONE HAS TO WONDER.
I'M AT LEAST HALF NORSE, SUPPOSEDLY.
KA-POK
NOT THAT I'M REALLY SURE ANYMORE.

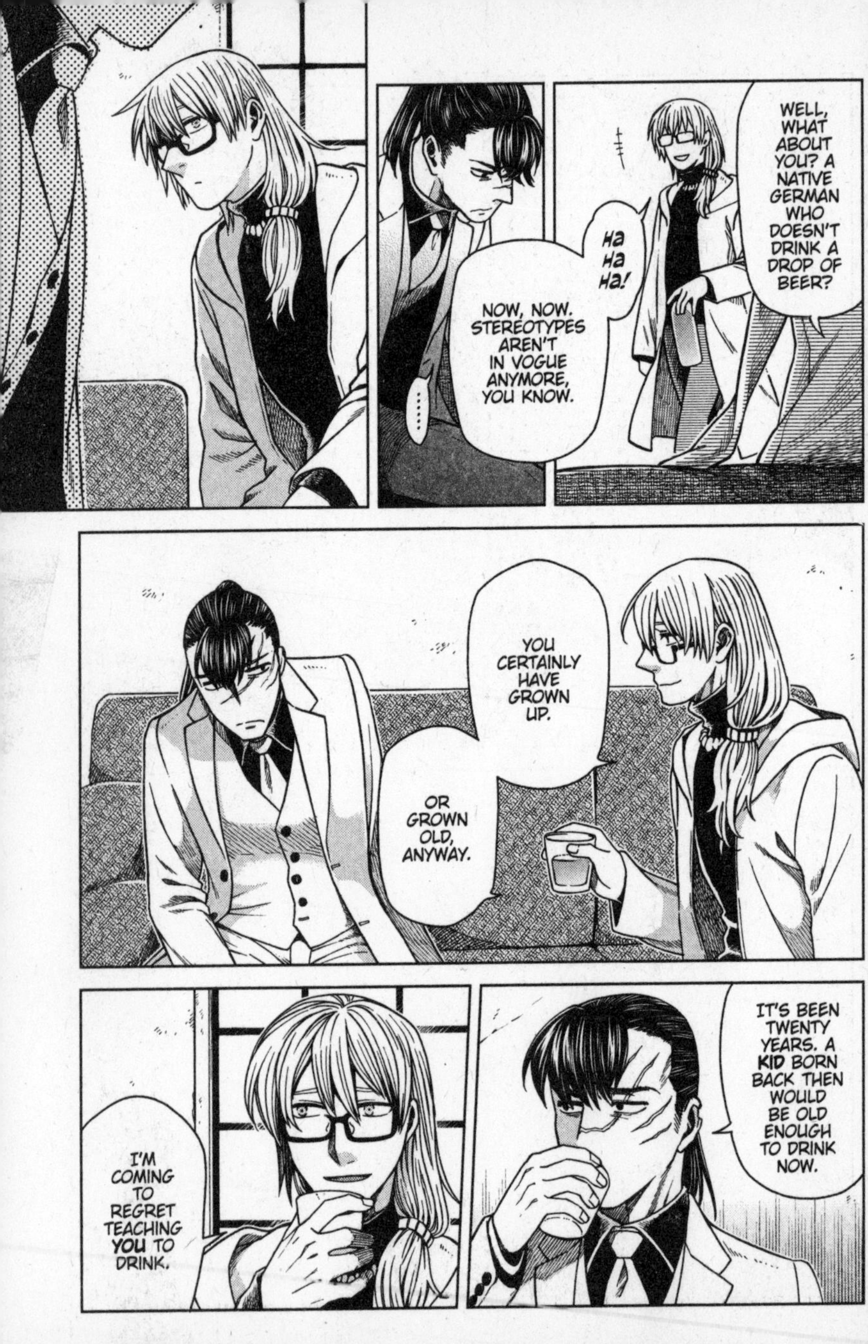
WELL, WHAT ABOUT YOU? A NATIVE GERMAN WHO DOESN'T DRINK A DROP OF BEER?
HA HA HA!
NOW, NOW. STEREOTYPES AREN'T IN VOGUE ANYMORE, YOU KNOW.
......
YOU CERTAINLY HAVE GROWN UP.
OR GROWN OLD, ANYWAY.
IT'S BEEN TWENTY YEARS. A **KID** BORN BACK THEN WOULD BE OLD ENOUGH TO DRINK NOW.
I'M COMING TO REGRET TEACHING **YOU** TO DRINK.

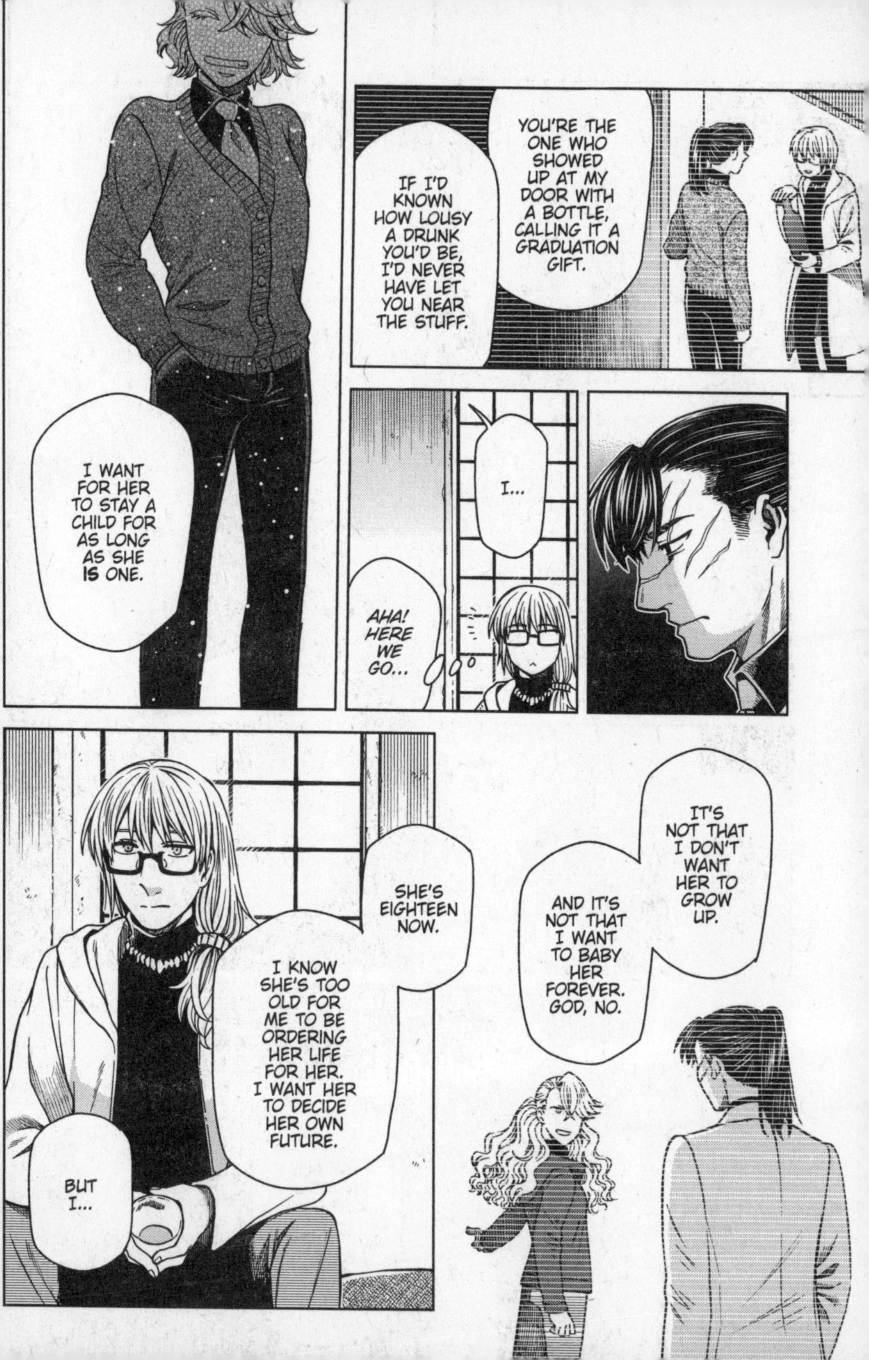
YOU'RE THE ONE WHO SHOWED UP AT MY DOOR WITH A BOTTLE, CALLING IT A GRADUATION GIFT.
IF I'D KNOWN HOW LOUSY A DRUNK YOU'D BE, I'D NEVER HAVE LET YOU NEAR THE STUFF.
I...
AHA! HERE WE GO...
I WANT FOR HER TO STAY A CHILD FOR AS LONG AS SHE **IS** ONE.
IT'S NOT THAT I DON'T WANT HER TO GROW UP.
AND IT'S NOT THAT I WANT TO BABY HER FOREVER. GOD, NO.
SHE'S EIGHTEEN NOW.
I KNOW SHE'S TOO OLD FOR ME TO BE ORDERING HER LIFE FOR HER. I WANT HER TO DECIDE HER OWN FUTURE.
BUT I...

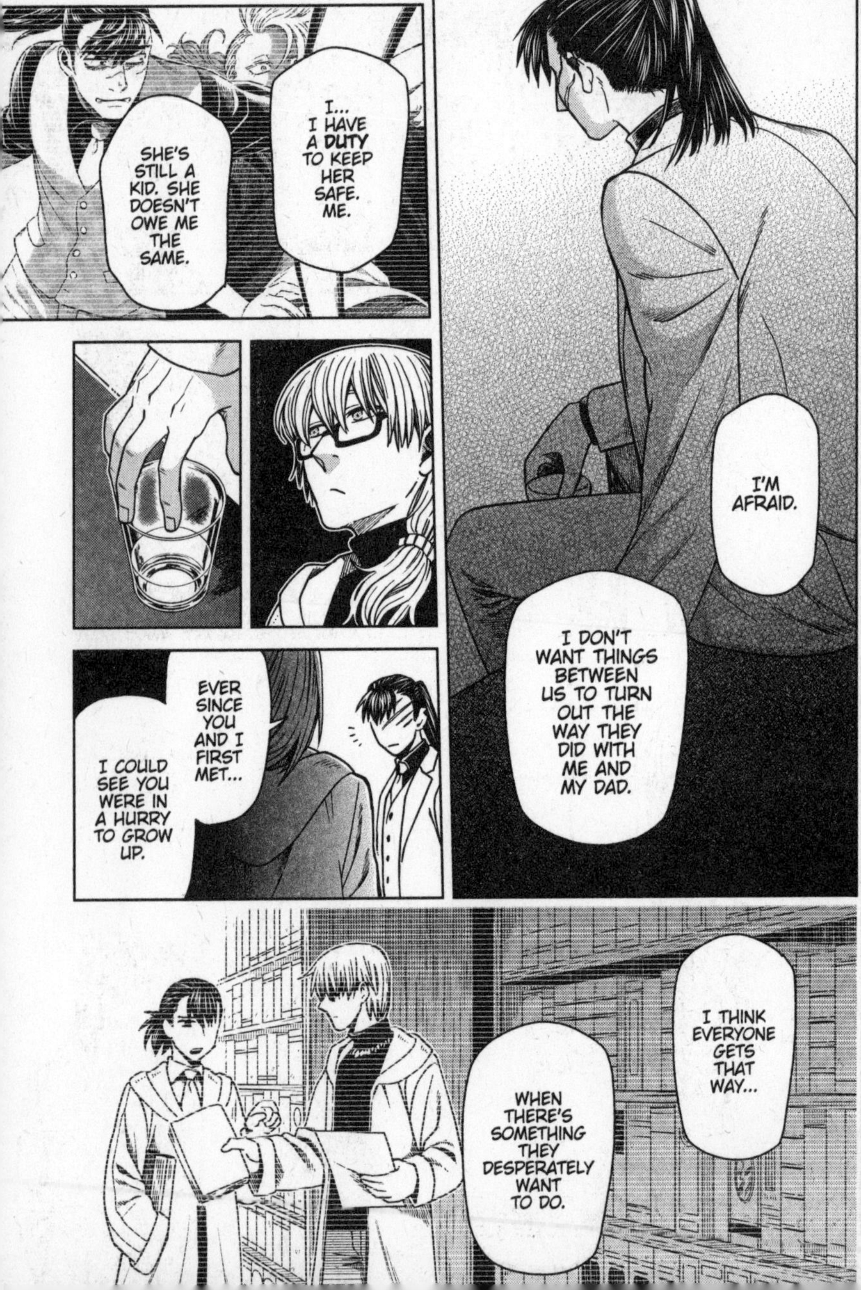
I'M AFRAID.
I DON'T WANT THINGS BETWEEN US TO TURN OUT THE WAY THEY DID WITH ME AND MY DAD.
I... I HAVE A **DUTY** TO KEEP HER SAFE. ME.
SHE'S STILL A KID. SHE DOESN'T OWE ME THE SAME.
EVER SINCE YOU AND I FIRST MET...
I COULD SEE YOU WERE IN A HURRY TO GROW UP.
I THINK EVERYONE GETS THAT WAY...
WHEN THERE'S SOMETHING THEY DESPERATELY WANT TO DO.

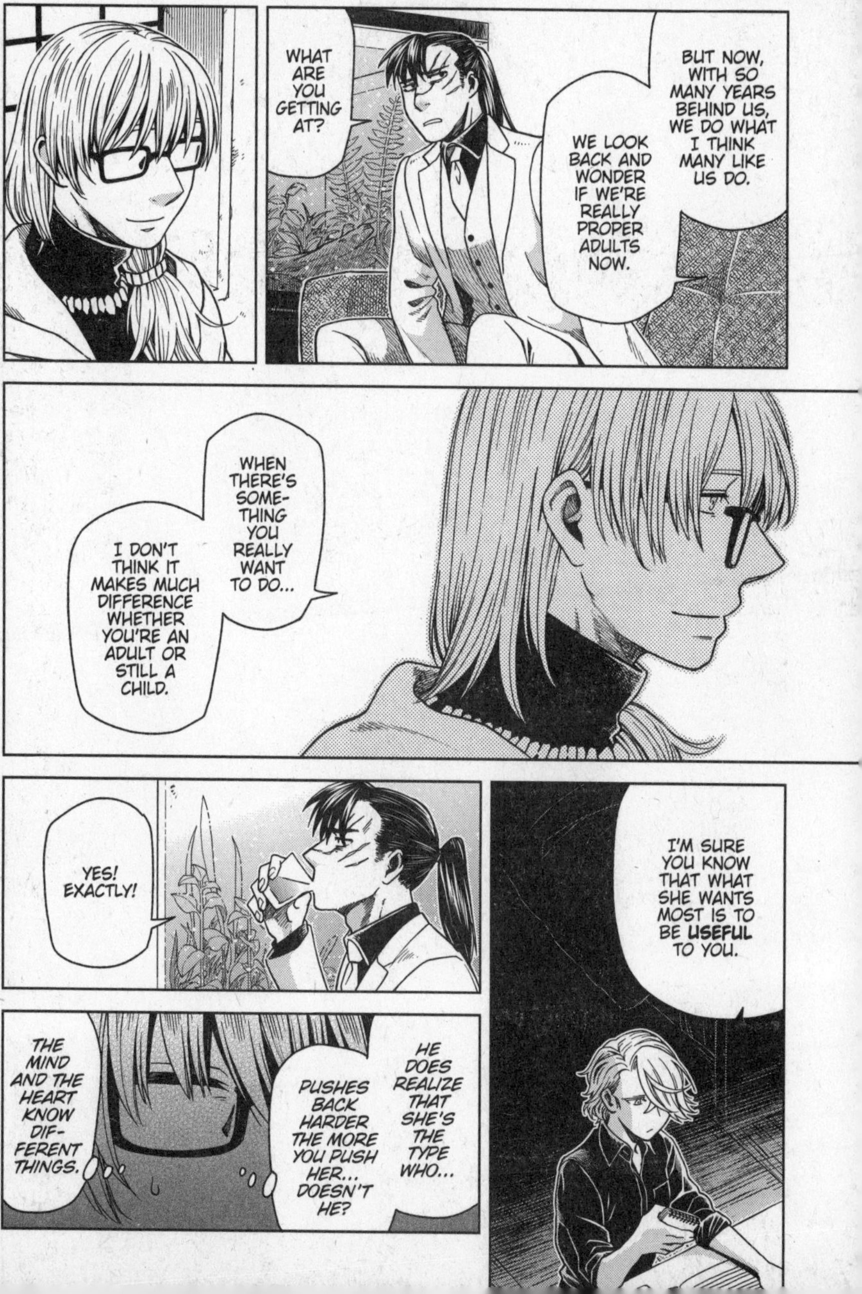
BUT NOW, WITH SO MANY YEARS BEHIND US, WE DO WHAT I THINK MANY LIKE US DO.
WE LOOK BACK AND WONDER IF WE'RE REALLY PROPER ADULTS NOW.
WHAT ARE YOU GETTING AT?
WHEN THERE'S SOME-THING YOU REALLY WANT TO DO...
I DON'T THINK IT MAKES MUCH DIFFERENCE WHETHER YOU'RE AN ADULT OR STILL A CHILD.
I'M SURE YOU KNOW THAT WHAT SHE WANTS MOST IS TO BE **USEFUL** TO YOU.
YES! EXACTLY!
HE DOES REALIZE THAT SHE'S THE TYPE WHO...
PUSHES BACK HARDER THE MORE YOU PUSH HER... DOESN'T HE?
THE MIND AND THE HEART KNOW DIF-FERENT THINGS.

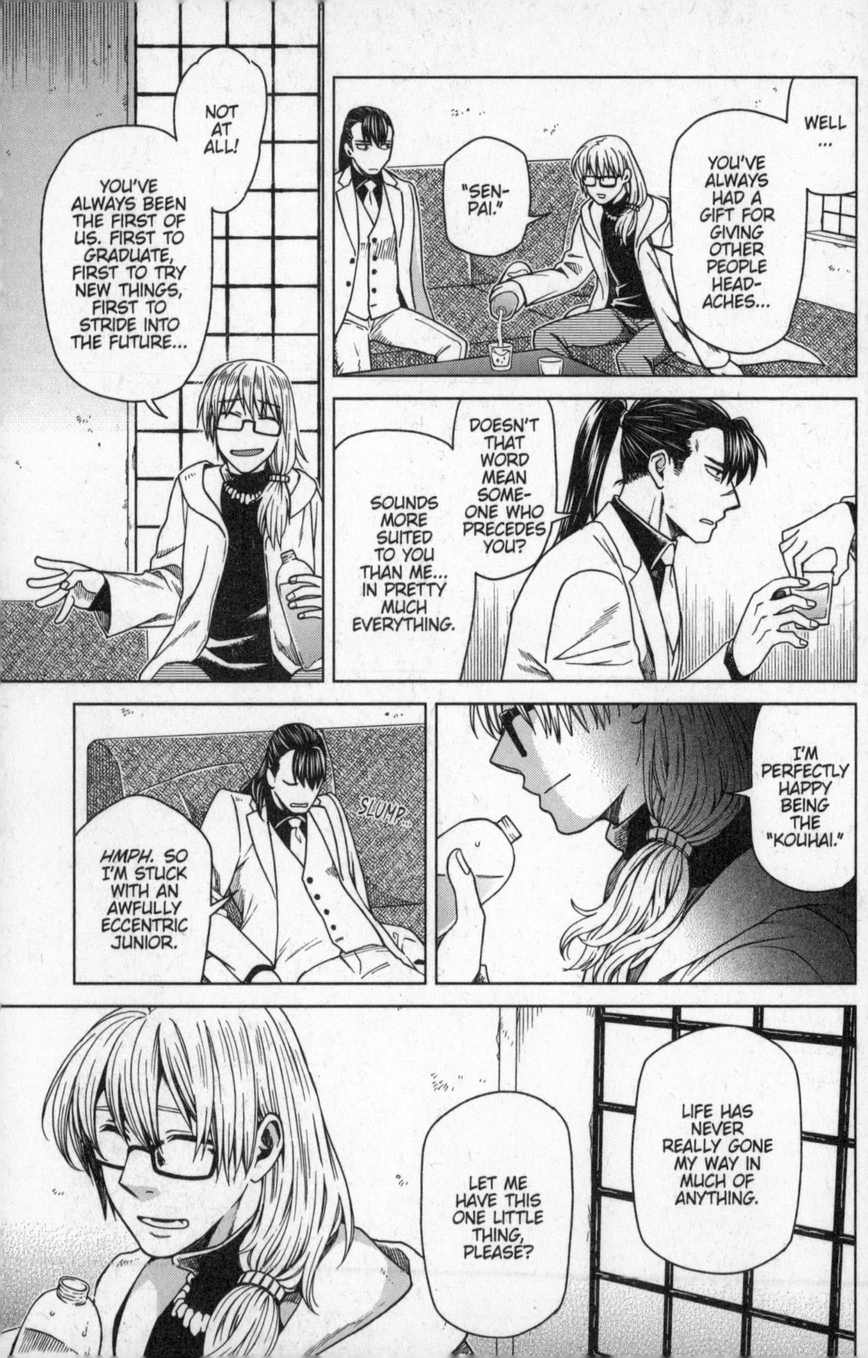
WELL ...
YOU'VE ALWAYS HAD A GIFT FOR GIVING OTHER PEOPLE HEAD-ACHES...
"SEN-PAI."
DOESN'T THAT WORD MEAN SOME-ONE WHO PRECEDES YOU?
SOUNDS MORE SUITED TO YOU THAN ME... IN PRETTY MUCH EVERYTHING.
NOT AT ALL!
YOU'VE ALWAYS BEEN THE FIRST OF US. FIRST TO GRADUATE, FIRST TO TRY NEW THINGS, FIRST TO STRIDE INTO THE FUTURE...
I'M PERFECTLY HAPPY BEING THE "KOUHAI."
SLUMP...
HMPH. SO I'M STUCK WITH AN AWFULLY ECCENTRIC JUNIOR.
LIFE HAS NEVER REALLY GONE MY WAY IN MUCH OF ANYTHING.
LET ME HAVE THIS ONE LITTLE THING, PLEASE?

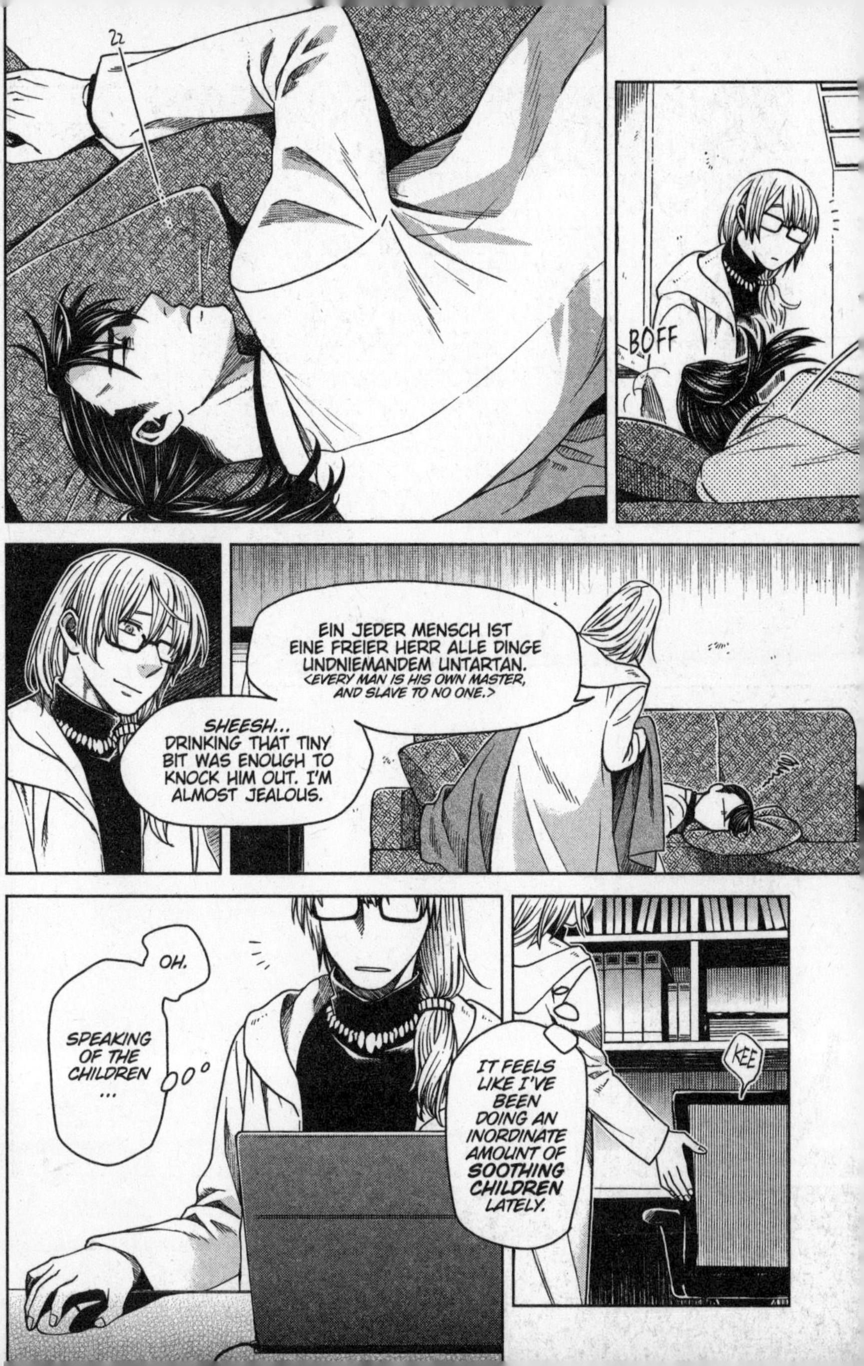
BOFF
EIN JEDER MENSCH IST EINE FREIER HERR ALLE DINGE UNDNIEMANDEM UNTARTAN.
<EVERY MAN IS HIS OWN MASTER, AND SLAVE TO NO ONE.>
SHEESH... DRINKING THAT TINY BIT WAS ENOUGH TO KNOCK HIM OUT. I'M ALMOST JEALOUS.
KEE
IT FEELS LIKE I'VE BEEN DOING AN INORDINATE AMOUNT OF SOOTHING CHILDREN LATELY.
OH.
SPEAKING OF THE CHILDREN ...

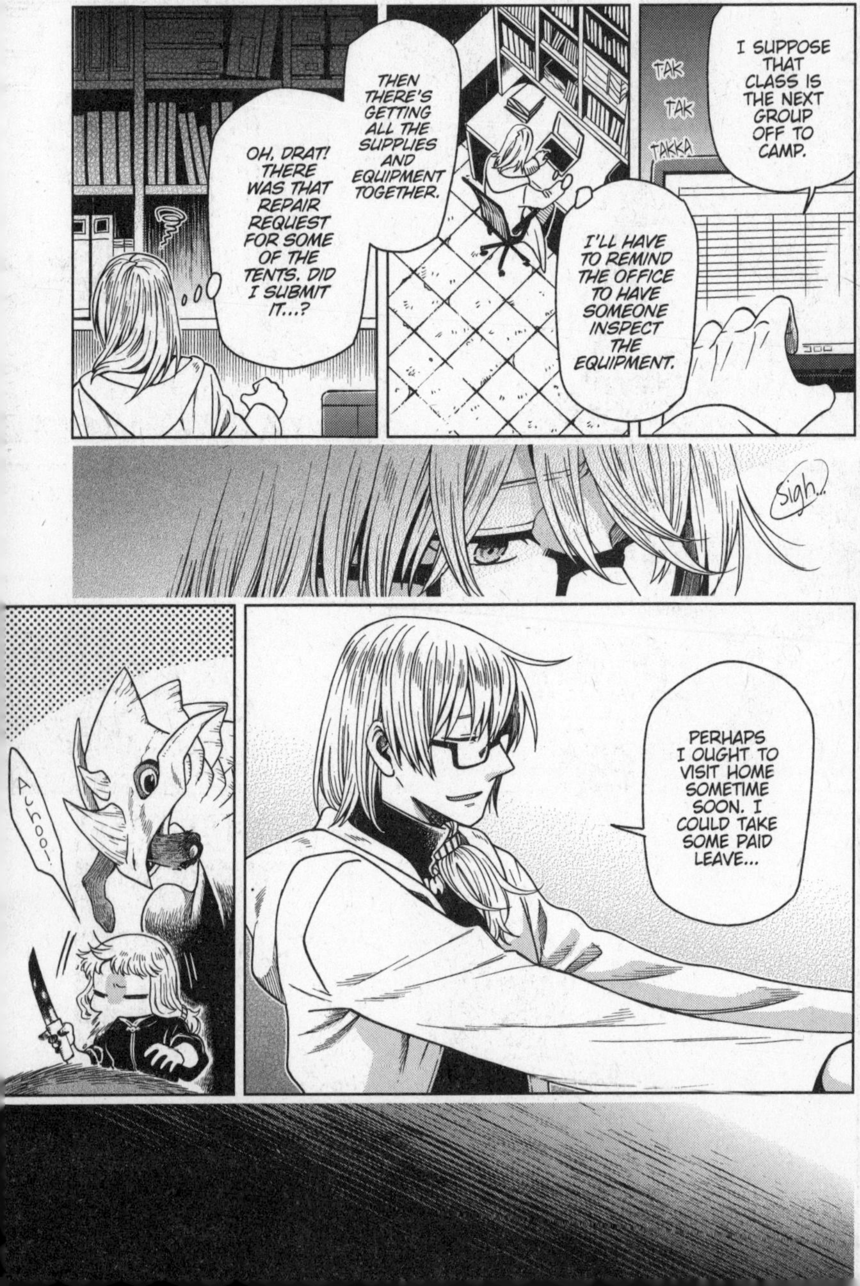

I SUPPOSE THAT CLASS IS THE NEXT GROUP OFF TO CAMP.
TAK
TAK
TAKKA
I'LL HAVE TO REMIND THE OFFICE TO HAVE SOMEONE INSPECT THE EQUIPMENT.
THEN THERE'S GETTING ALL THE SUPPLIES AND EQUIPMENT TOGETHER.
OH, DRAT! THERE WAS THAT REPAIR REQUEST FOR SOME OF THE TENTS. DID I SUBMIT IT...?
Sigh...
PERHAPS I OUGHT TO VISIT HOME SOMETIME SOON. I COULD TAKE SOME PAID LEAVE...
Achoo!

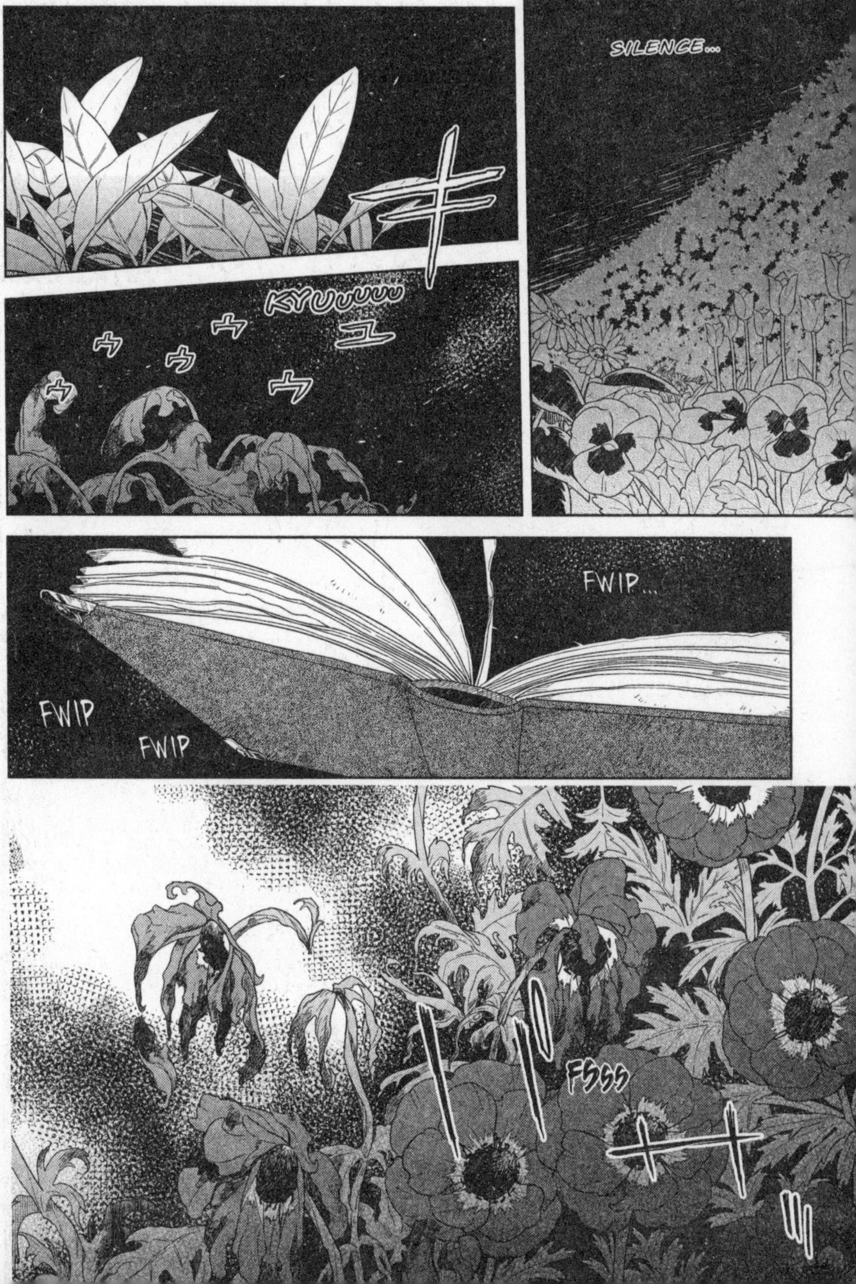
SILENCE...
キ
KYUUUUU
ウ
ウ
ウ
ウ
ユ
FWIP...
FWIP
FWIP
FSSS

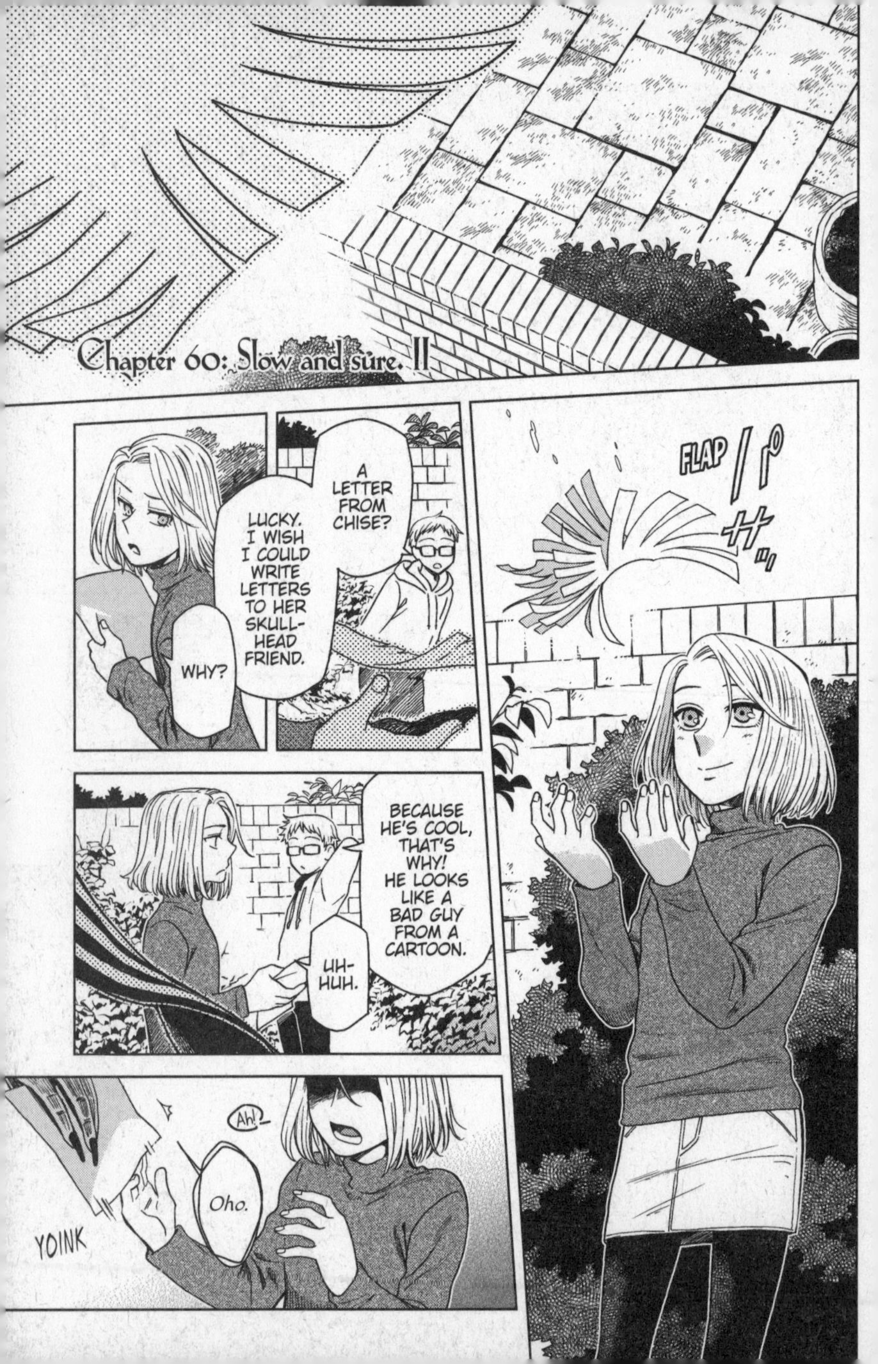
Chapter 60: Slow and sure. II
FLAP
A LETTER FROM CHISE?
LUCKY. I WISH I COULD WRITE LETTERS TO HER SKULL-HEAD FRIEND.
WHY?
BECAUSE HE'S COOL, THAT'S WHY! HE LOOKS LIKE A BAD GUY FROM A CARTOON.
UH-HUH.
Ah!
Oho.
YOINK

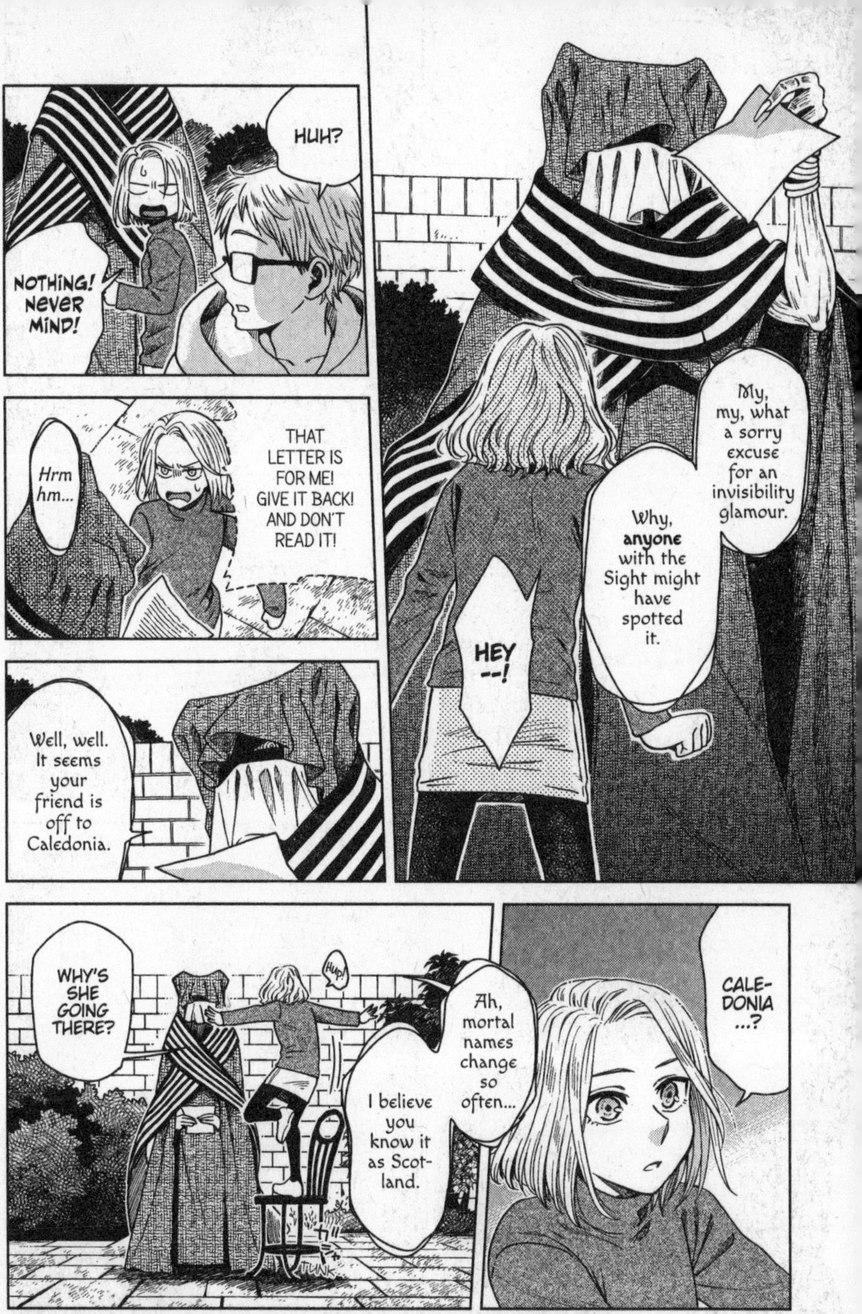
My, my, what a sorry excuse for an invisibility glamour.
Why, **anyone** with the Sight might have spotted it.
HEY --!
HUH?
NOTHING! NEVER MIND!
THAT LETTER IS FOR ME! GIVE IT BACK! AND DON'T READ IT!
*Hrm hm...*
Well, well. It seems your friend is off to Caledonia.
CALE-DONIA ...?
Ah, mortal names change so often...
I believe you know it as Scot-land.
Hup!
WHY'S SHE GOING THERE?
TUNK

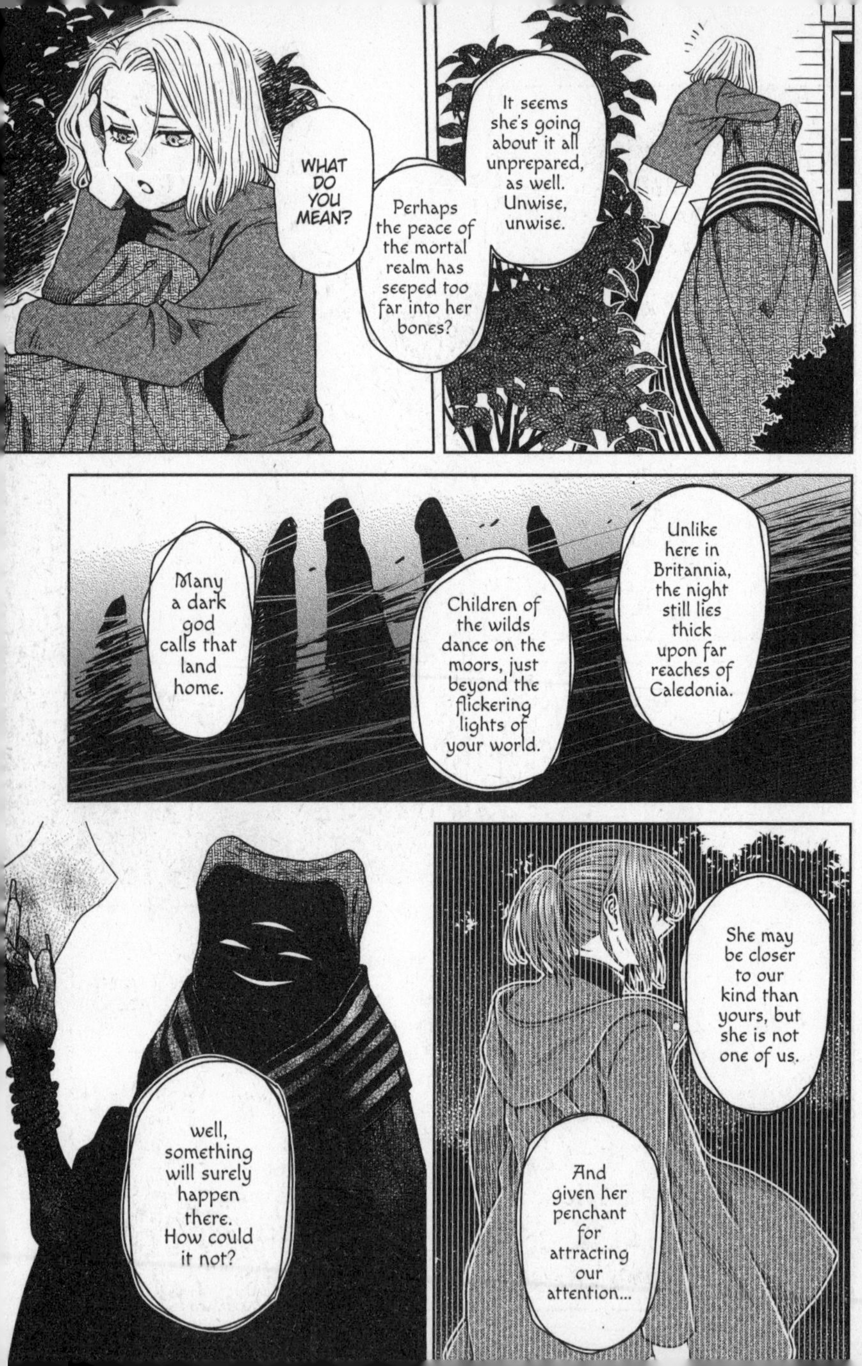
It seems she's going about it all unprepared, as well. Unwise, unwise.
Perhaps the peace of the mortal realm has seeped too far into her bones?
WHAT DO YOU MEAN?
Unlike here in Britannia, the night still lies thick upon far reaches of Caledonia.
Children of the wilds dance on the moors, just beyond the flickering lights of your world.
Many a dark god calls that land home.
She may be closer to our kind than yours, but she is not one of us.
And given her penchant for attracting our attention...
well, something will surely happen there. How could it not?

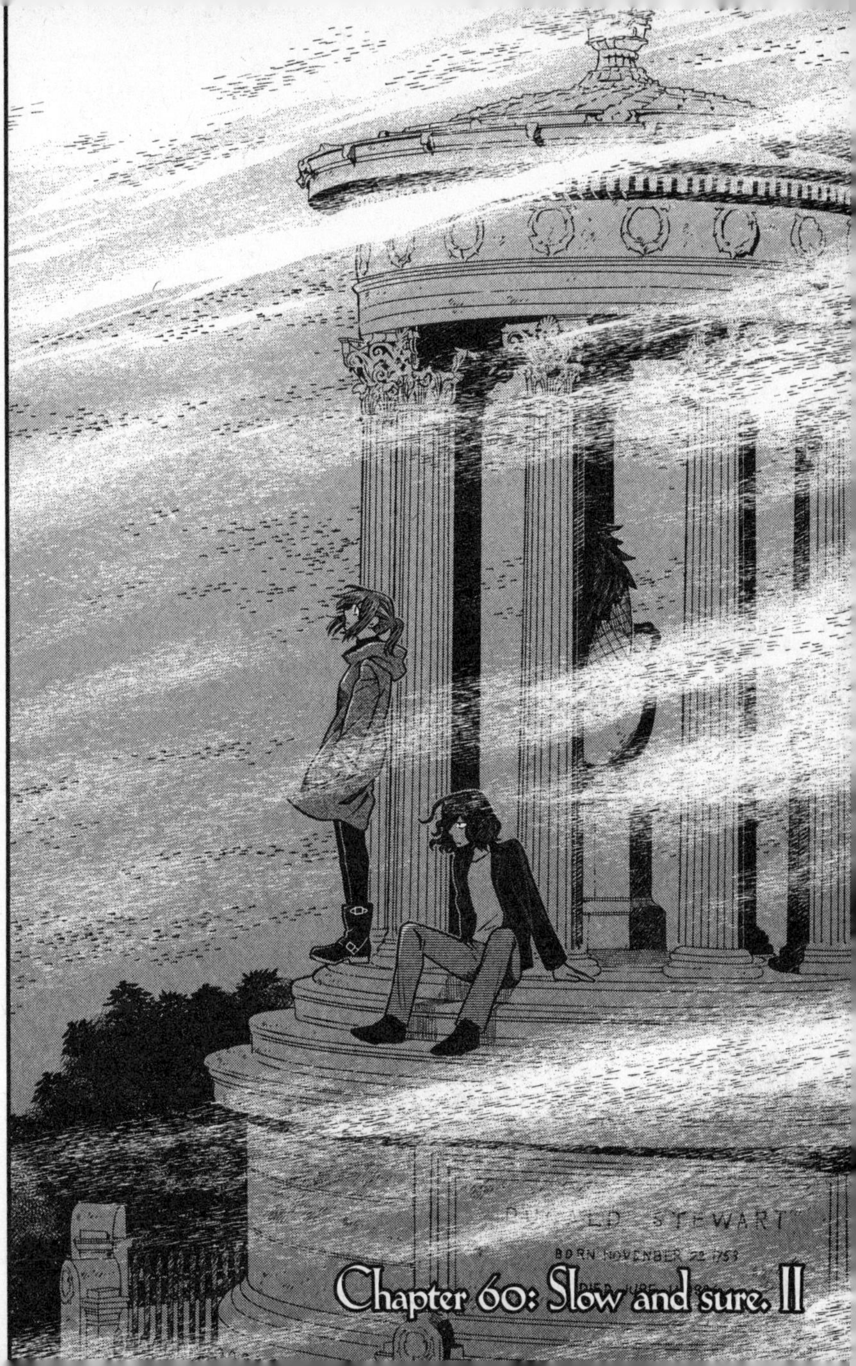
STEWART
BORN NOVEMBER 22 1753

# Chapter 60: Slow and sure. II

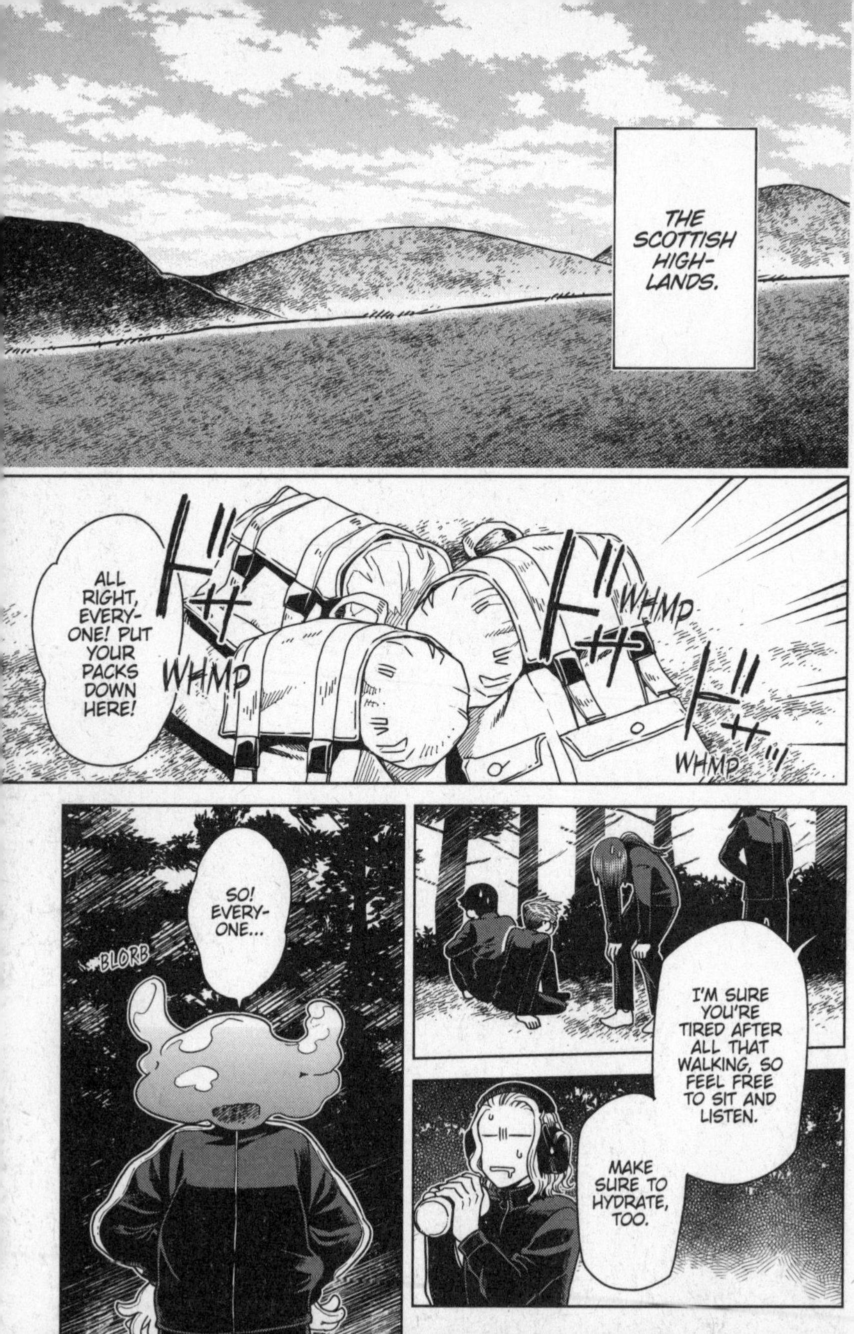
THE SCOTTISH HIGH-LANDS.
ALL RIGHT, EVERY-ONE! PUT YOUR PACKS DOWN HERE!
WHMP
WHMP
WHMP
I'M SURE YOU'RE TIRED AFTER ALL THAT WALKING, SO FEEL FREE TO SIT AND LISTEN.
MAKE SURE TO HYDRATE, TOO.
SO! EVERY-ONE...
BLORB

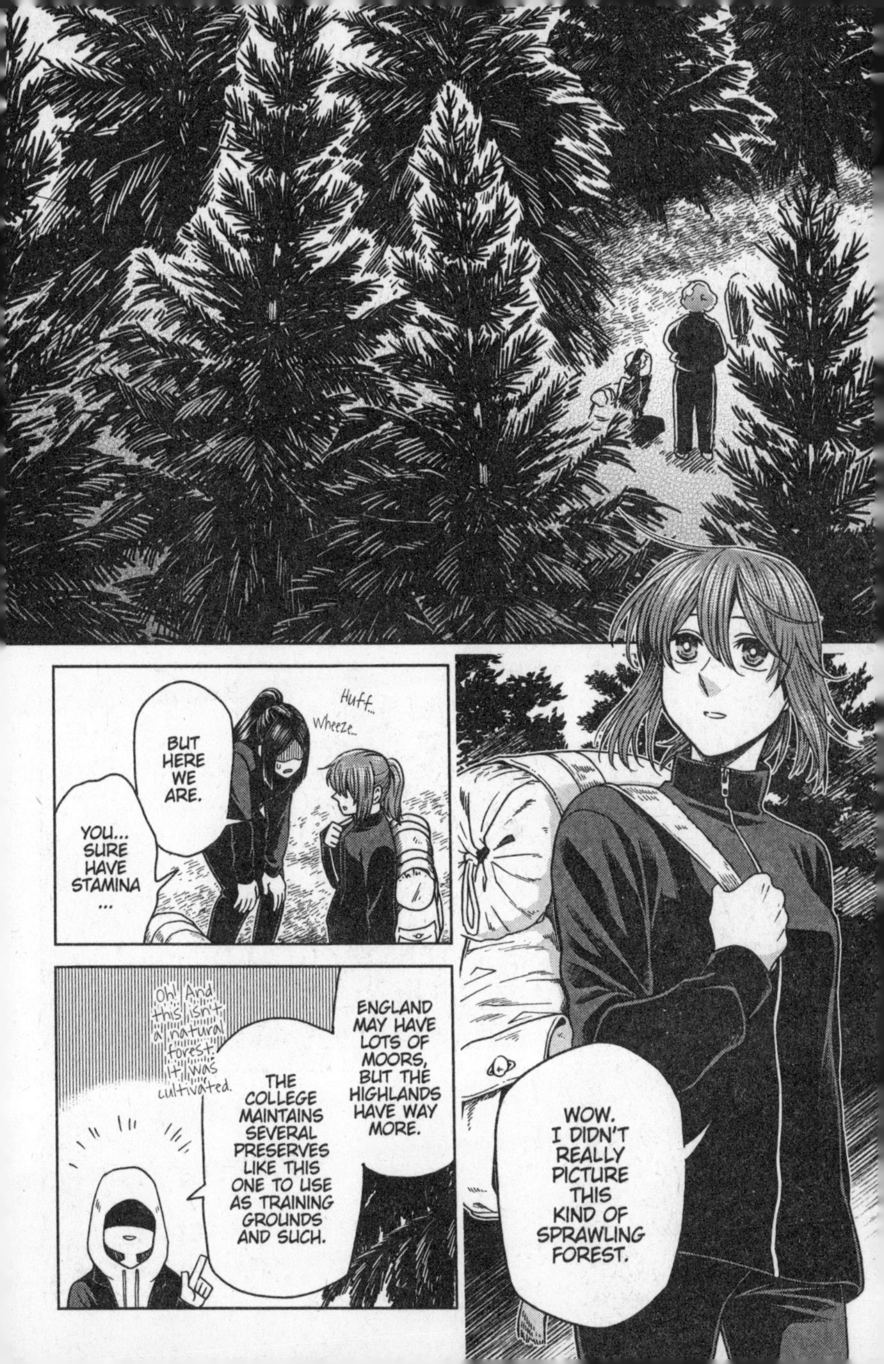
WOW. I DIDN'T REALLY PICTURE THIS KIND OF SPRAWLING FOREST.
Huff...
Wheeze...
BUT HERE WE ARE.
YOU... SURE HAVE STAMINA ...
ENGLAND MAY HAVE LOTS OF MOORS, BUT THE HIGHLANDS HAVE WAY MORE.
THE COLLEGE MAINTAINS SEVERAL PRESERVES LIKE THIS ONE TO USE AS TRAINING GROUNDS AND SUCH.
Oh! And this isn't a natural forest. It was cultivated.

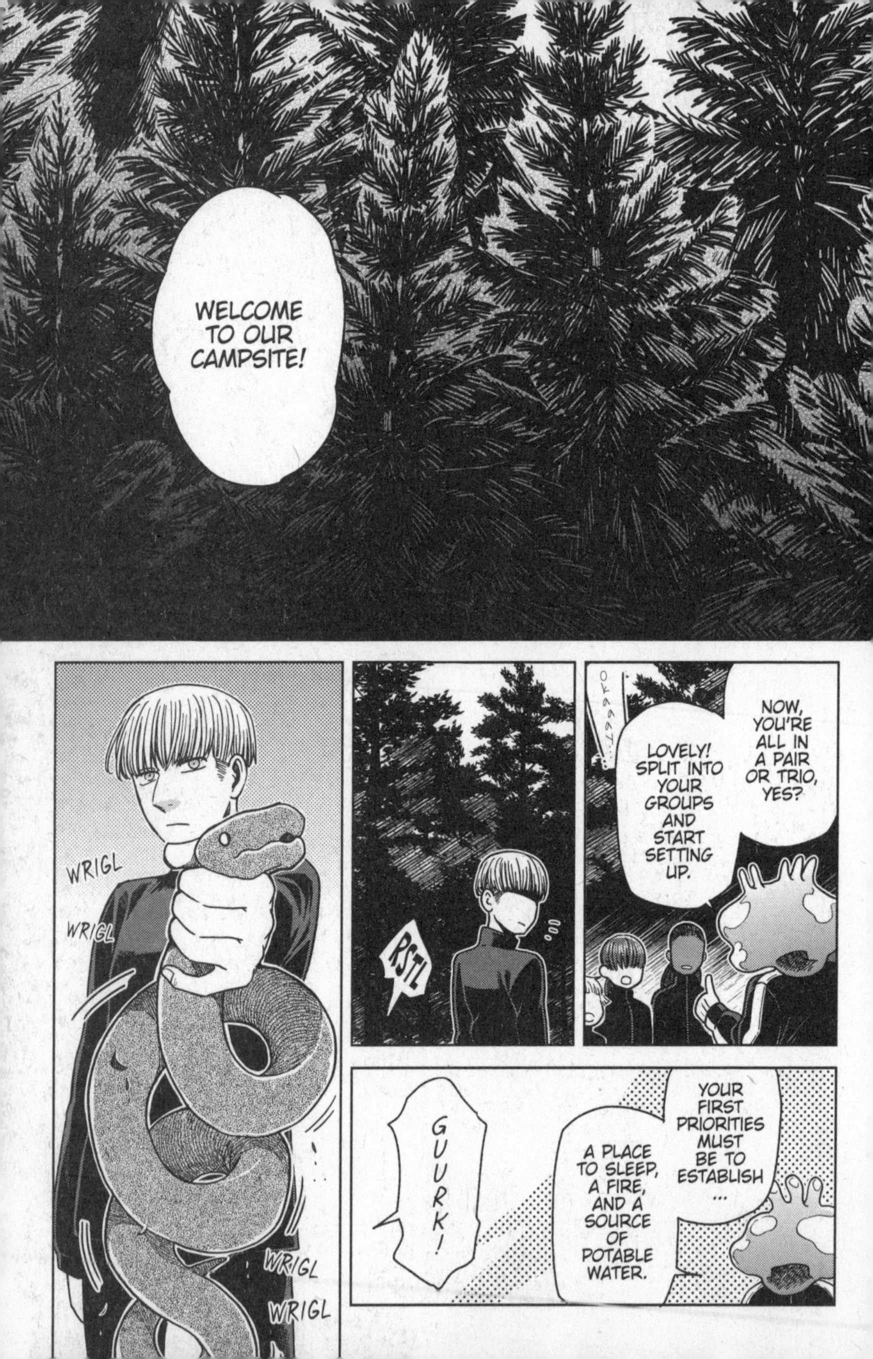
WELCOME TO OUR CAMPSITE!
NOW, YOU'RE ALL IN A PAIR OR TRIO, YES?
LOVELY! SPLIT INTO YOUR GROUPS AND START SETTING UP.
Okaaay...
RSTL
YOUR FIRST PRIORITIES MUST BE TO ESTABLISH...
A PLACE TO SLEEP, A FIRE, AND A SOURCE OF POTABLE WATER.
GUURK!
WRIGL
WRIGL
WRIGL
WRIGL

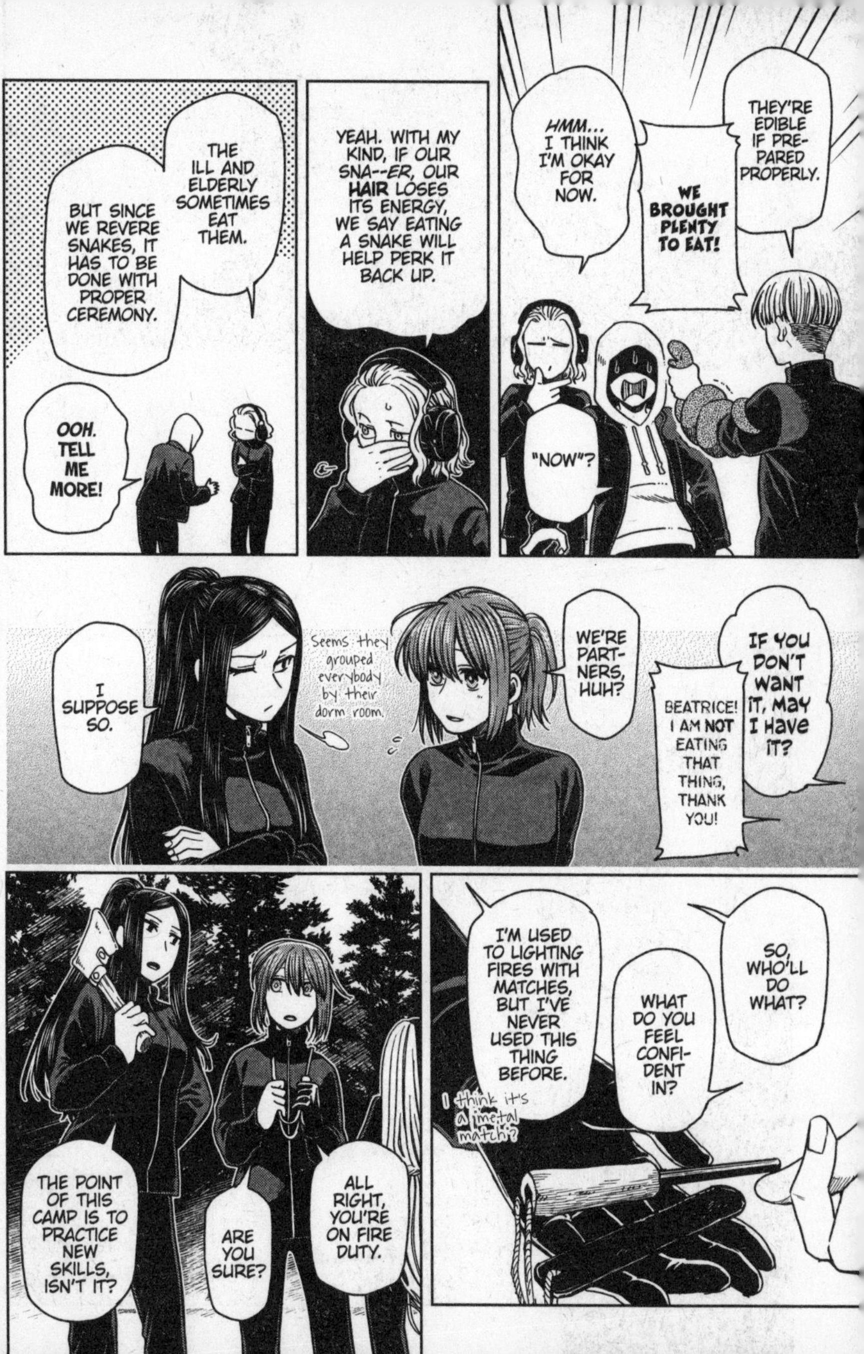
THEY'RE EDIBLE IF PRE-PARED PROPERLY.
WE BROUGHT PLENTY TO EAT!
HMM... I THINK I'M OKAY FOR NOW.
"NOW"?
YEAH. WITH MY KIND, IF OUR SNA--ER, OUR HAIR LOSES ITS ENERGY, WE SAY EATING A SNAKE WILL HELP PERK IT BACK UP.
THE ILL AND ELDERLY SOMETIMES EAT THEM.
BUT SINCE WE REVERE SNAKES, IT HAS TO BE DONE WITH PROPER CEREMONY.
OOH. TELL ME MORE!
IF YOU DON'T WANT IT, MAY I HAVE IT?
BEATRICE! I AM NOT EATING THAT THING, THANK YOU!
WE'RE PART-NERS, HUH?
Seems they grouped everybody by their dorm room.
I SUPPOSE SO.
SO, WHO'LL DO WHAT?
WHAT DO YOU FEEL CONFI-DENT IN?
I'M USED TO LIGHTING FIRES WITH MATCHES, BUT I'VE NEVER USED THIS THING BEFORE.
I think it's a metal match?
ALL RIGHT, YOU'RE ON FIRE DUTY.
ARE YOU SURE?
THE POINT OF THIS CAMP IS TO PRACTICE NEW SKILLS, ISN'T IT?

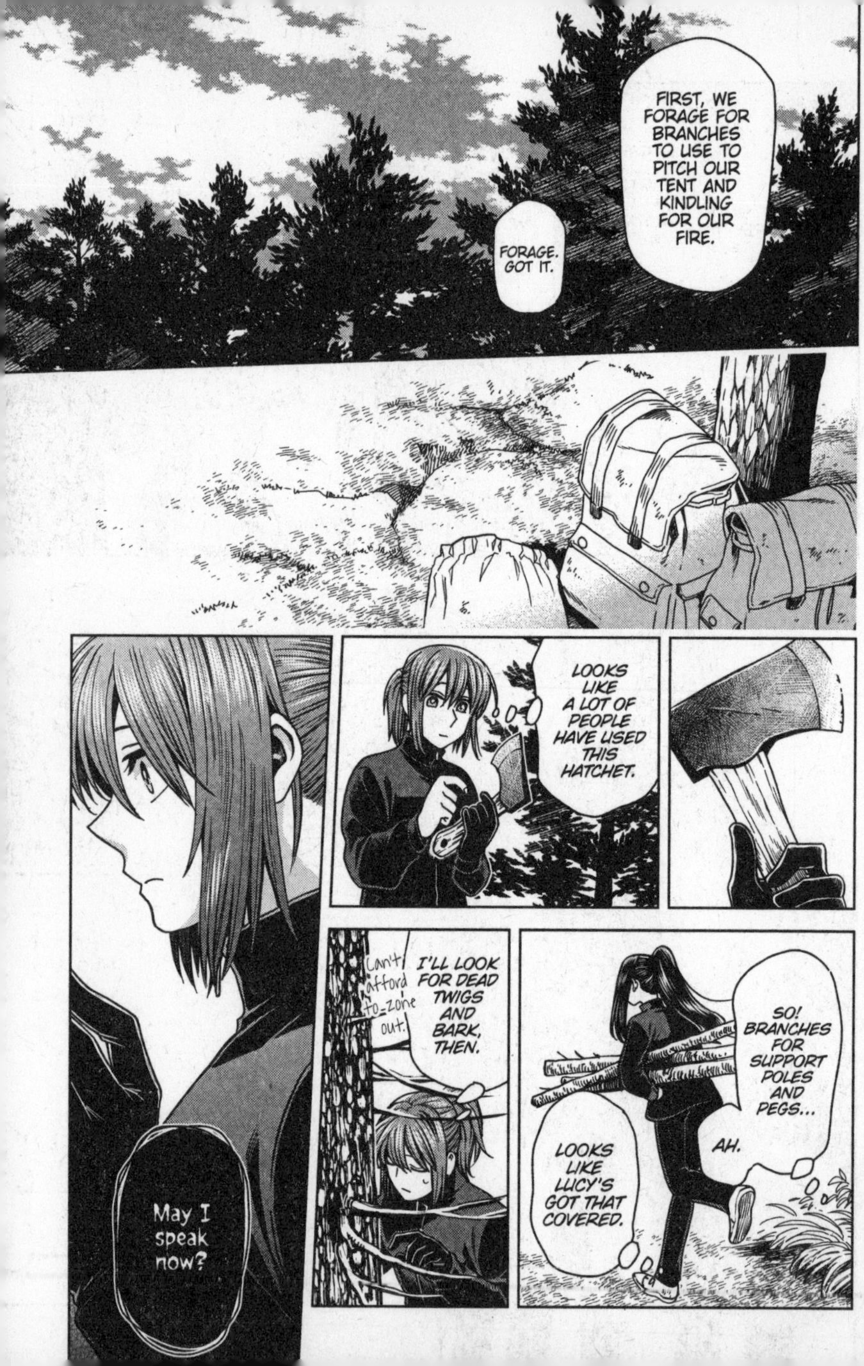
FIRST, WE FORAGE FOR BRANCHES TO USE TO PITCH OUR TENT AND KINDLING FOR OUR FIRE.
FORAGE. GOT IT.
LOOKS LIKE A LOT OF PEOPLE HAVE USED THIS HATCHET.
SO! BRANCHES FOR SUPPORT POLES AND PEGS...
AH.
LOOKS LIKE LUCY'S GOT THAT COVERED.
I'LL LOOK FOR DEAD TWIGS AND BARK, THEN.
Can't afford to zone out.
May I speak now?

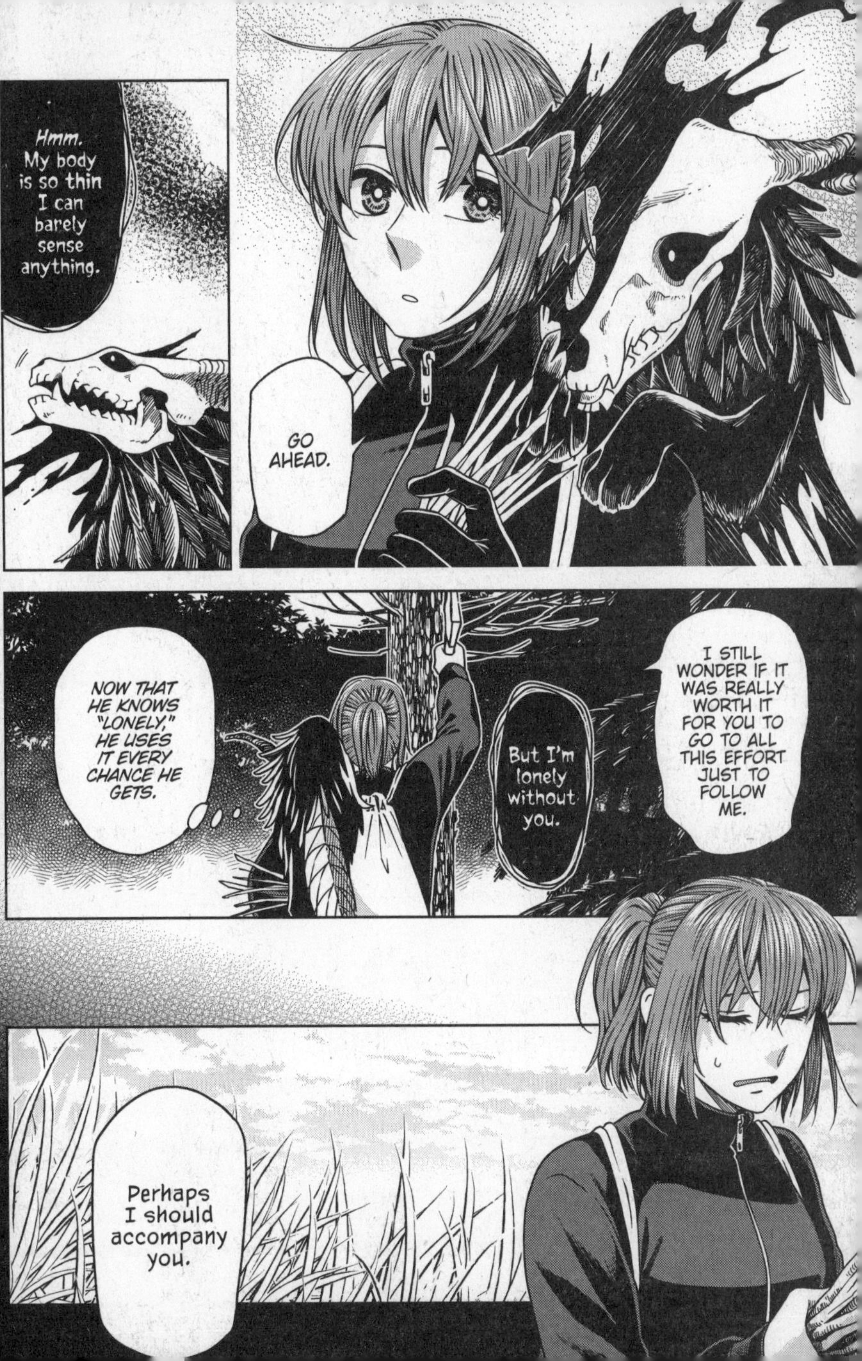
GO AHEAD.
Hmm. My body is so thin I can barely sense anything.
I STILL WONDER IF IT WAS REALLY WORTH IT FOR YOU TO GO TO ALL THIS EFFORT JUST TO FOLLOW ME.
But I'm lonely without you.
NOW THAT HE KNOWS "LONELY," HE USES IT EVERY CHANCE HE GETS.
Perhaps I should accompany you.

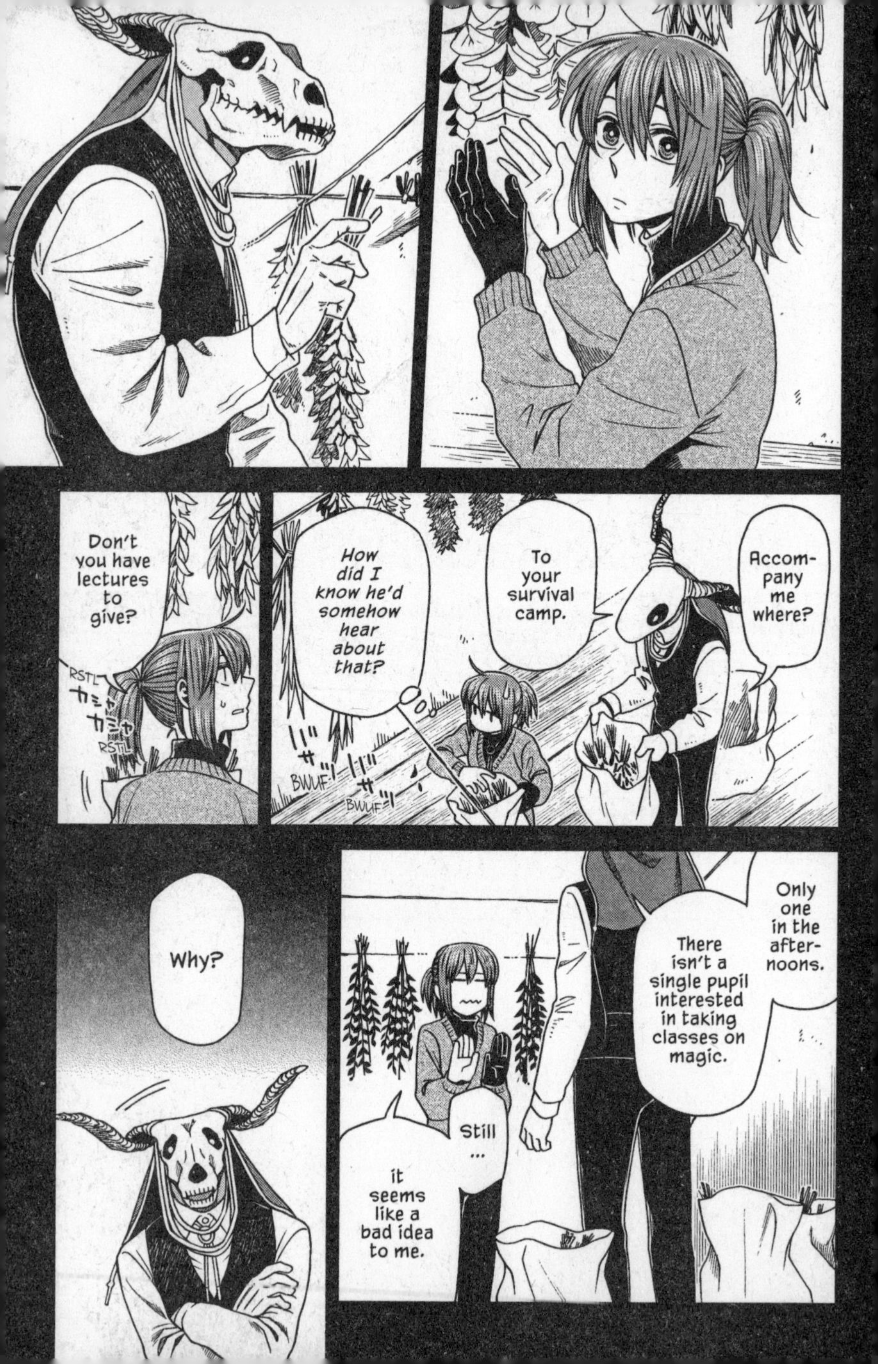
Accompany me where?
To your survival camp.
How did I know he'd somehow hear about that?
BWUF
BWUF
Don't you have lectures to give?
RSTL
RSTL
Only one in the afternoons.
There isn't a single pupil interested in taking classes on magic.
Still ...
it seems like a bad idea to me.
Why?

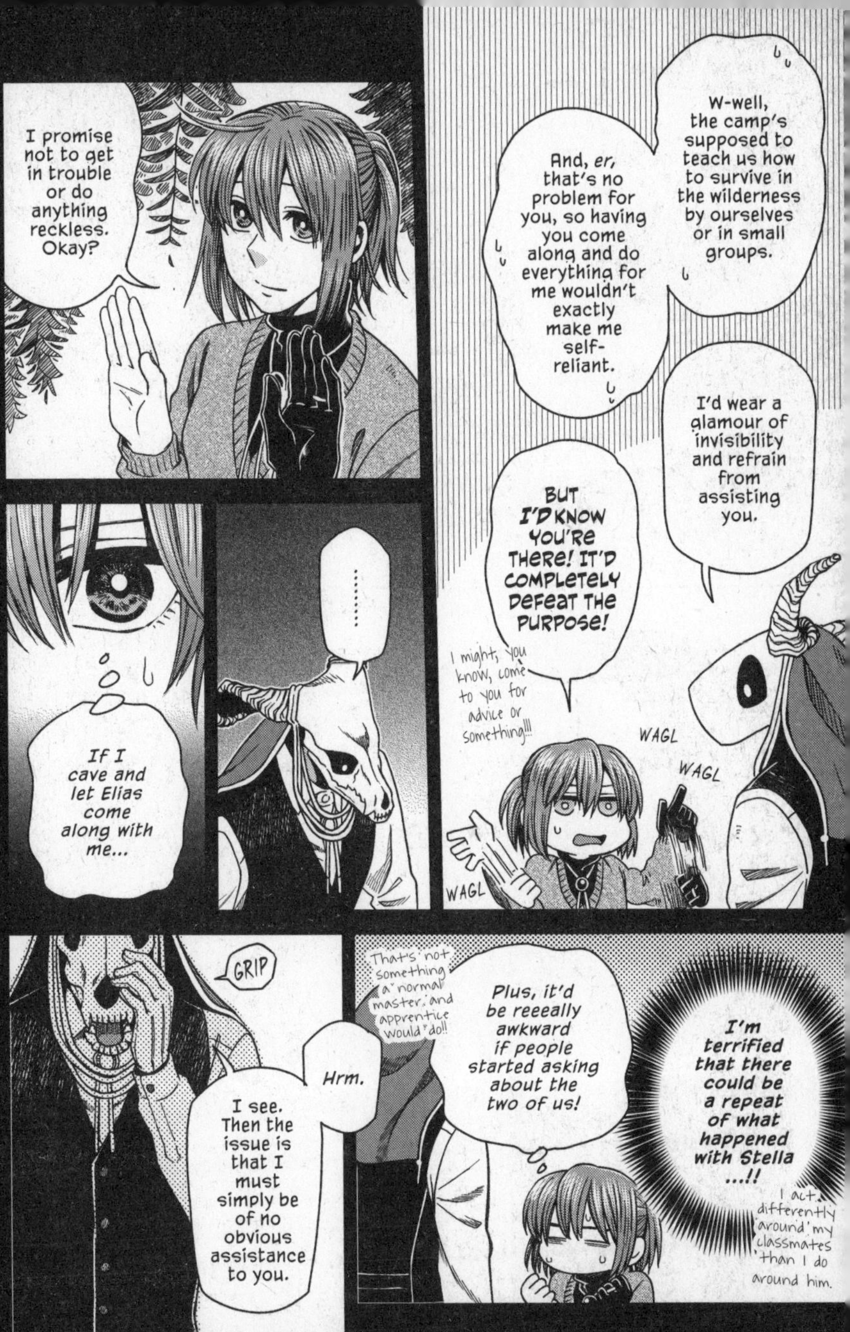
W-well, the camp's supposed to teach us how to survive in the wilderness by ourselves or in small groups.
And, *er*, that's no problem for you, so having you come along and do everything for me wouldn't exactly make me self-reliant.
I'd wear a glamour of invisibility and refrain from assisting you.
BUT *I'D* KNOW YOU'RE THERE! IT'D COMPLETELY DEFEAT THE PURPOSE!
I might, you know, come to you for advice or something!!!
WAGL
WAGL
WAGL
I promise not to get in trouble or do anything reckless. Okay?
......
If I cave and let Elias come along with me...
Plus, it'd be reeeally awkward if people started asking about the two of us!
That's not something a normal master and apprentice would do!!
I'm terrified that there could be a repeat of what happened with Stella ...!!
I act differently around my classmates than I do around him.
GRIP
Hrm.
I see. Then the issue is that I must simply be of no obvious assistance to you.

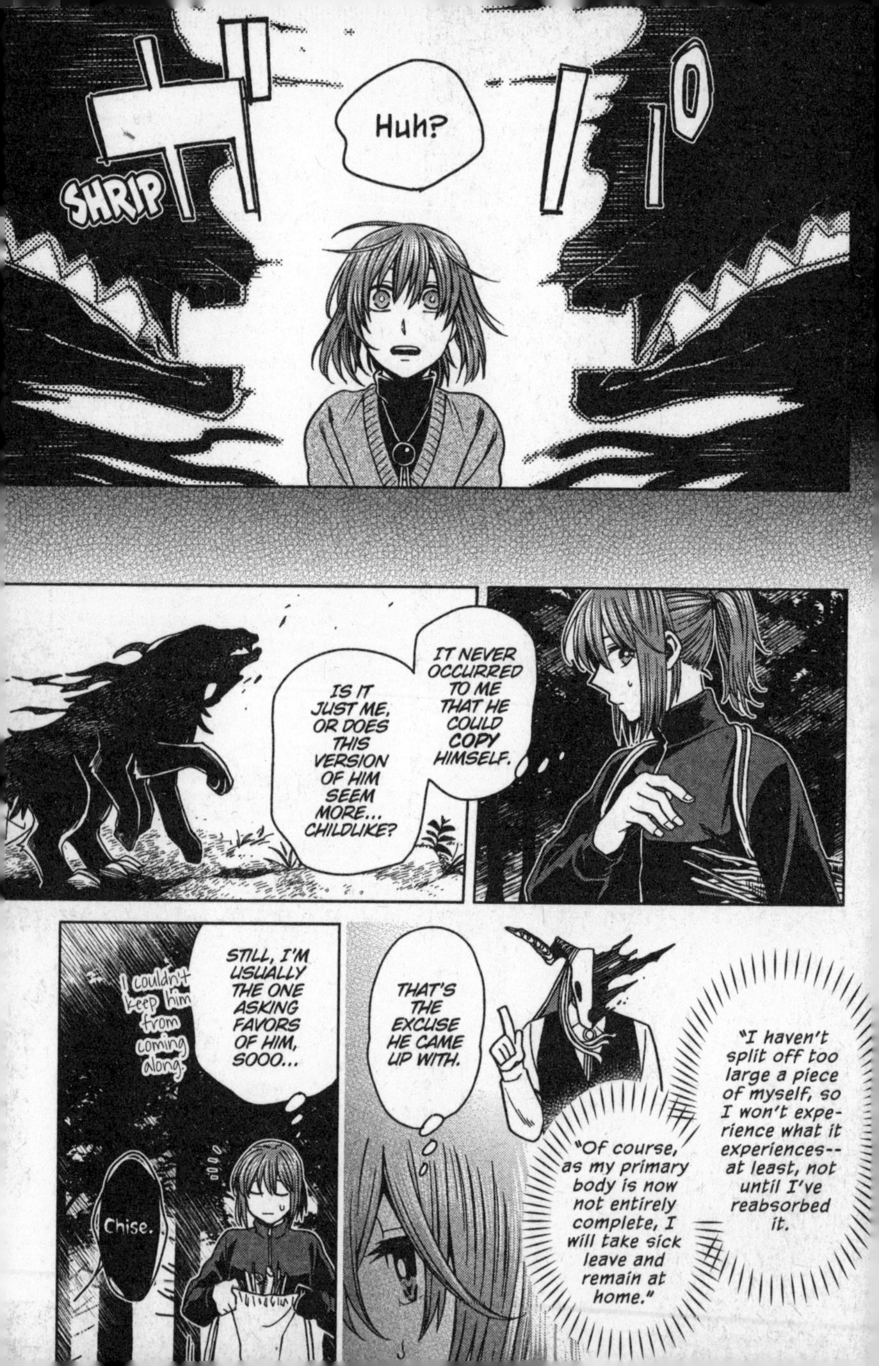
SHRIP
Huh?
IT NEVER OCCURRED TO ME THAT HE COULD COPY HIMSELF.
IS IT JUST ME, OR DOES THIS VERSION OF HIM SEEM MORE... CHILDLIKE?
"I haven't split off too large a piece of myself, so I won't experience what it experiences--at least, not until I've reabsorbed it.
"Of course, as my primary body is now not entirely complete, I will take sick leave and remain at home."
THAT'S THE EXCUSE HE CAME UP WITH.
STILL, I'M USUALLY THE ONE ASKING FAVORS OF HIM, SOOO...
I couldn't keep him from coming along.
Chise.

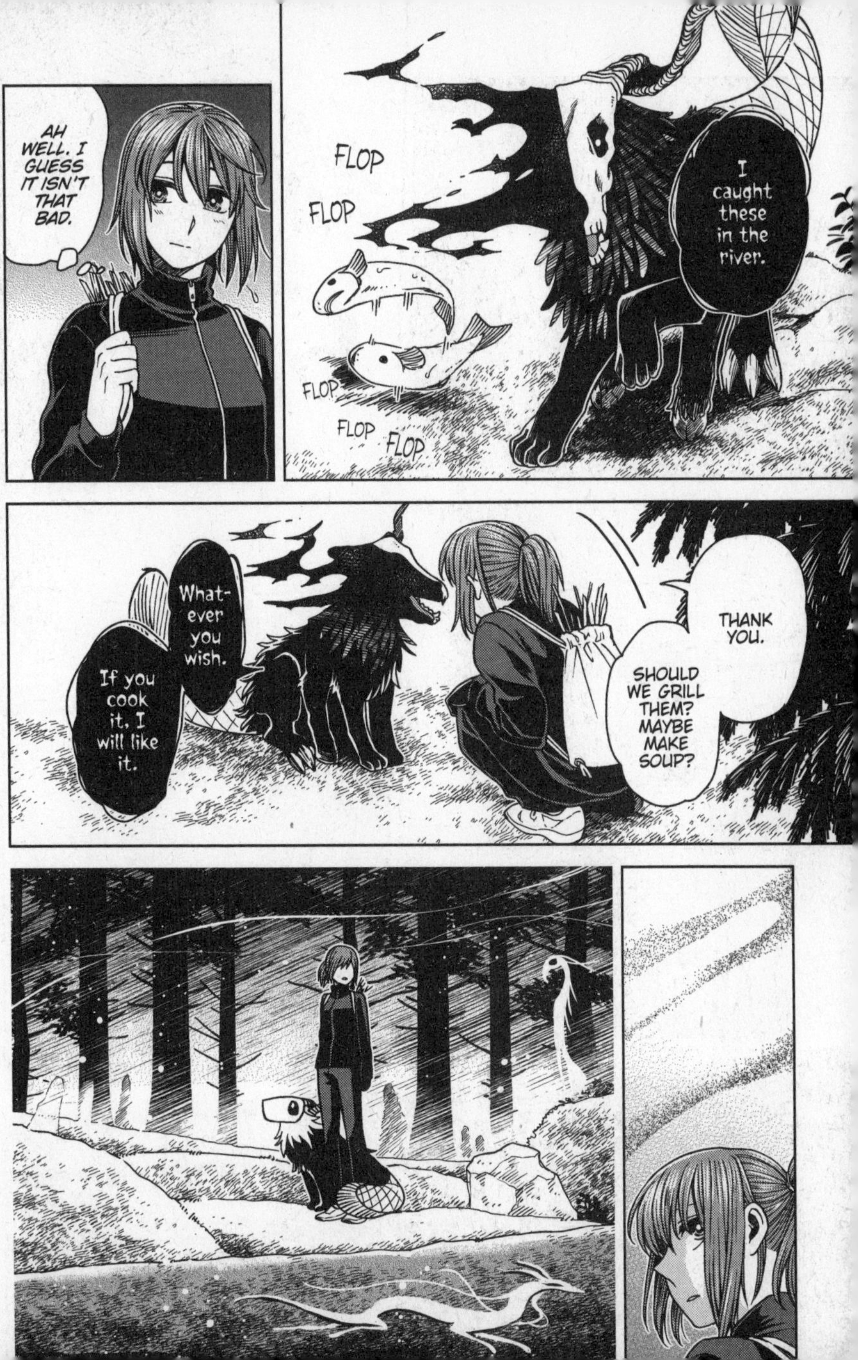
I caught these in the river.
FLOP
FLOP
FLOP
FLOP
FLOP
AH WELL. I GUESS IT ISN'T THAT BAD.
THANK YOU.
SHOULD WE GRILL THEM? MAYBE MAKE SOUP?
What-ever you wish.
If you cook it, I will like it.

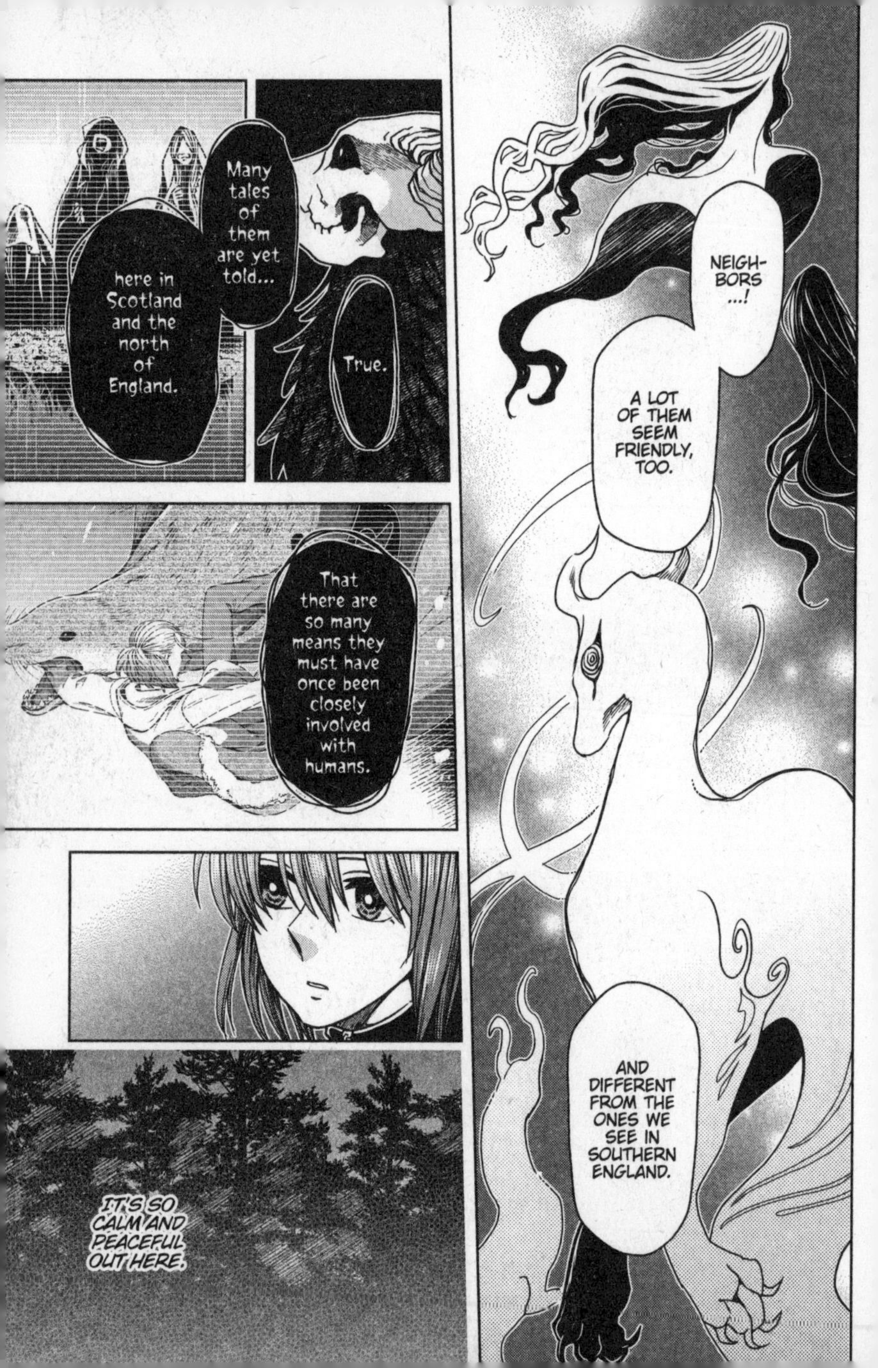
NEIGHBORS ...!
A LOT OF THEM SEEM FRIENDLY, TOO.
AND DIFFERENT FROM THE ONES WE SEE IN SOUTHERN ENGLAND.
Many tales of them are yet told...
here in Scotland and the north of England.
True.
That there are so many means they must have once been closely involved with humans.
IT'S SO CALM AND PEACEFUL OUT HERE.

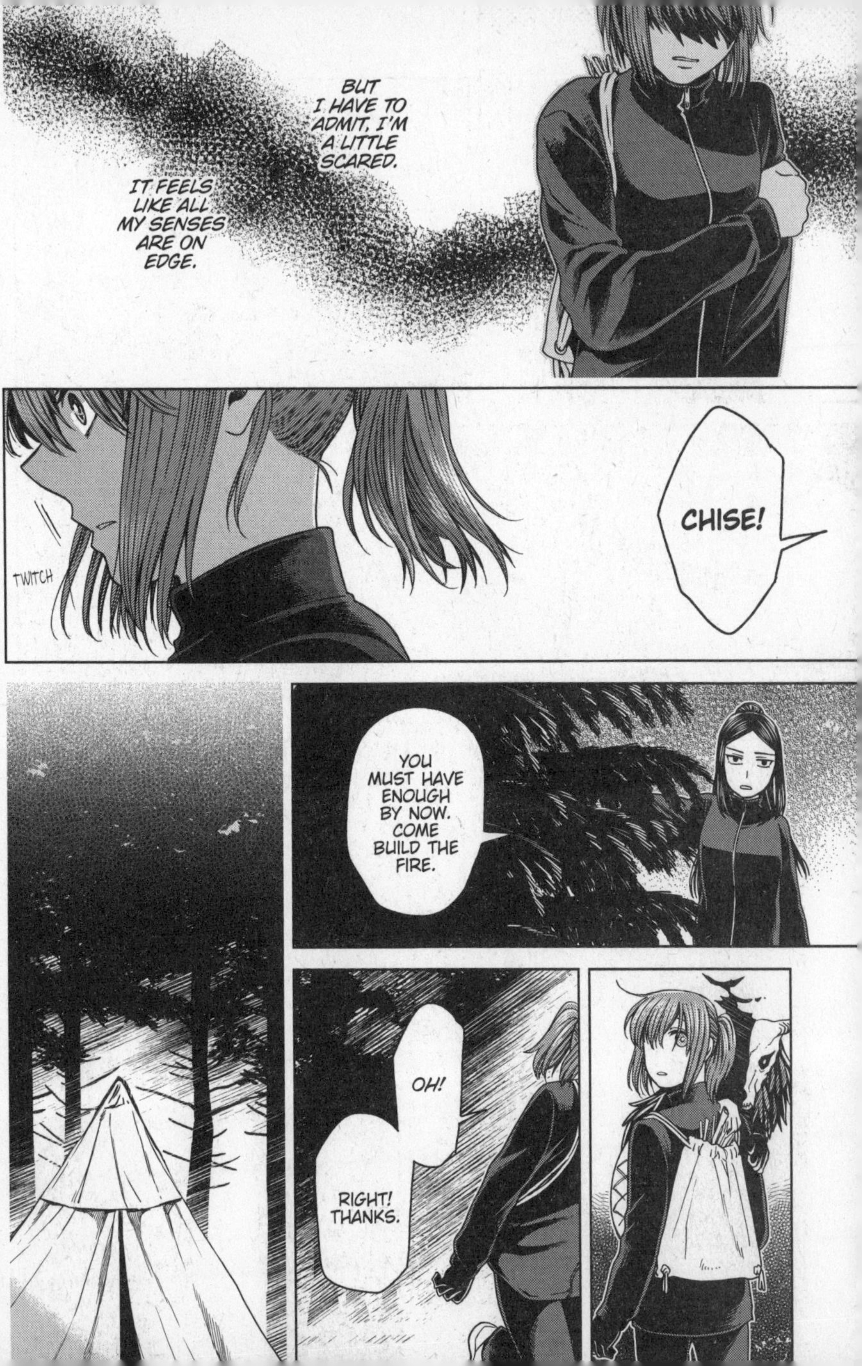
BUT I HAVE TO ADMIT, I'M A LITTLE SCARED.
IT FEELS LIKE ALL MY SENSES ARE ON EDGE.
CHISE!
TWITCH
YOU MUST HAVE ENOUGH BY NOW. COME BUILD THE FIRE.
OH!
RIGHT! THANKS.

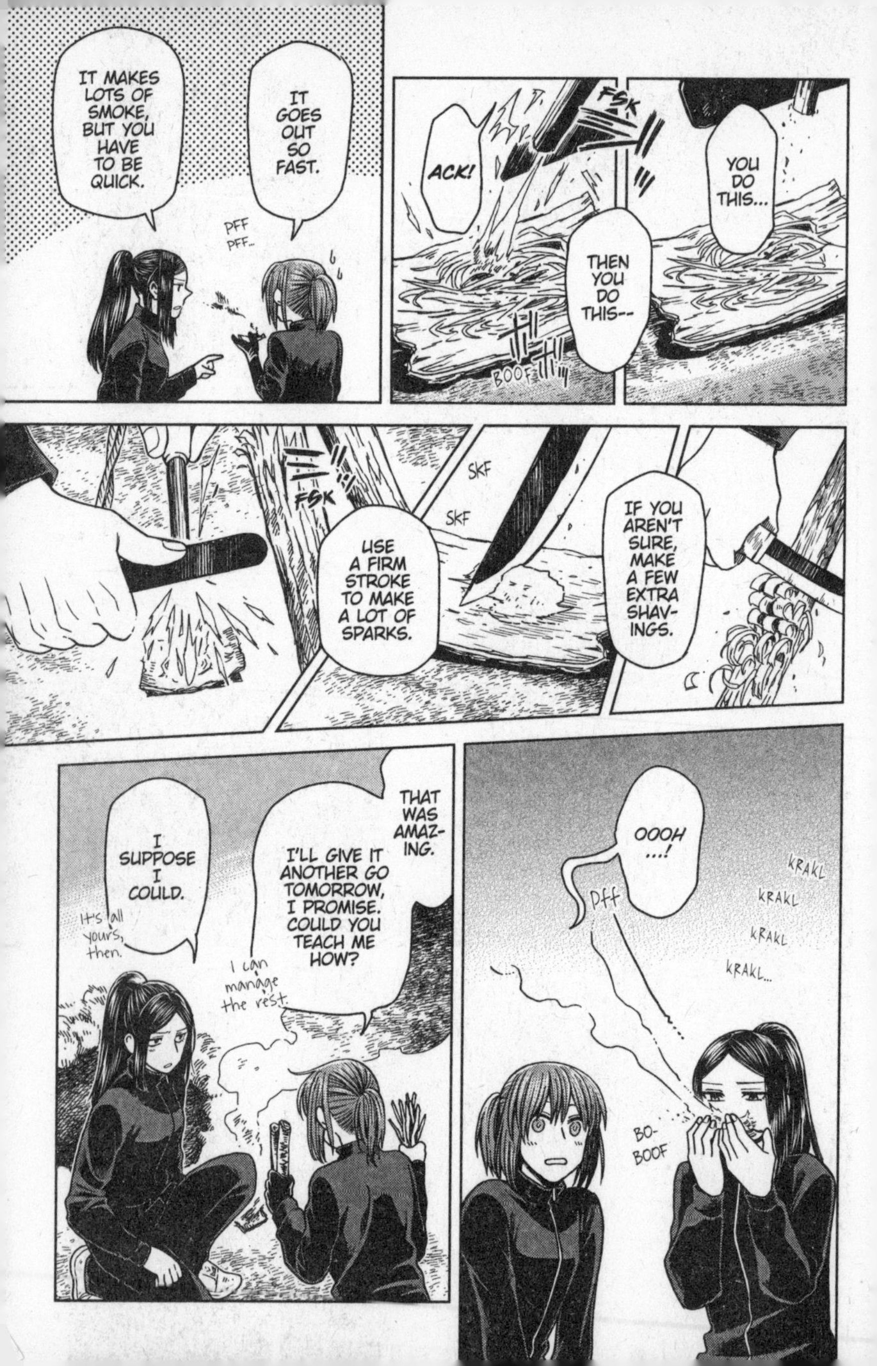
YOU DO THIS...
THEN YOU DO THIS--
BOOF
FSK
ACK!
IT GOES OUT SO FAST.
IT MAKES LOTS OF SMOKE, BUT YOU HAVE TO BE QUICK.
PFF PFF...
IF YOU AREN'T SURE, MAKE A FEW EXTRA SHAV-INGS.
SKF
SKF
USE A FIRM STROKE TO MAKE A LOT OF SPARKS.
FSK
OOOH ...!
Pff
KRAKL
KRAKL
KRAKL
KRAKL...
BO-BOOF
THAT WAS AMAZ-ING.
I'LL GIVE IT ANOTHER GO TOMORROW, I PROMISE. COULD YOU TEACH ME HOW?
I can manage the rest.
I SUPPOSE I COULD.
It's all yours, then.

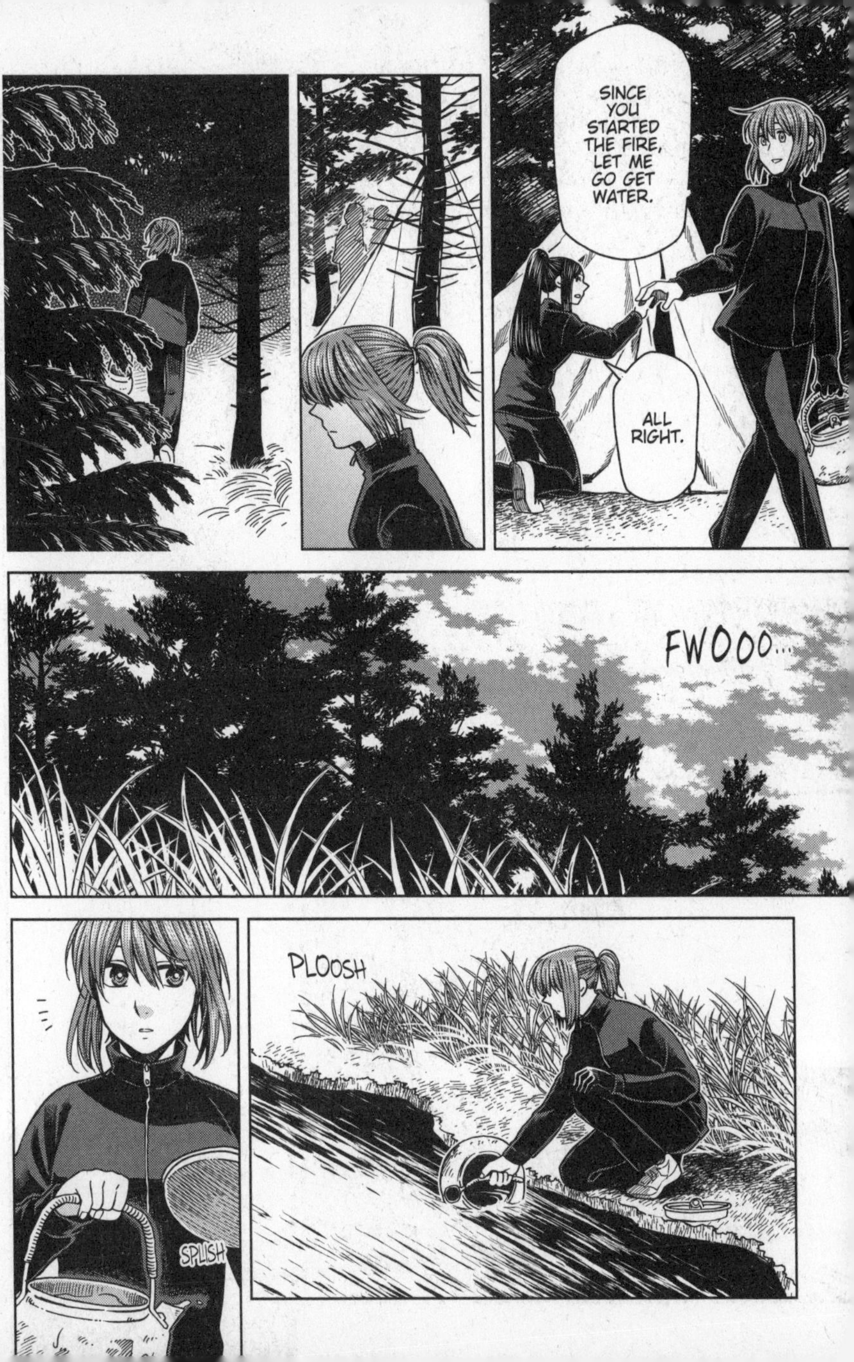
SINCE YOU STARTED THE FIRE, LET ME GO GET WATER.
ALL RIGHT.
FWOOO...
PLOOSH
SPLISH

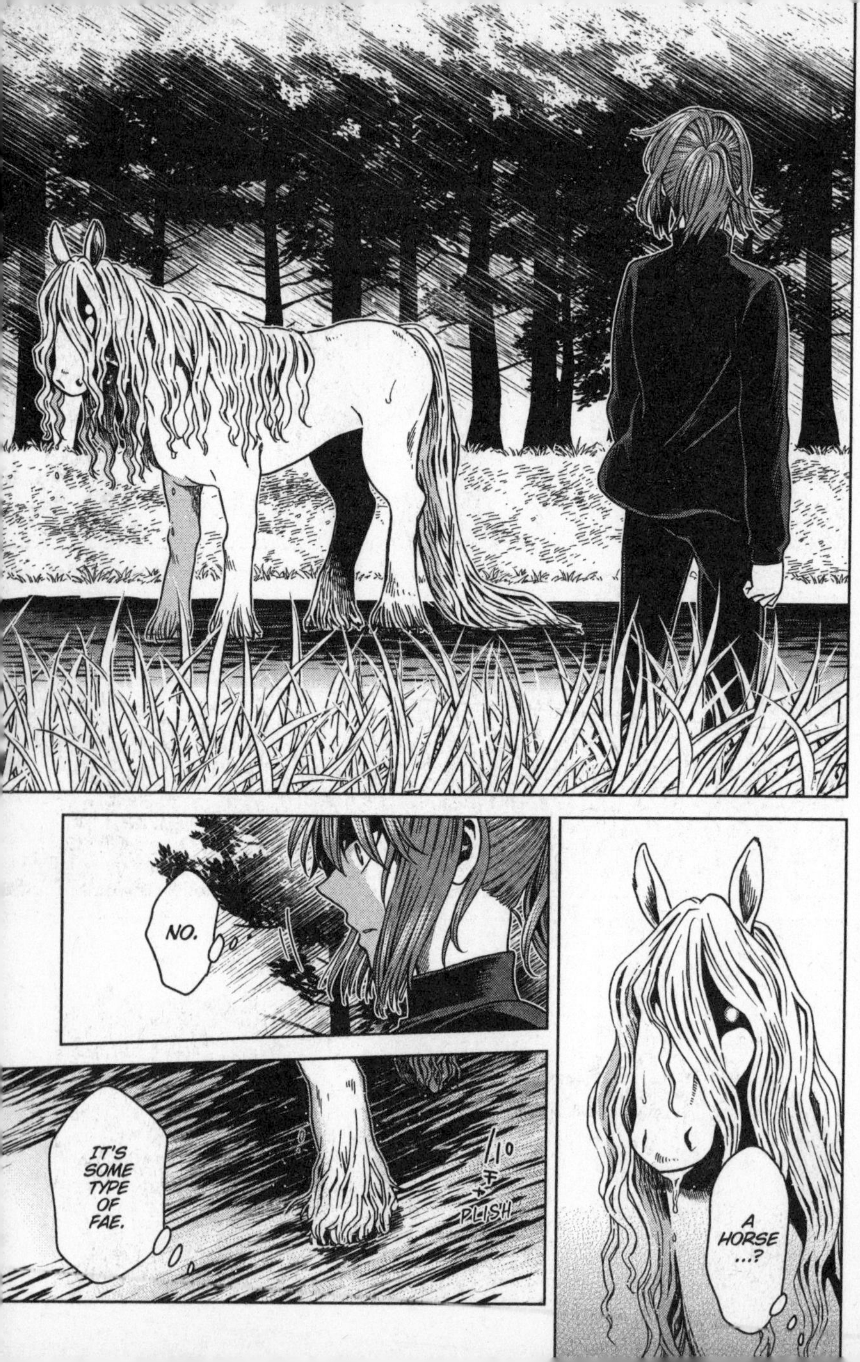
A HORSE ...?
NO.
IT'S SOME TYPE OF FAE.
PLISH

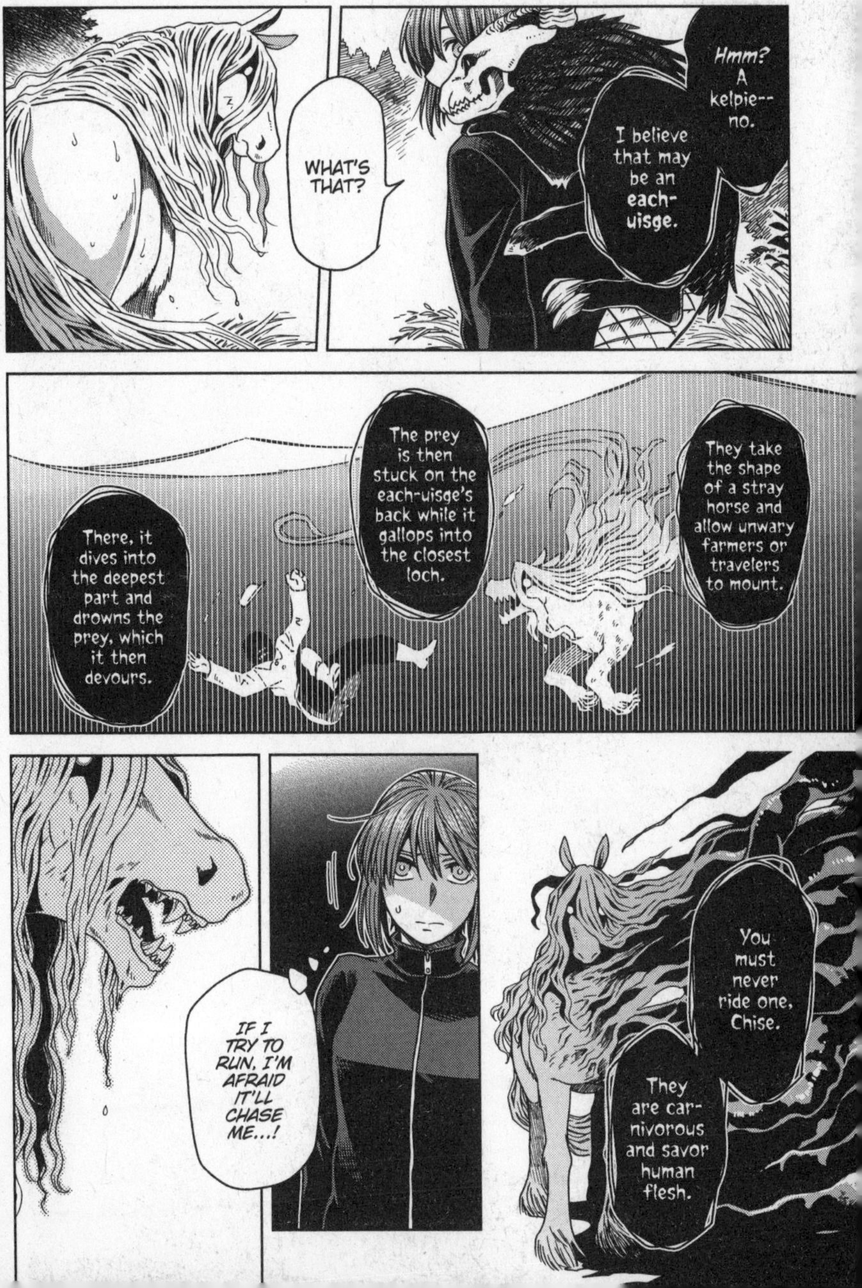
Hmm? A kelpie-- no.
I believe that may be an each-uisge.
WHAT'S THAT?
They take the shape of a stray horse and allow unwary farmers or travelers to mount.
The prey is then stuck on the each-uisge's back while it gallops into the closest loch.
There, it dives into the deepest part and drowns the prey, which it then devours.
You must never ride one, Chise.
They are carnivorous and savor human flesh.
IF I TRY TO RUN, I'M AFRAID IT'LL CHASE ME...!

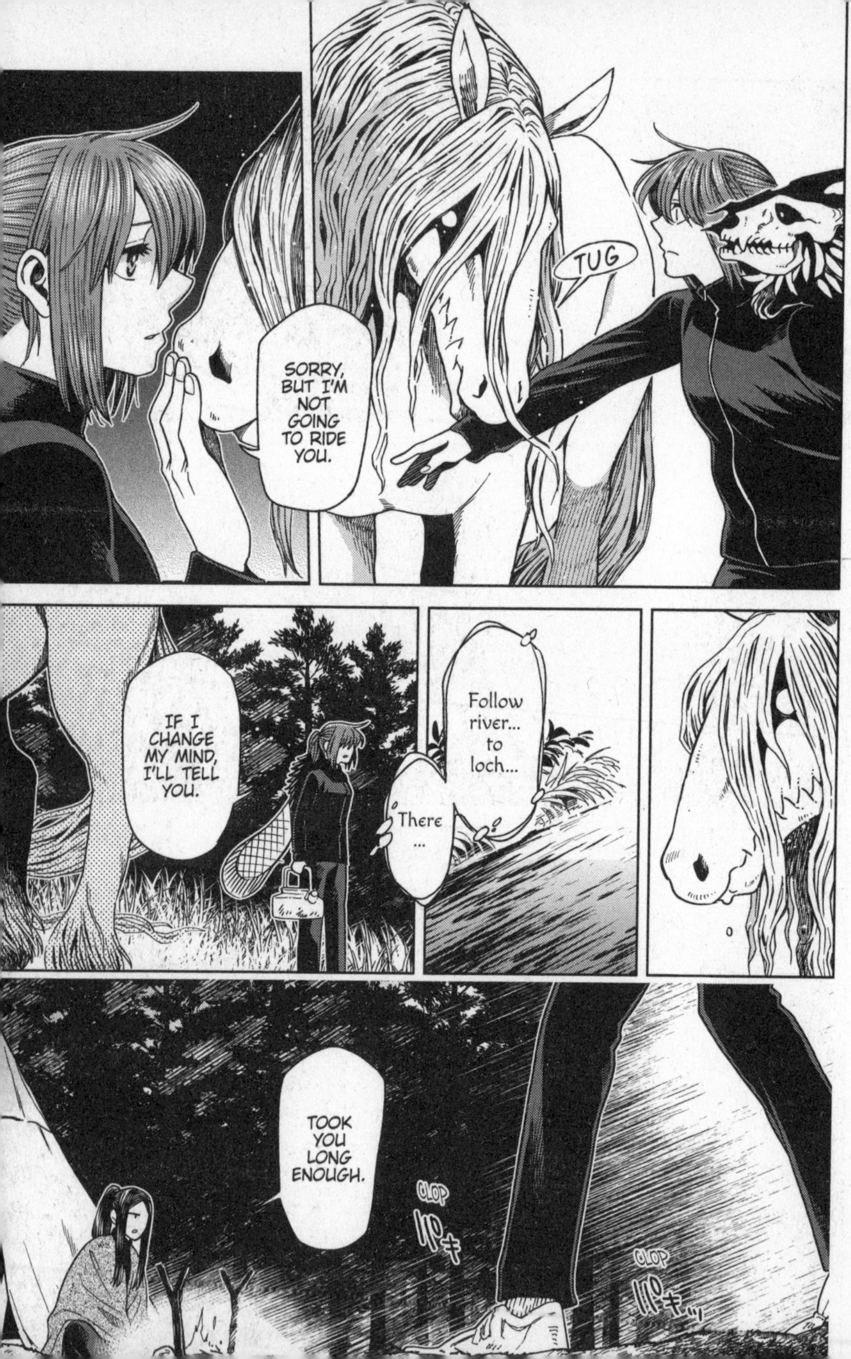
TUG
SORRY, BUT I'M NOT GOING TO RIDE YOU.
Follow river... to loch...
There ...
IF I CHANGE MY MIND, I'LL TELL YOU.
TOOK YOU LONG ENOUGH.
CLOP
パキ
CLOP
パキッ

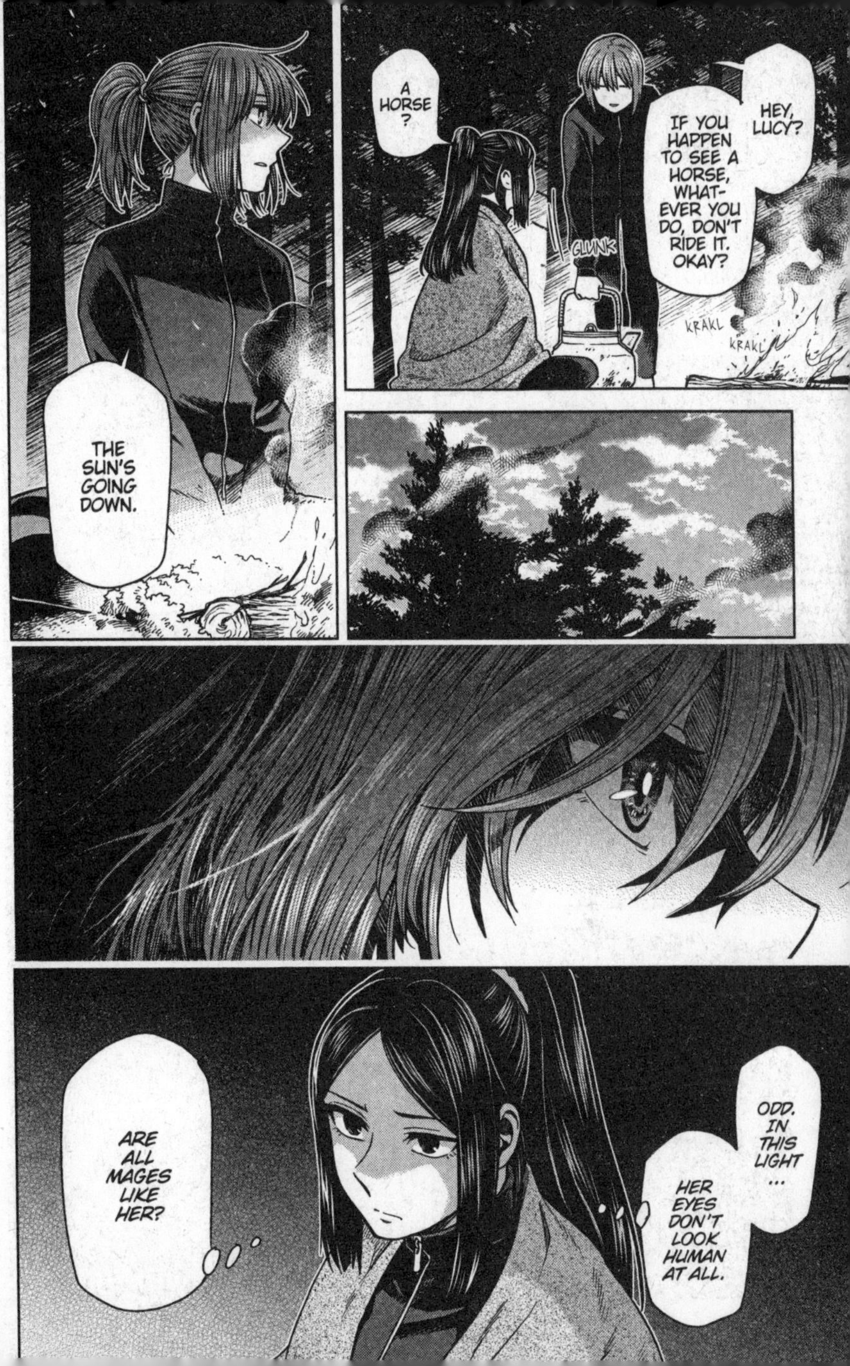
HEY, LUCY?
IF YOU HAPPEN TO SEE A HORSE, WHATEVER YOU DO, DON'T RIDE IT. OKAY?
A HORSE?
GLUNK
KRAKL
KRAKL
THE SUN'S GOING DOWN.
ODD. IN THIS LIGHT...
HER EYES DON'T LOOK HUMAN AT ALL.
ARE ALL MAGES LIKE HER?

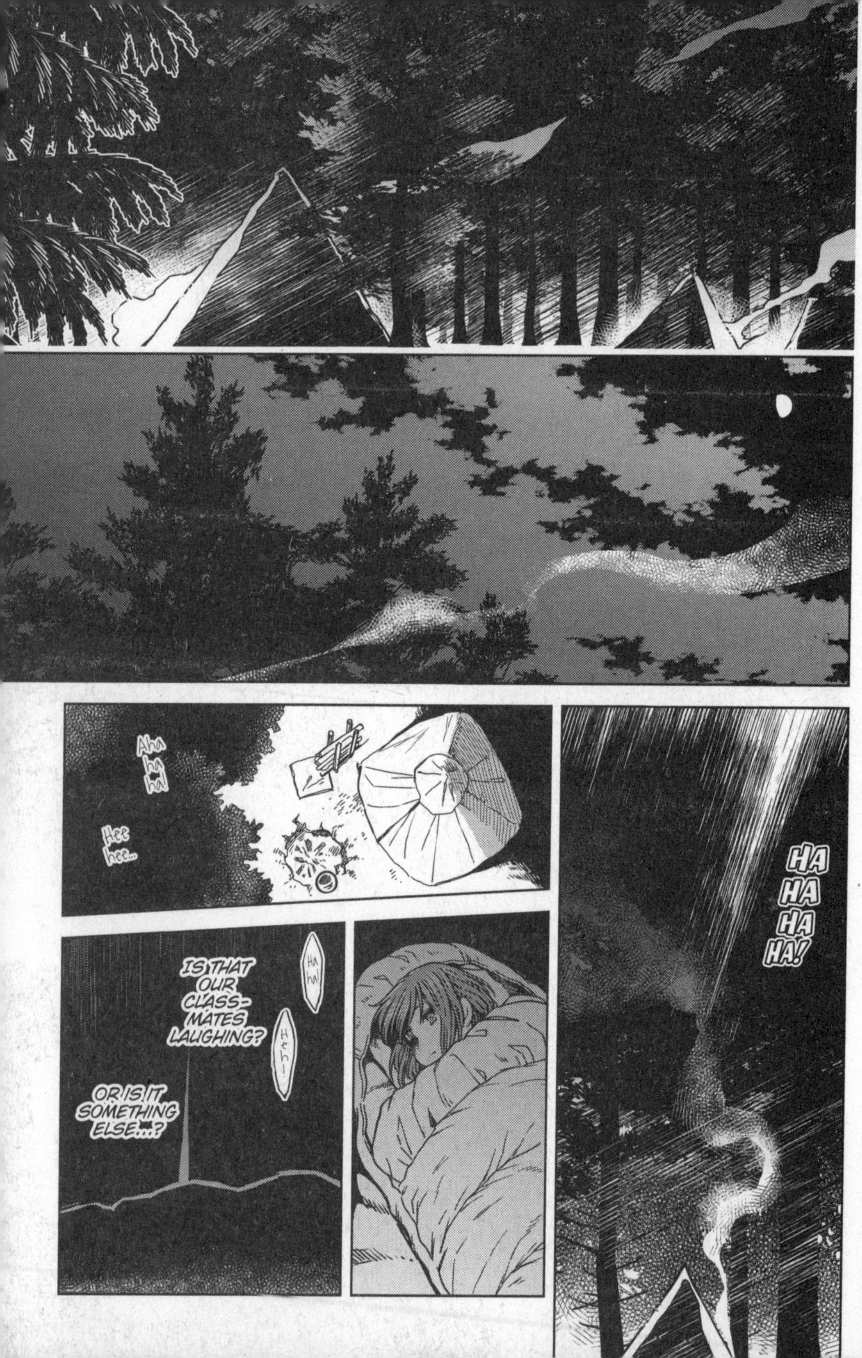
HA HA HA HA!
Aha ha ha!
Hee hee...
Ha ha!
Heh!
IS THAT OUR CLASS-MATES LAUGHING?
OR IS IT SOMETHING ELSE...?

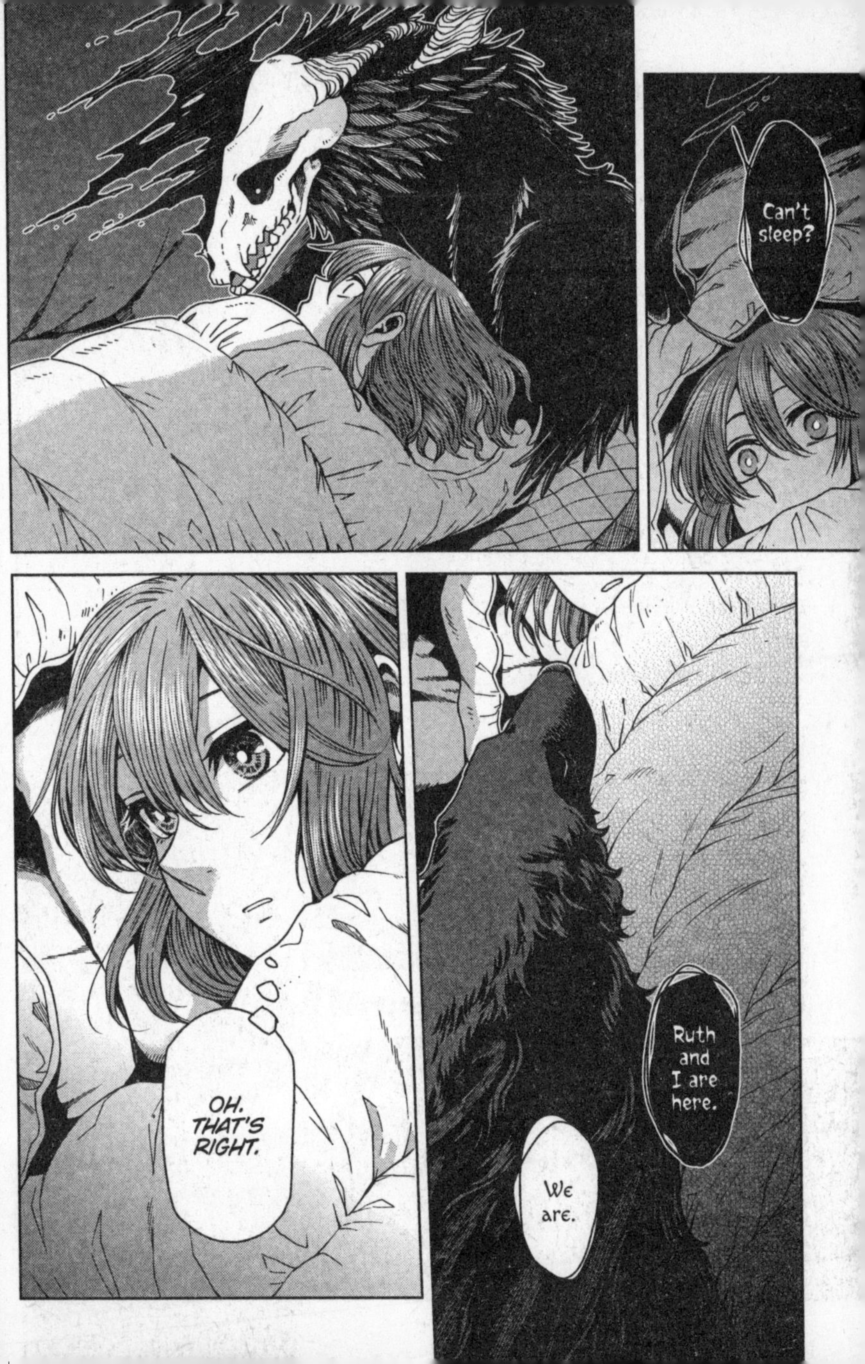
Can't sleep?
Ruth and I are here.
We are.
OH. THAT'S RIGHT.

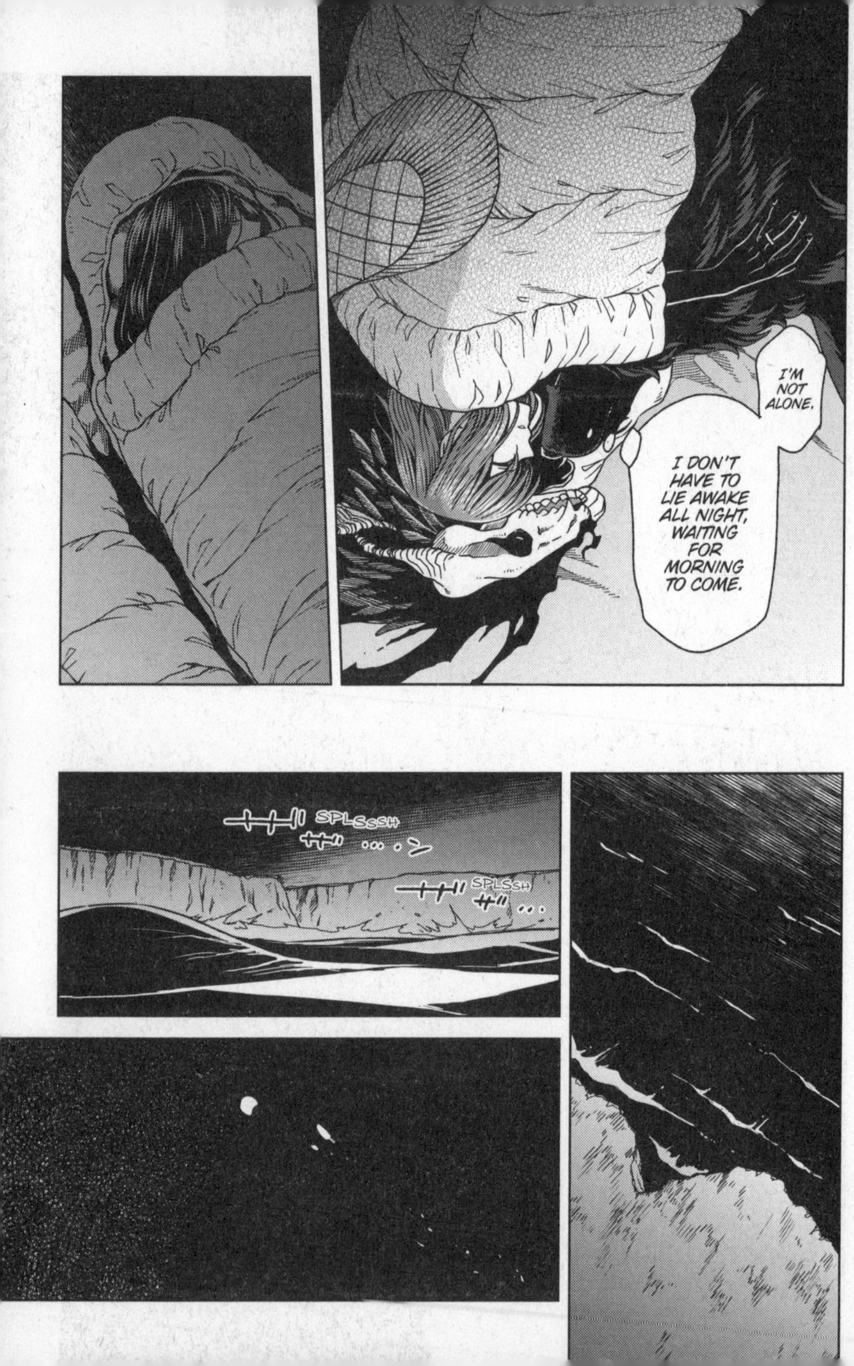
I'M NOT ALONE.
I DON'T HAVE TO LIE AWAKE ALL NIGHT, WAITING FOR MORNING TO COME.
SPLSSSH
SPLSSH

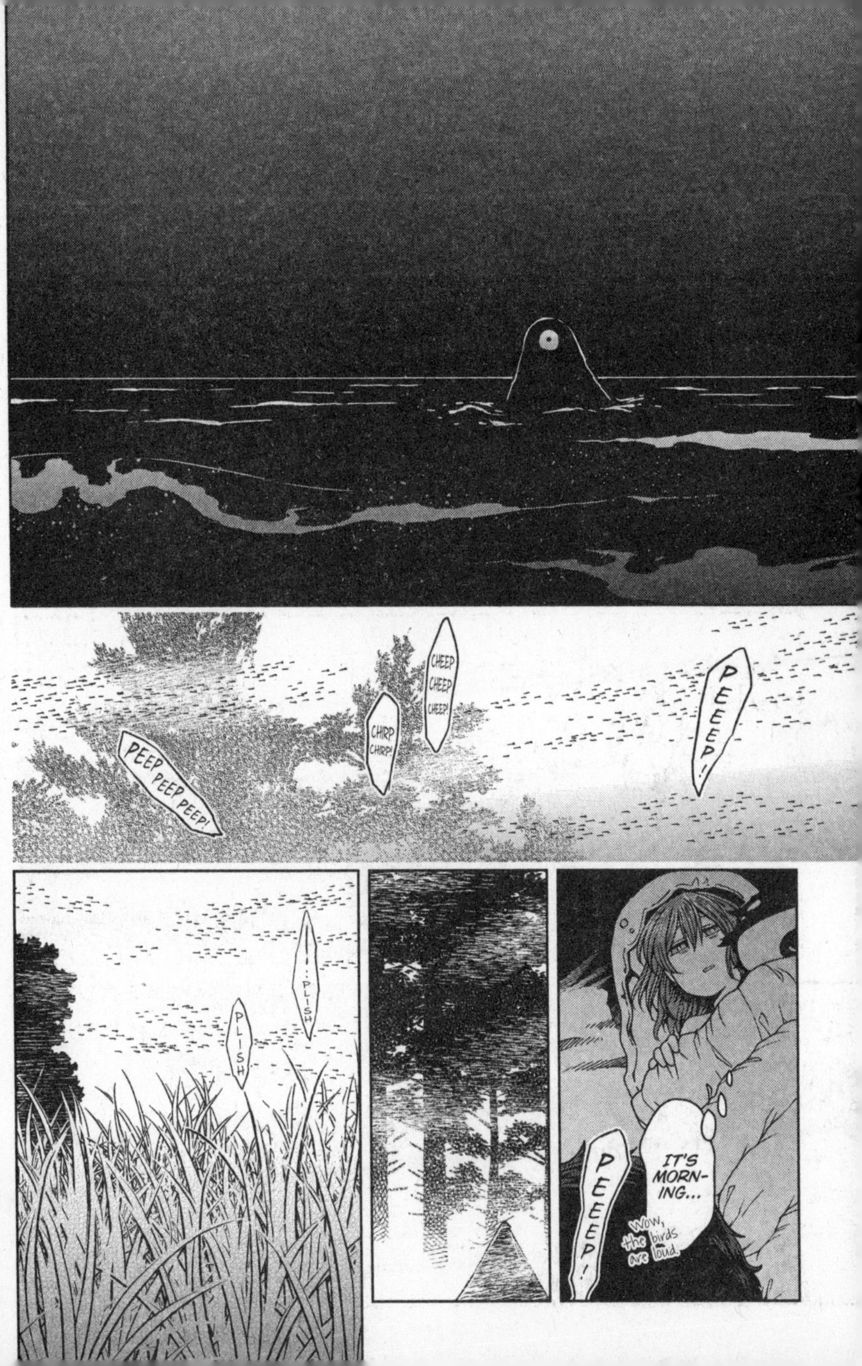
PEEEP!
CHEEP CHEEP CHEEP!
CHIRP CHIRP!
PEEP PEEP PEEP!
IT'S MORNING...
PEEEP!
Wow, the birds are loud.
...PLISH
PLISH

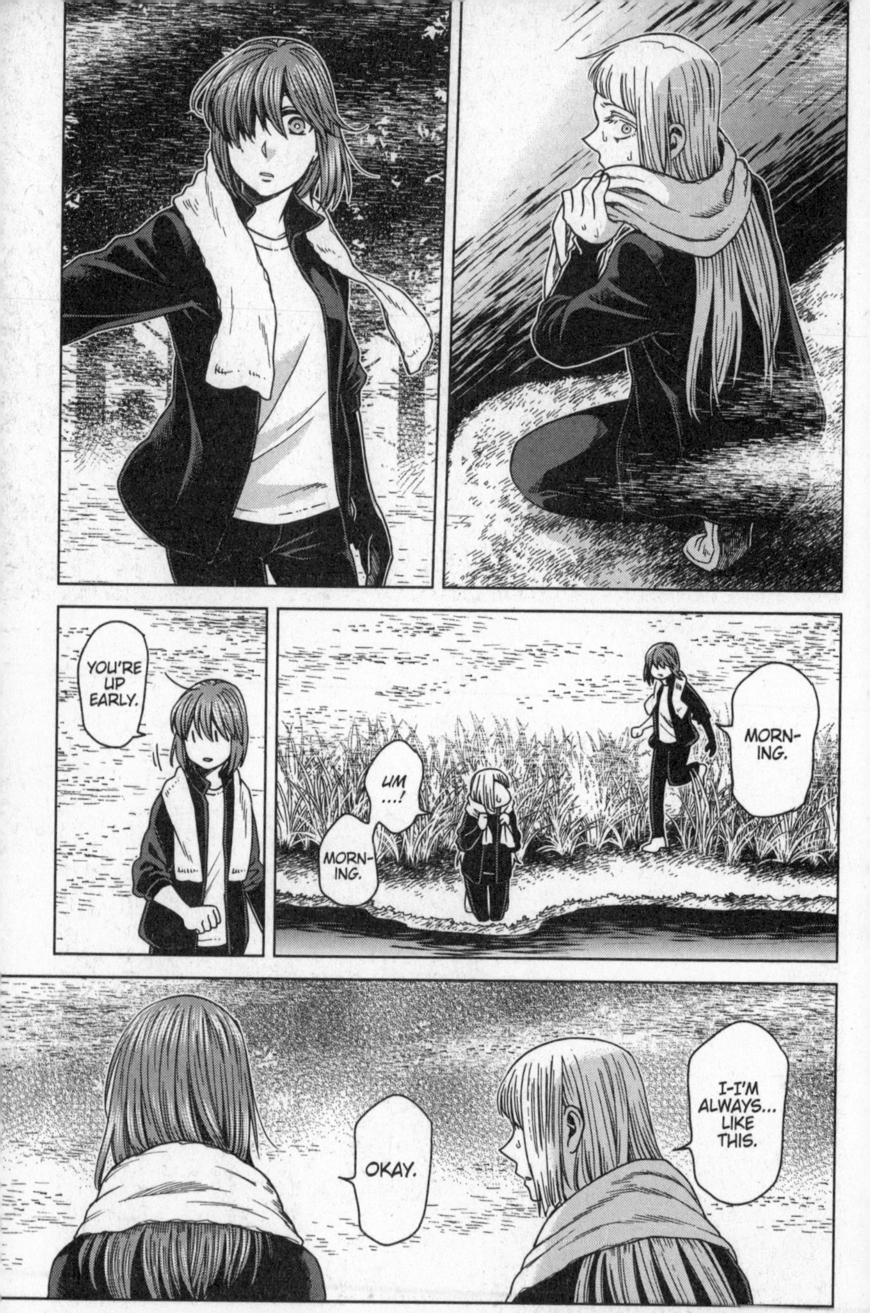
MORN-ING.
UM ...!
MORN-ING.
YOU'RE UP EARLY.
I-I'M ALWAYS... LIKE THIS.
OKAY.

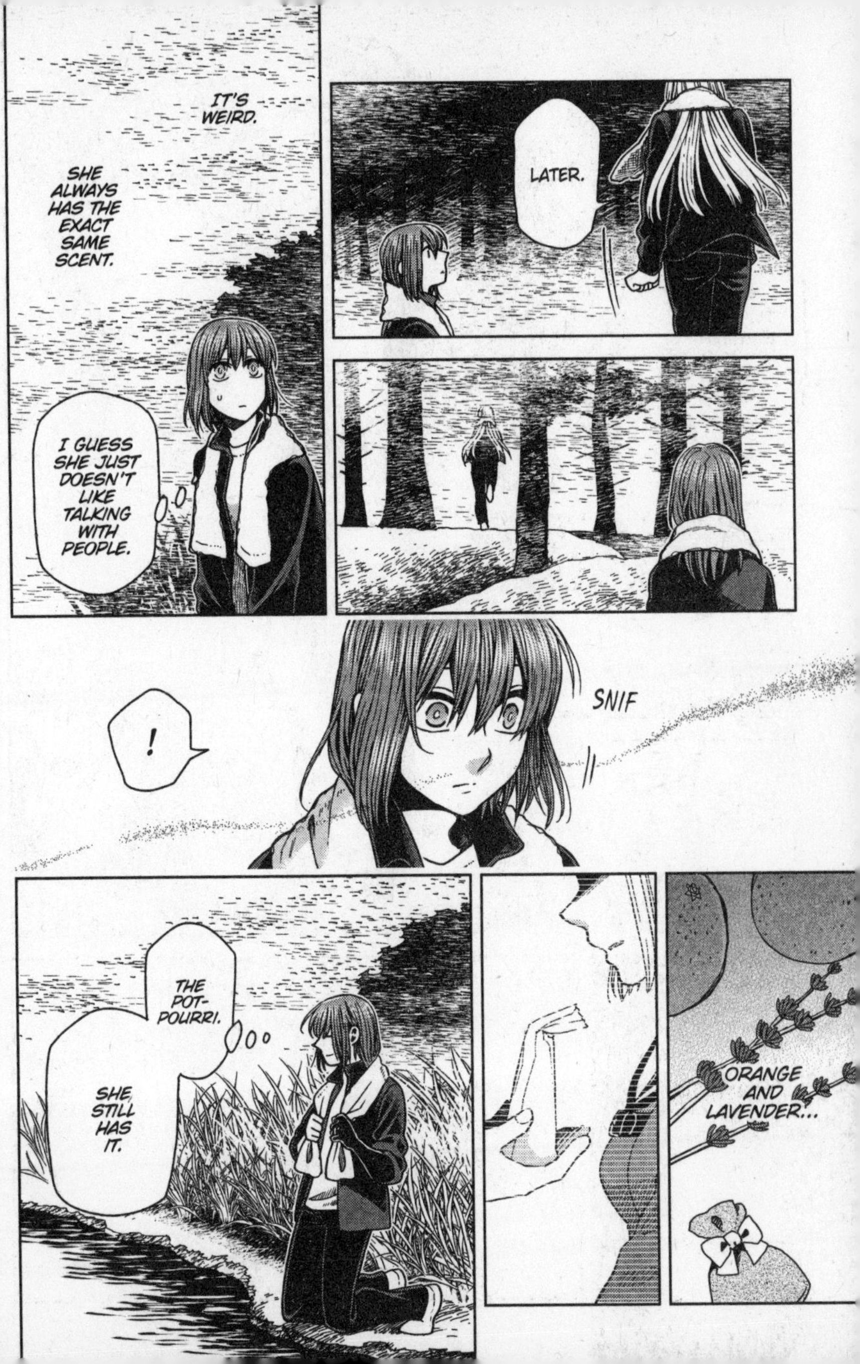
LATER.
IT'S WEIRD.
SHE ALWAYS HAS THE EXACT SAME SCENT.
I GUESS SHE JUST DOESN'T LIKE TALKING WITH PEOPLE.
SNIF
!
ORANGE AND LAVENDER...
THE POT-POURRI.
SHE STILL HAS IT.

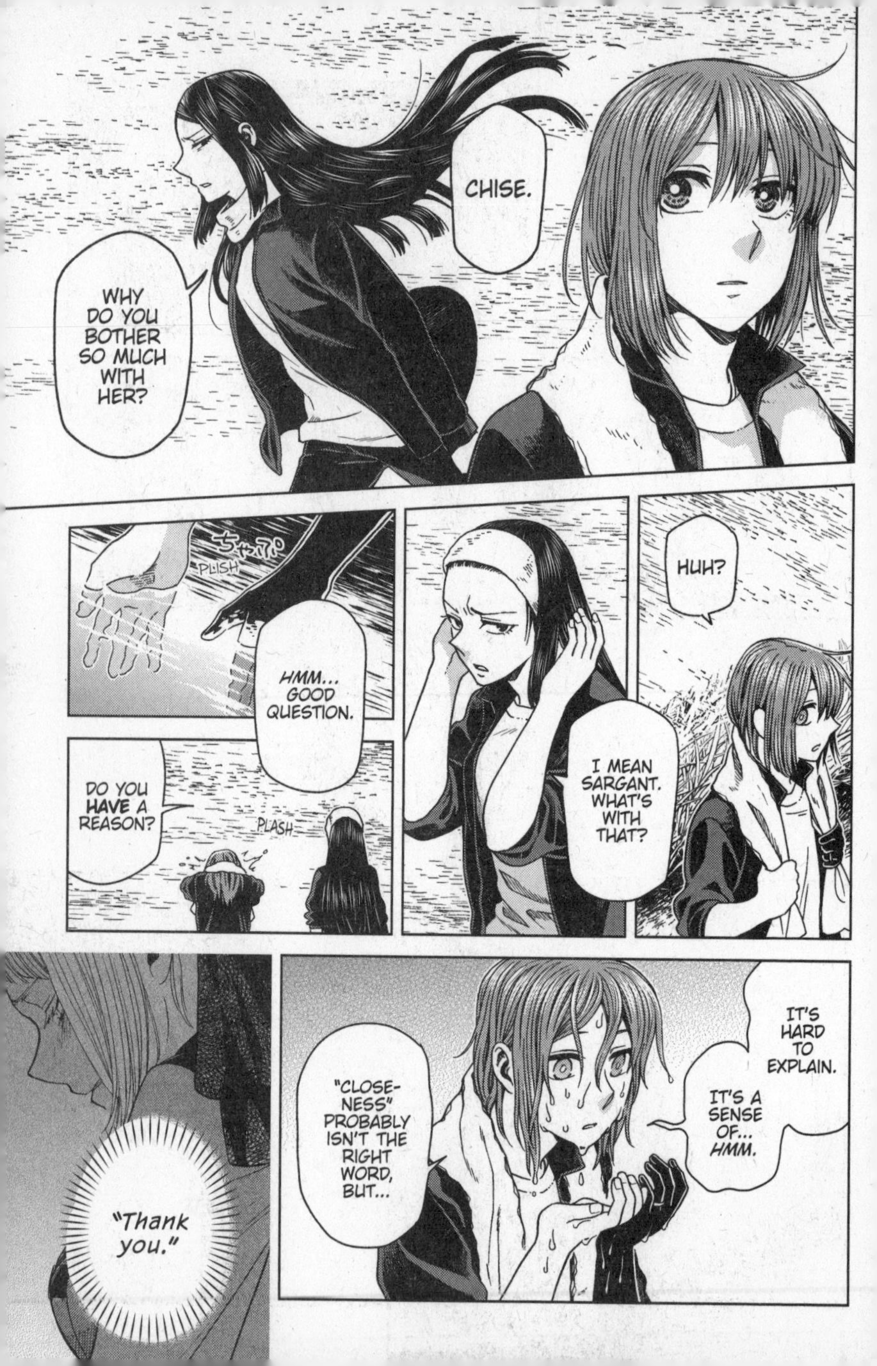
CHISE.
WHY DO YOU BOTHER SO MUCH WITH HER?
HUH?
I MEAN SARGANT. WHAT'S WITH THAT?
ちゃぷ
PLISH
HMM... GOOD QUESTION.
DO YOU HAVE A REASON?
PLASH
IT'S HARD TO EXPLAIN.
IT'S A SENSE OF... HMM.
"CLOSENESS" PROBABLY ISN'T THE RIGHT WORD, BUT...
"Thank you."

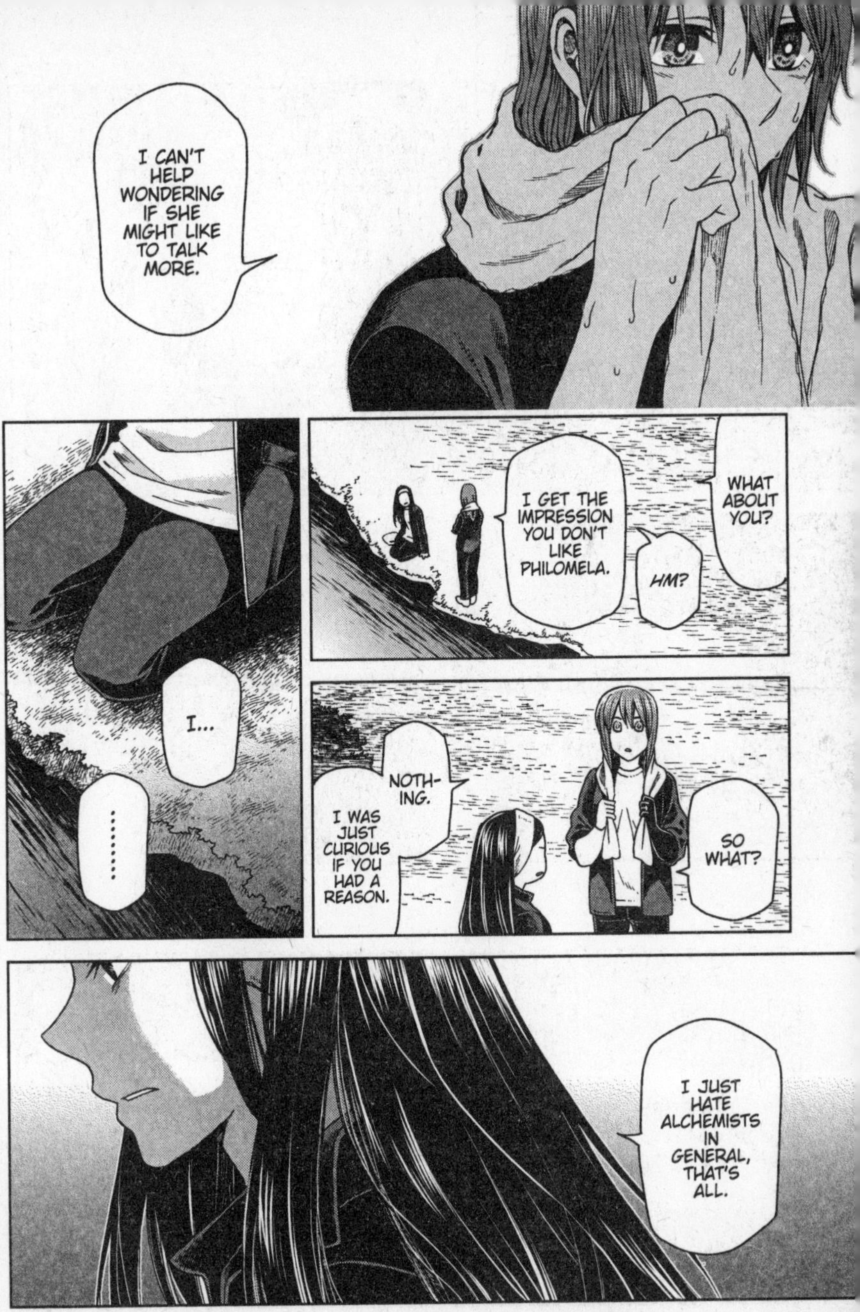
I CAN'T HELP WONDERING IF SHE MIGHT LIKE TO TALK MORE.
WHAT ABOUT YOU?
HM?
I GET THE IMPRESSION YOU DON'T LIKE PHILOMELA.
SO WHAT?
NOTHING.
I WAS JUST CURIOUS IF YOU HAD A REASON.
I...
.........
I JUST HATE ALCHEMISTS IN GENERAL, THAT'S ALL.

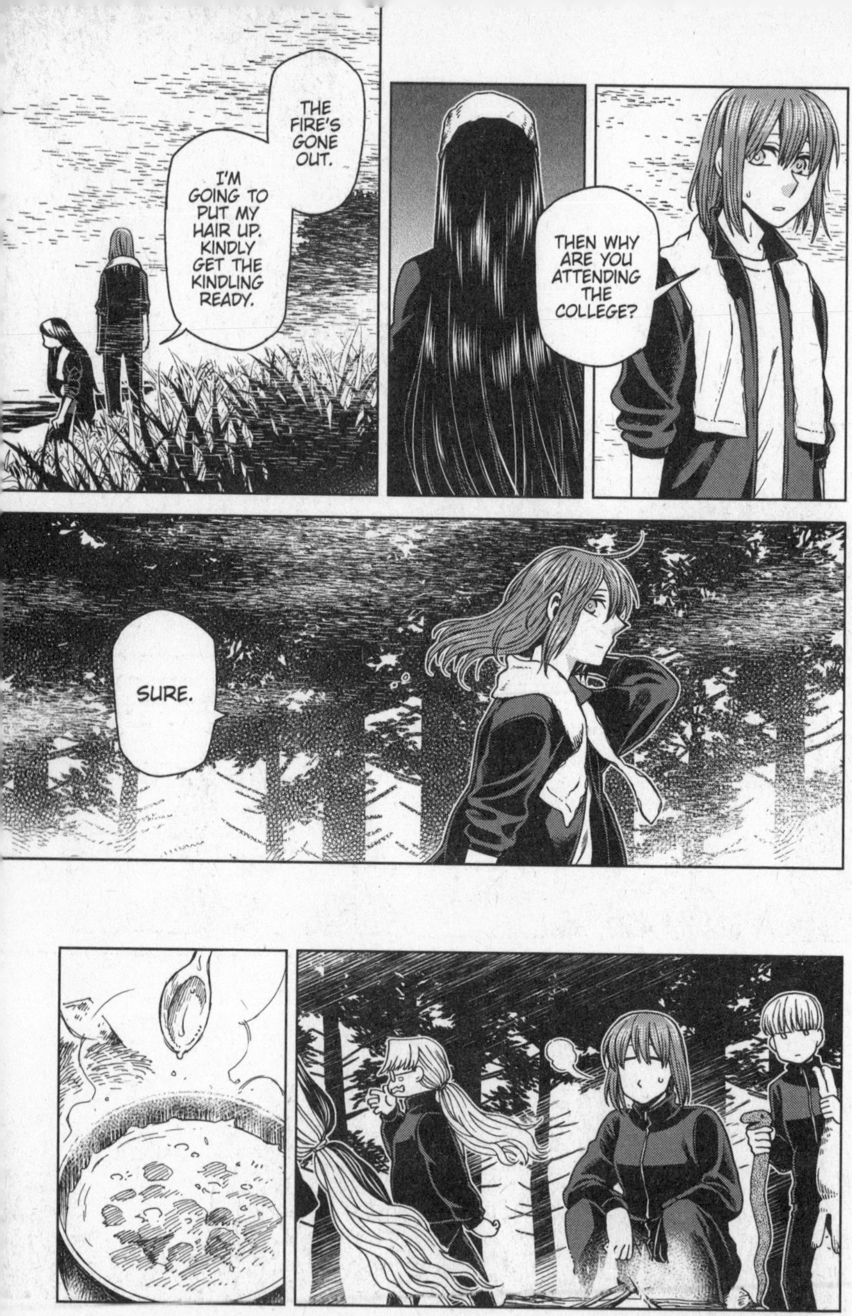
THEN WHY ARE YOU ATTENDING THE COLLEGE?
THE FIRE'S GONE OUT.
I'M GOING TO PUT MY HAIR UP. KINDLY GET THE KINDLING READY.
SURE.

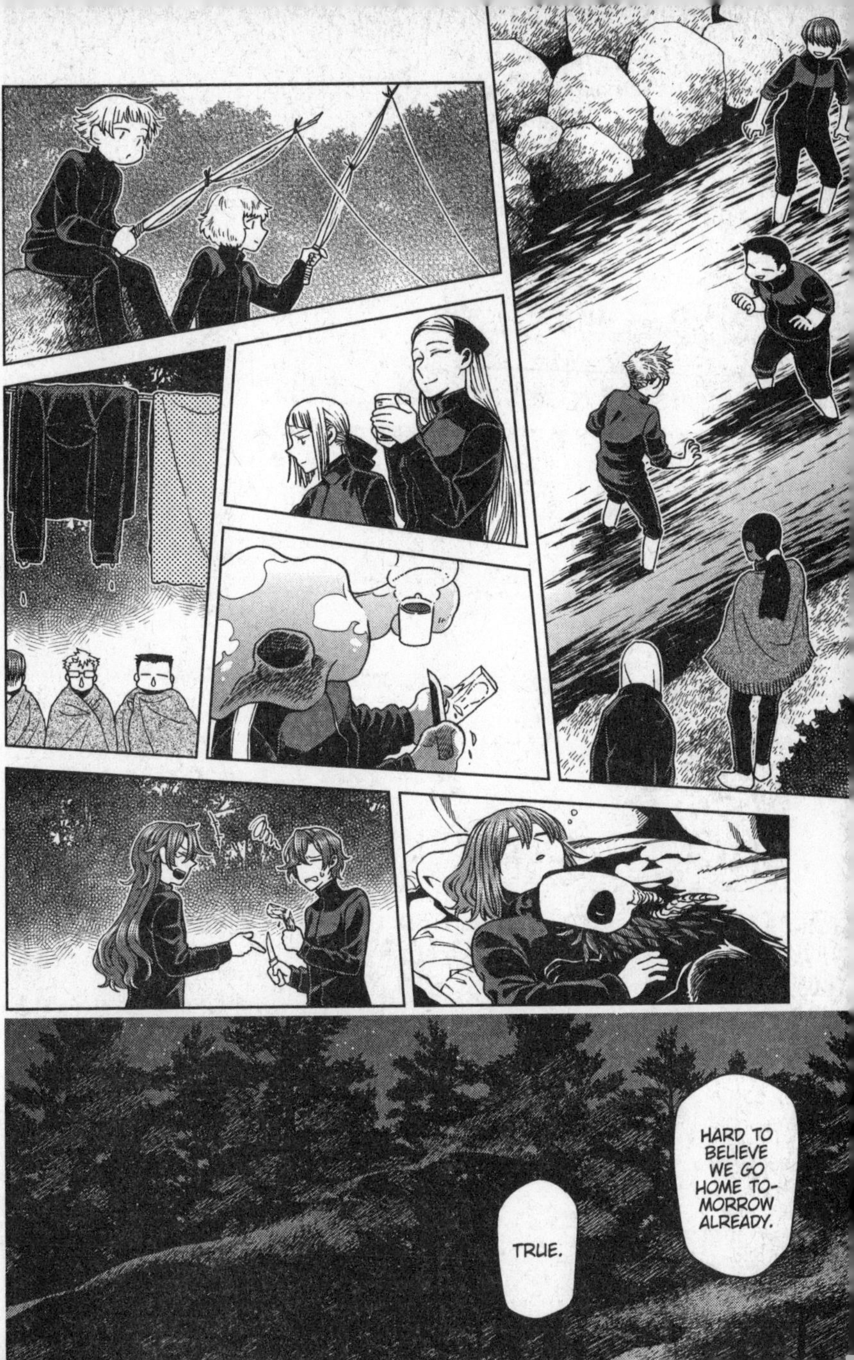
HARD TO BELIEVE WE GO HOME TO-MORROW ALREADY.
TRUE.

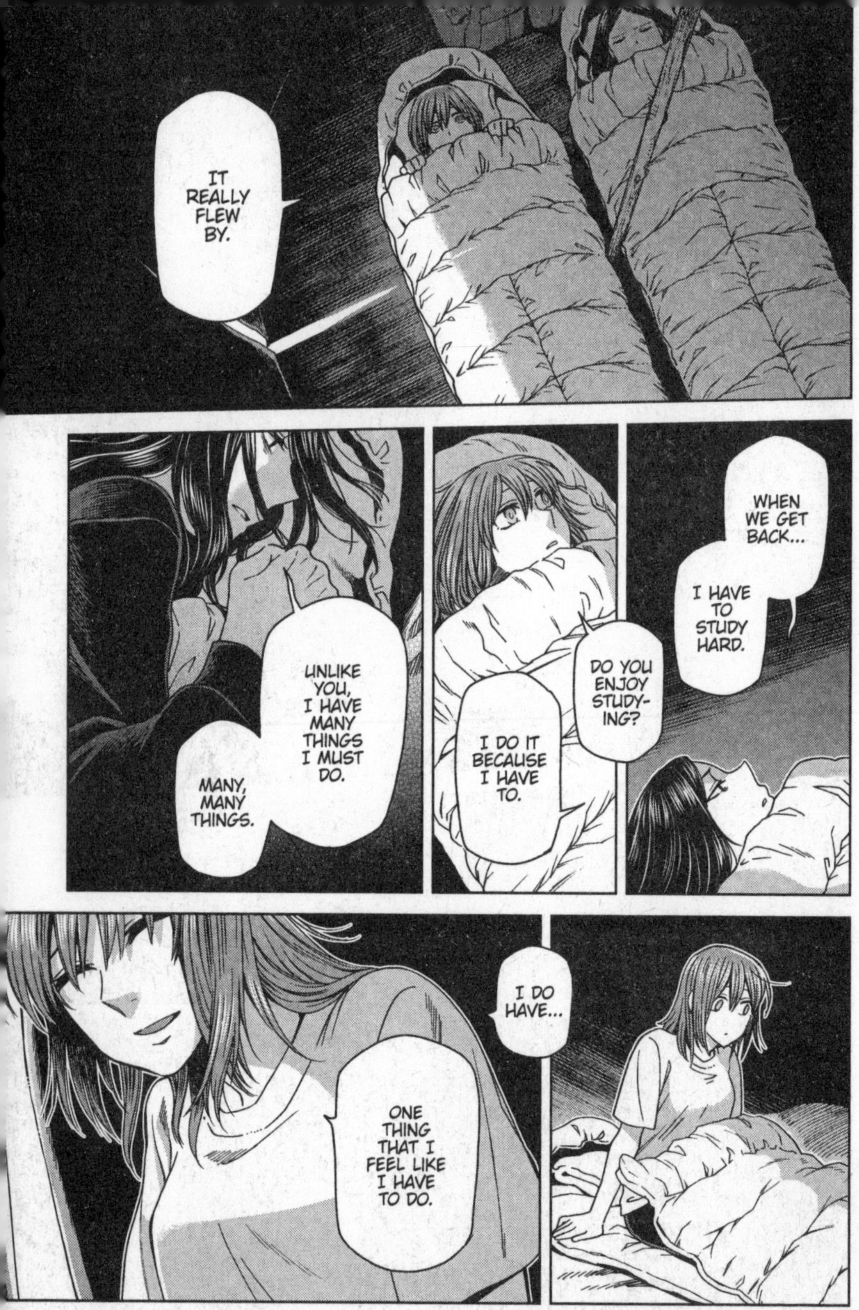
IT REALLY FLEW BY.
WHEN WE GET BACK...
I HAVE TO STUDY HARD.
DO YOU ENJOY STUDYING?
I DO IT BECAUSE I HAVE TO.
UNLIKE YOU, I HAVE MANY THINGS I MUST DO.
MANY, MANY THINGS.
I DO HAVE...
ONE THING THAT I FEEL LIKE I HAVE TO DO.

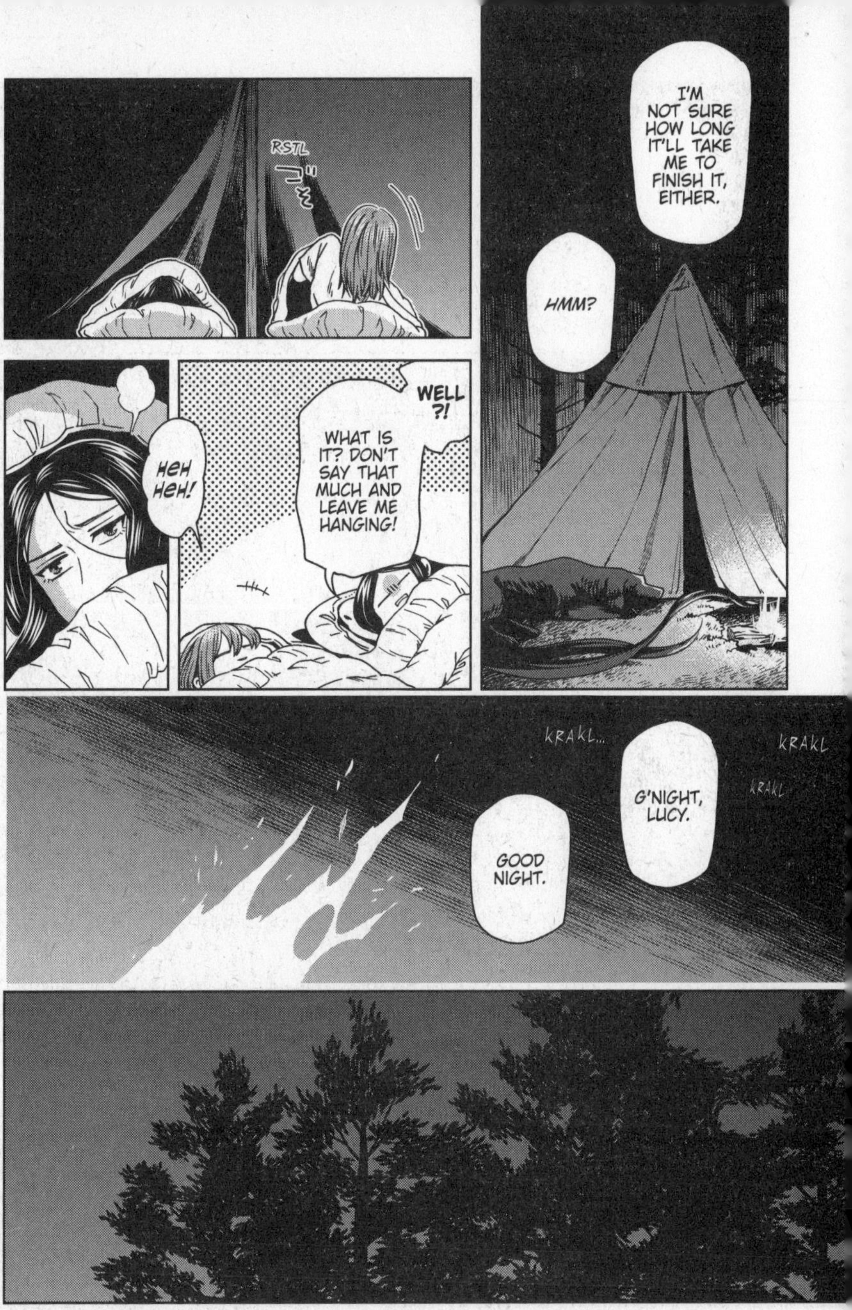
I'M NOT SURE HOW LONG IT'LL TAKE ME TO FINISH IT, EITHER.
HMM?
RSTL
WELL ?!
WHAT IS IT? DON'T SAY THAT MUCH AND LEAVE ME HANGING!
HEH HEH!
KRAKL
KRAKL
G'NIGHT, LUCY.
KRAKL...
GOOD NIGHT.

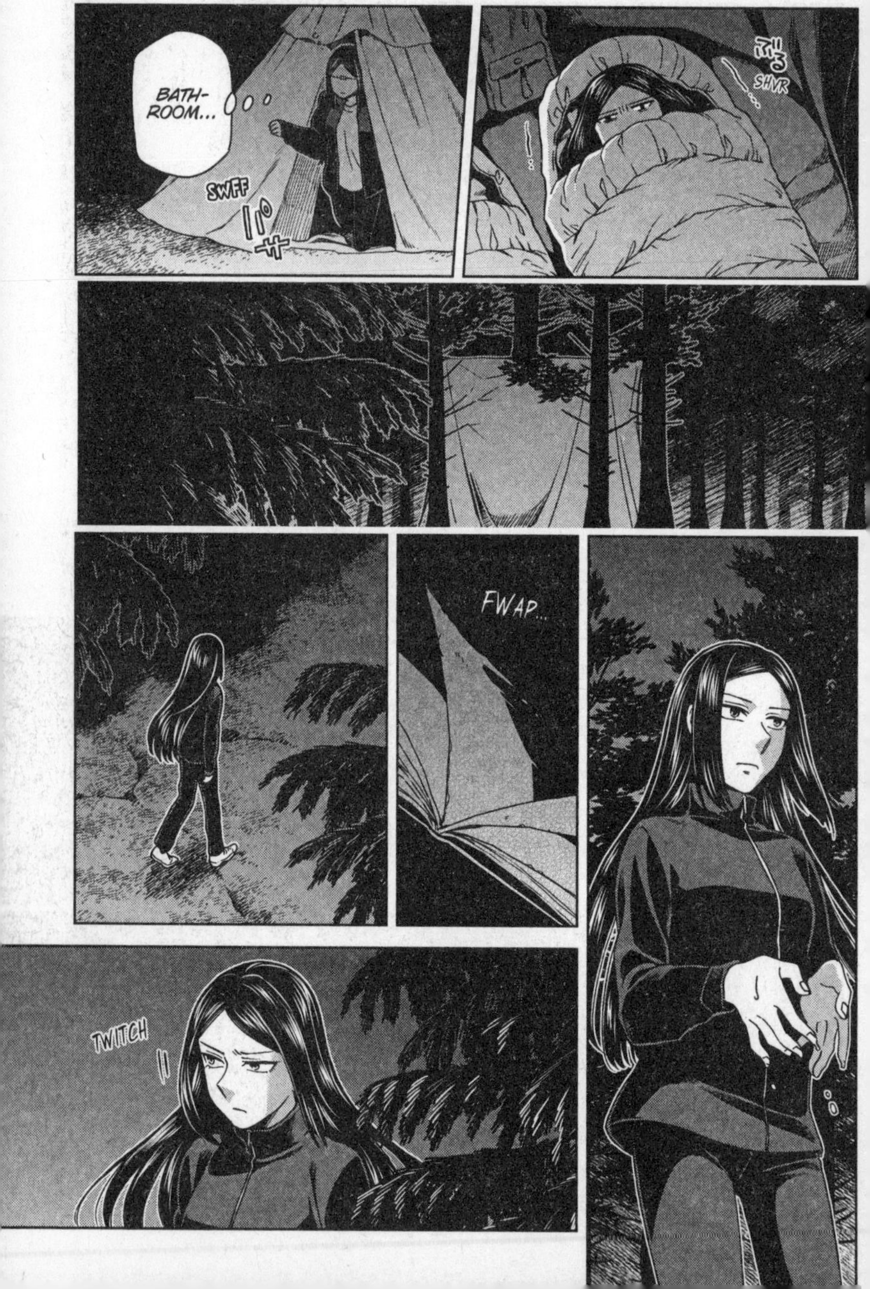
ぶる
SHVR
BATH-ROOM...
SWFF
FWAP...
TWITCH

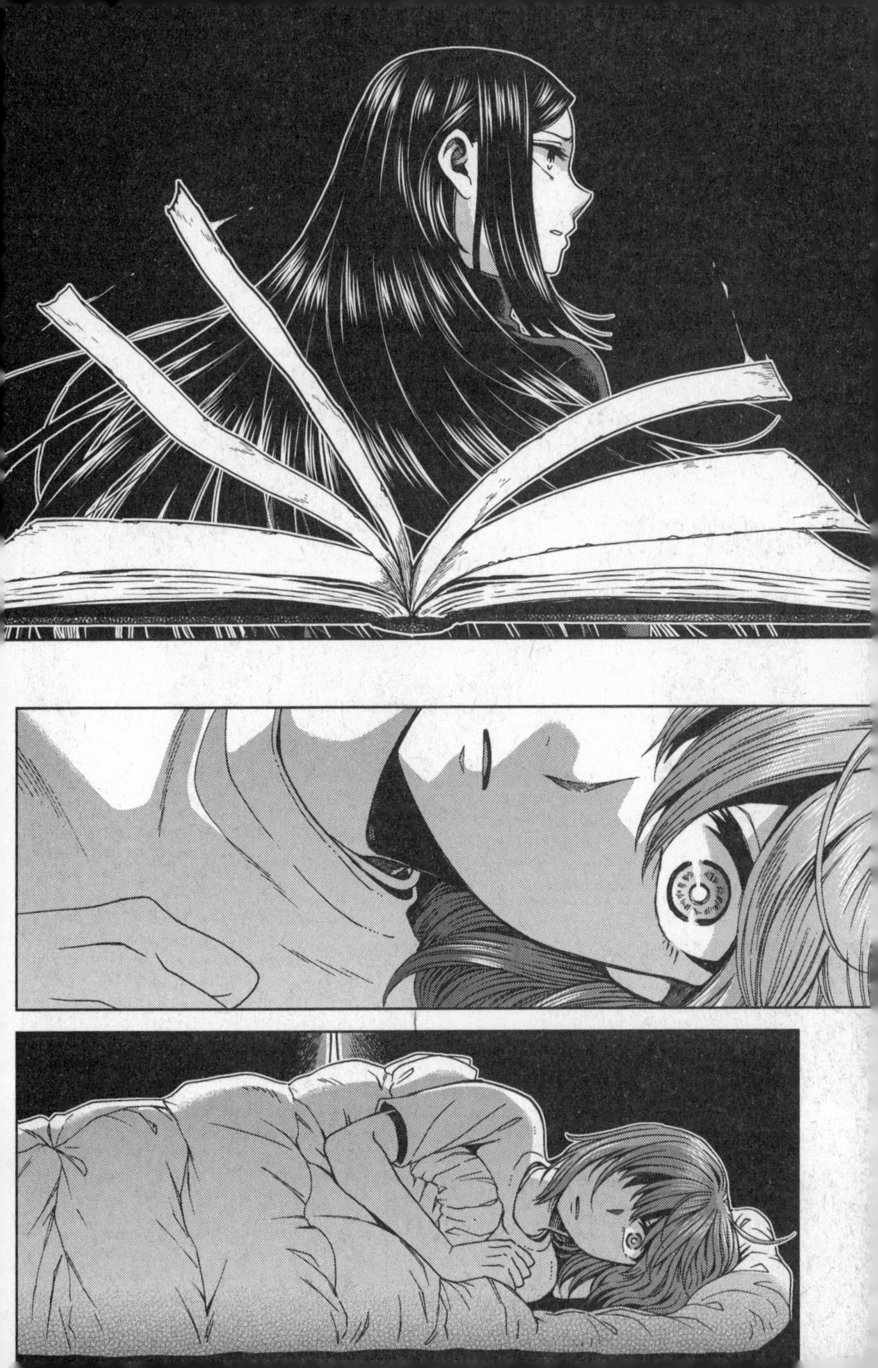

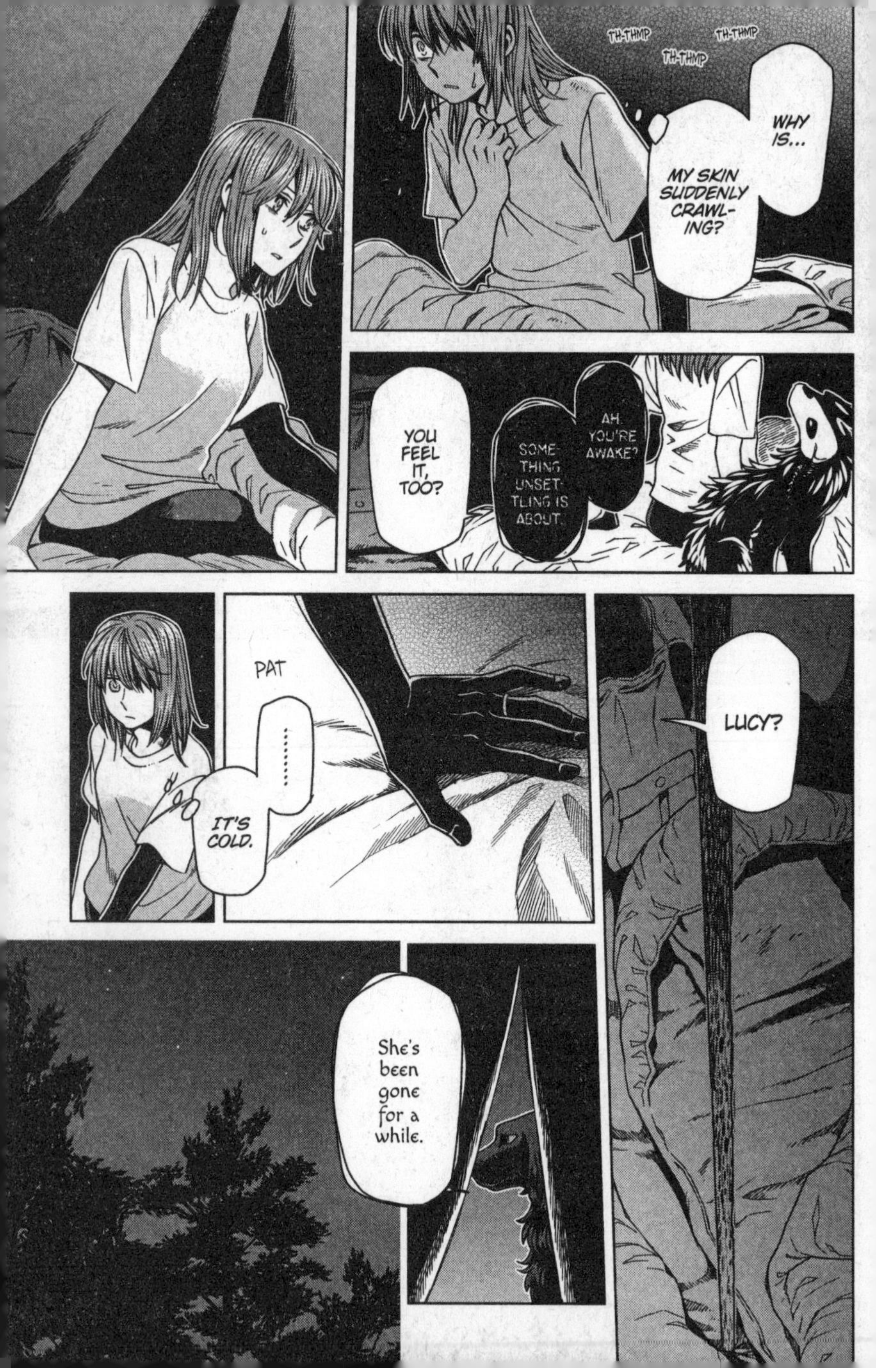
TH-THMP
TH-THMP
TH-THMP
WHY IS... MY SKIN SUDDENLY CRAWL-ING?
AH. YOU'RE AWAKE?
SOME-THING UNSET-TLING IS ABOUT.
YOU FEEL IT, TOO?
LUCY?
PAT
......
IT'S COLD.
She's been gone for a while.

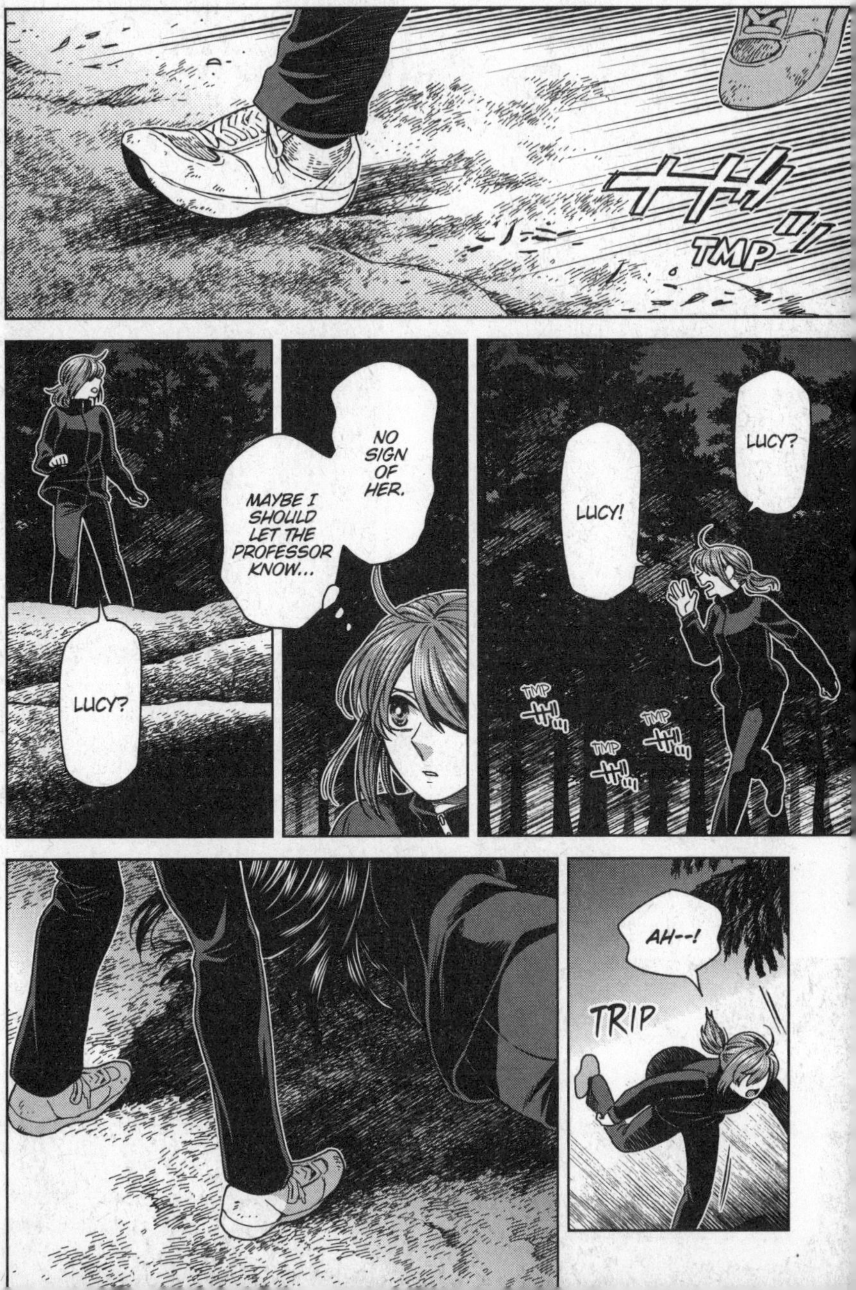
TMP
LUCY?
LUCY!
TMP
TMP
TMP
NO SIGN OF HER.
MAYBE I SHOULD LET THE PROFESSOR KNOW...
LUCY?
AH--!
TRIP

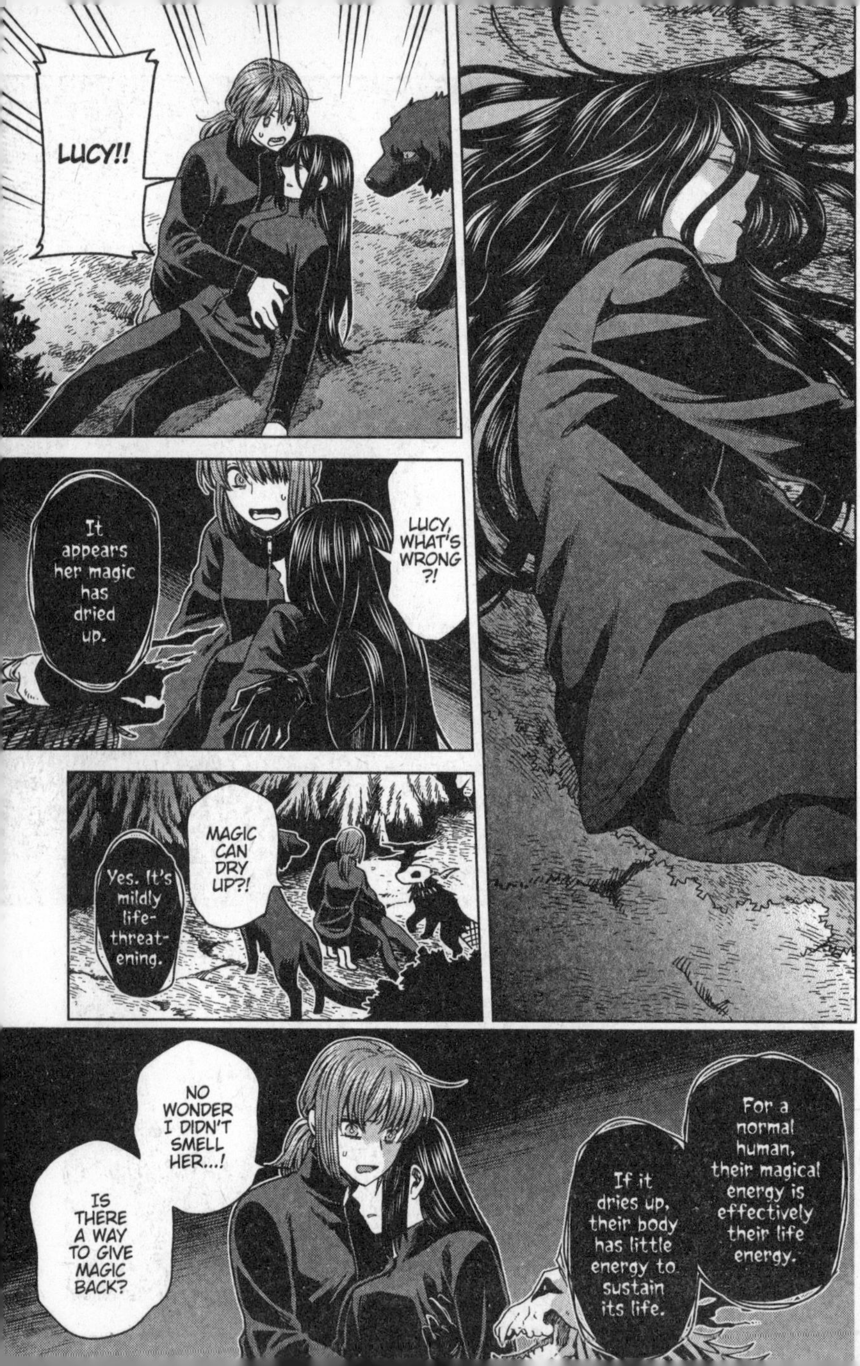
LUCY!!
LUCY, WHAT'S WRONG?!
It appears her magic has dried up.
MAGIC CAN DRY UP?!
Yes. It's mildly life-threatening.
For a normal human, their magical energy is effectively their life energy.
If it dries up, their body has little energy to sustain its life.
NO WONDER I DIDN'T SMELL HER...!
IS THERE A WAY TO GIVE MAGIC BACK?

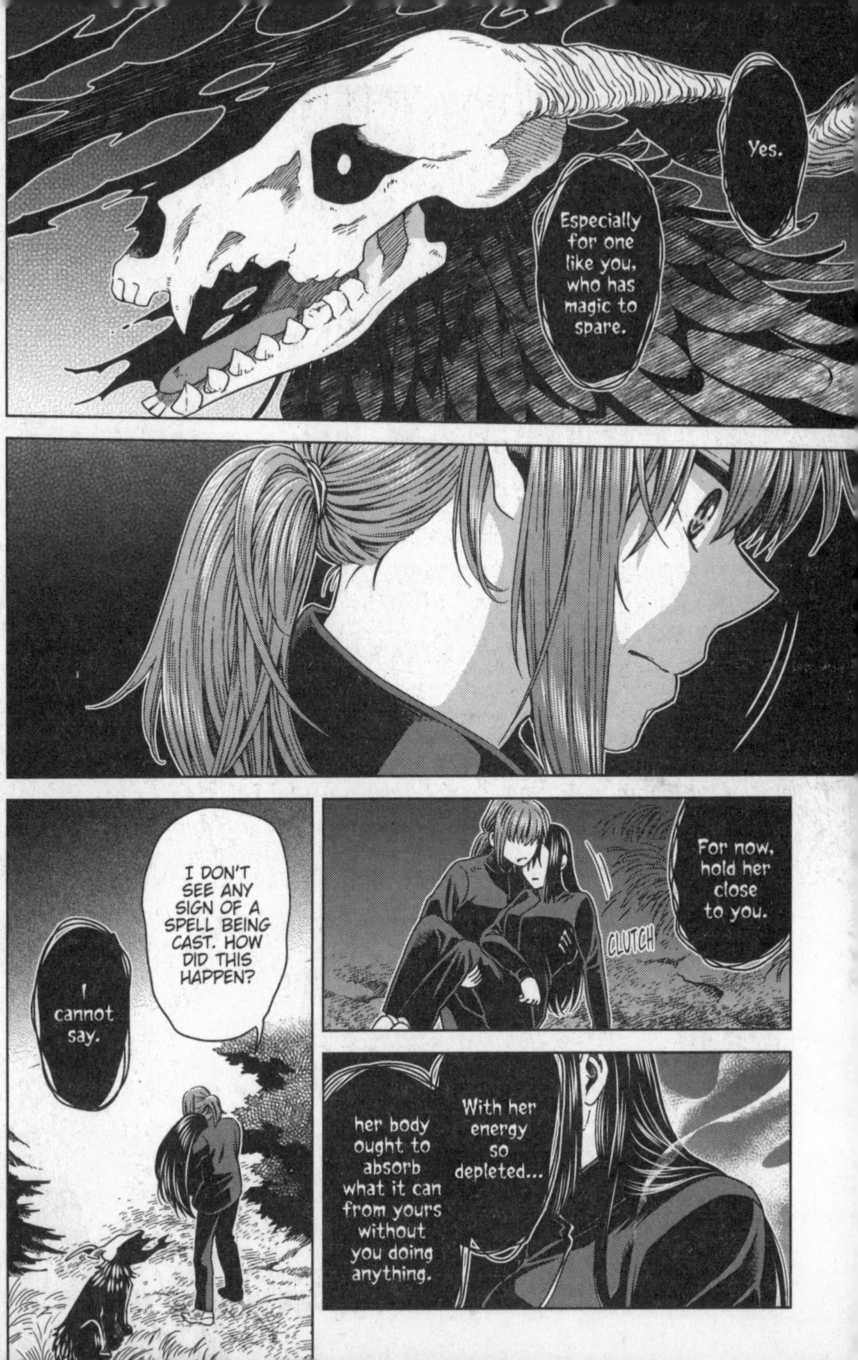
Yes.
Especially for one like you, who has magic to spare.
For now, hold her close to you.
CLUTCH
With her energy so depleted...
her body ought to absorb what it can from yours without you doing anything.
I DON'T SEE ANY SIGN OF A SPELL BEING CAST. HOW DID THIS HAPPEN?
I cannot say.

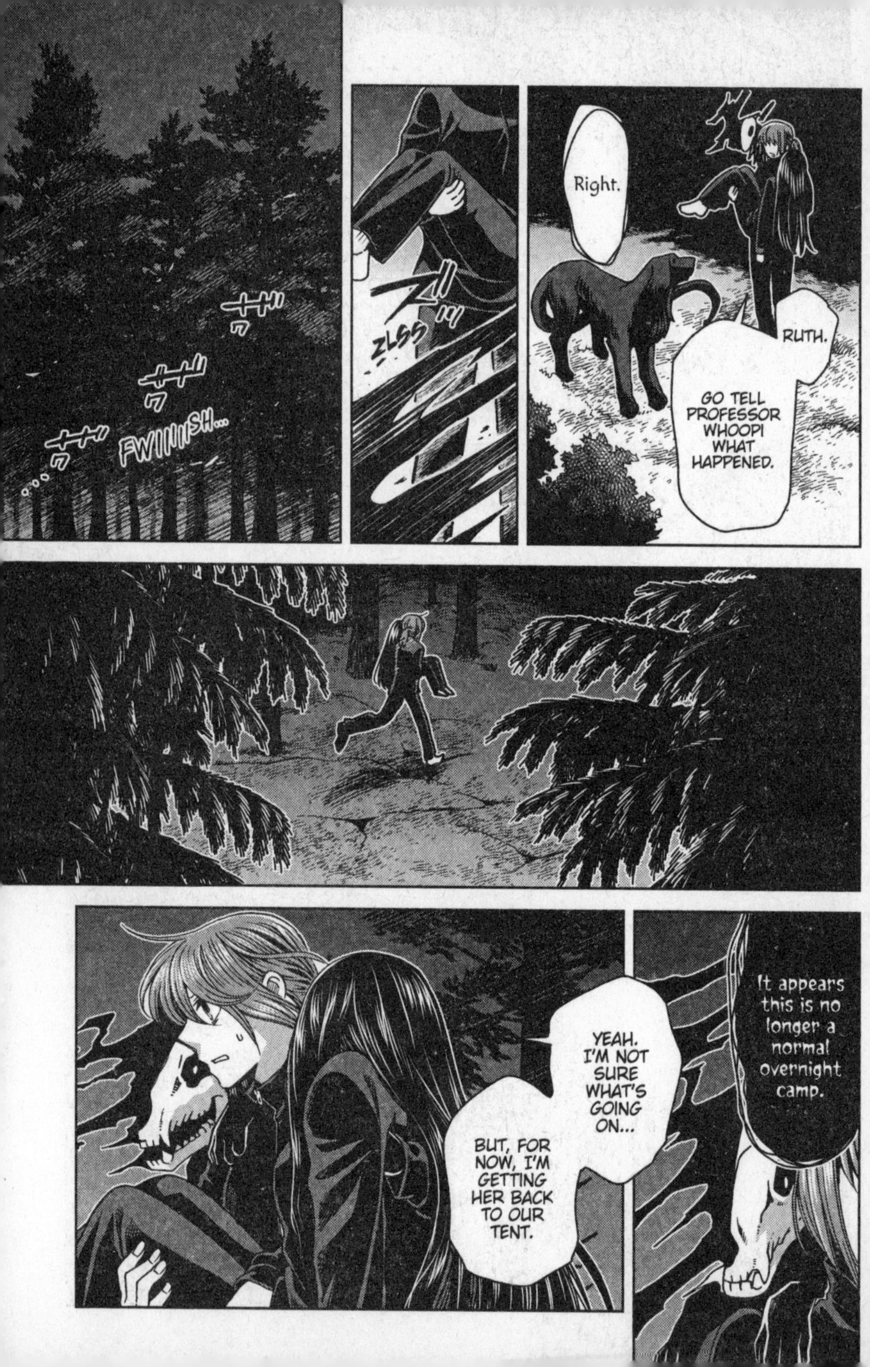
RUTH.
GO TELL PROFESSOR WHOOPI WHAT HAPPENED.
Right.
ZLSS
FWIIIISH...
It appears this is no longer a normal overnight camp.
YEAH. I'M NOT SURE WHAT'S GOING ON...
BUT, FOR NOW, I'M GETTING HER BACK TO OUR TENT.

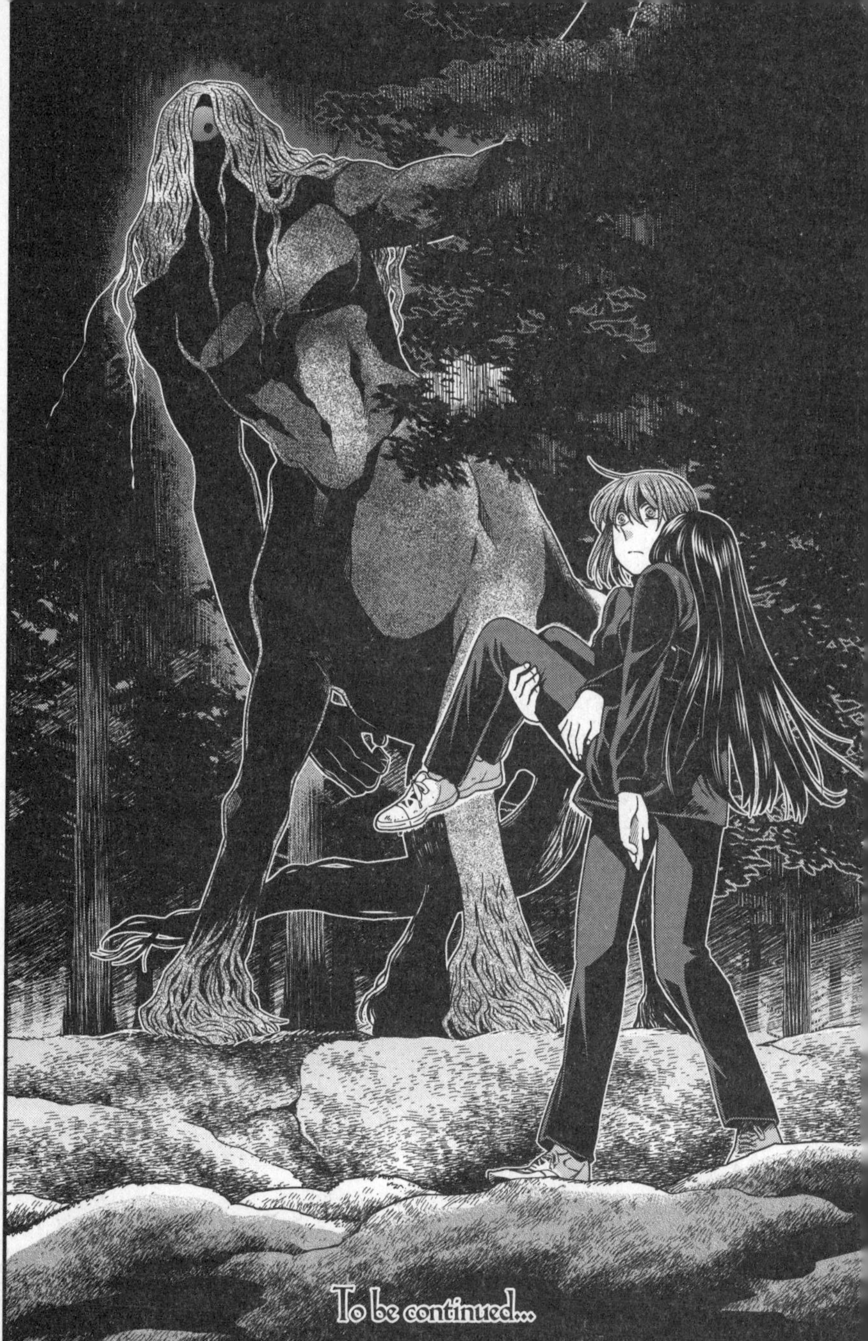
To be continued...

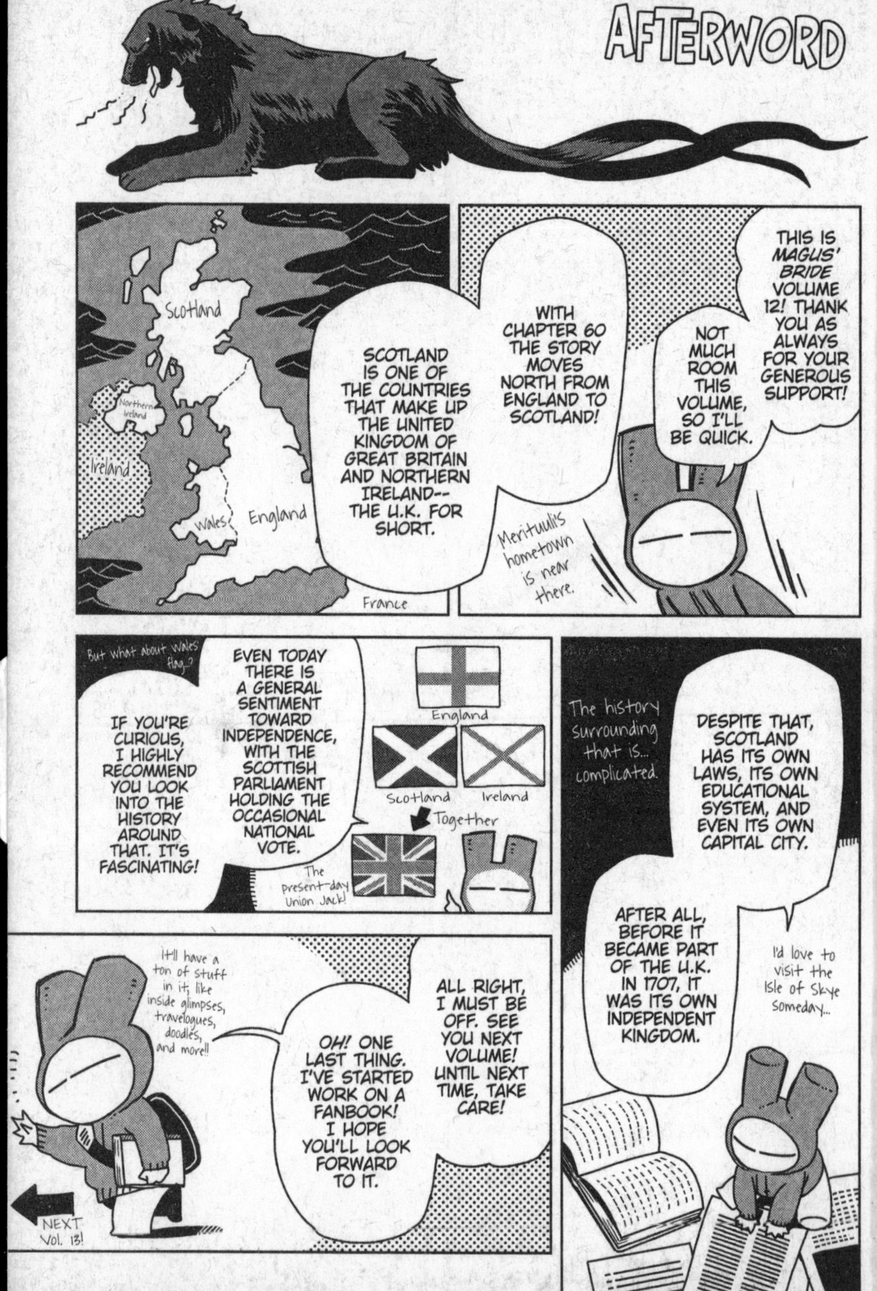
AFTERWORD
THIS IS MAGUS' BRIDE VOLUME 12! THANK YOU AS ALWAYS FOR YOUR GENEROUS SUPPORT!
NOT MUCH ROOM THIS VOLUME, SO I'LL BE QUICK.
WITH CHAPTER 60 THE STORY MOVES NORTH FROM ENGLAND TO SCOTLAND!
Merituuli's hometown is near there.
SCOTLAND IS ONE OF THE COUNTRIES THAT MAKE UP THE UNITED KINGDOM OF GREAT BRITAIN AND NORTHERN IRELAND-- THE U.K. FOR SHORT.
Scotland
Northern Ireland
Ireland
Wales
England
France
DESPITE THAT, SCOTLAND HAS ITS OWN LAWS, ITS OWN EDUCATIONAL SYSTEM, AND EVEN ITS OWN CAPITAL CITY.
The history surrounding that is... complicated.
AFTER ALL, BEFORE IT BECAME PART OF THE U.K. IN 1707, IT WAS ITS OWN INDEPENDENT KINGDOM.
I'd love to visit the Isle of Skye someday...
EVEN TODAY THERE IS A GENERAL SENTIMENT TOWARD INDEPENDENCE, WITH THE SCOTTISH PARLIAMENT HOLDING THE OCCASIONAL NATIONAL VOTE.
IF YOU'RE CURIOUS, I HIGHLY RECOMMEND YOU LOOK INTO THE HISTORY AROUND THAT. IT'S FASCINATING!
But what about Wales' flag..?
England
Scotland
Ireland
Together
The present-day Union Jack!
ALL RIGHT, I MUST BE OFF. SEE YOU NEXT VOLUME! UNTIL NEXT TIME, TAKE CARE!
OH! ONE LAST THING. I'VE STARTED WORK ON A FANBOOK! I HOPE YOU'LL LOOK FORWARD TO IT.
It'll have a ton of stuff in it, like inside glimpses, travelogues, doodles, and more!!
NEXT Vol. 13!

SEVEN SEAS ENTERTAINMENT PRESENTS

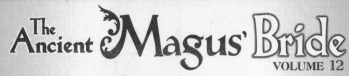

# The Ancient Magus' Bride

VOLUME 12

story and art by **KORE YAMAZAKI**

TRANSLATION
**Adrienne Beck**

ADAPTATION
**Ysabet Reinhardt MacFarlane**

LETTERING AND RETOUCH
**Lys Blakeslee**

COVER DESIGN
**Nicky Lim**

PROOFREADER
**Brett Hallahan**

EDITOR
**Alexis Roberts**

PREPRESS TECHNICIAN
**Rhiannon Rasmussen-Silverstein**

PRODUCTION MANAGER
**Lissa Pattillo**

MANAGING EDITOR
**Julie Davis**

ASSOCIATE PUBLISHER
**Adam Arnold**

PUBLISHER
**Jason DeAngelis**

THE ANCIENT MAGUS' BRIDE VOL. 12

Originally published in Japan in 2019 by MAG Garden Corporation, Tokyo.
English translation rights arranged through TOHAN CORPORATION, Tokyo.



Seven Seas press and purchase enquiries can be sent to Marketing Manager Lianne Sentar at press@gomanga.com. Information regarding the distribution and purchase of digital editions is available from Digital Manager CK Russell at digital@gomanga.com.



ISBN: 978-1-64505-201

Printed in Canada

First Printing: February

10 9 8 7 6 5 4 3 2

FOLLOW US ONLINE: ***www.sevenseasentertainment.com***

## READING DIRECTIONS

This book reads from ***right to left***, Japanese style. If this is your first time reading manga, you start reading from the top right panel on each page and take it from there. If you get lost, just follow the numbered diagram here. It may seem backwards at first, but you'll get the hang of it! Have fun!!

3
1
2
5
4
6
8
7
9

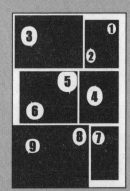